Behavioral Observation

Behavioral Observation

Technology and Applications in Developmental Disabilities

Travis Thompson, Ph.D.
John F. Kennedy Center for Research on Human Development
Vanderbilt University
Nashville, Tennessee

David Felce, Ph.D.
University of Wales College of Medicine
Cardiff, Wales, United Kingdom

and

Frank J. Symons, Ph.D.
Frank Porter Graham Child Development Center
University of North Carolina at Chapel Hill

·P·A·U·L·H·
BROOKES
PUBLISHING CO

Baltimore • London • Toronto • Sydney

Paul H. Brookes Publishing Co.
Post Office Box 10624
Baltimore, Maryland 21285-0624

www.brookespublishing.com

Typeset by Pro-Image Corp., Techna-Type Division, York, Pennsylvania.
Manufactured in the United States of America by
Hamilton Printing Company, Rensselaer, New York.

Chapter 3 is an updated version of Kahng, S., & Iwata, B.A. (1998). Computerized systems for collecting real-time observational data. *Journal of Applied Behavior Analysis, 31,* 253–261. Used with permission.

The case studies described herein are based on actual people and actual circumstances; but these individuals' names or initials and other identifying information have been changed to protect their identities, and no implications should be inferred.

Library of Congress Cataloging-in-Publication Data
Behavioral observation : technology and applications in developmental disabilities /
edited by Travis Thompson, David Felce, and Frank J. Symons.
    p. cm.
Includes bibliographical references and index.
ISBN 1-55766-451-X
    1. Developmental disabilities—Research—Methodology.   2. Observation (Psychology).
3. Developmentally disabled—Rehabilitation.   I. Thompson, Travis.   II. Felce, David.
III. Symons, Frank J.
    RC570.2 .B44   2000
    616.85'88—dc21

                                    99-23811
                                        CIP
British Library Cataloguing in Publication data are available from the British Library.

Contents

About the Editors

Travis Thompson, Ph.D., Professor of Psychology and Human Development, Special Education, and Psychiatry; Director, John F. Kennedy Center for Research on Human Development; and Co-Director, Institute on Genetics and Developmental Disabilities, John F. Kennedy Center for Research on Human Development, Vanderbilt University, Box 40 Peabody, Nashville, Tennessee 37203. Dr. Thompson received a doctoral degree in psychology from the University of Minnesota and has held visiting positions at the University of Maryland, Cambridge University, and the National Institute on Drug Abuse at the National Institutes of Health (NIH), U.S. Public Health Service. He has served on committees of the National Institute of Child Health and Human Development at the NIH, the U.S. Food and Drug Administration, the Hastings Center, the National Academy of Sciences National Research Council, the President's Committee on Mental Retardation, and the American Psychological Association (APA) committees concerning scientific and ethical issues related to developmental disabilities and medications. He is a past president of the Division of Psychopharmacology and Substance Abuse and the Division of Mental Retardation and Developmental Disabilities of the APA. In addition, Dr. Thompson is a recipient of the APA's Don Hake Award for exceptional contributions to basic behavioral research and its applications. He has received the American Association for Mental Retardation Research Award, The Arc Distinguished Research Award, and the Academy on Mental Retardation Career Scientist Award. Dr. Thompson has published more than 190 articles and 24 books concerning intellectual disabilities and pharmacology and has spoken in 40 states within the United States as well as in 14 other countries.

David Felce, Ph.D., Professor of Research in Learning Disabilities, Welsh Centre for Learning Disabilities, Applied Research Unit, Division of Psychological Medicine, University of Wales College of Medicine, Meridian Court–North Road, Cardiff CF4 3BL, Wales, United Kingdom. Dr. Felce's first research post, from 1973 through 1986, was at the University of Southampton, where he conducted research on the quality of residential services for people with mental retardation requiring extensive or pervasive support or other developmental disabilities, with a small excursion into the quality of residential accommodations for older adults with mental infirmities or who were physically frail. After 3 years as Director of the British Institute of Mental Handicap, he was appointed to his current post at the University of Wales College of Medicine. He maintains research interests in the measurement of quality of life, the determinants of quality in community housing services, the analysis and amelioration of challenging behavior, and service development generally in the field of intellectual disabilities. He is a co-editor of *Journal of Applied Research in Intellectual Disabilities* and serves on the editorial boards of seven other intellectual disability journals. In addition, he is a member of the council of the International Association for the Scientific Study of Intellectual Disabilities.

Frank J. Symons, Ph.D., Research Investigator, Frank Porter Graham Child Development Center, University of North Carolina at Chapel Hill, 105 Smith Level Road, CB #8180, Chapel Hill, North Carolina 27599. In addition to being a research investigator at the Frank Porter Graham Child Development Center, Dr. Symons is a clinical research scientist at the Center for Development and Learning and holds faculty research appointments in both the School of Education and the Department of Psychiatry at the University of North Carolina at Chapel Hill. He was formerly a research associate at the John F. Kennedy Center for Research on Human Development at Vanderbilt University, as well as a postdoctoral fellow at the Institute for Developmental Neuroscience at Vanderbilt University. He received his doctoral degree in education and human development (special education) from Vanderbilt University in 1996, and he was a distinguished junior scholar-in-residence at the Peter Wall Institute for Advanced Studies at the University of British Columbia in Vancouver, Canada, in 1999. His primary research activities are supported by the National Institute of Child Health and Human Development (NICHD) of the National Institutes of Health and focus on improving the assessment and treatment of severe self-injurious behavior of individuals with mental retardation requiring extensive or pervasive support and related disabilities. In this context, his specific research activities include the sequential analysis of observational data as a tool for determining the behavioral mechanisms of drug action. Dr. Symons is a past recipient of a Medical Research Council of Canada Research Training Grant (1993–1996) and was awarded a Steven Shapiro Fellowship from the International Association for the Scientific Study of Intellectual Disabilities (1996).

Contributors

Roger Bakeman, Ph.D.
Professor
Department of Psychology
Georgia State University
University Plaza
Atlanta, Georgia 30303

Maria L. Boccia, Ph.D.
Research Associate Professor
Frank Porter Graham Child
    Development Center
University of North Carolina at
    Chapel Hill
105 Smith Level Road
CB #8180
Chapel Hill, North Carolina 27599

William H. Brown, Ph.D.
Assistant Professor
Department of Educational
    Psychology
Wardlaw College of Education
Room 235C
University of South Carolina
Columbia, South Carolina 29208

Yvonne E.M. Bruinsma, M.A.
Research Assistant
Fairview Developmental Center
University of California, Irvine
16172 Nassau Lane
Huntington Beach, California 92649

Judith J. Carta, Ph.D.
Senior Scientist
Juniper Gardens Children's Project
University of Kansas
650 Minnesota Avenue, 2nd Floor
Kansas City, Kansas 66101

Harriett Dawson
Research Assistant
Juniper Garden's Children's Project
University of Kansas
650 Minnesota Avenue, 2nd Floor
Kansas City, Kansas 66101

Elizabeth M. Delaney, Ed.D.
Assistant Professor
College of Education
University of Illinois at Chicago
1040 West Harrison Street
MC 147
Chicago, Illinois 60614

Mark Egli, Ph.D.
Research Associate
John F. Kennedy Center for Research
    on Human Development
Vanderbilt University
Box 156 Peabody
Nashville, Tennessee 37203

Eric Emerson, Ph.D.
Professor of Clinical Psychology in
    Intellectual Disability
Hester Adrian Research Centre
University of Manchester
Oxford Road
Manchester M13 9PL, England
United Kingdom

Sara S. Ezell, M.Ed.
Assistant Director for Disability
    Services
Opportunity Development Center
Vanderbilt University
108 Baker Building
110 21st Avenue South
Nashville, Tennessee 37203

Paddy C. Favazza, Ed.D.
Associate Professor
Department of Instruction and
    Curriculum Leadership
University of Memphis
Box 520617
Memphis, Tennessee 38152

Irene D. Feurer, Ph.D.
Research Assistant Professor of
    Psychiatry
Coordinator of Quantitative and
    Observational Methodology
John F. Kennedy Center for Research
    on Human Development
Vanderbilt University
Box 156 Peabody
Nashville, Tennessee 37203

Charles R. Greenwood, Ph.D.
Senior Scientist
Juniper Gardens Children's Project
University of Kansas
650 Minnesota Avenue, 2nd Floor
Kansas City, Kansas 66101

Scott Hall, Ph.D.
Research Fellow
School of Psychology
University of Birmingham
Edgbaston
Birmingham B15 2TT, England
United Kingdom

Terry B. Hancock, Ph.D.
Research Associate
Department of Special Education
John F. Kennedy Center for Research
    on Human Development
Vanderbilt University
Box 328 Peabody
Nashville, Tennessee 37203

Peggy P. Hester, Ph.D.
Associate Professor
Department of Early Childhood,
    Speech-Language Pathology,
    and Special Education
Child Study Center
Old Dominion University
Norfolk, Virginia 23527

Eva M. Horn, Ph.D.
Assistant Professor
Department of Special Education
John F. Kennedy Center for Research
    on Human Development
Vanderbilt University
Box 328 Peabody
Nashville, Tennessee 37203

Carolyn Hughes, Ph.D.
Associate Professor
Department of Special Education
John F. Kennedy Center for Research
    on Human Development
Vanderbilt University
Box 328 Peabody
Nashville, Tennessee 37203

Brian A. Iwata, Ph.D.
Professor
Department of Psychology
University of Florida
369 Psychology Building
Post Office Box 112250
Gainesville, Florida 32611

SungWoo Kahng, Ph.D.
Psychologist
Neurobehavioral Unit
Kennedy Krieger Institute
707 North Broadway
Baltimore, Maryland 21205

Ann P. Kaiser, Ph.D.
Professor
Department of Special Education
John F. Kennedy Center for Research
    on Human Development
Vanderbilt University
Box 328 Peabody
Nashville, Tennessee 37203

Sarah Walsh Lorden, M.Ed.
Employment Specialist
Jewish Vocational Service
26 West Street
Boston, Massachusetts 02111

Jason Ly
Research Assistant
Fairview Developmental Center
University of California, Irvine
2501 Harbor Boulevard, Box 5-A
Costa Mesa, California 92626

William E. MacLean, Jr., Ph.D.
Professor
Departments of Psychology and
    Biological Sciences
University of Wyoming
16th and Gibbon Streets, Room 35
Post Office Box 3415
Laramie, Wyoming 82071

Sarah DeBoard Marion, M.A.
Research Assistant
Departments of Psychiatry and
    Human Behavior and Pediatrics
Fairview Developmental Center
University of California, Irvine
2501 Harbor Boulevard, Box 5-A
Costa Mesa, California 92626

Samuel L. Odom, Ph.D.
Otting Professor of Special Education
Department of Curriculum and
    Instruction
School of Education
Indiana University
3234 W.W. Wright Education Building
201 North Rose Avenue
Bloomington, Indiana 47405

Chris Oliver, Ph.D.
Professor of Clinical Psychology
School of Psychology
University of Birmingham
Edgbaston
Birmingham B15 2TT, England
United Kingdom

Vincenç Quera, Ph.D.
Profesor Titular
Departamento de Metodología de las
    Ciencias del Comportamiento
Universidad de Barcelona
Paseo Valle de Hebrón, 171
E-08035 Barcelona
Spain

David J. Reeves, Ph.D.
Research Fellow
Hester Adrian Research Centre
University of Manchester
Oxford Road
Manchester M13 9PL, England
United Kingdom

Jane Elizabeth Roberts, Ph.D.
Investigator
Frank Porter Graham Child
    Development Center
University of North Carolina at
    Chapel Hill
105 Smith Level Road
CB #8180
Chapel Hill, North Carolina 27599

Julia Robinson, M.A.
Professor
Department of Architecture
College of Architecture and Landscape
    Architecture
University of Minnesota
110 Architecture Building
89 Church Street SE
Minneapolis, Minnesota 55455

Michael S. Rodi, M.Ed.
Research Analyst
American Institutes for Research
1000 Thomas Jefferson Street, NW
Washington, D.C. 20007

Gene P. Sackett, Ph.D.
Professor
Regional Primate Research Center
University of Washington
Box 357330
Seattle, Washington 98195

Curt A. Sandman, Ph.D.
Professor
Departments of Psychiatry and
    Human Behavior and Pediatrics
Fairview Developmental Center
University of California, Irvine
2501 Harbor Boulevard, Box 5-A
Costa Mesa, California 92626

Jay L. Saunders
Bluestem Technologies
9816 West 132nd Terrace
Overland Park, Kansas 66213

Richard R. Saunders, Ph.D.
Professor and Senior Scientist
Schiefelbusch Institute for Life Span
    Studies
Parsons Research Center
University of Kansas
2601 Gabriel
Campus Box 738
Parsons, Kansas 67357

JaneDiane Smith, Ph.D.
Assistant Professor
Department of Counseling, Special
    Education, and Child Development
University of North Carolina at
    Charlotte
9201 University City Boulevard
Charlotte, North Carolina 28223

Ned A. Solomon
Research Analyst
Department of Special Education
John F. Kennedy Center for Research
    on Human Development
Vanderbilt University
Box 328 Peabody
Nashville, Tennessee 37203

Jon Tapp
Director of Computer Services
John F. Kennedy Center for Research
    on Human Development
Vanderbilt University
Box 40 Peabody
Nashville, Tennessee 37203

Paul E. Touchette, Ed.D.
Professor and Principal Psychologist
Departments of Psychiatry and
    Human Behavior and Pediatrics
University of California, Irvine
18 Mendel Court
Irvine, California 92612

Tedra A. Walden, Ph.D.
Professor
Department of Psychology and
    Human Development
Vanderbilt University
Box 512 Peabody
Nashville, Tennessee 37203

Steven F. Warren, Ph.D.
Professor of Special Education and
    Psychology
Deputy Director
John F. Kennedy Center for Research
    on Human Development
Vanderbilt University
Box 328 Peabody
Nashville, Tennessee 37203

Joseph H. Wehby, Ph.D.
Assistant Professor
Department of Special Education
John F. Kennedy Center for Research
    on Human Development
Vanderbilt University
Box 328 Peabody
Nashville, Tennessee 37203

Paul J. Yoder, Ph.D.
Research Associate Professor
Department of Special Education
Director, Quantitative and
    Observational Methodology
John F. Kennedy Center for Research
    on Human Development
Vanderbilt University
Box 328 Peabody
Nashville, Tennessee 37203

Foreword

Although people have always watched others in order to learn about them, technologies of systematic observation emerged only during the second half of the 20th century. Other methods, such as controlled laboratory testing, standardized inventories, general surveys, and behavior checklists, are perhaps used more widely. However, the description of ongoing behavior and its relationship to events in the environment allows one to ask detailed questions and derive a type of quantitative answer that cannot be achieved by using other methods.

The description of moment-to-moment changes in specific behaviors promotes the development of concepts of the way in which behavior is organized over brief periods of time. This attribute is particularly useful as part of the modern study of neuroscience because it allows the association of behavior change with short-term changes in the physiology of the brain.

Because observation methods traditionally have emphasized the study of the person or the animal in everyday situations, they also foster an ecological approach. Investigation of the relationships between patterns of environmental events and behavioral change has yielded improved understanding of the complex processes not only of everyday adaptation but also of behavioral evolution.

Observation methods originally were developed for the study of animal, nonverbal communication and the behavior of children and adults who have no speech. This special use of observation methods has perhaps been their most unique feature. The fields of animal behavior, emotional expression, and early child psychology would not have been possible without observational technology.

Behavioral technologies have developed rapidly since the 1960s. *Behavioral Observation: Technology and Applications in Developmental Disabilities* provides a picture of the results of developments in this field in the 1980s and 1990s. Methods of data analysis, developments in the use of microcomputers for data acquisition, and examples of research results are this book's main features. Remarkable new computer technologies make it possible to collect and manage vast quantities of observational data as well as facilitate quantitative treatment of raw data in ways that have had significant theoretical implications. The chapters are written by individuals who have been responsible for the increased sophistication of the approach.

It is notable that almost all of the chapters of this book are written by individuals who work in the national centers for research on mental retardation in the United Kingdom and the United States. Government-supported mental retardation research centers have been the national focus for much of the world's research on the biological, psychological, and social aspects of mental retardation. Observational technologies are a natural result of their research on people with severe mental retardation.

Although many of the developments in observational methodology toward the end of the 20th century had their source in the study of people with mental retardation, this book is also a demonstration of how research about people with mental retardation developed out of studies of other groups (e.g., young children, animals). It also points to the future of detailed quantitative description of patterns of moment-to-moment changes in behavior.

Gershon Berkson
University of Illinois at Chicago

Preface

Accurate, reliable information about the behavior of individuals with intellectual and other developmental disabilities in relation to their surroundings and their health status and in response to treatments (e.g., medications) is essential to understanding people with disabilities and devising and evaluating interventions for them. In 1976, the Lake Wilderness Conference on Applications of Observational-Ethological Methods to the Study of Mental Retardation was convened near Seattle, Washington, under the auspices of the National Institute of Child Health and Human Development (NICHD), National Institutes of Health, to explore state-of-the-art methods for obtaining such information about the lives of individuals with intellectual disabilities. That landmark conference led to the publication in 1978 of the two-volume proceedings of the conference, entitled, *Observing Behavior: Proceedings of the Conference "Application of Observational/ Ethological Methods to the Study of Mental Retardation,"* edited by Gene P. Sackett.

In March 1997, a group of researchers heavily involved in behavioral observation research met in Riverside, California, at the Gatlinburg Conference on Research and Theory in Mental Retardation and Developmental Disabilities. That conference, also sponsored by the NICHD, explored changes that had occurred in the theory and practice of using observational methods since the 1978 Lake Wilderness Conference and included some of the Lake Wilderness Conference participants (e.g., Sackett, Berkson, Bakeman) as well as a new generation of researchers. At the conclusion of that conference, it became obvious that significant developments had occurred in both theory and practice in behavioral observation methods, which called for the publication of an update of *Observing Behavior.* With that in mind, the participants of the 1997 conference, joined by others who were involved actively in behavioral observation research methods development, agreed to contribute to *Behavioral Observation: Technology and Applications in Developmental Disabilities.*

Several trends make this book especially timely. An enormous amount has been learned about the nature of disabilities, including the specificity of the behavioral features of various developmental disabilities, the interdependence of the behavior of people with disabilities and their surroundings, and the close ties between subjective concepts such as quality of life and objective measures obtained in natural environments.

Second, theory in the field of intellectual disabilities has become decidedly biobehavioral and transactional at an individual level. In 1976, observational research in the field of disabilities was driven largely by ethological theory (i.e., evolutionary function) and the ecological tradition of Roger Barker and colleagues. At the turn of the 21st century, the emphasis is much heavier on functional analysis and assessment in natural environments in the tradition of experimental and applied behavioral analysis and in the integration of behavior analytic and biobehavioral perspectives. Interest in setting conditions or state variables that can be quantified independently and objectively (see Chapter 7) has created renewed interest in the moderating influence of motivation, affect, arousal, and overt behavior, which are very old concerns in the history of psychology.

Finally, the availability of relatively inexpensive computer technologies and the associated software with accompanying data-analytic packages has revolutionized the kinds of questions that can be asked and answered about the relationships between behavior and environment, behavior and biological states, and behavior and treatments. These technologies have spawned new theoretical analyses (see Chapters 18 and 19) that would have been inconceivable without the ability to manage and analyze enormous amounts of data relatively effortlessly. Even though, as Sackett points out in Chapter 2, not all of this information has yet filtered down to practitioners and researchers in institutions and community environments, the diversity and vitality of the work described in this book attest to the rapidly expanding influence that these methods have.

The proof of the pudding is in the degree to which these new observation strategies improve the understanding of disabilities and contribute to improving the lives of individuals with disabilities and their families. The editors and contributors of this book believe that these strategies have already done so and are optimistic that there are many more developments to come.

Note to the Reader: The reader will find inconsistencies in the use of specific terms throughout this book, reflecting the international nature of the contributions. In the United Kingdom and much of Europe, the terms *intellectual disabilities* and *learning disabilities* have largely replaced *mental retardation* as the latter term has been used in the United States. Rather than attempt to impose a single, consistent nomenclature, the editors decided to recognize the facts that these terms are in transition and that no single set of terms has been adopted universally.

Travis Thompson
Nashville, Tennesee

REFERENCE

Sackett, G.P. (Ed.). (1978). *Observing behavior: Proceedings of the conference "Application of Observational/Ethological Methods to the Study of Mental Retardation"* (2 vols.) [NICHD mental retardation research centers series]. Baltimore: University Park Press.

Acknowledgments

Gene P. Sackett was the moving force behind the Lake Wilderness Conference in 1976, and we are grateful for his continuing contribution to this endeavor. The 1997 Gatlinburg Conference on Research and Theory in Mental Retardation and Developmental Disabilities in Riverside, California, grew out of conversations that took place over the course of several years with Gershon Berkson, longtime champion of behavioral science research in the field of intellectual disabilities and a second intellectual moving force behind the 1976 Lake Wilderness Conference.

Neither conference would have been convened, nor would this book exist, without the continued commitment of the National Institute of Child Health and Human Development (NICHD) of the National Institutes of Health in its support of behavioral science research in the field of mental retardation and related intellectual and developmental disabilities. Because of the efforts of NICHD Director Duane Alexander, Mental Retardation and Developmental Disabilities Branch Chief Felix de la Cruz and NICHD Staff Member Marie Bristol, this effort has borne fruit. We are grateful to all of them for their continued efforts on behalf of behavioral science research. The support of the core grant (No. P30 HD 15052) of the John F. Kennedy Center for Research on Human Development, Vanderbilt University, from the NICHD is gratefully acknowledged.

We are most grateful to the contributors to this book who have, with exceptional competence and diligence, prepared outstanding chapters and accepted our editorial suggestions graciously. To Jennifer Lazaro Kinard, who served as an editor for Paul H. Brookes Publishing Co. through November 1998, we express our gratitude for her patient guidance, and to Jessica Allan, Ms. Lazaro Kinard's replacement at Brookes, we express our sincerest gratitude for seeing this project through to completion. The meticulous work of preparing the final manuscript for submission fell to Valorie Corley, who did so with exceptional skill, and to whom we express our gratitude.

Finally, we acknowledge the support of our spouses—Anneke Thompson, Jan Felce, and Stacy Coleman Symons, respectively—whose patient understanding was immeasurably helpful during the course of this project.

I

Principles of Behavioral Observation

Principles of Behavioral Observation

Assumptions and Strategies

Travis Thompson,
Frank J. Symons, and
David Felce

Francis Bacon's *Novum Organum* (1620/1994) provided an apologia for inductive science based on the observation of nature. Before 1600, it was common practice to make knowledge claims about natural phenomena by seeking the wisdom of authority rather than by drawing conclusions based on direct observation. Although Bacon set the rudder on the course to enlightenment, it was not until the mid-1800s that experimental science based on observation became established. Claude Bernard, the founder of the experimental method in physiology, wrote that "Observers . . . must be photographers of phenomena; their observations must accurately represent nature" (1865/1949, p. 22).

Interest in obtaining systematic quantitative observations of the behavior of people with intellectual disability and related developmental disabilities is relatively recent. Wilhelm T. Preyer (1888/1973), in his two volumes on *The Mind of the Child*, provided qualitative observations in the tradition of Darwin's observations on the Galapagos Islands; but basically he relied on anecdotal evidence for his largely theoretical analysis. Perhaps the most detailed quantitative examination of typical development was Mary Margaret Shirley's *The First Two Years* (1931–1933), a three-volume study of the lives of typically developing children conducted at

This chapter was supported in part by National Institute of Child Health and Human Development Grant No. P30 HD15052 to Vanderbilt University.

the Institute of Child Development at the University of Minnesota. Shirley studied the development of 24 children from birth to 2 years of age, focusing on the ages at which children displayed specific skills, such as lifting their heads or the number of vocabulary words used. It was the first detailed study of its kind. Like Goodenough's (1926) earlier study of drawing by young children, much of Shirley's work was designed to evaluate the most appropriate standardized testing procedures for assessing motor, perceptual, and intellectual skills to evaluate a given child's development against a set of well-documented norms. This early work on normative child development set the stage for a major tradition within the field of developmental disabilities, which emerged in large part from the study of typical child development. That tradition emphasized standardized, norm-referenced tests to evaluate the behavior of people with developmental disabilities.

Beginning in the 1950s and 1960s, three traditions emerged that increasingly shaped the measurement of the behavior of individuals with intellectual disabilities in natural environments. Two were represented in Sackett's (1978a, 1978b) *Observing Behavior*: 1) ethological theory and methods and 2) ecological theory and methods. Not represented was the rapidly growing field of applied behavior analysis, which had already begun to bear practical fruit in interventions to improve the lives of people with developmental disabilities (cf. Bijou, Peterson, & Ault, 1968; Risley & Wolf, 1967; Thompson & Grabowski, 1972). The three traditions had different roots and focused on different issues, which are reflected in their respective approaches to obtaining behavioral observations.

The ethological tradition assumed behavior of the person with a developmental disability occurred because of an adaptive reason and ultimately served an evolutionary function (Charlesworth, 1978). The ecological tradition (Schoggen, 1978) assumed complex transactional relationships between the person being observed and his or her environment. The unit of analysis for the ethologist was the reflex, fixed action pattern or some similar component of behavior believed to serve an adaptive function. The units of relevance to the ecologist were molar person-environment complex variables. For the ethologist, maintaining detailed records of the individual's sequences of responses after an eliciting event (e.g., a nipple touching an infant's cheek) was a common measurement strategy. To the ecologist, the specimen record and the behavior-setting survey were essential to interpreting an individual's behavior in his or her natural environment (Barker & Wright, 1955).

The behavioral units of interest in applied behavior analysis were defined two ways. They were of practical and social importance to the person and to others around the individual (Baer, Wolf, & Risley, 1968). Being able to feed oneself and choose preferred foods is of practical social significance. Behavior of only theoretical significance generally was not a focus of attention. Second, the behavior was assumed to serve some function, not in the evolutionary sense but an immediate reinforcing function. It is assumed that behavior (both adaptive and maladaptive) occurs for a good reason in the immediate environment and serves a purpose. The individual learns to use a spoon correctly if that skill allows him or her to gain access to preferred foods when he or she wants them. A man with severe developmental delay stops striking others with his fists if he is able to induce others to stop shoving him as he gets into the van by using a gesture to indicate that he wants them to move away from him. Functional units (cf.

Thompson & Lubinski, 1986) are not defined by their size or their appearance; rather, they are viewed as components of an individual's actions that serve a common purpose or are controlled by a common consequence.

These three traditions have led to different measurement strategies, but all agree on one thing: Standardized tests do not adequately characterize how an individual functions in his or her natural environment, nor do they reveal the reasons people with developmental disabilities do the things they do. Checklists, rating scales, and similar instruments have shortcomings when they are used to evaluate intervention outcomes. Even today, however, there is great disagreement among professionals about the role of direct behavioral observation as opposed to the use of standardized, norm-referenced tests. From diagnostic decisions, to evaluating the adequacy of environments for individuals with specific developmental characteristics, to determining treatment outcomes, there are vast differences in the underlying assumptions about the role of behavioral observation among professionals.

Issues such as these led a group of researchers specializing in the study of the behavior and psychological status of people with intellectual disability to convene a conference in June 1976 sponsored by the National Institute of Child Health and Human Development. The meeting was held at the Lake Wilderness Conference Center near Seattle, Washington. It was intended to explore state-of-the-art knowledge about the "Application of Observational-Ethological Methods to the Study of Mental Retardation." The main questions before the 40 researchers who participated in that conference concerned the adequacy of observational theory and methods for quantifying critical features of intellectual disability. A two-volume set based on the conference, entitled *Observing Behavior* (edited by Gene P. Sackett), was published in 1978.

The conference proceedings referred to promising new computer technologies that were not then generally available but that participants anticipated would make accumulating and summarizing observational data far more manageable. A handheld protocomputer (the DATAMYTE) with a keyboard for recording observational data was just being developed but was not widely used. In 1976, when the conference was held, behavioral observations were recorded by using a pencil and paper attached to a clipboard. Aggregating, summarizing, and analyzing the resulting raw data were extraordinarily labor-intensive. As a result, few researchers attempted any but the simplest of observational studies.

PURPOSE OF THIS BOOK

Behavioral Observation: Technology and Applications in Developmental Disabilities reassesses the state of knowledge concerning the use of observational methods to understand the nature of intellectual disabilities and developmental disabilities, to evaluate transactions between individuals with developmental disabilities and their surroundings, and to assess the use of observational methods to measure intervention outcomes. As with the Lake Wilderness Conference volumes, this volume grew out of a 3-day workshop at the annual Gatlinburg Conference on Research and Theory in Mental Retardation and Developmental Disabilities, held in Riverside, California, in March 1997. Although the focus is on individuals with intellectual disabilities and related developmental disabilities, most of the material is applicable to other fields as well, such as child care, mental health, services for people with dementia, and other areas of general and special education. Two major forces have driven the decision to create this volume. An enormous amount has been learned since the mid-1970s about the nature of various developmental disabilities and the relationships of individuals with intellectual disabilities with their surroundings. This new knowledge base has changed what is being observed, how and when it is observed, and how the resulting data are analyzed. Equally important, computer technology has revolutionized behavioral observational research. The availability of handheld optical bar code readers; palmtop, laptop, and desktop computers; and lightweight, flexible videotape technologies has revolutionized behavioral observational research. It has made it possible to obtain quantitative behavioral observations of a wider array of people under a broader range of circumstances than was possible in 1976. The use of computer databases and data analysis packages has made it possible to sort, aggregate, and analyze prodigious volumes of data in a minimal amount of time with minimal effort. This has led to new theories and applications of improved quantitative methods to explore the relationships between behavior and environmental events in real time.

The purpose of this book is fourfold: Section I summarizes past and current observational methods and research findings and their relevance for understanding and improving observational methods. Section II presents an array of computer-assisted observational systems, both hardware and software, being used by professionals in various fields of developmental disabilities. Sections III and IV illustrate the use of computer-assisted technologies in an array of community environments and demonstrate the flexibility of these technologies for a broad range of applied research questions. Finally, Section V explores theoretical and methodological issues in the quantification of observational data obtained via computer-assisted systems.

PURPOSES OF OBSERVING BEHAVIOR

Behavior is observed directly for applied reasons as well as for use as a tool in research. Behavioral observation can be an essential tool in differential diagnosis and in understanding variability. In using norm-referenced tests, variability is a problem. In direct behavioral observation, however, variability is often the clue that leads investigators or practitioners to identify the factors responsible for individual differences. A cluster of behavioral features that co-vary among some people within a given diagnostic category (see, e.g., the *Diagnostic and Statistical Manual of Mental Disorders, Fourth Edition* [DSM-IV]; American Psychiatric Association, 1994) but not others within that same taxon can provide essential information that can be related to genotypic abnormalities. Behavioral observations can be used to evaluate the role of adverse living environments in shaping the behavior of individuals with developmental delays (see Chapters 8 and 11 on quality of life in residential settings). Behavioral observation can help us understand the circumstances under which some students profit from specific education practices but others do not (see Chapters 13 and 15). Behavioral observation procedures can be the most effective tool for evaluating the effects of social, educational, and pharmacological interventions and treatments (see Chapters 12, 15, and 17).

ASSUMPTIONS UNDERLYING BEHAVIORAL OBSERVATION

Prior to beginning to observe behavior, several assumptions need to be examined. It might seem obvious what the researcher or practitioner should observe, but in reality it may not be clear precisely which aspects of behavior will be most informative. In addition, the most appropriate and effective measurement approach must be selected, a direct versus an indirect measurement approach (e.g., checklist, rating scale). Finally, certain behavior problems do not lend themselves to direct observational methods, because they are difficult to observe or because of ethical considerations. In this section, we explore some of these assumptions.

Choosing What to Observe

Certain types of behavior are of concern because of their practical importance. The number of words per minute read correctly by a child with dyslexia during special education reading instruction, the number of potatoes sliced per hour in a fast-food job setting, and the number of assaults against other people in a residential environment are all inherently significant. These behavioral measures are not important because they indicate anything else; they are significant in their own right. Reading fluently, keeping up with the pace required at one's job, and injuring others are intrinsically meaningful and socially relevant.

Other types of activity (e.g., making verbal threats against others) may be important not because of the threats per se but because intimidation can be viewed as a member of a larger class of aggressive behaviors, some of which eventually can cause bodily harm to others. It is assumed that threats are correlated with the probability of occurrence of other behaviors within the broader functional class—namely, behavior that causes harm or submission by others (i.e., aggression). We (Lubinski & Thompson, 1986) argued elsewhere that such dispositional clusters or response families involve groups of behavioral instances that may appear different in form but that share common controlling variables and serve similar functions. It is seldom possible to predict with accuracy which member of a dispositional cluster will actually occur on a given occasion, but the fact that one member of a class will occur often can be stated with considerable accuracy. In a verbal association test, if the stimulus is "cat," the listener will be likely to respond by saying "dog," "kitten," or "mouse." Only one verbal utterance can occur at any moment, however (e.g., "dog"). The number of constituent responses defining a dispositional cluster can be determined only by observing a person's behavior for an extended period and under a wide range of circumstances. When we say "He seems very aggressive" after a verbal threat, we are subjectively estimating the likelihood that the individual will strike another resident, pinch a staff member, or scratch his or her teacher, all of which are viewed as members of a single dispositional response class (i.e., aggression).

Direct and Indirect Behavioral Measurement Approaches

The task of assessing the nature and strength of a person's major response tendencies can be a formidable undertaking. It can involve detailed observation for an extended period under a wide range of circumstances, some of which may involve invasion of privacy. In practice, since the mid-1900s the solution to this problem has been to use rating scales and checklists to estimate response dispositions. Consider the following Likert rating scale: from 0 to 5, where 0 indicates not at all aggressive and 5 indicates dangerous. Using such a scale, the rater estimates the relative frequency and intensity of aggressive behavioral outbursts that might have been observed had it been possible to observe a given individual for many weeks under a wide array of circumstances. A behavioral rating scale is an estimate of the behavior one would actually have observed in practice were it possible to do so. The validity of rating scales depends on the adequacy with which items are included that sample most members of the dispositional response class. The same is true of direct behavioral observations. In assessing the effects of a treatment (e.g., a new medication to reduce aggression), several members of the seemingly heterogeneous group of responses called *aggressive* must be included in the response class being observed.

Raters estimate the strength, or the probability, of occurrence of members of a cluster of responses by periodically observing the individual, by talking with others (e.g., parents, teachers) who interact with the individual, and by reviewing documents, all of which collectively create an impression that shapes a rating. In practice, the rater may actually observe the individual being rated infrequently and may witness only one or two instances of the cluster of responses in question. Nonetheless, the rater will make an estimate of the strength of a cluster of response tendencies. Ratings are powerfully influenced by many different factors, some of which are unrelated to the behavior being observed. Sanger, MacLean, and Van Slyke (1992) showed that maternal ratings of a child's behavior problems using standardized checklists were influenced by psychological distress and marital adjustment. This suggests that findings derived from child behavior scales should be interpreted relative to the overall family context. In psychopathology research, Rutter (1997) noted that not only is there generally weak agreement between ratings by different informants but the patterns of correlates vary by informants. In addition, recency effects may result in raters' devaluing events that occur over several days or over a longer interval (Schwartz, 1999). A rating of an individual's aggressive behavior during the preceding week may be determined largely by the outburst that led to a staff injury earlier that morning, although the individual may have displayed few instances of aggression for the previous 6 days.

Definitions of response classes are usually explicit when using direct behavioral observations, but often they are not carefully developed when using ratings to estimate the strength of response tendencies. In direct observational approaches, verbal descriptions of each type of behavior being recorded are used and agreed on by all observers. Each behavioral description is referred to as a behavioral *code*, and the process of recording such instances (e.g., from a videotape recording) is called *coding*. Without carefully specified criteria for determining when a particular type of behavior is or is not a member of the class in question, considerable variability can result. Aggression can mean different things to different people, depending on personal experience and social background. An observer who grew up in a tough neighborhood and had previously worked as a counselor in a correctional facility may have a high threshold for considering an action aggressive. Another observer may believe that a socially insensitive remark about another person's appearance is an aggressive comment. Although it is possible to clarify such differences before using rating scales, in practice that is almost never done. Operational definitions (i.e., behavioral codes) are always a part of direct, systematic observational systems.

Rating scales often are used because norms may be available for various groups of individuals (e.g., typically developing children, adult psychiatric patients). Thus, these ratings are especially useful because they show how the response tendencies of a group of people being studied differ from those of a reference group. In addition, they show how those tendencies change over time or in response to an experimental intervention such as medication or an educational procedure. Professionals trained in clinical psychology, school psychology, and psychiatry are so accustomed to using standardized rating scales as part of their professional activities in evaluating clients, students, and patients that they often forget that such instruments are estimates of what they would see if they observed the individuals systematically.

It is often assumed that rating scales are inherently superior measures, but this is not necessarily the case. In practice, such indirect methods give variable information that is often less sensitive to the behavior of a given individual, especially in the evaluation of intervention outcomes. Schroeder, Rojahn, and Reese (1997) showed that the majority of instruments used to evaluate drug effects on self-injurious behavior are insensitive to changes in daily rates of target behaviors. Rating scales overemphasize the validity of the reference categories (e.g., taxons) and the factors associated with those categories (e.g., subscales within a given taxon), which often is not warranted (Bussing, Schuhmann, Belin, Widawski, & Perwien, 1998; Mahoney et al., 1998). If, for example, one were to score the presence or absence of various component signs and symptoms of attention-deficit/hyperactivity disorder (ADHD) using the DSM-III (American Psychiatric Association, 1980), DSM-III-R (American Psychiatric Association, 1987), DSM-IV, International Classification of Diseases-9 (World Health Organization, 1975), and International Classification of Diseases-10 (World Health Organization, 1992) with the same group of children, one would arrive at different diagnoses for many of the same individuals. Yet, during the time that each diagnostic system was in use by child psychiatrists, child psychologists, and pediatricians, researchers behaved with great certainty about the meaningfulness of diagnoses of ADHD using each of these diagnostic tools. In reality, ratings based on these varying diagnostic features of ADHD often have been of questionable validity, especially when used as measures of treatment outcome.

Rating scales, standardized diagnostic interviews, and other paper-and-pencil tests usually assume an underlying psychological or psychiatric construct that may be causally linked to specific behavioral instances. Typically, groups of items that are related to a hypothesized common underlying construct are developed and evaluated by using factor-analytic methods to determine their ability to distinguish people who have been sorted into categories by using an independent criterion (e.g., experienced clinical judgment). Circular reasoning such as "He is out of his seat frequently because he has ADHD" is commonplace. Too often, the speaker fails to realize that being out of one's seat frequently is part of the defining characteristic of being diagnosed as having ADHD, so such a statement adds nothing.

Direct behavioral observations usually use the individual's behavior or the behavior of members of the dyad being studied as the unit of analysis. A change in frequency or probability of observed behavior following intervention is compared with those same measures during preintervention baseline. The mean change from baseline to postintervention is interpreted in the context of variability of those measures under each condition. Change scores may be averaged across individuals for certain purposes. To facilitate comparison of populations across studies, it may be worthwhile to use a standardized rating scale to characterize several children with ADHD before beginning treatment with a new medication. It does not follow, however, that changes in scores on that same test are most useful in determining whether and how those children benefited from treatment or which side effects emerged. Key target responses with demonstrated educational or clinical face validity can be more useful in determining whether a child profited from treatment and in which ways.

Appropriate and Inappropriate Circumstances
for Use of Direct Behavioral Observation Methods

Practical considerations mitigate against the use of direct behavioral observation methods to measure treatment effects when it may be unsafe or unethical to do so. Behaviors such as fire setting, sexual assault, and severe self-injury (e.g., in Lesch-Nyhan syndrome) cannot be allowed to occur and simply be recorded to assess frequency before, during, and after intervention. There may be circumstances under which the behavior of concern cannot be observed for ethical reasons. Attempting to observe, for example, intimate sexual interactions, personal hygiene activities, illicit drug use, or confidential conversations poses significant ethical problems. Some behaviors, such as theft, are surreptitious and fleeting and therefore do not lend themselves to direct observation assessment methods. The behavior of stealing personal items from fellow residents in a community residential program for adults with developmental delays is rarely observable. The theft is discovered when the personal items are found to be missing, and at a later time the pilfered items are found among the perpetrator's possessions, hidden in a drawer or closet. The act of stealing itself is not observable. Behavior that is infrequent but any occurrence of which is of serious concern (e.g., suicide attempts) is not appropriate for measurement and evaluation by using routine applications of direct behavioral observation methods.

Other psychological processes cannot be observed directly, but behavior associated with them may be observable at times. The hallucinations of an individual with schizophrenia are not observable; but the behavior of a person with schizophrenia who is seen seeming to be talking to someone whom no one else sees, or who is seen picking insects off a wall when no one else in the room sees insects on the wall, is observable and can be recorded. Similarly, delusional thinking cannot be observed directly, but delusional statements (e.g., "God wants me to punish sinners!") can be observed and recorded. Affective states cannot be observed, but behavior associated with those states—such as crying, making self-deprecating statements, making comments of a discouraged and depressive nature, and sighing repeatedly—can be observed. Hand wringing, skin picking, twirling of hair, pacing, and spontaneous statements about feeling nervous or being worried can be recorded as behavioral measures correlated with the presumed mood state of anxiety.

DIFFERENT STRATEGIES TO DIRECTLY OBSERVE AND RECORD BEHAVIOR

The process of behavioral recording unfolds in a predictable although not invariant sequence of steps. This sequence begins with informal observations and later includes operationally defining specific behaviors; developing unique codes; pilot work to evaluate the definitions and the behavioral codes; calibration and observer training; and, finally, implementing the observational protocol according to a specific strategy. To some degree, all of the steps in this process are guided by the question(s) being asked, regardless of whether the observations are being conducted to test theory, evaluate treatments, or appraise program quality. The selected observation strategy should relate directly to the specific nature of the question being asked or the problem to be solved. Questions may concern how often a peer initiates a social interaction (i.e., frequency), how long before someone appears happy during a favorite activity (i.e., latency), how damaging an act of aggression is (i.e., intensity), or how long an individual persists at completing work in a supported employment environment (i.e., duration). In each case, a specific property or dimension of behavior is of importance that must be defined and measured. Thus, an operational definition describes uniquely the specific dimension or dimensions of behavior that result in the behavior being recorded, whether that recording is done by making a mark with a pencil on a sheet of paper, scanning a bar code with an optical bar code reader, or pushing a key on the keyboard of a palmtop computer.

Sampling Rules

After deciding what to observe, decisions regarding who, where, and when to observe must be made. Such decisions are often referred to as *sampling rules* (for a more detailed overview, including the strengths and weaknesses associated with each approach, see Martin & Bateson, 1993). In general, there are four different approaches to deciding which people to observe and when. The terms used to describe these approaches are encountered more frequently in ethology and ecology, but their logic is common to behavioral observation research in intellectual disability and developmental disabilities. The first, *ad libitum sampling,* refers to a strategy whereby no systematic constraints are placed on the observer, who simply records whatever is apparent and relevant during the observation session. Clearly, there are weaknesses associated with this type of observation, depending on the reasons for conducting systematic observations in the first place. Such a strategy can be beneficial during preliminary, informal observations, however. In *focal sampling* an individual or dyad (or some other unit) is observed for a specific amount of time, and all instances of the individual's behavior are recorded. Typically, the behavioral codes are distributed into several different categories. Practical problems associated with the focal individual moving out of view can be lessened if explicit rules are agreed to before the start of an observation session. *Scan sampling* refers to scanning a group of individuals rapidly at fixed intervals. The behavior of each individual is coded at the instant of scanning. In behavioral observation research this strategy is best illustrated by Placheck recording in behavior analysis and special education research (Hall, 1971; LeLaurin & Risley, 1972). Placheck is used when recording group behavior. Similar to conventional time sampling, the total observation period is divided into equal or variable intervals. At the completion of each interval, the observer counts and records 1) the number of individuals engaged in the target behavior and 2) the number of people who *should* be engaged in the target behavior. By dividing the former by the latter, the proportion of subjects engaged in the target behavior at the end of each interval can be determined. Finally, *behavior sampling* refers to situations in which the observer watches a group of individuals and records specific occurrences of particular types or categories of behavior and notes the details surrounding their occurrence (e.g., who was involved). This sampling strategy is more common in formal ethology and ecology research traditions, but its logic is implicit in many applied behavior research projects involving classroom observations or other settings with groups of people and single target behaviors of interest (e.g., acts of aggression, acts of cooperation).

Recording Strategies

There are numerous strategies to guide the timing and procedure by which behavior is recorded (i.e., the "how" of behavioral recording). There are two general approaches, each with its own subset of specific procedures. Behavior can be either continuously recorded or time sampled. *Continuous recording* refers to recording the onset and offset of each instance of a defined behavior during each observation session. *Time sampling* refers to periodic sampling of defined or target behaviors during the observation session. Both strategies have strengths and weaknesses and specific methods associated with them, which are elaborated briefly in the following paragraphs.

Narrative recording consists of a written account of the events occurring in any given situation or setting. Typically, but not always, the narrative includes the impressions of the observer, the time of day or the time within the observation session that the behavior occurred, the condition of the recording area, and the number of people present. The most frequently encountered method is found in the familiar antecedent-behavior-consequence event-recording technique. An observer records events according to 1) the occurrence of the target behavior, 2) the antecedent conditions, and 3) the consequent events after the target behavior (Bijou et al., 1968).

Event counting during continuous recording requires that each discrete occurrence of the target behavior be recorded. From this record, frequency and rate data can be calculated. *Frequency* is simply the total number of times that the target behavior occurred, whereas rate of response is calculated by dividing the frequency by the duration of the observation period. By convention, much of the direct behavioral observation research in developmental disabilities uses rate per minute (Tawney & Gast, 1984).

Continuous observations also can rely on *duration recording,* in which the duration of each defined target behavior is recorded. The onset of the behavior and the total time that the individual is engaged in the target response are recorded continuously. By summing all occurrences and dividing by the total observation time, the observation data can be transformed into the percentage of time that a given behavior occurs during an observation session (Barton & Johnson, 1990).

Narrative, frequency, and duration recording can provide accurate, reliable measures of behavior. Each method yields direct indices of the duration of responding or the length of time the target behavior occurred. These procedures, however, can be labor-intensive (requiring the constant attention of the observer) and typically capture a limited number of variables at one time, although with the advent of computer-assisted technologies, this problem has diminished. Efforts to improve efficiency without sacrificing accuracy have resulted in additional methods of direct observation that either sample time or record in real time with computer-assisted devices.

Time sampling divides the observation period into short intervals. The occurrence or nonoccurrence of the defined target behaviors is coded within each time interval. Three general forms of time sampling are used. *Whole-interval time sampling* requires that a session be divided into equal time intervals and that an observer code an occurrence of behavior only if the target behavior occurs for the entire duration of the recording interval (e.g., 10, 15, or 20 seconds). During a study of preschool prosocial classroom behavior, for example, instances of a child with disabilities interacting with a peer without disabilities may be coded only if the interaction occurs for the entire duration of the recording interval. *Partial-interval time sampling* allows the observer to code the occurrence of a target behavior if the target behavior occurs at any time within the time interval (e.g., one occurrence within the specified second interval). In keeping with the example used previously, any instance of interaction with a peer during the observation interval would be counted. The third form of time sampling, referred to as *momentary time sampling*, requires the observer to ignore all behavior that occurs before a fixed moment in time (i.e., at the end of an interval) and to record the presence or absence of the target behavior at that moment in time. Thus, only instances of peer interaction that occur at the end of the time interval are recorded.

In general, it is preferable to use numerous short sampling intervals (e.g., 5–10 seconds) separated by a nonsampling period of three to four times the length of the sampling interval (e.g., 30–40 seconds) rather than to use fewer longer sampling intervals. The observe/record interval sizes are determined, in part, by the base rate of the target behavior. With high rate behavior of short duration, small time intervals are required, whereas low rate behavior and behavior with long durations require larger time intervals. For individual recording, when behaviors are of moderate duration and sampling is done repeatedly, momentary time sampling of intervals up to 30 seconds appears to be accurate. In group research, however, momentary time sampling can both overestimate and underestimate occurrences of behavior an equal number of times at intervals of up to 4 minutes (for a detailed review of the research concerning the strengths and weaknesses of time-sampling procedures, see Repp, Barton, & Brulle, 1987).

Recording observation data in real time involves both the frequency and the duration of the specified target behaviors as they occur. This method of recording allows for the coding of onsets and offsets of behavior in direct relation to the passage of time, enabling more elaborate and sophisticated analyses (e.g., examining cycles of responding, behavioral clustering, broad patterns, transitional probabilities). Recording in real time provides the advantages of both frequency and duration recording with none of the limitations associated with time-sampling procedures (e.g., underestimating or overestimating actual occurrences of behavior). Because of advances in computer-assisted software and hardware, collecting data in real time has become a reality, permitting the simultaneous recording of multiple behaviors and analysis of the relationships among them.

RELIABILITY AND VALIDITY OF OBSERVATIONAL MEASURES

As in other measurement systems, reliability and validity are of paramount importance in the direct observation of behavior. If the data collected via direct observation are suspected to be unreliable or invalid, they are of little use in evaluating a treatment outcome, monitoring a program's quality, or providing important diagnostic and assessment information. Furthermore, with the advent of innovations in computer-assisted observation software and complex recording schemes, issues of reliability and validity have important technical and conceptual implications (Vyse & Mulick, 1990).

Reliability

The *reliability* of direct behavioral observation measures refers to the degree to which the measure and its result can be repeated consistently. In this sense, reliable measures are precise, sensitive, and consistent (for a more detailed discussion, see Martin & Bateson, 1993). *Precise measures* are those that are free of random errors and are indexed by the number of figures in the measurement. In psychophysiological recording, for example, measurement precision is reflected in milliseconds rather than in seconds when recording heart activity in relation to behavioral state (see Chapter 7). In behavioral recording, measurement precision is reflected by quantifying the occurrence of behavior by rate rather than by relying on less-precise qualitative statements (e.g., "He does it a lot"). *Sensitive measures* are those that change reliably when changes occur in the variable being measured. In behavioral and psychopharmacological treatment research, it appears that observing some forms of severe behavior problems directly (e.g., self-injury) may be a more sensitive means of detecting behavior change than indirect measures that rely on recall or personal judgment (see Chapter 10). Finally, *consistent measures* refer to those that, when repeated, produce the same results. A system based on direct observation must be able to produce consistent findings in similar situations at different times. If behavior is measured (directly or indirectly) by systems that are imprecise, insensitive, or inconsistent, then real relationships among behavioral and environmental variables are likely to be overlooked or missed and real effects are likely to be ignored or misinterpreted.

Validity

Validity refers to the degree to which a measure or measurement system records or measures the variables it purports to measure and the degree to which the information that is gained is useful for its intended purpose. Behavior can be reliably measured but not valid. Consider a case in which a young girl with a specific reading disability is observed in her classroom using a coding system that records out-of-seat behavior, teacher and peer interaction, and affect (e.g., happy, sad). After repeated observation sessions, her out-of-seat behavior, interactions with teachers and peers, and proportion of time spent in different affective states are quantified precisely and consistently. This can be important information if we are interested in knowing about her social behavior. If our original interest concerns the nature of her reading disability and, specifically, her reading behavior, then our measurement system provides little useful information. It is invalid for our original and intended purpose. Valid measurement systems are accurate, specific, and scientifically or clinically useful (for a more detailed discussion, see Martin & Bateson, 1993). Direct behavioral observation measurement systems should be *accurate* and free of systematic errors (i.e., those that consistently bias outcomes in one direction or another). In other words, direct observational coding schemes should correspond as closely as possible with the true state of affairs. In this regard, valid measurement systems are *specific* and describe what they claim to describe and nothing else. The greater the degree to which a direct observational measure is specific to what it is intended to measure, the more confidence one can have in the validity of the recordings. *Scientific validity* refers to whether the measures used reveal anything important about a person's behavior (Martin & Bateson, 1993). Whether the measure does (or does not) depends on whether the behavior of the person is being observed and recorded for purposes of diagnosis, assessment, evaluation, or treatment monitoring.

CONCLUSIONS

In behavioral observation, one size does not fit all. In designing behavioral observation systems, it is essential to be aware of the basic operating assumptions underlying the phenomenon being assessed, to be cognizant of the basic principles of behavioral observation, and to thoroughly explore alternative strategies for obtaining the necessary information. Tailoring the observation and quantification systems to the unique properties of the behavioral and environmental circumstances under examination is the sine qua non.

REFERENCES

American Psychiatric Association (APA). (1980). *Diagnostic and statistical manual of mental disorders* (3rd ed.). Washington, DC: Author.

American Psychiatric Association (APA). (1987). *Diagnostic and statistical manual of mental disorders* (3rd ed. rev.). Washington, DC: Author.

American Psychiatric Association (APA). (1994). *Diagnostic and statistical manual of mental disorders* (4th ed.). Washington, DC: Author.

Bacon, F. (1994). *Novum organum: With other parts of the great insaturation* (P. Urbach & J. Gibson, eds. & trans.). Chicago: Open Court. (Original work published 1620)

Baer, D.M., Wolf, M.M., & Risley, T.R. (1968). Some current dimensions of applied behavior analysis. *Journal of Applied Behavior Analysis, 1,* 91–97.

Barker, R.G., & Wright, H.F. (1955). *Midwest and its children: The psychological ecology of an American town.* Hamden, CT: Archon Books.

Barton, L.E., & Johnson, H.A. (1990). Observational technology. In S.R. Schroeder (Ed.), *Ecobehavioral analysis and developmental disabilities: The twenty-first century* (pp. 201–227). New York: Springer-Verlag New York.

Bernard, C. (1949) *Experimental medicine* (H.C. Greene, Trans.). New Brunswick, NJ: Transaction Publishers. (Original work published as *Introduction to the Study of Experimental Medicine* in 1865)

Bijou, S.W., Peterson, R.F., & Ault, M.H. (1968). A method to integrate descriptive and experimental field studies at the level of empirical concepts. *Journal of Applied Behavior Analysis, 1,* 175–191.

Bussing, R., Schuhmann, B.A., Belin, T.R., Widawski, M., & Perwien, A.R. (1998). Diagnostic utility of two commonly used ADHD screening measures among special education students. *Journal of the American Academy of Child and Adolescent Psychiatry, 37,* 74–82.

Charlesworth, W. (1978). Ethology: Its relevance for observational studies of human adaptation. In G.P. Sackett (Ed.), *Observing behavior: Vol. 1. Theory and applications in mental retardation* (pp. 7–31). Baltimore: University Park Press.

Goodenough, F.L. (1926). *Measurement of intelligence by drawings.* New York: Arno Press.

Hall, R.V. (1971). *Managing behavior: Behavior modification: The measurement of behavior.* Lawrence, KS: H & H Enterprises.

LeLaurin, K., & Risley, T.R. (1972). The organization of day-care environments: "Zone" vs. "man-to-man" staff assignments. *Journal of Applied Behavior Analysis, 5,* 225–232.

Lubinski, D., & Thompson, T. (1986). Functional units of human behavior and their integration: A dispositional analysis. In T. Thompson & M.D. Zeiler (Eds.), *Analysis and integration of behavioral units.* Mahwah, NJ: Lawrence Erlbaum Associates.

Mahoney, W.J., Szatmari, P., MacLean, J.E., Bryson, S.E., Bartolucci, G., Walter, S.D., Jones, M.B., & Zwaigenbaum, L. (1998). Reliability and accuracy of differentiating pervasive developmental disorder subtypes. *Journal of the American Academy of Child and Adolescent Psychiatry, 37,* 278–285.

Martin, P.R., & Bateson, P.P.G. (1993). *Measuring behavior: An introductory guide* (2nd ed.). New York: Cambridge University Press.

Preyer, W.T. (1973). *The mind of the child: Parts I and II* (H.W. Brown, trans.) (Classics in psychology series). New York: Arno Press. (Original work published as *The Mind of the Child . . . Observations Concerning the Mental Development of the Human Being in the First Years of Life* in 1888)

Repp, A.C., Barton, L., & Brulle, A. (1987). An applied behavior analysis perspective on naturalistic observation and adjustment to new settings. In S. Landesman, P.M. Vietze, & M.J. Begab (Eds.), *Living environments and mental retardation* (pp. 151–172). Washington, DC: American Association on Mental Retardation.

Risley, T.R., & Wolf, M. (1967). Establishing functional speech in echolalic children. *Behaviour Research and Therapy, 5,* 73–88.

Rutter, M. (1997). Child psychiatric disorder: Measures, causal mechanisms, and interventions. *Archives of General Psychiatry, 54,* 785–789.

Sackett, G.P. (Ed.). (1978a). *Observing behavior: Vol. 1. Theory and applications in mental retardation.* Baltimore: University Park Press.

Sackett, G.P. (Ed.). (1978b). *Observing behavior: Vol. 2. Data collection and analysis methods.* Baltimore: University Park Press.

Sanger, M.S., MacLean, W.E., & Van Slyke, D.A. (1992). Relation between maternal characteristics and child behavior ratings: Implications for interpreting behavior checklists. *Clinical Pediatrics, 31,* 461–466.

Schoggen, P. (1978). Ecological psychology and mental retardation. In G.P. Sackett (Ed.), *Observing behavior: Vol. 1. Theory and applications in mental retardation* (pp. 33–62). Baltimore: University Park Press.

Schroeder, S.R., Rojahn, J., & Reese, R.M. (1997). Brief report: Reliability and validity of instruments for assessing psychotropic medication effects on self-injurious behavior in mental retardation. *Journal of Autism and Developmental Disorders, 27,* 89–102.

Schwartz, N. (1999). Self-reports: How the questions shape the answers. *American Psychologist, 54,* 93–105.

Shirley, M.M. (1931–1933). *The first two years: A study of twenty-five babies* (3 vols.). Westport, CT: Greenwood Publishing Group.

Tawney, J.W., & Gast, D.L. (1984). *Single subject research in special education.* Upper Saddle River, NJ: Merrill.

Thompson, T., & Grabowski, J. (1972). *Behavior modification of the mentally retarded.* New York: Oxford University Press.

Thompson, T., & Lubinski, D. (1986). Units of analysis and kinetic structure of behavioral repertoires. *Journal of Experimental Analysis of Behavior, 46,* 219–242.

Vyse, S.A., & Mulick, J.A. (1990). Ecobehavioral assessment: Future directions in the planning and evaluation of behavioral intervention. In S.R. Schroeder (Ed.), *Ecobehavioral analysis and developmental disabilities: The twenty-first century* (pp. 64–81). New York: Springer-Verlag New York.

World Health Organization (WHO). (1975). *International classification of diseases* (9th rev.). Geneva: Author.

World Health Organization (WHO). (1992). *International classification of diseases* (10th rev.). Geneva: Author.

2

Observational Research in Mental Retardation

American Journal of Mental Deficiency and American Journal on Mental Retardation, 1940–1995

Gene P. Sackett

The most honest "Methods" section, 1940–1995:

> Ten cases were selected because they make a nice round number and do not unduly extend the length of the paper.
> A.M. Gordon (*American Journal of Mental Deficiency*, 1946, p. 409)

A milestone in my career, and perhaps also an event of importance to behavioral studies in mental retardation, was a conference held in June 1976 on the observation of behavior. The National Institute of Child Health and Human Development sponsored and funded the conference[1] along with the University of Washington Child Development and Mental Retardation Center.[2] More than 30 distinguished researchers in the fields of child development, clinical psychology,

---

[1]My thanks to Drs. Michael Begab and Theodore Tjossem, National Institute of Child Health and Human Development Mental Retardation Branch, for their support of the Lake Wilderness Conference and the subsequent publication of the proceedings.

[2]Now named the University of Washington Center on Human Development and Disability.

This review, and my longtime interest in mental retardation and observational research, was supported by National Institutes of Health (NIH) Grant No. HD08633 to the Center on Human Development and Disability and NIH Grant No. RR00166 to the Washington Regional Primate Research Center. I also thank Kate Elias for her editorial expertise.

and mental retardation attended the 4-day meeting held at the University of Washington's Lake Wilderness facility. The setting was many miles from any extraneous influences or entertainment, so the participants had to entertain each other. The result was a two-volume work entitled *Observing Behavior*, which presented empirical studies illustrating applications of observational methods to problems in mental retardation and reviewed a number of fundamental methodological topics related to quantitative behavioral observation (Sackett, 1978).

This chapter is based on a talk presented at the Gatlinburg Conference on Research and Theory in Mental Retardation and Developmental Disabilities held in Riverside, California, in March 1997. After I accepted an invitation to participate in the conference workshop on observational methods, I realized that I had done almost no work on the topic for more than a decade. I had wondered for many years, however, whether *Observing Behavior* had had an impact on the quantity or the quality of observational research in the mental retardation field. So, I decided to approach an answer by reviewing 55 years' worth of research studies in the *American Journal of Mental Deficiency* (*AJMD*), since renamed the *American Journal on Mental Retardation* (*AJMR*) in 1987, which I have designated collectively as *AJMD(R)*. I selected the years 1940–1995 because they provide a good time range for the assessment of trends before and after the publication of *Observing Behavior*—and, not incidentally, because Volume 45 (1940) was the earliest available volume in the University of Washington libraries. I read the abstract and methods sections of all research studies published in these volumes, and, in the case of papers on observational methods, I read the whole article. My primary hypotheses were that, after 1980, there would be an increase in published quantitative observational research and that these studies would be more sophisticated than those from before 1980.

WHY ENGAGE IN QUANTITATIVE BEHAVIORAL OBSERVATION STUDIES?

The implementation of quantitative observational studies is often a complex, time-consuming, and potentially expensive endeavor. Although important advances have occurred since the 1970s with respect to the development of coding systems, assessment and maintenance of observer reliability, management of large databases, and statistical analysis (e.g., Altmann, 1974; Bakeman & Gottman, 1997; Bakeman & Quera, 1995; Fleiss, 1981; Martin & Bateson, 1993; Sackett, 1979; Suen & Ary, 1989; Taplin & Reid, 1973), initiating and completing a quantitative observational study can be a daunting experience. Then why perform such studies? Why not simply devise standardized psychological tests, questionnaires, or controlled experiments to determine what an individual is capable of doing, to place an individual's test performance in some relation to that of other individuals in a population, or to study group differences under varied conditions?

The answer is simple, even if attaining that answer is not. The main purpose of systematic quantitative observation is to measure what individuals actually do during their daily life activities. Although these methods are also applied in controlled situations, the strength of modern quantitative observational techniques lies in their application to the study of individual and group differences under naturalistic or seminaturalistic conditions. Other methods, such as laboratory experiments with automated measures, questionnaires, standardized tests, medical histories, and clinical interviews, measure what an individual can do, what an individual might be able to do, or even what an individual might have done in the past; but these methods do not quantitatively document what individuals actually are doing during a typical—or even an atypical—day.

CHARACTERISTICS OF THE REVIEW

In conducting this review, I had two goals in mind: 1) to determine how many of the total number of research studies in the *AJMD(R)* used quantitative behavioral observation and 2) to measure some important characteristics of these observational studies. My basic assumption was that these observational studies represented the state of the art in mental retardation research at the time that they were conducted.

Total Studies Count

An article was considered to be a research study if it was a data-based paper and contained results and some type of statistical summary or analysis. An article was not counted if it was a review, editorial, or comment on social policy; a description of an institution or a geographical area; a description of educational plans or therapy regimens; a simple case study; a sociometric rating study that did not compare any independent variables; a descriptive study that measured a single response, such as correct or incorrect responses on a task; or a descriptive epidemiological study that made no comparisons between independent variables.

Observational Studies

Two types of observational studies were counted. Type 1 involved real-time or time-sampled behaviors yielding quantitative scores: true frequencies and/or durations, modified frequencies (1-0 scores), or time-point frequencies. These studies were almost always done by professional personnel trained in a behavioral science or nursing or by their students or laboratory assistants. Type 2 involved rating-scale measures. These studies were included only if the ratings were done at or near the time of observation. The maximum time between observation and rating for these studies was 1 week, although even this is probably too long. These studies often were done by caregiver personnel, nurses, or other medical staff; but some were done by behavioral scientists and their students. Many other studies made ratings at monthly, quarterly, or even yearly intervals. These were not considered to be objective observational studies involving what people actually did during their daily activities.

The quantitative and rating studies also were categorized by whether they were purely descriptive or actually tested a hypothesis. The latter were identified by a statement of the hypothesis and/or by the presence of at least a single one-tailed statistical test. Any study that had no hypothesis was categorized as descriptive. A study using two-tailed tests was always considered descriptive, even if a hypothesis seemed to be presented.

Other Measures

Observational studies varied in terms of the type of testing situation. Some studies assessed free behavior (i.e., activities occurring with minimal or no supervision or structure). Examples include play periods for children and after-dinner evening activities in a ward or home environment. Other studies assessed behavior in more structured settings, such as at mealtime, in school or other learning environments, or in a work situation. The general characteristic of a structured setting is to restrict the range of activities, usually emphasizing behaviors related to one or more goals. The third situational variation involved experimental manipulations. A familiar example of this type of study is the Ainsworth "strange situation," in which a series of scenarios is set up to assess an infant's or a child's responses to a strange person, to being alone, or to being reunited with a parent or other caregiver. Another example is the assessment of the social behavior of children with mental retardation while they interact in a playroom with similar children, with children without mental retardation, or with mixed groups.

Observational studies also varied in terms of the primary type of behavior measured. This included social behavior and its appropriate adaptive activities; atypical, deviant, or maladaptive activities; language behavior; and "other" topics. The "Other" category included the caregiver's behavior; skill learning usually performed in structured situations; operant behavior modification studies that included more than one subject and a number of measures, not simply one target response; and the behavior of a supervisor or other "superior" staff member. Some studies measured several of these behavior types. The primary emphasis of the work usually was obvious. If it was not, as in the case of studies involving atypical activities and one of the other categories, I flipped a coin to determine the primary behavior type.

My most subjective category involved "could-haves." These were studies that I believed could have benefited from the use of direct observation, often because the purpose and/or the hypothesis involved a group's typical behaviors, but instead the researcher used a nonobservational technique. For example, investigators often used the Vineland Adaptive Behavior Scales (Sparrow, Balla, & Cicchetti, 1984) to measure the adaptive abilities of a group of people with mental retardation versus those of a group of people without mental retardation rather than actually observe each individual's activities in real time. Studies that were specifically designed to assess some technical property, such as the reliability of a particular instrument or the correlations between several instruments, were not considered to be could-haves.

The categories measured in this review are summarized in Table 1. All were based on frequency counts and are presented in Figures 1–6 as either frequencies or percentages derived from the counts. Each measure was made for each issue of the *AJMD(R)*, Volumes 45–100. The data were then summarized as either means per volume or percentages per 5-year period, except for the 6-year period 1940–1945.[3]

FINDINGS

The findings for each measured category as well as my reliability in measuring them are presented next.

---

[3]The *AJMD(R)* has a peculiar split cycle per volume. The first two issues are in the last half of a year and the last two issues are in the first half of the next year. For example, Volume 100 starts in July 1995 and ends in June 1996. This constitutes the year 1995 for this review. Therefore, the beginning of each 5-year period in this review is actually the last 6 months of the first year in the period. The end of the 5-year period is actually the first 6 months of the year after the end of the period. I hope the reader is not as confused as I was when I first tackled this job.

Table 1.   Frequency measures used in this review

Category	Description
Totals	Pages Research studies Observational research studies
Type of observational study	Quantitative observations Ratings Test of a hypothesis Descriptive
Type of test situation	Free behavior Structured Experimental manipulations
Type of behavior	Social-adaptive Abnormal-deviant Language Other
Could-have	Could have used observational methods but did not

Each measure was made for all issues of the *American Journal of Mental Deficiency* and the *American Journal on Mental Retardation,* Volumes 45–100.

Reliability

The first challenge of any measurement system based on human judgment concerns intraobserver reliability, the degree to which one observer can generate the same scores on repeated measurements of the same material. This is obviously more important than the more common interobserver reliability measures presented in most observational research articles. If one observer cannot generate the same measurements consistently and reliably, how can one expect two observers to agree with one another?

I assessed intraobserver reliability by remeasuring six categories of information in 11 individual volumes. Table 2 presents the results in terms of Pearson correlations and the mean differences between the 11 pairs of measurements. The correlations seemed reasonable and the mean differences were respectable, being less than one study difference per year for total observational studies and less than 2.5% difference for the quantitative and hypothesis-testing study types. As I expected, given its subjective nature, the could-have category had a relatively low

Table 2.   Intraobserver reliability

Measure	Pearson *r*	Mean difference (per year)
Total pages	1.00	0 studies
Total studies	0.95	2.3 studies
Total observational studies	0.96	−.37 studies
Quantitative studies	0.92	2.1%
Testing hypotheses	0.91	2.4%
Could-have	0.82	−6.9%

Resurvey of years 1945, 1950, 1955, 1960, 1965, 1970, 1975, 1980, 1985, 1990, and 1995.

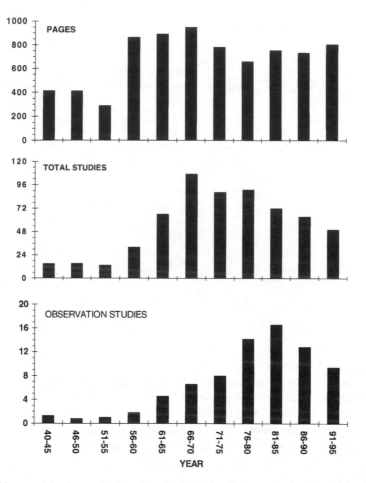

Figure 1.   Mean number of pages (top), total studies (middle), and observational studies (bottom) per yearly volume in each 5-year period of the *AJMD(R)* from 1940 to 1995.

correlation and a fairly large percentage difference, although both measures for this category seemed acceptable for this type of work. In summary, the review measurement system appeared to have good intraobserver reliability, at least with me as the observer.

Overall Frequencies

Figure 1 presents mean frequency measures per volume per 5-year period. From 1956–1960 through 1991–1995, the number of pages per volume was similar at about 700–900 per year. The total number of studies declined after the 1966–1970 period, indicating that articles were getting longer, especially after the 1976–1980 period. The frequency of observational studies began to increase steadily after the 1956–1960 period and peaked in the 1981–1985 period, but then declined. With respect to my hypothesis, it seems that *Observing Behavior* was part of a general trend toward increased interest in doing observational studies rather than a cause of the trend. Unfortunately, there seems to be a fairly marked trend toward a decrease in observational work on mental retardation. It would be of some interest to determine whether this trend is related to a decline in the availability of

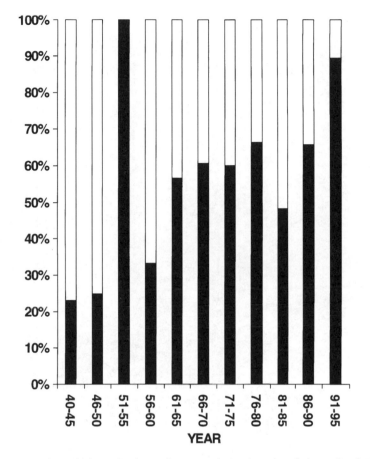

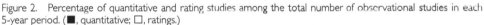

Figure 2.   Percentage of quantitative and rating studies among the total number of observational studies in each 5-year period. (■, quantitative; □, ratings.)

funds for observational studies in the mental retardation field or in behavioral sciences in general.

Type of Study

Figure 2 presents the percentage of quantitative and rating observational studies among the total number of observational studies per volume per period. With the exception of 1951–1955, quantitative studies increased over rating research during most periods. Unfortunately for my hypothesis, the 1981–1985 period actually showed a small decrease in quantitative studies from the previous long-term trend.

Figure 3 presents the percentage of observational studies that were descriptive versus those that tested a hypothesis. With the exception of those published during 1956–1960 and 1971–1975, almost all of the observational studies were descriptive. The overall average of studies that tested a hypothesis was about 20% per 5-year period. This suggests that mental retardation researchers often do not use theories on which to base research hypotheses with respect to the repertoire of behaviors that may be expected from the individuals under study.

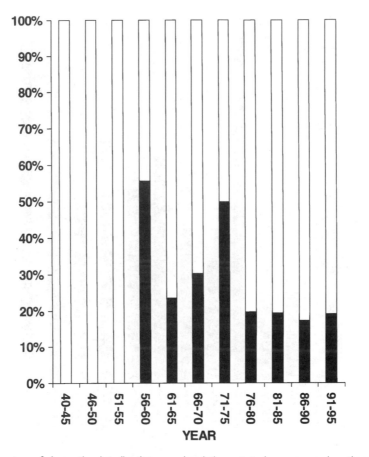

Figure 3.   Percentage of observational studies that were descriptive or tested one or more hypotheses in each 5-year period. (■, hypothesis testing; □, descriptive.)

Test Situations

Figure 4 presents percentages for the three types of testing situations relative to the total number of observational studies. In general, free behavior settings declined during the 55 years of the review period. Experimental studies showed an increase through 1981–1985 but a decline from 1986 to 1995. Structured settings had the highest percentage during this final 10-year period reviewed. These trends seem to contradict the idea that the main strength of observational research is that it involves measurement in relatively unstructured, free behavior situations. It seems that mental retardation researchers do not have a great deal of interest in free behavior studies or that there may be insufficient funding for such work.

Behavior Types

Figure 5 presents percentages by content type. Studies of social-adaptive and atypical-deviant behaviors constituted a large majority of the observational studies during the years reviewed. The "Other" category largely disappeared during the final 15 years of the review, whereas language studies may be on the increase. It seems clear that the main concern of research aimed at understanding the

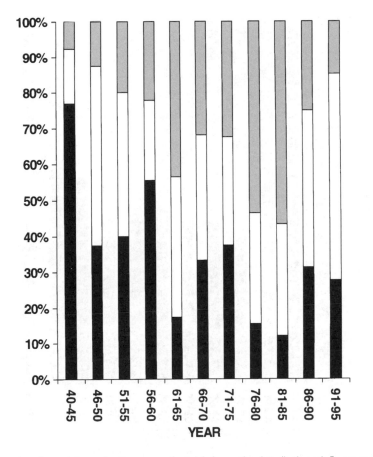

Figure 4.   Percentage for each type of setting among the total observational studies in each 5-year period. (■, free behavior; □, structured; ▨, experimental.)

behavioral repertoire of people with mental retardation has been, and remains, social and atypical behavior. This seems unfortunate because major advances have been made in understanding the brain mechanisms involved in learning and memory and in the neuropsychology of developmental processes (e.g., Diamond, 1991; Goldman-Rakic, 1994; Greenough & Black, 1992; Roberts & Pennington, 1996). These research areas could certainly benefit from data concerning how cognitive abilities and language are actually used by people with mental retardation during their typical activities and in social and adaptive behavior.

Could-Haves

Figure 6 shows the percentage of observational studies among the total number of research studies and the percentage of studies that could have used observational methods but did not do so among the total number of studies minus the number of observational studies. In general, the percentage of could-have studies was lower than that of observational studies. A trend may have appeared, however, starting in the 1981–1985 period, for an increase in studies that could have benefited from the use of observation but did not use these methods. It also should be noted that the percentage of observational studies declined markedly in the 1991–1995 period.

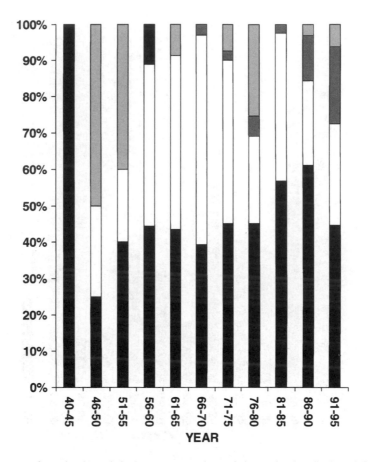

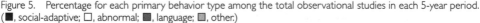

Figure 5.   Percentage for each primary behavior type among the total observational studies in each 5-year period. (■, social-adaptive; □, abnormal; ■, language; ▩, other.)

No-Show or Almost No-Show Topics

A number of important topics in the development and use of observational systems were not found or occurred very rarely in the *AJMD(R)*. These topics are discussed in the following paragraphs.

1.   No observational study presented a statistical power analysis or even discussed the relation between the findings and the variability of the data with regard to the magnitude of statistical effect that could be detected. This is especially important with respect to studies that had marginal observer reliability, a major source of statistical error (e.g., Suen, 1987).

2.   Of the hundreds of observational studies reviewed, only three presented intercorrelations between all of the behavioral categories measured. Therefore, readers had no idea which of the often large number of comparisons made in the study were actually independent. Of course, this criticism can be leveled at many observational studies, regardless of the journal in which they appear.

3.   Few studies assessed learning and problem-solving abilities during an individual's everyday activities. This would seem to be a requisite validity study

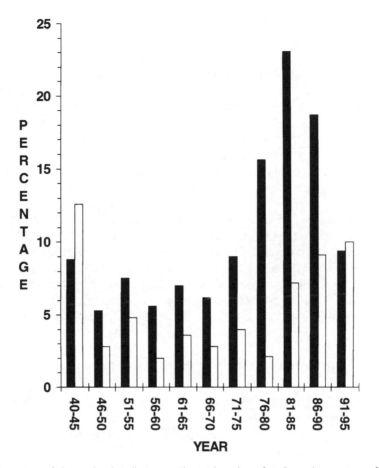

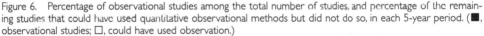

Figure 6.   Percentage of observational studies among the total number of studies, and percentage of the remaining studies that could have used quantitative observational methods but did not do so, in each 5-year period. (■, observational studies; □, could have used observation.)

for any educational training program attempting to teach skills that are to be used in "real life."

4.   There were almost no studies that attempted to measure behavioral organization within and/or between individuals. Such studies involve sequential analysis methods (e.g., Sackett, 1979) and social systems analyses (e.g., Sameroff, 1995; Thelen & Smith, 1994). This seems surprising, given that social behavior is the modal observational study topic in almost every 5-year period reviewed.

5.   Most important, almost no studies used state-of-the-art techniques to assess observer reliability. In fact, the majority of studies presented no reliability analyses whatsoever.

These five "no-show" areas suggest that the sophistication of observational research in the mental retardation field—at least as illustrated by articles published in the *AJMD(R)*—has a long way to go to catch up with advances in observational research methods since the 1970s.

Observational Study "Firsts" in the AJMD(R)

A second type of information related to the sophistication of observational research concerns the date of the first use of state-of-the-art methods and procedures. For example, the first sophisticated observational study was a relatively early one that Tizard published in 1953. The work involved the effects of different types of supervision on the behavior of people with mental retardation in a sheltered workshop. The method included 10-second 1-0 (i.e., modified frequency) time sampling, daily conduct and work activity ratings, 1-minute samples of distracting talk, monthly rankings of behavioral traits, formal reliability checks using Kendall coefficients of concordance, and the use of repeated-measure analyses of variance. This study was ahead of its time because many of these methods were not yet common in child development or other psychological research.

The first real-time observational study was not published until 1976. In that study, Frankel and Graham used an Esterline-Angus chart recorder to measure event frequencies. I had used this technique in the precomputer days of 1963 to measure real-time frequencies, durations, and sequences in my first study of rhesus monkeys in Harlow's laboratory at the University of Wisconsin. I note, however, that Harlow never used real-time recording, preferring modified frequency methods using paper and pencil. Maybe Harry Harlow knew what he was doing?

Some other important firsts include the following:

1. Buiun, Rynders, and Turnure reported the first maternal language study in 1974.

2. Browning, Campbell, and Spence reported the first complex behavioral organization measurement scheme in 1974. They measured triadic interaction patterns, although the patterns were predefined rather than detected through sequential analysis methods.

3. The important methodological advance of comparing retrospective ratings with direct observation measures was reported for the first time by Millham, Chilcutt, and Atkinson in 1978.

4. The first report to use behavioral duration as the primary dependent variable was presented by Carsrud, Carsrud, Henderson, Alisch, and Fowler in 1979. It might also be noted that this was the first report to use the phrase *retarded persons* in its title.

5. The first observational study using videotape methods was reported by Guralnick and Paul-Brown in 1980.

6. Stoneman, Brody, and Abbott published the first sequential analysis study in 1983. However, they used analysis of variance procedures to study group differences in frequencies rather than the conditional probabilities used in current research.

7. The first study to actually present a sequential analysis based on conditional probabilities was reported by Maurer and Sherrod in 1987. However, these conditional values were not adjusted for or compared with any "chance" expected probabilities or other base rate measures, even though there were more than a decade's worth of relevant statistical articles available at the time of the study.

8. The first observational study of cognitive skill use during free behavior was published by Malone and Stoneman in 1990. This occurred after at least 50 years of published articles that had attempted to teach a cognitive skill in a structured educational or experimental environment.

9. In 1993, Guess et al. published the first use of sequential analysis with correct expected values and a statistical description of behavioral cyclicity. Few investigators followed this seminal work with other sophisticated observational research on behavioral organization. This is unfortunate because much pharmacological research and other types of therapeutic research are aimed at altering the organization of an individual's behavior. Direct observation of such behavior is the most objective means of assessing both the validity and the safety of therapeutic efforts.

CONCLUSIONS

This review has produced several interesting findings and a few possible conclusions.

1. Twenty-five years of increased numbers and percentages of observational studies published in *AJMD(R)* peaked in the 1981–1985 period. This peak was followed by a decline in both the number of observational studies per volume and the percentage per 5-year period. This pattern did not support my hypothesis that the publication of *Observing Behavior* (Sackett, 1978), the first book that specifically addressed observational research theory, content, and methodology for mental retardation studies, triggered an increase in the number of observational studies in this field.

2. Study topics related to mental retardation have changed little since 1940. Social, adaptive, and atypical behaviors continue to be the main topics. Studies that express clear hypotheses, as opposed to descriptive research, constitute a small minority of the observational research during the review period. This suggests that few observational researchers in the mental retardation field base their work on testable theory. Given the advances in the neurobiology of behavior, social systems theory, and general systems theory since the 1980s (e.g., Dawson, 1994; Parke & Ladd, 1992; and citations in the preceding sections "Behavior Types" and "Could-Haves"), it might be concluded that observational research on mental retardation lacks the theoretical sophistication of such research in many other behavioral and psychobiological sciences.

3. Quantitative studies of real-time behavior did overtake rating studies. This suggests that the researchers engaged in observational work are interested in directly measuring what individuals are doing in their research environments. However, those environments have become primarily structured ones rather than the free behavior environments that can tell researchers what individuals are doing during their daily lives.

4. There has been an increase in the percentage of studies that could have used direct observation but did not. Many of these studies involved educational, training, or therapeutic goals. The measures in these studies were most often standard test scores, quarterly or even yearly ratings, or a specific behavior in a struc-

tured or experimental environment. This was especially true of studies that used pharmacological or other medically based therapies. The basic validity and utility of such studies depends on the ability to generalize behavior change from the structured or experimental research environment to the everyday behavior of the individuals receiving the therapy, education, or training. As a simple example, suppose an individual with mental retardation learns to read in a school environment. Does that individual actually do any reading outside of that environment? A naturalistic study using quantitative observation can answer this question.

In summary, the overall conclusion of this review is that there have been fewer quantitative, naturalistic or seminaturalistic, hypothesis-testing studies in the mental retardation field since the 1980s. The studies that have been done are often methodologically unsophisticated and atheoretical. Almost all of them concern social-adaptive and atypical behavior as opposed to the use of learning, memory, and language skills in daily life.

There are several possible nonexclusive explanations for these findings. Perhaps most mental retardation researchers who publish in the *American Journal on Mental Retardation,* or the editors and reviewers of that journal, are not interested in what individuals with mental retardation do during their daily lives. Maybe most mental retardation studies using observation are too unsophisticated in methodology or theory to pass editorial review, thereby not warranting publication in *AJMR.* It is also possible that the National Institutes of Health and other funding agencies and their reviewers may have little interest in the technically demanding, often longitudinal studies that use observational methods. One hopes that this review will serve to remotivate some policy makers, scientists, and funding agencies to consider that knowledge about everyday behavior constitutes valuable information. Identification of behavioral traits may play an especially important role in the discovery of the genetic causes of mental retardation. This information is also critical for evaluating the ultimate success or failure of therapeutic and educational efforts involving individuals with mental retardation.

REFERENCES

Altmann, J. (1974). Observational study of behavior: Sampling methods. *Behaviour, 49,* 227–267.

Bakeman, R., & Gottman, J.M. (1997). *Observing interaction: An introduction to sequential analysis* (2nd ed.). New York: Cambridge University Press.

Bakeman, R., & Quera, V. (1995). *Analyzing interaction: Sequential analysis with SDIS and GSEQ.* New York: Cambridge University Press.

Browning, P.L., Campbell, D.R., & Spence, J.T. (1974). Counseling process with mentally retarded clients: A behavioral exploration. *American Journal of Mental Deficiency, 79,* 292–296.

Buiun, N., Rynders, J., & Turnure, J. (1974). Early maternal linguistic environment of normal and Down's syndrome language-learning children. *American Journal of Mental Deficiency, 79,* 52-58.

Carsrud, A.L., Carsrud, K.B., Henderson, D.P., Alisch, C.J., & Fowler, A.V. (1979). Effects of social and environmental change on institutional mentally retarded persons: The relocation syndrome reconsidered. *American Journal of Mental Deficiency, 84,* 266–272.

Dawson, G. (1994). Frontal electroencephalographic correlates of individual differences in emotional expression in infants: A brain systems perspective on emotion. *Monographs of the Society for Research in Child Development, 59*(2–3), 135–151, 250–283.

Diamond, A. (1991). Guidelines for the study of brain-behavior relationships during development. In H.S. Levin, H.M. Eisenberg, & A.L. Benton (Eds.), *Frontal lobe function and dysfunction* (pp. 339–378). New York: Oxford University Press.

Fleiss, J.L. (1981). *Statistical methods for rates and proportions* (2nd ed.). New York: John Wiley & Sons.

Frankel, F., & Graham, V. (1976). Systematic observation of classroom behavior of retarded and autistic preschool children. *American Journal of Mental Deficiency, 81,* 73–84.

Goldman-Rakic, P.S. (1994). *Neurobiology of mental representation.* Reading, MA: Addison Wesley Longman.

Gordon, A.M. (1946). Some aspects of idiocy in Mongolism. *American Journal of Mental Deficiency, 50,* 402–410.

Greenough, W.T., & Black, J.E. (1992). Induction of brain structure by experience: Substrates for cognitive development. In M.R. Gunnar & C.A. Nelson (Eds.), *Developmental Behavioral Neuroscience: The Minnesota Symposia on Child Psychology, 24,* 155–200.

Guess, D., Roberts, S., Siegel-Causey, E., Ault, M., Guy, B., & Thompson, B. (1993). Analysis of behavior state conditions and associated environmental variables among students with profound handicaps. *American Journal on Mental Retardation, 97,* 634–653.

Guralnick, M.J., & Paul-Brown, D. (1980). Functional and discourse analysis of nonhandicapped preschool children's speech to handicapped children. *American Journal of Mental Deficiency, 84,* 444–454.

Malone, D.M., & Stoneman, Z. (1990). Cognitive play of mentally retarded preschoolers: Observations in the home and school. *American Journal on Mental Retardation, 94,* 475–487.

Martin, P.R., & Bateson, P.P.G. (1993). *Measuring behavior: An introductory guide* (2nd ed.). New York: Cambridge University Press.

Maurer, H., & Sherrod, K.B. (1987). Context of directives given to young children with Down syndrome and nonretarded children: Development over two years. *American Journal of Mental Deficiency, 91,* 579–590.

Millham, J., Chilcutt, J., & Atkinson, B.L. (1978). Comparability of naturalistic and controlled observation assessment of adaptive behavior. *American Journal of Mental Deficiency, 83,* 52–59.

Parke, R.D., & Ladd, G.W. (Eds.). (1992). *Family-peer relationships: Modes of linkage.* Mahwah, NJ: Lawrence Erlbaum Associates.

Roberts, R.J., Jr., & Pennington, B.F. (1996). An integrative framework for examining prefrontal cognitive processes. *Developmental Neuropsychology, 12,* 105–126.

Sackett, G.P. (Ed.). (1978). *Observing behavior: Proceedings of the conference "Application of Observational/Ethological Methods to the Study of Mental Retardation"* (2 vols.) [NICHD mental retardation research centers series]. Baltimore: University Park Press.

Sackett, G.P. (1979). The lag sequential analysis of contingency and cyclicity in behavioral interaction research. In J.D. Osofsky (Ed.), *Handbook of infant development* (pp. 623–649). New York: John Wiley & Sons.

Sameroff, A.J. (1995). General systems theory and developmental psychopathology. In D. Cicchetti & D.J. Cohen (Eds.), *Developmental psychopathology: Vol. 1. Theory and methods* (pp. 659–695). New York: John Wiley & Sons.

Sparrow, S.S., Balla, D.A., & Cicchetti, D.V. (1984). *Vineland Adaptive Behavior Scales (VABS).* Circle Pines, MN: American Guidance Service.

Stoneman, Z., Brody, G.H., & Abbott, D. (1983). In-home observation of young Down syndrome children with their mothers and fathers. *American Journal of Mental Deficiency, 87,* 591–600.

Suen, H.K. (1987). Agreement, reliability, accuracy, and validity: Toward a clarification. *Behavioral Assessment, 10,* 343–366.

Suen, H.K., & Ary, D. (1989). *Analyzing quantitative behavioral observation data.* Mahwah, NJ: Lawrence Erlbaum Associates.

Taplin, P.S., & Reid, J.B. (1973). Effects of instructional set and experimenter influence on observer reliability. *Child Development, 44,* 547–554.

Thelen, E., & Smith, L.B. (1994). *A dynamic systems approach to the development of cognition and action.* Cambridge, MA: MIT Press.

Tizard, J. (1953). The effects of different types of supervision on the behavior of mental defectives in a sheltered workshop. *American Journal of Mental Deficiency, 58,* 143–161.

II

New Technologies
for Behavioral Observation

3

Computer Systems for Collecting Real-Time Observational Data

SungWoo Kahng and
Brian A. Iwata

Technological advances have led to a proliferation of computer applications in behavioral research (for a review, see Farrell, 1991). One area of particular interest to applied behavior analysts is the development of semiautomated systems for collecting real-time observational data. These systems have the potential to facilitate the task of observation by improving the reliability and accuracy of recording relative to traditional but cumbersome methods based on paper and pencil and to improve the efficiency of data calculation and graphing (Donát, 1991; Eiler, Nelson, Jensen, & Johnson, 1989). Thus, the use of computers to both record and analyze data has become increasingly important in clinical work and research.

As the technology has improved, these systems have incorporated more advanced features and become increasingly user-friendly. Unfortunately, information about available options is not widely accessible and is shared primarily through informal networks. Therefore, we conducted a survey of developers of computerized real-time observation systems. Fifteen developers responded to an initial request for information published in the *Journal of Applied Behavior Analysis* and subsequently completed more detailed surveys, the results of which are summarized below. A critical review of the systems, which would require comparisons under a number of different but standardized situations, was beyond the scope of this report. Our intent was merely to describe the key characteristics of each sys-

This chapter is an updated version of Kahng, S., & Iwata, B.A. (1998). Computerized systems for collecting real-time observational data. *Journal of Applied Behavior Analysis, 31,* 253–261. Used with permission.

tem as reported by its developer. The summaries are presented in alphabetical order. A table listing the major features of each system, along with information for obtaining additional information, is presented in the Appendix. We recommend that potential users compare features and costs for systems with similar capabilities, contact several developers for more complete descriptions of their current systems, and query colleagues who use these or similar systems.

BEHAVIORAL EVALUATION STRATEGY AND TAXONOMY (BEST)

BEST (1996) is software that allows the user to record up to 36 different responses during a session. It has the ability to record response frequency, duration, intervals (variable duration), time samples, latency, interresponse time (IRT), and discrete trials. A text feature allows the recording of notes for unique or atypical event occurrences. In addition, a pause feature permits the interruption of observation sessions if the need arises, and entry errors made while recording can be edited.

The data analysis program gives the user the option of calculating response frequency (total number and rate), duration, latency, IRT, percentage of intervals, percentage of trials, and conditional probabilities. The user can also define subgroups that contain various combinations of responses (A or B, A and B). *BEST* can calculate central tendencies (mean and median), variability (range and frequency distribution), and statistical significance (z-score transformations). A reliability program allows the comparison of interobserver agreement (overall agreement and *kappa*). *BEST* also can create frequency, duration, rate, and percentage charts; percentage pie charts; and multiple behavior temporal graphs. In addition, the data and graphs can be exported to commercial graphics applications (e.g., Windows *Paint, Delta Graph*).

BEST requires an IBM-compatible personal computer (PC) with a minimum 386 processor running DOS or Windows. It has minimal random access memory (RAM) and hard disk requirements. Demonstration copies are available upon request for 90–120 days. Individual purchase of the software costs $750. Institutional purchases (i.e., site license), which include multiple copies of the software and a guarantee of free upgrades, are available for $1,250. Included with the package are instruction manuals and technical support.

DATACAP, HARCLAG, AND HARCREL

DATACAP (Emerson, 1995a) is software for real-time recording of observational data on Psion Series 3 or Workabout handheld computers. It allows recording of up to 40 different responses using frequency or duration measures. The data are saved as ASCII files for uploading to IBM-compatible PCs for storage or further analysis.

HARCLAG (Emerson, 1995b) is a DOS-based program that can also run with Windows. It has the ability to calculate response frequency (total number and rate), duration, latency, IRT, and conditional probabilities. It also has the ability to calculate cumulative frequency distributions and time-based lag subgroups that contain various combinations of responses (A or B, A and B) for further analysis. A Windows-based reliability program, *HARCREL* (Emerson, 1995c), permits the calculation of interobserver agreement (overall, occurrence, and nonoccurrence agreement as well as *kappa*). Both *HARCLAG* and *HARCREL* have minimal memory requirements and require an IBM-compatible PC with a minimum 386 processor. All software is free and includes an instruction manual.

DATA COLLECTION ASSISTANT (DCA)

DCA (1997) uses TimeWand I or DuraTrax bar code scanners to collect real-time data. Data can be recorded as frequency, duration, and discrete trials for an infinite number of responses (more than 2 million). In addition, the observer can use DCA to collect Likert scale data, prompt sequences, and yes/no entries. Customized templates can be created to facilitate data collection. Entry errors made while recording can be edited.

The data analysis option allows the user to calculate response frequency (total number and rate), duration, and percentage of trials. The user can also graph the data and identify central tendencies (mean and median) as well as determine the range and frequency distribution. The user also can annotate data collected and graphs with relevant comments.

DCA requires an IBM-compatible PC (Windows) with at least a 486/33 processor, 8 megabytes (MB) of RAM, and 8–10 MB of hard disk space. The costs of the TimeWand I and DuraTrax scanners are $348 and $625, respectively. An instruction manual and technical support are included with the package.

DIRECT OBSERVATION DATA SYSTEM (DODS)

Using separate programs, DODS (Johnson, 1993) has the ability to capture frequency, duration, interval (variable duration), time sample, latency, and antecedent-behavior-consequences data for three different responses. In addition, it can aid in the selection of data collection measures as well as interpret student progress, refine an intervention, and confirm the mastery of an objective.

When the observation is complete, the program summarizes the data as response frequency (total number and rate), duration, latency, or percentage of intervals. The utilities program allows the user to retrieve files, graph data, and write and print reports of graphs. If the need arises to collect pencil-and-paper data, DODS can construct and print data collection forms.

DODS requires a computer running MacOS (System 6.0.5 or later version) and HyperCard. The user can also develop a remote recording device that consists of an adapted Macintosh mouse, a radio transmitter, and a radio receiver for use when a desktop computer is not available. The software is available free of charge.

ECOBEHAVIORAL ASSESSMENT SYSTEMS SOFTWARE (EBASS)

EBASS (Greenwood, 1993) is a series of three observational programs, each of which is designed specifically for a client's educational level. All allow the user to record interval data (10–20 seconds) for more than 100 different responses.

The data analysis feature allows the user to calculate the percentage of intervals, conditional probabilities, mean, range, and frequency distribution. In addition, responses can be combined (A and B) for further analysis. Interobserver agreement (overall and occurrence agreement) can also be calculated. The raw data, as well as session statistics, can be stored to disk or graphed. EBASS requires an IBM-compatible PC (DOS or Windows) and has minimal memory requirements. The cost of the software alone is $350. The cost of the complete package is $750 and includes an instruction manual and instructional videotapes as well as technical support. Site licenses are also available.

EVENT-PC

EVENT-PC (Ha, 1992a) is designed for use with multiple platforms (DOS, MacOS, Windows, Commodore 64, and Tandy 100/102). The observer can record frequency, duration, latency, and IRT for 40 different responses.

The data analysis feature has the ability to calculate total number and duration of response. *EVENT-PC* can also calculate means, ranges, and standard deviations. With a supplemental program, *SEQ* (Ha, 1992b), the user can perform additional statistical tests (e.g., chi-square test). All results can be printed, viewed on the screen, or saved to disk. Disk outputs are compatible with most spreadsheets and statistical packages. *EVENT-PC* has the ability to graph interval relations for visual inspection. All platform versions have minimal memory requirements. The DOS, MacOS, and Windows versions of *EVENT-PC* are available for $50. The price includes an instruction manual and technical support.

MULTIPLE OPTION OBSERVATION SYSTEM FOR EXPERIMENTAL STUDIES (MOOSES)

MOOSES (1999) has the ability to capture frequency, duration, interval (variable duration), and time-sampling data for 200 different responses. Code sets for individual projects are defined in a file by the user of the program. Entry errors can be edited at the end of the observation session.

The user can calculate response frequency (total number and rate), duration, percentage of intervals, percentage of trials, and conditional probabilities. The user can define subgroups that contain various combinations of responses (A and B, A or B). Furthermore, interobserver agreement (smaller/larger, overall, occurrence, and nonoccurrence agreement) can be calculated.

MOOSES requires an IBM-compatible PC (DOS) and has minimal memory requirements. The software program is free of charge. A complete package, which includes an instruction manual and support, is available for $450. A program for recording data from video (*PROCODER*) is also available at an extra cost.

OBSERVATIONAL DATA ACQUISITION PROGRAM (ODAP)

ODAP (Hetrick, Isenhart, Taylor, & Sandman, 1991) allows simultaneous recording of up to 20 different responses in a given observation session. It permits the recording of response frequency, duration, intervals (variable duration), time samples, latency, and IRT. In addition, deletion of entry errors can be made while recording. Data output is provided in two formats: a raw data file and a summary file that is appended after each observation session, with session identifiers as well as response frequency (total number and rate) and duration. *ODAP* requires an IBM-compatible PC (DOS) and has minimal memory requirements. The software is free and includes an instruction manual.

OBSERVATIONAL DATA COLLECTION AND ANALYSIS FOR WINDOWS (ObsWin)

ObsWin (Oliver, 1998) is an integrated data collection and analysis software package. It has the ability to capture frequency and duration data for up to 86 different behaviors. The user can create up to seven mutually exclusive code sets to facilitate data collection. Errors in data collection can be marked for future editing, and notes may be written during an observation session and saved with data files.

The data analysis option allows the user to calculate response frequency (total number and rate), duration, latency, IRT, and conditional probabilities. The user can also define various combinations of responses (A and B, A or B) for further analysis. *ObsWin* has the ability to compute central tendencies (mean and median), variability (range and frequency distribution), and interobserver agreement (smaller/larger, overall, occurrence, nonoccurrence, and exact agreement) and to perform lag sequential analyses. It also can download data collected using other existing data collection programs.

All data (raw, session statistics, and reliability statistics) can be saved to disk or printed. The user can create occurrence graphs, cumulative onset graphs, frequency per interval graphs, and summary statistic bar charts. All graphs may be saved as Windows metafiles or bitmaps.

The basic data collection program requires an IBM-compatible computer (DOS) and has minimal memory requirements. The analysis program, which also includes a program for data collection from video, requires Windows 3.1, 4 MB of RAM, and a 386 processor. The cost of the system is approximately $750–$800. The package includes an instruction manual and technical support. The purchaser is permitted to use one copy of the Windows-based program on a single computer, but the DOS-based program can be freely distributed on any number of computers.

!Observe

!Observe (1994) uses hand-held computers (Apple Newton) to record behavioral data by touching "buttons" created on the screens. The user can access templates (i.e., code sets) already created for a number of observational contexts. Furthermore, the user can customize the templates or create new templates by choosing from a list of behaviors provided by the system or by writing directly on the buttons. These templates allow the recording of up to 24 different responses during a session. With *!Observe* the user can record response frequency, duration, intervals (minimum of 3 seconds), time samples, latency, IRT, and discrete trials.

The data analysis option of *!Observe* has the ability to calculate response frequency (total number and rate), duration, latency, IRT, percentage of intervals, and percentage of trials using the hand-held computer. The user can also define subgroups that contain various combinations of responses (A or B, A and B) for further analysis. Interobserver agreement (overall, occurrence, and nonoccurrence agreement) can be calculated when using Apple Newton hand-held computers by linking them via their infrared data transfer systems. The raw data, as well as session and reliability statistics, can be downloaded to a MacOS or Windows-based PC for storage or further manipulation by spreadsheets, graphing programs, databases, or statistical software.

!Observe requires an Apple Newton hand-held computer with at least 2 MB of RAM. The cost of the software alone is $149.95. However, Psychsoft offers grants of free software to students and faculty who wish to use the system at their academic institutions. Included with the purchase price are an instruction manual and technical support.

The Observer

The Observer's (1993) program tasks are divided into several subprograms. *The Observer* can collect frequency, duration, interval (variable duration), time sample, latency, and IRT data for a maximum of 999 different responses. Entry errors can be marked for later editing, and text notes for unique or atypical events can be written during an observation session if the need arises. In addition, the session timer can be adjusted during data collection. Data for all observation sessions are stored on a disk, and the user is notified when the threshold of disk space is about to be reached.

The data analysis feature has the ability to calculate the total number of responses, duration, latency, IRT, percentage of intervals, and conditional probabilities. The user can also define subgroups that contain various combinations of responses (A or B, A and B). The user also has the options of 1) calculating other statistics, such as interobserver agreement (overall and exact agreement, *kappa*), mean, range, standard deviation, and standard error; and 2) performing lag sequential analyses. In addition, the user can construct a graph of the observational data against elapsed time. All data can be saved to disk; printed; or exported to a number of spreadsheets, databases, or statistical packages. The price of the base package, which includes *The Observer* software, is $1,740. *The Observer* can be used on any PC running DOS (minimal memory requirements), Windows (minimum 4 MB of RAM, 10-MB hard disk, 386DX processor), or MacOS (minimum 4 MB of RAM, 10-MB hard disk, system 6.0.7). Supplemental software packages that allow the user to collect data on a variety of different hand-held computers (*Observational Research Kit*), such as the Psion Organizer and Workabout, or from video (*Video Tape Analysis System*) are available for an additional cost. All packages include an instruction manual and technical support.

PORTABLE COMPUTER SYSTEMS (PCS)

PCS (1989) consists of separate data collection and analysis programs. The data collection program allows the observer to record response frequency, duration, latency, and IRT for up to 45 different events and to capture discrete trial data. Entry errors made while recording can be edited. The data collector has the option to disable the keys and timer temporarily if the need arises and to enter text notes about the observation session.

The data analysis program can calculate response frequency (total number and rate), duration, latency, IRT, and conditional probabilities. In addition, *PCS* can conduct lag sequential analyses. The user can define combinations of responses (A and B, A or B) for further analysis. A reliability program allows the comparison of data files using overall, occurrence, and nonoccurrence agreement. *PCS* requires an IBM-compatible PC (DOS) and has minimal memory requirements. *PCS* is available for $400 and includes an instruction manual.

PROFESSIONAL BEHAVIOR EVALUATION SYSTEM (ProBES)

ProBES (Ricketts, 1995) operates on a Psion Series 3a hand-held computer. It enables the observer to collect frequency, duration, interval (1–999 seconds), and time-sampling data for six different responses. The user can create templates for different types of observation sessions to facilitate data collection. The data analysis option can calculate response frequency (total number and rate), duration, percentage of intervals, percentage of trials, conditional probabilities, and means. All of these can be viewed within *ProBES* immediately after completion of a session, downloaded to a desktop computer as a text file, or printed using any standard printer. The cost of the system is $695. Included with the system are a Psion Series 3a hand-held computer, all software, an instruction manual, and technical support.

SOCIAL INTERACTION CONTINUOUS
OBSERVATION PROGRAM FOR EXPERIMENTAL STUDIES (SCOPES)

SCOPES (Shores, 1997) permits the recording of up to 21 different responses during a given observation session and can capture response frequency and duration. In addition, entry errors made during collection can be edited. The data analysis feature allows the user to calculate response frequency (total number and rate), duration, and conditional probabilities and to conduct lag sequential analyses. Interobserver agreement (overall, occurrence, nonoccurrence, and exact agreement) also can be calculated. *SCOPES* requires an IBM-compatible PC (DOS or Windows) and has minimal memory requirements. The program is available free of charge.

VIRTUAL BEHAVIOR ANALYST (VBA)

VBA (1995) is a template used in *Microsoft Word 6.0* that allows the collection of up to 16 different responses. *VBA* captures response frequency, duration, interval (1 second to 60 minutes), time sample, latency, and IRT data. Entry errors can be edited while recording. A separate program (*The Enabler Series*) can be used to record discrete trial data. The data analysis option allows the user to calculate response frequency (total number and rate), duration, latency, IRT, percentage of intervals, and conditional probabilities. In addition, the raw data and session statistics can be stored to disk or imported into *Microsoft Excel* for further analysis or graphing.

VBA requires an IBM-compatible PC with at least 8 MB of RAM, a 386 processor, and *Microsoft Office*. A stand-alone version is in production. *VBA* retails for $69.95 and includes an instruction manual and technical support. Interested users can download ScreenCam demonstrations of the program from the Behavior Analysis Archive at the University of Wisconsin–Madison (ftp://alphal.csd.uwm.edu/pub/psychology/BehaviorAnalysis/software/research).

REFERENCES

Behavioral Evaluation Strategy and Taxonomy (BEST) [Software]. (1996). West Lafayette, IN: Educational Consulting.

Data Collection Assistant (DCA) [Software]. (1997). Overland Park, KS: Bluestem Technologies.

Donát, P. (1991). Measuring behavior: The tools and the strategies. *Neuroscience and Behavioral Review, 15,* 447–454.

Eiler, J.M., Nelson, W.W., Jensen, C.C., & Johnson, S.P. (1989). Automated data collection using bar code. *Behavior Research Methods, Instruments & Computers, 21,* 53–58.

Emerson, E. (1995a). *DATACAP* [Software]. Manchester, England: University of Manchester, Hester Adrian Research Centre.

Emerson, E. (1995b). *HARCLAG* [Software]. Manchester, England: University of Manchester, Hester Adrian Research Centre.

Emerson, E. (1995c). *HARCREL* [Software]. Manchester, England: University of Manchester, Hester Adrian Research Centre.

Farrell, A.D. (1991). Computers and behavioral assessment: Current applications, future possibilities, and obstacles to routine use. *Behavioral Assessment, 13,* 159–179.

Greenwood, C.R. (1993). *Ecobehavioral Assessment Systems Software (EBASS)* [Software]. Kansas City, KS: University of Kansas, Juniper Gardens Children's Project.

Ha, J. (1992a). *EVENT-PC* [Software]. Seattle: University of Washington.

Ha, J. (1992b). *SEQ* [Software]. Seattle: University of Washington.

Hetrick, W.P., Isenhart, R.C., Taylor, D.V., & Sandman, C.A. (1991). ODAP: A stand-alone program for observational data acquisition. *Behavior Research Methods, Instruments, and Computers, 23,* 66–71.

Johnson, H. (1993). *Direct Observation Data System (DODS)* [Software]. Trenton: The College of New Jersey.

Multiple Option Observation System for Experimental Studies (MOOSES) [Software]. (1999). Hermitage, TN: Jon Tapp & Associates.

!Observe [Software]. (1994). Denton, TX: Psychsoft.

The Observer [Software]. (1993). Sterling, VA: Noldus Information Technology.

Oliver, C. (1998). *Observational Data Collection and Analysis for Windows (ObsWin)* [Software]. Birmingham, England: University of Birmingham.

Portable Computer Systems (PCS) [Software]. (1989). DeKalb, IL: Communitech.

Ricketts, R. (1995). *Professional Behavior Evaluation System (ProBES)* [Software]. Abilene, TX: Author.

Shores, R. (1997). *Social Interaction Continuous Observation Program for Experimental Studies (SCOPES)* [Software]. Parsons: University of Kansas.

Virtual Behavior Analyst (VBA) [Software]. (1995). Coral Springs, FL: World Enabling Resources.

Appendix

Summary of the Main Features of Computerized Observation Systems

Program	Behavioral Evaluation Strategy and Taxonomy (BEST)	DATACAP, HARCLAG, HARCREL	Data Collection Assistant (DCA)
Address	Tom Sharpe Educational Consulting Inc. 7870 Kipp Farm Road Lafayette, Indiana 47905	Eric Emerson Hester Adrian Research Centre University of Manchester Manchester M13 9PL, England United Kingdom	Jay L. Saunders Bluestem Technologies 9816 West 132nd Terrace Overland Park, Kansas 66213
Telephone Fax Internet	(765) 494-0048 (765) 496-1239 tsharpe@skware.com http://www.skware.com	+44 0161 275 3335 +44 0161 275 3333 eric.emerson@man.ac.uk	(913) 685-0065 N/A bluestem@pchelponline.com
Data collection hardware	User supplied (laptop computer)	User supplied (hand-held computer)	TimeWand I DuraTrax by Videx
Operating system	DOS Windows	DOS Windows	Windows
Data collection[a]	F, D, I, S, L, IRT, T	F, D	F, D, T
Data analysis[a]	F, R, D, I, L, IRT, T, P	F, R, D, L, IRT, P	F, R, D, T
Reliability statistics[b]	OV, K	OV, OCC, NON, K	None
Price	$750	Free	$348–$625

[a]F = frequency, R = rate, D = duration, I = interval, S = time sample, L = latency, IRT = interresponse time, T = discrete trial, P = conditional probability.
[b]SL = smaller/larger, OV = overall, OCC = occurrence, NON = nonoccurrence, EX = exact, K = kappa.

Program	Direct Observation Data System (DODS)	Ecobehavioral Assessment Systems Software (EBASS)	EVENT-PC
Address	Happy Johnson College of New Jersey Hillwood Lakes, CN 4700 Trenton, New Jersey 08650	Charles Greenwood Juniper Gardens Children's Project 650 Minnesota Avenue 2nd Floor Kansas City, Kansas 66101	James Ha University of Washington Regional Primate Research Center Box 357330 Seattle, Washington 98195
Telephone Fax Internet	(609) 771-2998 (609) 771-3434 johnsha@tcnj.edu	(913) 321-3143 (913) 371-8522 greenwood@kuhub.cc.ukans.edu http://www.lsi.ukans.edu/jg/ ebass.htm	(206) 543-2420 (206) 685-8606 jcha@u.washington.edu
Data collection hardware	User supplied (laptop computer or remote-control device)	User supplied (laptop computer)	User supplied (laptop computer)
Operating system	MacOS Windows	DOS Windows	DOS MacOS Windows
Data collection[a]	F, D, I, S, L	I	F, D, L, IRT
Data analysis[a]	F, R, D, I, L, T	I, P	F, D
Reliability statistics[b]	None	OV, OCC, K	None
Price	Free	$350–$750	$50

[a] F = frequency, R = rate, D = duration, I = interval, S = time sample, L = latency, IRT = interresponse time, T = discrete trial, P = conditional probability.
[b] SL = smaller/larger, OV = overall, OCC = occurrence, NON = nonoccurrence, EX = exact, K = kappa.

Program	Multiple Option Observation System for Experimental Studies (MOOSES)	Observational Data Acquisition Program (ODAP)	Observational Data Collection and Analysis for Windows (ObsWin)
Address	Jon Tapp Jon Tapp & Associates 103 Hal Drive Hermitage, Tennessee 37076	William Hetrick Department of Psychology Indiana University Psychology Building 131 1101 East 10th Street Bloomington, Indiana 47405	Chris Oliver School of Psychology University of Birmingham Edgbaston Birmingham B15 2TT, England United Kingdom
Telephone Fax Internet	(615) 443-0535 (615) 322-8236 jon.tapp@vanderbilt.edu http://miles.kc.vanderbilt.edu/ ~jont/mooses.html	(812) 855-2311 (812) 856-4544 whetrick@indiana.edu http://www.indiana.edu/~clinpsy/	+44 0121 414 4909 +44 0121 414 4897 c.oliver@bham.ac.uk http://psgsuni.bham.ac.uk/ obswin.htm
Data collection hardware	User supplied (hand-held or laptop computer)	User supplied (laptop computer)	User supplied (laptop computer)
Operating system	DOS Windows	DOS	DOS Windows
Data collection[a]	F, D, I, S	F, D, I, S, L, IRT	F, D
Data analysis[a]	F, R, D, I, T, P	F, R, D	F, R, D, L, IRT, P
Reliability statistics[b]	SL, OV, OCC, NON, K	None	SL, OV, OCC, NON, EX
Price	Free	Free	$750–$800

[a] F = frequency, R = rate, D = duration, I = interval, S = time sample, L = latency, IRT = interresponse time, T = discrete trial, P = conditional probability.
[b] SL = smaller/larger, OV = overall, OCC = occurrence, NON = nonoccurrence, EX = exact, K = kappa.

Program	!Observe	The Observer	Portable Computer Systems (PCS)
Address	Sandy Martin Psychsoft Inc. Box 307393 UNT Station Denton, Texas 76203	Noldus Information Technology, Inc. 6 Pidgeon Hill Drive Suite 180 Sterling, Virginia 20165	Peggy Williams Department of Special Education Northern Illinois University Dekalb, Illinois 60115
Telephone Fax Internet	(800) 536-4996 (940) 321-1292 psycsoft@aol.com http://www.psycsoft.com/	(800) 355-9541 (703) 404-5507 info@noldus.com http://www.noldus.com	(815) 753-0657
Data collection hardware	User supplied (hand-held computer)	User supplied (hand-held or laptop computer)	User supplied (laptop computer)
Operating system	MacOS Windows	DOS MacOS Windows	DOS
Data collection[a]	F, D, I, S, L, IRT, T	F, D, I, S, L, IRT	F, D, L, IRT, T
Data analysis[a]	F, R, D, I, L, IRT, T	F, D, L, IRT, I, P	F, R, D, L, IRT, P
Reliability statistics[b]	OV, OCC, NON	OV, EX, K	OV, OCC, NON
Price	$149.95	$1,740	$400

[a] F = frequency, R = rate, D = duration, I = interval, S = time sample, L = latency, IRT = interresponse time, T = discrete trial, P = conditional probability.
[b] SL = smaller/larger, OV = overall, OCC = occurrence, NON = nonoccurrence, EX = exact, K = kappa.

Program	Professional Behavior Evaluation System (ProBES)	Social Interaction Continuous Observation Program for Experimental Studies (SCOPES)	Virtual Behavior Analyst (VBA)
Address	Robert Ricketts 241 Pine Street Suite 15LB Abilene, Texas 79601	Richard Shores University of Kansas at Parsons 2601 Gabriel Parsons, Kansas 67357	Merrill Winston World Enabling Resources 5231 Pine Tree Road Coral Springs, Florida 33067
Telephone Fax Internet	(915) 676-1052 N/A ricketts@camalott.com	(316) 421-6550 ext. 1859 N/A	(954) 341-2878 (954) 977-0409 sales@weru.com http://www.weru.com
Data collection hardware	User supplied (Psion Series 3a)	User supplied (laptop computer)	User supplied (laptop computer)
Operating system	OPL	DOS Windows	Windows (Microsoft Office)
Data collection[a]	F, D, I, S	F, D	F, D, I, S, L, IRT
Data analysis[a]	F, R, D, L, IRT, P	F, D, L, IRT, P	F, R, D, L, IRT, I, P
Reliability statistics[b]	None	OV, OCC, NON, EX	None
Price	Free	Free	$69.95

[a] F = frequency, R = rate, D = duration, I = interval, S = time sample, L = latency, IRT = interresponse time, T = discrete trial, P = conditional probability.
[b] SL = smaller/larger, OV = overall, OCC = occurrence, NON = nonoccurrence, EX = exact, K = kappa.

4

Palmtop Computer Technologies for Behavioral Observation Research

Eric Emerson,
David J. Reeves, and
David Felce

The ready availability of powerful and sophisticated palmtop computers has for the first time made real-time, multiple-category data collection in the natural environment practically possible. There is nothing inherently different between palmtop and laptop observational technology (see Chapter 20) other than the portability of the former and the potential it thereby establishes to observe people as they move freely about their environment. This chapter is structured in four sections: 1) assumptions about the nature of the data to be captured and the division between data capture and analysis; 2) the development of handheld computers as input devices; 3) an illustrative data capture and analysis suite of programs; and 4) future directions.

ASSUMPTIONS ABOUT THE DATA CAPTURE TASK

Before the advent of computer-assisted data capture, quantitative observational research in the natural environment was restricted to relatively simple, albeit often adequate, recording methods. However, paper-and-pencil and timer-based methods of event recording, duration recording, and time sampling have significant limitations (Suen & Ary, 1989). Event recording is insensitive to variation in duration. Duration recording is unwieldy when several behaviors or environmental events or states are recorded. The various time-sampling procedures are insensitive to frequency of occurrence, may inaccurately reflect duration, and by definition do not produce a complete record of behavior.

The application of computer technology to the observational task has two advantages. First, it simplifies the observer's task by eliminating the need to attend to an independent timer. Second, it allows for automated data summary. These advantages can have a significant effect on the complexity of the observational schema that can be pursued and the efficiency with which results can be produced. In particular, they make real-time recording of multiple events practicable. As a result, it has become possible for observers to produce an exhaustive record of the flow of behavioral and environmental events of interest. This, in turn, opens up the possibility of using considerably more sophisticated statistical techniques to identify conditional and sequential relationships among the behaviors and events under study (see Chapters 19 and 20).

Our first assumption, therefore, is that one requires a system of data capture that allows the onsets and offsets of each occurrence of several events to be preserved in precise temporal sequence. This is achieved simply by programming key depressions (which signal the onset or offset of event codes) to be recorded by the computer's internal clock as elapsed times from the beginning of the session. When combined with information on the total length of a session, such a record permits, for each independent code, the relatively simple calculation of the frequency of its occurrence (number of onsets), its rate (frequency per total session time), event duration (offset time minus preceding onset time), cumulative duration (sum of each offset time minus preceding onset time), percentage duration (100 times cumulative duration divided by total session time), and interevent duration (onset time minus preceding offset time). The data obtained are amenable to secondary analysis of concurrent and sequential association between two or more behaviors or events.

The range and complexity of possible relevant analyses mean that, powerful though palmtop computers have become, data analysis is best thought of as a separate series of operations rather than as part of the data capture program. Our second assumption, therefore, is that the main function of the palmtop device is for data capture and temporary file storage. Data files are then transferred to a desktop machine for permanent storage and analysis. The output format for the data capture program and the input format for the analysis program provide a common link. This assumption is likely to become redundant as the power of palmtop computers increases.

DEVELOPMENT OF HAND-HELD COMPUTERS AS INPUT DEVICES

Kahng and Iwata (1998) (see Chapter 3) describe 15 computerized systems for collecting real-time observational data. Three of these systems are direct successors to a suite of programs written for the Epson HX20 in the early 1980s (Repp & Felce, 1990; Repp, Harman, Felce, Van Acker, & Karsh, 1989; Repp, Karsh, Van Acker, Felce, & Harman, 1989; see also Kratochwill, Doll, & Dickson, 1985). The Epson HX20 was one of the first truly portable, battery-driven computers. Approximately the size of a closed laptop computer, it was relatively robust, with a small liquid crystal display mounted centrally above a QWERTY keyboard, rather than a hinged screen. It also had a microcassette drive for the storage of program and data files and a small integral printer similar to those in supermarket cash registers. For data capture and summary, it was completely self-contained. Its major drawbacks were its size, weight, and battery and memory capacities (a meager 16 kilobytes of random access memory, which could be expanded with a sizable bolt-on unit to 32 kilobytes). Despite the memory limitations, however, it was possible to design a data capture program that met the requirements described above and produced a summary analysis of the frequency, rate, cumulative duration, and percentage time of occurrence of each code.

Among the analysis programs written at the same time were prototype editing and reliability programs. In addition to allowing for the correction of errors, the editing program permitted the combination or union of events (A and B, A or B) to be defined as new codes. The reliability program contained two procedures: one to explore the extent of agreement on the precise timing of the onsets and offsets recorded for each code (within a tolerance set by the investigator) and the other to compare agreement on whether a code was occurring on a second-by-second basis. We return to issues of reliability in more detail in the next section.

Since then, however, things have changed considerably. The review by Kahng and Iwata (1998) describes a variety of capture devices based on bar code scanners, DOS- or Windows-based computers, computers using MacOS, and Psion Series 3 computers. Although the majority of these are DOS or Windows applications written for laptop computers, the relatively minimal memory requirements of the data capture programs mean that the majority of these programs could be used on available PC-compatible palmtop devices. The systems described by Kahng and Iwata (1998) vary in a number of dimensions, including data analysis, reliability calculation, and graphing and exporting capabilities. They also vary in price. Readers are referred to the review in question for further details.

Developments in palmtop computers during the 1990s include Windows CE devices such as the Casio Cassiopeia A-20E, Ericsson MC12, Hewlett-Packard HP 360LX and 620LX, Sharp HC-4100, and the Philips Velo 500 (reviewed in *PC Magazine*, Vol. 7[7], pp. 92–135). The Psion Series 3c, Sienna, and Series 5 are also reviewed, as are the 3Com PalmPilot and the IBM Workpad 8602-10U. On the whole, Windows CE devices were more expensive, larger, heavier, and less efficient in conserving battery life than the Psion or Palm Pilot/Workpad devices, which were both preferred in the review. Two software systems were developed for the Psion Series 3, and a third had optional software for a Psion, available at an additional cost. These will require some modification to make them compatible with the Series 5, which has the advantage of a much better keyboard, 8 megabytes (MB) of random access memory, a touch-sensitive screen, and improved (infrared) communication with a PC. One system was developed for a US Robotic Pilot and may be compatible with the more recent Palm Pilot/Workpad devices. Otherwise, there are at least nine DOS-based or Windows-based software systems that could be used with Windows CE devices.

AN ILLUSTRATIVE SYSTEM

In this section, we illustrate some of the potential of computer-assisted data collection with reference to the system currently used by the Hester Adrian Research Centre, University of Manchester, England, and the Welsh Centre on Learning Disabilities, University of Wales College of Medicine in Cardiff. This system, a direct descendant of the Epson HX20 suite described above, evolved during a

series of studies to investigate the quality of care provided in residential estab-
lishments for people with severe and complex intellectual disabilities (Emerson,
Beasley, Offord, & Mansell, 1992; Emerson, Hatton, Robertson, Henderson, &
Cooper, 1999; Hatton, Emerson, Robertson, Henderson, & Cooper, 1995; Mansell,
1994; McGill, Hewson, & Emerson, 1994) and from descriptive analyses of challenging behaviors shown by people with severe intellectual disabilities (Emerson,
Reeves, Thompson, Henderson, & Robertson, 1996; Emerson, Thompson, Reeves,
Henderson, & Robertson, 1995). More recently, it has been used in studies to investigate such diverse issues as the effects of reducing psychotropic medication
(Ahmed et al., in press), the effect of staff training (Jones et al., 1999), the costs and
benefits of residential treatment models for people with severe challenging behavior (Felce et al., 1998), and the effect of peripatetic outreach teams on the care of
elderly people (Proctor et al., 1998) and people with intellectual disabilities and
severe challenging behavior (Lowe, Felce, & Blackman, 1996).

Hardware

The system uses Psion palmtop computers (Psion Series 3c or Psion Workabout)
for data capture and IBM-compatible PCs for data analysis. The Psion Series 3c is
a small (17 centimeters by 9 centimeters by 2 centimeters), light (280 grams) palmtop computer with a hinged lid housing a backlit monochrome screen (12 centimeters by 4 centimeters) of 480 pixels by 160 pixels. The lower half of the shell
contains a small QWERTY keyboard. Internal memory varies from 1 to 2 MB
depending on the model, with optional expansion through 1 MB solid-state disks.
It uses standard disposable AA batteries, and the manufacturer claims a battery
life of approximately 40 hours. The operating language (OPL) is unique to Psion.
Data transfer to PCs is accomplished via a serial port connection using a communications package (*PsiWin*) supplied by the manufacturer. More recent models
(e.g., Psion Series 5) allow for data transfer using infrared communication.
Overall, we find the Psion palmtop computers to be well balanced for hand-held
use. They are small enough to hold with two hands and reach all of the keys with
the thumbs or to balance in one hand and key with the other. The Psion
Workabout is similar in its internal and communications specifications. However,
it is arranged as an extremely robust single unit, with a rectangular liquid crystal
display screen above a set of keys in a calculator-like arrangement, surrounded by
a hand grip.

Data Capture

DATACAP software is used for data capture. It provides for the recording of up to
43 independent codes without using the shift key to access further symbols. The
software is not dedicated to any particular observational schema. In practice,
the letters, numerals, or punctuation symbols on the keys distinguish codes.
(Descriptive code labels may be stuck to or above the keys, if preferred.)

The program allows for the three keying options contained in the original
Epson program. First, keys may operate independently. Depression of the key
records the onset of an event; the next depression of the key records its offset.
Second, keys may be grouped into mutually exclusive and exhaustive sets. Within
each set only one key may be "active" at any time. Depression of a key within the
set records the onset of that event and automatically records the offset of any
active key within the set. Third, keys may be designated to record short events

(allocated notional durations of 1 second), a single depression recording the time of occurrence. Once the operative keys and keying options are defined, the resulting version of the data capture can be saved as a custom-made application. The computer will accept entry only of designated keys.

After each onset, the keyboard symbol corresponding to the code is displayed on the screen, which provides a record of all active keys. Depression of an event key causes the corresponding symbol to appear on the screen and then move progressively to the left until it disappears. In addition to keys being defined to represent behaviors and events of interest, keys may be used to mark keying errors and/or designated to mark an interruption of the observation session (e.g., if the individual is out of view). Files are automatically saved to the Psion using unique identifiers at the end of each observational session.

Data Transfer and Editing

Given the considerable storage capacity of the Psion, file transfer is necessary only for purposes of data analysis and security. Transfer to PCs is accomplished via a serial port connection using a manufacturer-supplied "drag-and-drop" Windows-based communications package (*PsiWin*) running on the PC. Once files are transferred to a PC, editing for errors can be undertaken by loading the files into any word-processing package or text editor.

Data Analysis

Further file editing (e.g., the creation of new variables based on existing observational codes) and data analysis are accomplished with the DOS-based program *HARCLAG* (Reeves, 1994a, 1994b). Before briefly describing the analytic procedures available within *HARCLAG*, an important point needs to be made about the nature of real-time observational records. Any observational session represents a slice of time with an arbitrary beginning and end (and possible interruptions within). Most behavioral events within the observed period will have definite onset and offset times entered by the observer as they happen. However, the onset times of events that were occurring when the observational session began will be unknown. The offset times of events occurring at the end of the session also will be unknown. As a result, the bout length of such events is indefinite. In addition, each interruption within the observation session causes another set of indefinite offsets and onsets. *HARCLAG* separates such indefinite bouts and allows them to be either included in or excluded from the analysis. As a general rule, it is advisable to exclude them when calculating specific bout durations or when analyzing the sequential dependence between the onsets (or offsets) of coded events. *HARCLAG* allows any key reserved for suspending observation temporarily to be defined as such for the purposes of the analysis. Intervals containing an interrupt code are excluded from the analysis. Periods of observation between interruptions are analyzed, and bouts made indefinite by the interruption are treated as such.

Below, we briefly describe the main components of the *HARCLAG* program. This is presented as an example of the type of operation we have found to be of value during the last decade in studies of the behavioral ecology of residential environments and descriptive analyses of challenging behaviors.

Management of Data Files   A menu option allows data files relating to the same observational session to be merged into one file (e.g., simultaneous but independent records taken by two observers of pupil and teacher behaviors).

Visual Inspection of Selected Aspects of Data Files   HARCLAG presents a graphical display of the occurrence or nonoccurrence of selected codes across consecutive intervals, either in the original "uncollapsed bins" of 1-second duration or in "collapsed bins" of 2-second duration or more. Each code is displayed as occurring throughout the interval, partially occurring, or not occurring.

Selection of Sets or Portions of Files for Analysis   It is frequently desirable to undertake analyses on sets of files (e.g., all files pertaining to a particular individual, time of day, or setting) or portions of files. A menu option allows the creation of a file set. Any analysis can then be applied to every file in the set as a single operation, and the results can be obtained for each file and for the set as a whole. Portions of files also can be selected for analysis by either time or the presence of selected coded behaviors, events, or states. The use of a time filter allows a section of a file or the same section of a set of files to be analyzed separately by restricting the analysis to specified start and end times. For example, setting the time filter to between 1 and 1,800 seconds would provide an analysis of the first half hour of every file included. Similarly, the use of a variable (or code) filter allows the analysis to be restricted to those intervals in a file or file set when a particular variable (code) is either present or absent. Most observational protocols for real-time data capture contain at least one key (code) to denote that the person cannot be observed (e.g., the observer's view of the person is temporarily blocked, the person has entered a private area). Use of the absence of such a code as a variable filter (i.e., not unobserved) would appropriately restrict all analyses to periods in which the person was observed.

Variable (or code) filters are particularly useful in the investigation of behavioral responding, given a range of other behavioral events or longer-lasting states. Thus, one might be interested in the behavior of pupils under a number of teacher conditions: teacher not present, teacher present but not interacting with the pupils, teacher making instructional demands of the pupils, and other forms of teacher interaction (e.g., Emerson, Reeves, et al., 1996; Emerson, Thompson, et al., 1995). As long as the relevant teacher conditions were also encoded, behavioral observations of pupils could be analyzed according to the prevailing conditions by using these teacher conditions as filter variables. Figure 1 presents such data showing variation in the rate of self-injurious behavior by a 13-year-old girl with severe developmental disabilities.

Simultaneous use of combinations of filter variables allows more complex situational analyses. For example, the effect of different curriculum subjects or biological states could be added to the example above.

Creation of New Variables   It is frequently desirable during data analysis to create new variables from the original variables coded. These include 1) the absence of an observed code (e.g., X = not A), 2) combinations based on the presence or absence of two or more observed events, and 3) "episodes" of coded events.

Combinations may be defined as the union or intersection of codes. For example, one may want to define a behavioral category such as engagement in nonsocial functional activity as the union (combination) of domestic (household), personal (self-help), leisure, or "other" activities. In this example the new code would occur within the modified observational record whenever any of the constituent codes occurred. Alternatively, one may be interested in the intersection (co-occurrence) of self-injury and negative vocalization (e.g., crying, whining) and

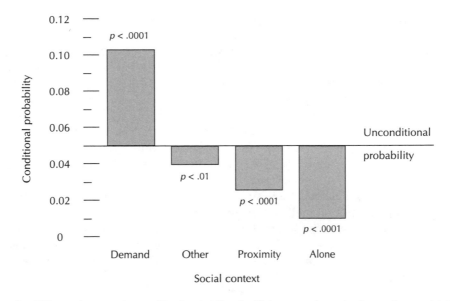

Figure 1. Difference between the conditional probability of self-injury occurring under four environmental states and the overall (unconditional) probability of self-injury. (p, probability.)

want to separate instances when either behavior occurs alone from instances when they occur together. Created variables themselves can be used in further combinations. For example, one may be interested in a person's social interaction while engaged and while not engaged in some functional activity. A code for the absence of social interaction can be created based on the absence of the social interaction code, a code for engagement in nonsocial functional activities can be created as in the example given above, and another code for its absence also can be created. New combinations then can be defined using these new codes, including the intersection of social interaction and nonsocial functional activities, the intersection of social interaction and the absence of nonsocial functional activities, the intersection of the absence of social interaction with the occurrence of non-social functional activities, and the nonoccurrence of either type of activity.

Within the observational record all variables occur as a series of bout (from onset to offset) and interbout (from offset to onset) intervals. For certain purposes some bout lengths or interbout intervals might be deemed insignificant. For example, one may be interested in the extent to which teachers attend to their pupils while they are engaged in activities germane to the lesson. One might decide to exclude as trivial periods of pupil engagement in education-related tasks of less than 30 seconds. Alternatively, one might be interested in a person's repetitious self-injury. Such instances may have been recorded as a series of discrete events (e.g., hits, slaps), but one may be interested in analyzing them in terms of longer episodes of self-injury. *HARCLAG* allows the creation of *episodic variables* for these eventualities. In creating an episodic version of the variable, the investigator specifies two parameters: the shortest length that an episode can be and the interval length between events that is required for them to be considered separate episodes. Any occurrences shorter than the former will be eliminated, and any intervals shorter than the latter will be treated as if the variable continued to occur.

Data Summary   At its most basic level, analysis will involve the generation of descriptive statistics for each code and created variable that occurs in the file or file set. In *HARCLAG* these include number of onsets (frequency of occurrence), probability of onset (rate per second), intervals present (cumulative duration), probability present (proportion of time), number of offsets, and probability of offset (which may differ from the data on onsets if the analysis is restricted to bouts with definite onsets and offsets). Provision is also made for the analysis of bout length, interbout intervals (offsets to next onset), intervals between onsets, and intervals between offsets. The analysis provides a summary of frequency, percentage occurrence, cumulative frequency, and cumulative percentage occurrence for each quantity.

Time-Based Lag Sequential Analysis   *HARCLAG* contains a number of routines to enable the application of methods of time-based lag sequential analysis (Sackett, 1979, 1987) to the data encoded by *DATACAP*. Several options can be considered when determining the sequential association between one variable (the base or criterion variable) and another (the conditional or target variable) across time (lag sizes).

1.   Lagging may be specified to stem from the onset, offset, or presence of the base variable and to search for the onset, offset, or presence of the conditional variable.

2.   Lags may be calculated in either direction in time, forward (positive lag sizes, e.g., onset plus 1 second, onset plus 2 seconds) and backward (negative lag sizes).

3.   Lags may be calculated on the raw data (equivalent to 1-second bins) or on collapsed intervals (e.g., 5-second bins). For collapsed intervals the conditional probabilities calculated relate to the likelihood of the conditional (target) variable occurring for at least a single 1-second interval within the wider bin.

4.   Five options are available within *HARCLAG* to control the way in which lagging is applied. *Unrestricted lagging* calculates the conditional probability of the conditional variable over every specified lag size from the base variable, irrespective of the repetition of either variable within that range of intervals. The *base variable restricted model* treats every instance of the base variable as a potential influence over the conditional variable only until the next occurrence of the base variable. Instances of lag sizes from an occurrence of the base variable that overlaps with or goes beyond the next onset of the base variable are excluded from the calculation of conditional probability. The *conditional variable restricted model* restricts lagging to one occurrence of the conditional variable, on the rationale that the influence of the base event extends only to the immediately occurring conditional event and not to events that occur subsequently. The *base and conditional variables restricted model* applies both restrictions. For each instance of the base variable, lagging stops at whichever restriction occurs first. For example, suppose the data in Figure 2 represent the occurrence of teacher prompts and self-injurious behavior for 21 consecutive 1-second intervals. Episodes of teacher prompts were recorded as commencing at seconds 2, 8, 11, and 16 of the observational record, and self-injurious behavior was recorded at seconds 4, 7, 13, and 21. The lower four rows of the table indicate 1) whether self-injurious behavior occurred at lag plus 5 sec-

Second	1	2	3	4	5	6	7	8	9	10	11	12	13	14	15	16	17	18	19	20	21	Occurrences	Base (N)	Conditional probability
Teacher prompts	X	X	X	X				X	X		X	X	X	X		X	X	X						
Self-injurious behavior				S			S						S								S			
Unrestricted							1						1			0					1	3	4	0.75
Base variable restricted							1						n2			0					1	2	3	0.67
Conditional variable restricted							n1						1			n1					1	2	2	1
Base and conditional variable restricted							n1						n2			n1					1	1	1	1

Figure 2. Hypothetical data illustrating different approaches to the calculation of the conditional probability of self-injurious behavior (SIB) at lag plus 5 seconds after the onset of teacher prompts. (n1, Lag plus 5-second data not included because of the occurrence of the conditional variable [self-injurious behavior] at lag plus 2 seconds; n2, Lag plus 5-second data not included because of the occurrence of the conditional variable [self-injurious behavior] at lag plus 3 seconds; X, occurrence of teacher prompt; S, occurrence of self-injury; 0 or 1, occurrence of self-injury 5 seconds following onset of teacher prompt [1] or nonoccurrence [0].)

onds after the onset of teacher prompts (1 or 0); 2) the number of occurrences of self-injurious behavior at a given lag; 3) the base sample size (i.e., the number of times it could have occurred); and 4) the conditional probability of self-injurious behavior after the onset of teacher prompts at lag plus 5 seconds. As can be seen, one possible effect of restricting the lagging process is to reduce the base sample size. Finally, *HARCLAG* allows calculation of conditional probabilities according to a *change of state model*. This produces two tables of probabilities with reference to the change of the base variable from being absent to being present and vice versa. Negative lags in the first analysis correspond to times before the onset of the base variable, with lagging restricted to the base variable being absent. The zero lag and positive lags correspond to times after onset, with lagging restricted to the base variable being present. Negative lags and the zero lag in the second analysis relate to times before offset, with lagging constrained to the base variable being present, and positive lags relate to times after offset, with lagging restricted to continued base variable absence. Such an option might be chosen to investigate the conditional occurrence of a student's engagement before, during, and after the occurrence of teacher instruction (Figure 3; Emerson et al., 1999).

HARCLAG calculates conditional probabilities of the conditional variable occurring given the base variable occurrence at a given lag size. It also calculates the unconditional probability of the conditional variable, 95% and 99% confidence intervals, corresponding z-scores, and the sample size for the base variable. It is important to note that the z-scores and significance levels are based on assumptions that most data sets probably violate and, therefore, should be viewed with caution. When analyses are performed on a file set, probabilities are based on the number of occurrences of the conditional and base variables in all files, and the

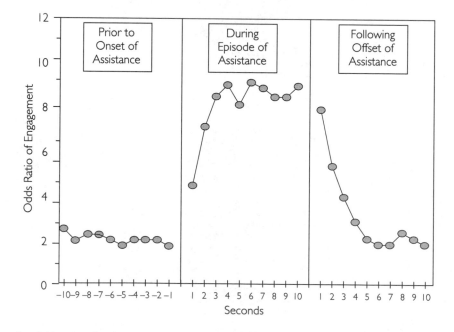

Figure 3.   Odds ratios of student engagement before, during, and after episodes of instructor assistance.

resulting overall probability is in effect weighted for occurrence. Other descriptive statistics such as odds ratios and Yule's Q can be calculated directly from the data provided in the probability table.

Calculating Reliability   Continuous observation requires ways of calculating interobserver agreement appropriate to its structure. Events are defined by their onset, continued occurrence (occupation of 1-second bins), and offset. *HARCREL* (Reeves, 1994b) compares the records of two observers and calculates kappa coefficients for the extent of agreement of three quantities for each code in the observational system: agreement over onsets, agreement over offsets, and agreement over second-by-second presence throughout the session. Because observers can differ in the time it takes to interpret events and depress the relevant codes, the two records may be essentially similar but the times of events may differ by 1 or 2 seconds. *HARCREL*, therefore, allows the investigator to specify a tolerance of a few seconds to create a window within which a corresponding entry will be taken as agreement. Hence, a tolerance of 2 seconds will create a 5-second window, defined by 2 seconds before and after the time of occurrence of the event in one observer's record, in which to look for a similar occurrence in the second observer's record. Setting a tolerance is clearly applicable to the investigation of onsets and offsets, in which the moment at which the key is depressed is the only salient issue, irrespective of the subsequent or preceding duration of the event or the agreement between observers of the extent of its occurrence. It also applies to short-duration behaviors, particularly those established as "event" keys. However, one would not want to set a tolerance when investigating second-by-second agreement of the presence of events that have a moderate to long duration. When a tolerance is set, the kappa coefficient is adjusted to take account of the changed possibilities of "chance" agreement.

FUTURE DIRECTIONS

On the basis of existing trends it seems plausible to suggest that palmtop computers will continue to improve in such areas as processor speed, memory capacity, reliability, battery life, usability of keyboards and screens, and ease of connectivity with laptop and desktop PCs. A new series of devices for Windows is expected, as are developments using a Macintosh operating system. Already, entirely portable computer-assisted, real-time data collection is possible. Further development of hardware can only make it a matter-of-fact reality. Whether this will radically alter the conceptualization of the observation and analysis task, however, is less clear.

The main barrier to increasing the sophistication of the observational task appears to lie in the reliance on keyboards (miniaturized or not) for data entry. Although clearly superior to pencil and paper, observers find the accurate operation of such devices for real-time, multiple data entry demanding. Two developments in procedures for data entry may be worthy of exploration. First, the use of touch-sensitive screens (with or without additional "handwriting" recognition; cf. US Robotic Pilot) may have some ergonomic advantages over key pressing. If nothing else, it may add a sense of reassuring familiarity for observational researchers reared on paper-and-pencil methods. Second, developments in voice recognition software already, at least in theory, allow for the possibility of data capture through observers providing a running verbal commentary using key words to describe real-time sequences of events. Given the verbal ability of human observers, it is likely that voice-activated data capture may replace manual entry in the first decade of the 21st century.

REFERENCES

Ahmed, Z., Fraser, W.I., Kerr, M., Kiernan, C., Emerson, E., Robertson, J., Felce, D., Allen, D., Baxter, H., & Thomas, J. (in press). The effects of reducing antipsychotic medication in people with a learning disability. *British Journal of Psychiatry.*

Emerson, E., Beasley, F., Offord, G., & Mansell, J. (1992). Specialised housing for people with seriously challenging behaviours. *Journal of Mental Deficiency Research, 36,* 291–307.

Emerson, E., Hatton, C., Robertson, J., Henderson, D., & Cooper, J. (1999). A descriptive analysis of the relationships between social context, engagement and stereotypy in residential services for people with severe and complex disabilities. *Journal of Applied Research in Intellectual Disabilities, 12,* 11–29.

Emerson, E., Reeves, D., Thompson, S., Henderson, D., & Robertson, J. (1996). Time-based lag sequential analysis in the functional assessment of severe challenging behaviour. *Journal of Intellectual Disability Research, 40,* 260–274.

Emerson, E., Thompson, S., Reeves, D., Henderson, D., & Robertson, J. (1995). Descriptive analysis of multiple response topographies of challenging behavior. *Research in Developmental Disabilities, 16,* 301–329.

Felce, D., Lowe, K., Perry, J., Baxter, H., Jones, E., Hallam, A., & Beecham, J. (1998). Service support to people in Wales with severe intellectual disabilities and the most severe challenging behaviours: Processes, outcomes and costs. *Journal of Intellectual Disability Research, 42,* 390–408.

Hatton, C., Emerson, E., Robertson, J., Henderson, D., & Cooper, J. (1995). The quality and costs of services for adults with multiple disabilities: A comparative evaluation. *Research in Developmental Disabilities, 16,* 439–460.

Jones, E., Perry, J., Lowe, K., Felce, D., Toogood, S., Dunstan, F., Allen, D., & Pagler, J. (1999). Opportunity and the promotion of activity among adults with severe mental retardation living in community residences: The impact of training staff in active support. *Journal of Intellectual Disability Research, 43,* 164–178.

Kahng, S., & Iwata, B.A. (1998). Computerised systems for collecting real-time observational data. *Journal of Applied Behavior Analysis, 31,* 253–261.

Kratochwill, T.R., Doll, E.J., & Dickson, W.P. (1985). Microcomputers in behavioral assessment: Recent advances and remaining issues. *Computers in Human Behavior, 1,* 277–291.

Lowe, K., Felce, D., & Blackman, D. (1996). Challenging behaviour: The effectiveness of specialist support teams. *Journal of Intellectual Disability Research, 40,* 336–347.

Mansell, J. (1994). Specialized group homes for persons with severe or profound mental retardation and serious behavior problem in England. *Research in Developmental Disabilities, 15,* 371–388.

McGill, P., Hewson, S., & Emerson, E. (1994). *CTS: A software package for the collection of observational data on Psion organisers* [Software]. Canterbury, United Kingdom: CAPSC, University of Kent.

Proctor, R., Stratton-Powell, H., Burns, A., Tarrier, N., Reeves, D., Emerson, E., & Hatton, C. (1998). An observational study to evaluate the impact of a specialist outreach team on the quality of care in nursing and residential homes. *Aging and Mental Health, 2,* 232–238.

Reeves, D. (1994a). *Calculating inter-observer agreement and Cohen's kappa on time-based observational data allowing for "natural" measurement error.* Manchester, United Kingdom: Hester Adrian Research Centre, University of Manchester.

Reeves, D. (1994b). *HARCLAG: A program for the sequential analysis of observational data* [Computer software]. Manchester, United Kingdom: Hester Adrian Research Centre, University of Manchester.

Repp, A.C., & Felce, D. (1990). A micro-computer system used for evaluative and experimental behavioural research in mental handicap. *Mental Handicap Research, 3,* 21–32.

Repp, A.C., Harman, M.L., Felce, D., Van Acker, R., & Karsh, K.G. (1989). Conducting behavioral assessments on computer-collected data. *Behavioral Assessment, 11,* 249–268.

Repp, A.C., Karsh, K.G., Van Acker, R., Felce, D., & Harman, M. (1989). A computer-based system for collecting and analysing observational data. *Journal of Special Education Technology, 9,* 207–217.

Sackett, G.P. (1979). The lag sequential analysis of contingency and cyclicity in behavioral interaction research. In J.D. Osofsky (Ed.), *Handbook of infant development* (1st ed., pp. 301–340). New York: John Wiley & Sons.

Sackett, G.P. (1987). Analysis of sequential social interaction data: Some issues, recent developments, and a causal inference model. In J.D. Osofsky (Ed.), *Handbook of infant development* (2nd ed., pp. 855–878). New York: John Wiley & Sons.

Suen, H.K., & Ary, D. (1989). *Analyzing quantitative behavioral observation data.* Mahwah, NJ: Lawrence Erlbaum Associates.

5

PROCODER

A System for Collection and Analysis of Observational Data from Videotape

Jon Tapp and
Tedra A. Walden

PROCODER (Tapp & Walden, 1993) is a software system for DOS-compatible computers that facilitates the collection and analysis of data obtained from observing social interaction processes and/or individuals. The system consists of the software, a personal computer, an edit-quality videotape deck, a video monitor, and a computer/tape deck controller interface box. We have attempted to create a system that is versatile enough to meet the needs of any project that uses real-time observation to gather data. As events are entered into the computer data files they are automatically marked with an entry time code from the tape. The system collects data of two different types: 1) *event data,* in which events and related times (frame numbers) are entered into a data stream; and 2) *interval data,* in which a code is entered at fixed intervals (e.g., every 30 seconds). These different data types can be collected for an observation session and later merged for analytic purposes. Interval data can be collected without missing any time because the system plays an interval, stops for data entry, and then plays the next interval. Event data can be collected easily because several passes of a single session can be coded and then the data are automatically sorted by beginning frame number.

This chapter was supported in part by National Institute of Child Health and Human Development Grant No. P30HD15052.

PROCODER is available for free via the Internet on the *PROCODER* World Wide Web site: http://miles.kc.vanderbilt.edu/~jont/procoder.html.

TIME CODING OF TAPES

During the development of the *PROCODER* system we learned a great deal about how time code is written to tapes. Having a code actually written on the tape enables the user to find events or sections of tape very reliably. The time code we use is accurate to the frame rate of the tape deck, which is 30 frames per second. This means that our measurements can be accurate to one-thirtieth of a second, if so desired.

The time code refers to a signal that is written to the tape that indicates to the apparatus (described further on in this chapter) what frame number the tape is currently displaying on the monitor. The time codes available on the market in the early 1990s, when we developed the system, were of two general types: codes written on the video portion of the tape and codes written on one of the two audio channels of the tape. The equipment that we first used wrote the time code on one of the audio channels. We found that this time code was subject to drift problems that, after repeated use, caused the frame numbers to no longer match the video frames. This drift is attributable to the fact that the small edge of the tape used for audio is subject to stretching as the tape is used repeatedly. Time code that is written on the video signal is and remains accurate to the frame. We looked at other types of time coding as well but found that most other types were not standardized and could be used only with specific equipment.

The standard created by the Society of Motion Picture and Television Engineers (SMPTE) written on the video signal in the vertical interlace area (vertical interlace time code, or VITC) is the best for our use for a number of reasons. First, it provides frame-accurate consistent time values for tapes. Second, any editing shop can read SMPTE standard time code in the VITC area and use that to find sections of tape. This standard is still the most widely used for analog tapes, but the digital formats are slowly taking over the market. The cost per tape for digital tapes is still high enough to be prohibitive for our use.

APPARATUS

The equipment needed consists of a computer that controls a tape deck using a tape controller. Each piece of equipment is described briefly in the following subsections. Figure 1 shows the connections between the various devices.

Computer Requirements

As mentioned previously, *PROCODER* was written for DOS. The computer requirements for *PROCODER* are minimal; all that is needed is a DOS-compatible computer with an 80286 processor or better, at least 640 kilobytes of random access memory, as least one free serial port that must be addressable as COM1: or COM2:, and a small hard drive. The program takes up less than 500 kilobytes of disk space and even can be run from a floppy disk, although a hard drive is highly recommended. The program has been tested with Windows 95 and runs fine as a DOS application.

Tape Controllers

The tape controller that is required is connected to the computer using a standard RS-232 serial cable of the type that is normally used with modems. The controller allows the computer to control the tape deck and is hooked to the tape deck with

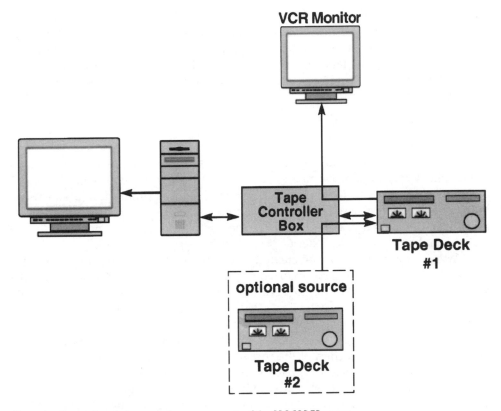

Figure 1.   Connections between various components of the *PROCODER* system.

a standard 50-pin edit controller patch cable. The controller also reads the time code from the tape in the form of frame numbers and reports this information to the computer. While in Time Code Write mode, the controller can write the time code on tapes as they are being dubbed. This Time Code Write function requires a source tape deck or camera to provide source video for a time-coded copy of the tape. The tape controller is made by AEC Electronics. In a previous article (Tapp & Walden, 1993), we described the system using the control equipment made by a company named BCD, for which we first designed the system. The AEC tape controller has far better capabilities because it uses VITC time code; therefore, BCD equipment is no longer supported (additional information concerning pricing and availability is available from the first author).

Tape Decks

Any tape deck that is supported by the AEC tape controller will work with *PROCODER*. The software communicates with the tape controller and not with the tape deck directly. There are a number of models that have edit controller patches on the back of the tape deck. The AEC tape controller supports several models from Sony and Panasonic. These decks are high-quality decks and are expensive. When purchasing new decks, consider a reputable high-end videotape equipment supplier that will guarantee maintenance. The model we currently recommend and use is the Panasonic AG-7450. These high-end decks are required because of the enormous amount of shuttling and searching that is inherent in coding. If no other options exist for putting the SMPTE standard time code on tapes in the VITC area, an additional tape deck or camera will be required that can be used as a source of video while making copies. We recommend that users make copies of their original tapes in any case and code the tapes from the copy. It is much cheaper to make another copy than to return to the field and record the activity of interest again.

USING THE SYSTEM

After copying the source tape while adding time code to the copy, the events on the duplicate tape are ready to be coded. Event coding is best accomplished by describing the types of files needed to record data. The program operates using menus selected by using the arrow keys and pressing <Enter>. When this program was developed in the early 1990s, the use of a mouse was not widespread on personal computers, so *PROCODER* does not support a mouse.

At least three files must be created to use the system: a code file, a segment file, and either an event or an interval file. The code file is needed to enable the system to determine whether the codes being entered are "legal" for the coding scheme in use. The segment file is needed to provide the program with information on which sections of the tape are to be coded. In connection with the code file, the segment file provides a way for the system to determine if a given code is legitimate in a certain section of the segment being coded (i.e., codes about a toy are not legitimate when there is no toy present). We designed this extensive checking capability to eliminate as many coding errors as possible. We found from experience that errors in coding lead to problems with reliability and analysis that are extremely difficult to find and correct after the fact.

CODE FILE

PROCODER allows for the code file to be developed using the Code File Setup screen. Selections are made from the side menu to add, change, and delete codes; to move between the different code types; and to change to a different code file or create a new code file. The code file is not linked to the data files in any way except for its use in checking code input. This means that the code file can be changed at any time without affecting data already entered. Four types of codes can be used with *PROCODER*. Each code type is described in the following subsections. The user may enter up to 100 of each code type, but all codes must be unique. In other words, a code for a time interval cannot be the same as a code for an event. However, as many codes as necessary may be written.

Event Codes

Event codes are used to code normal tape events. Each code line consists of the code itself (up to 10 characters), an associated 25-character description, and a status code that indicates where in the tape segment the code can be legally entered (status codes are explained more fully under the "Checking by Time Value" heading further on in this chapter). When data are being collected, event codes are entered into the data file with an associated start and stop time (in frames) to code what type of event of interest is happening on the tape during that period.

Event Codes with Ratings

In some cases, the user may want to add a qualifier to the event code. An example would be if one were coding smiles and wanted to assign a rating number to describe the "happiness" value of the smile, with a very big smile indicated by "10" and a slight smile indicated by "1." For this type of coding scheme we have incorporated the ability for a "rating" number to be added to the event codes. It is important to remember that the event code and any potential ratings should not exceed 10 characters in length. If the code exceeds 10 characters, it will be truncated to 10 characters before it is entered into the event stream.

Interval Codes

Interval codes are used differently from event codes. Interval codes are used to record data about intervals of any desired duration. For example, the user might want to know whether a smile occurred in each 10 seconds of a tape segment. During coding of intervals *PROCODER* will play 10 seconds of tape, stop the tape, wait for a code to be entered, and then play the next 10 seconds, stop the tape, and wait again. This process is repeated for the entire segment. In this case one could have an interval code for "smile" and a code for "no smile."

Interval Codes with Ratings

As with event codes the user may want to have some ratings for interval codes as well. In our example, one may want not only to code the fact that a smile occurred or did not but also to attach a "happiness" rating to the smile, as described previously in the discussion of rated event codes.

Checking by Time Value

The status codes are used to check the times of codes being entered to ensure that the code occurs at an appropriate time within the segment being coded. We have found that this time checking can greatly reduce time-consuming coding errors. The segment file can contain up to three "breakpoints" within the segment that define where certain events happen. These breakpoints are simply a time (in frames) within the segment at which significant events happen (e.g., the parent enters the room, a toy robot enters the area). The status code tells *PROCODER* where within the breakpoints of the tape segment the code can be entered. For example, parent codes can be disallowed when the parent is not present or toy codes can be disallowed when the toy is not present.

SEGMENT FILES

Segment files consist of a starting frame, up to three breakpoints, an ending frame, and a condition code for each segment of videotape that the user wishes to code. Condition codes can be used for later quantification of any attribute one wants to consider. The breakpoints allow designation of sets of allowable codes for different portions of a segment. For example, a code with a status variable of zero is allowed at any point in a segment, whereas a status code of one is allowed only between the start of the segment and breakpoint one, and so forth.

Coders mark tape segments while viewing the tape by depressing a "mark" key on the computer keyboard. The mark key puts the current frame number from the tape into the currently selected time area on the screen. For example, to mark the beginning of a segment, the cursor is moved to the start frame position on the screen for the current segment, and the mark key is pressed when the tape reaches the beginning of the segment. The tape is controlled from a pop-up menu of tape controls or by using one of the many defined "hot" keys (e.g., Alt-P for play).

EVENT FILES

Event files are created using the Code Events selection from the main menu. An event in *PROCODER* consists of a code, a start time in frames, and a stop time in frames. The current time on the tape (in frames) is displayed in the corner of the screen and can be put into the currently selected event code's data record with one keystroke (called the *mark key*). It is usually best to mark the time of an event first and then enter the code for it. Events can be replayed using the "instant replay" key for a judgment to be made. A flexible and user-selectable amount in frames called the *preroll* is used to rewind the tape to a place slightly before the event and then replay the event for a coding judgment. After the file is saved or the Sort option is chosen from the Edit menu, the codes are sorted in order by start frame. This quick sorting allows the user to code events without being concerned with the order in which they appear on the tape.

We have developed several methods for entering event codes. The general strategy is to move the cursor on the screen to the code or time that needs to be entered or changed and then make the entry as in a spreadsheet program. If codes are to be mutually exclusive there is a "quick keys" mode that can be used to code the tape using single keystrokes. We find that most coders develop their own style of coding and interacting with the system because it is very flexible and coding can be accomplished in several ways. Because the codes are easily sorted and merged together, coding can be completed by making several passes on the same segment of tape (e.g., first, watch for smiles, then make another pass for crying). Codes are checked as they are entered to ensure that they are allowed and that they are in the correct time segment as defined by the code and segment files.

INTERVAL FILES

Interval files are created using the Code Intervals selection from the main menu. Interval files consist of only one event code per entry. The time of the interval is determined by selectable interval duration and by the distance from the start of the tape segment being coded. For example, if a segment starts at frame 1000 and the interval length is set to 900 frames (30 seconds), then the first interval will start at 1000 and end at 1900, the second interval will start at 1900 and end at 2800, and so forth. The instant replay key plays the current interval as selected by the cursor and then stops the tape. The rater then enters a code, moves the cursor to the next interval, and hits the instant replay key again. Interval and event codes can be merged and sorted by time for use in further analyses.

OUTPUT, PRINTING, AND ANALYSIS OPTIONS

PROCODER has the ability to process event and interval files to obtain frequencies, duration, or percentage of intervals by code. Results from all analyses can be sent to the printer, a disk file, or the screen. The program also can compare two files and output the degree to which they agree with one another for an analysis of interrater agreement. A report by code is available for interval data and event data. For duration measures we calculate agreement for each frame by code. For interval data the percentage of intervals of agreement is calculated. For event frequency a "windowing" method, described in a previous report (MacLean, Tapp, & Johnson, 1985), is used.

For simplicity and flexibility, all files are stored in Text Only or ASCII format. The system can create a merged output file containing the raw event data for use with statistical packages or with other programs for more extensive analyses. The files can be printed in several different ways to aid in data presentation. Results of analyses also can be printed to files for use in subsequent analyses if, for example, only frequency and/or duration values are needed in an analysis of variance.

SAMPLE STUDIES USING *PROCODER*

PROCODER can be used to structure coding, set up data files, and perform analyses on different types of research questions. One question that has been pursued by the second author focuses on the contingency of parental responses after young children's bids for interaction. We have been interested in assessing the contingency of parental responses so that we might compare parental responsiveness across different groups of participants (e.g., typically developing, developmentally delayed). Furthermore, we have attempted to link variations in responsiveness to children's subsequent behavior. For this project, data were collected in several studies of infant social referencing, and both parent and child behaviors were coded using event codes that denoted the occurrence of each target behavior.

PROCODER was used to identify target child behaviors that occurred in the stream of coded data. The data were searched forward and backward to locate the target parental behaviors of interest. Sequences were categorized as being either "contingent" or "noncontingent." Contingency ratings were then linked to several child outcomes to determine whether parents' contingency influenced their children's behavior. In a series of studies on this topic, we first discovered that parents of children with developmental delays were significantly less contingently responsive than parents of children without delays (Walden & Knieps, 1996; Walden, Knieps, & Baxter, 1991). We also found that children with developmental delays were less likely to learn the appropriate social regulation of their behavior based on social referential information than children who were developing typically. However, the children with developmental delays whose parents responded contingently were able to regulate their behavior appropriately. Thus, parental contingency was important for young children to learn to regulate their behavior toward an event based on their parents' responses to that event. In subsequent work we found that the children with developmental delays produced social signals that were significantly more difficult to detect than the signals produced by children who were developing typically; thus, the lower parental contingency may have resulted from the difficulty in responding contingently to social behavior that is difficult to detect (Walden, 1996). We also have identified a similar relation between parental contingent responsiveness and behavior regulation among children without developmental delays, although this effect is weaker (Carpenter & Walden, 1999).

POTENTIAL RESEARCH APPLICATIONS

We searched the literature to identify published studies that addressed the kinds of research questions that could be examined using *PROCODER* coding and analysis techniques to quantify observational data. A wide range of interesting and important research questions were identified. One category of questions involves sequences of behaviors of interacting dyads, often comparing such sequences for groups with some known disability and groups without disability. Some examples of these studies include face-to-face interaction between infants with orofacial clefts and their mothers in which sequences of mother and infant behaviors were coded and compared across groups of children with and without disabilities (Endriga & Speltz, 1997), caregivers' sensitivity to the communicative and linguistic needs of their deaf infants (Robinshaw & Evans, 1995), sequences of communication between family members (Dadds, Barrett, & Rapee, 1996), teachers' strategies for intervening in disputes between children (Bayer, Whaley, & May, 1995), and studies of relationship structure (Hinde, Tamplin, & Barrett, 1993).

A number of studies have focused on the effect of parental behaviors on children's linguistic and/or reading performance. These include studies on the nature of reciprocal sequential relations in conversations between parents and children with developmental delays (Yoder & Davies, 1990), the effect of adult continuing "wh-" questions (what, where, and who) on children's conversational participation (Yoder, Davies, Bishop, & Munson, 1994), adult–child discourse in the construction of a story theme (Shugar, 1996), discourse repairs (Gardner, 1997), verbal interactions of drug-exposed children and their mothers (Heller, Sobel, & Tanaka-Matsumi, 1996), and children's responsiveness in the organization of parent–infant interactions during picture book reading (Senechal, Cornell, & Broda, 1995).

A third category of studies involved coding observational data and examining sequences of affective behaviors and affective communications. Examples of such studies include those on affect regulation and synchrony in mother–infant face-to-face interaction (Feldman & Greenbaum, 1997), relational control patterns and expressed emotion in families of individuals with schizophrenia and bipolar disorder (Wuerker, 1994), the development of laughter in mother–infant dyads using timing parameters and temporal sequence patterns that elicited laughter (Nwokah, Hsu, Dobrowolska, & Fogel, 1994), and gender-based differences in styles of maternal sensitivity and dyadic balance of control (Biringen, Robinson, & Emde, 1994).

FUTURE DIRECTIONS

PROCODER was created relatively early in the evolution of personal computer and related operating systems. Text Only files and methods for dealing with them are time consuming and awkward by today's standards of mouse-driven operating systems and menu-driven statistical packages. The software also has the drawback of having small code fields and therefore is not useful for some needs, such as language transcription. For these reasons we are developing a new generation of software for coding from tapes based on the Windows 95/NT operating system and using larger data fields and database files. We anticipate using the same tape equipment with a slightly better computer system. We also anticipate incorporating digital tape decks and other protocols, in addition to the AEC tape controller, as they become available and as tape costs decline.

CONCLUSIONS

We have tried to create a system that is flexible enough to aid in many areas of study that use videotape for direct observational research. The *PROCODER* software program is freely available from the authors or via the Internet. The only costs associated with this system are equipment costs. However, compared with the time costs incurred using traditional tape decks and hand-held remote-controlled systems, and because of the higher quality of data that can be achieved using this coding system, we believe that the additional costs are minimal in the long run.

REFERENCES

Bayer, C.L., Whaley, K.L., & May, S.E. (1995). Strategic assistance in toddler disputes: II. Sequences and patterns of teachers' message strategies. In M. Killen (Ed.), Conflict resolution in early social development [Special issue]. *Early Education and Development, 6,* 405–432.

Biringen, Z., Robinson, J.L., & Emde, R.N. (1994). Maternal sensitivity in the second year: Gender-based relations in the dyadic balance of control. *American Journal of Orthopsychiatry, 64,* 78–90.

Carpenter, K. & Walden, T.A. (1999). *The effect of parental contingency on infant behavior and affect.* Manuscript submitted for publication.

Dadds, M.R., Barrett, P.M., & Rapee, R.M. (1996). Family process and child anxiety and aggression: An observational analysis. *Journal of Abnormal Child Psychology, 24,* 715–734.

Endriga, M.C., & Speltz, M.L. (1997). Face to face interaction between infants with orofacial clefts and their mothers. *Journal of Pediatric Psychology, 22,* 439–453.

Feldman, R., & Greenbaum, C.W. (1997). Affect regulation and synchrony in mother–infant play as precursors to the development of symbolic competence. *Infant Mental Health Journal, 18,* 4–23.

Gardner, H. (1997). Are your minimal pairs too neat? The dangers of phonemicisation in phonology therapy. *European Journal of Disorders of Communication, 32,* 167–175.

Heller, M.C., Sobel, M., & Tanaka-Matsumi, J. (1996). A functional analysis of verbal interactions of drug-exposed children and their mothers: The utility of sequential analysis. *Journal of Clinical Psychology, 52,* 687–697.

Hinde, R.A., Tamplin, A., & Barrett, J. (1993). A comparative study of relationship structure. *British Journal of Social Psychology, 32,* 191–207.

MacLean, W.E., Jr., Tapp, J.T., & Johnson, W.L. (1985). Alternate methods and software for calculating interobserver agreement for continuous observation data. *Journal of Psychopathology and Behavioral Assessment, 7,* 65–73.

Nwokah, E.E., Hsu, H.C., Dobrowolska, O., & Fogel, A. (1994). The development of laughter in mother–infant communication: Timing parameters and temporal sequences. *Infant Behavior and Development, 17,* 23–35.

Robinshaw, H.M., & Evans, R. (1995). Caregivers' sensitivity to the communicative and linguistic needs of their deaf infants. *Early Child Development and Care, 109,* 23–41.

Senechal, M., Cornell, E.H., & Broda, L.S. (1995). Age-related differences in the organization of parent-infant interactions during picture-book reading. *Early Childhood Research Quarterly, 10,* 317–337.

Shugar, G.W. (1996). The social construction of enacted stories: Adult-child collaboration on transformation of a story schema. *Polish Psychological Bulletin, 27,* 201–216.

Tapp, J.T., & Walden, T.A. (1993). PROCODER: A professional tape control, coding and analysis system for behavioral research using videotape. *Behavior Research Methods, Instruments, & Computers, 25,* 53–56.

Walden, T.A. (1996). Social responsivity: Judging signals of young children with and without developmental delays. *Child Development, 67,* 2079–2085.

Walden, T.A., & Knieps, L.J. (1996). Reading and responding to social signals. In M. Lewis & M.W. Sullivan (Eds.), *Emotional development in atypical children* (pp. 29–42). Mahwah, NJ: Lawrence Erlbaum Associates.

Walden, T.A., Knieps, L.J., & Baxter, A. (1991). Contingent provision of social referential information by parents of normally-developing and delayed children. *American Journal of Mental Retardation, 96,* 177–187.

Wuerker, A.M. (1994). Relational control patterns and expressed emotion in families of persons with schizophrenia and bipolar disorder. *Family Process, 33,* 389–407.

Yoder, P.J., & Davies, B. (1990). Do parental questions and topic continuations elicit replies from developmentally delayed children? A sequential analysis. *Journal of Speech and Hearing Research, 33,* 563–573.

Yoder, P.J., Davies, B., Bishop, K., & Munson, L. (1994). Effect of adult continuing wh- questions on conversational participation in children with developmental disabilities. *Journal of Speech and Hearing Research, 37,* 193–203.

6

Observational Software for Laptop Computers and Optical Bar Code Readers

Jon Tapp and
Joseph H. Wehby

Advances in the computer hardware and software industries have resulted in an increased number of technological applications within the behavioral sciences field. Kahng and Iwata (1998) reported on 15 computer programs used to collect and analyze observational data (see Chapter 3). As these technological advances continue, hardware and software systems for the study of behavior should become increasingly more sophisticated and user-friendly for researchers and clinicians alike. The purpose of this chapter is to describe the development of two computer-assisted observational systems that use this advanced technology. The *Multiple Option Observation System for Experimental Studies* (*MOOSES*; Tapp, Wehby, & Ellis, 1995) is a software program designed for the collection of observational data using laptop computers. The *Wand Analysis* (*WANDA*) (Tapp & Symons, 1995) program is a software program that is designed to manage data collected via hand-held optical bar code scanning devices. The chapter is organized into four sections. A brief introduction and overview is presented for both the *MOOSES* and *WANDA* programs. Next, brief technical descriptions of the data collection procedures for both programs are highlighted. The third section reviews a common set of data analysis procedures that can be implemented for

This chapter was supported in part by National Institute of Child Health and Human Development Grant No. P30HD15052.

both software programs. In the final section, a brief summary of research projects using *MOOSES* and *WANDA* is presented.

OVERVIEW OF *MOOSES*

The *MOOSES* system consists of software for the collection and analysis of data gathered in real-time observations. The *MOOSES* program outputs the results of the analyses to a printer, a disk file, or the computer screen. Each of these steps is described in detail below. The original version is available for DOS-compatible personal computers and laptop computers and requires a minimum of 640 kilobytes of memory. In addition, there is a Windows 95 version that requires 16 megabytes of memory to run efficiently. Both versions are programmed in *Visual Basic* (Version 6.0). Finally, the collection program can be run separately on a very basic machine and the files uploaded to a desktop personal computer for later analysis.

OVERVIEW OF *WANDA*

The *WANDA* program was developed to facilitate the analysis and management of observational data collected from time wand bar code data collectors. Time wands are handheld optical bar code scanning devices. The time wand software program manages two types of event-based data: 1) *continuously collected data*, wherein events are scanned in real time as observed in a setting, and 2) *fixed-interval data*, wherein a set interval for observation is defined in seconds and a set interval is defined for recording the observations. The *WANDA* program is a data-processing program that sorts and performs analyses on observational data and outputs the results of the analyses to a printer, a disk file, or the computer screen. Each of these steps is described in detail below. The program is Macintosh based and is run by simply launching it from the Finder icon by double clicking or by selecting Open from the Finder's file menu while *WANDA* is selected. The program then operates by making selections from the Macintosh menu bar.

A NOTE ON TIME WANDS

Time wands were designed for the collection of inventory data in stores and warehouses. Physically, time wands are very compact and portable. The programming that can be done to the wand by the user, however, is limited. The primary programmable options are for controlling the prompts that are presented to the user when the Scan button is pressed and for providing data checks and rejecting scans that do not conform to a predetermined character pattern or that are not found in a table (called *Xref tables*) located in the wand's memory. Because of the time wand's limited memory and the need to use it for a long time without downloading, programming is minimized so that the majority of its memory is dedicated to data collection rather than to prompts and Xref tables.

   Symbology refers to the set of symbols that are used to represent data characters in the form of small bars of different widths. Bar code symbology is based on modular arithmetic and abstract algebra's group theory. The word *symbology* simply refers to the way in which the bars are arranged. A now-standard symbology is the universal product code used in retail sales. The time wands can read and decode many different types of symbologies. In our time wand application, we use Code 3 of 9 symbology because a Macintosh font for this symbology is provided; thus, we can construct and adapt the scan code sheets in our laboratory as needed.

In our application of time wands during daily observational sessions in residential treatment facilities, special education classrooms, and group homes for children and adults with mental retardation and related disabilities, a number of practical problems have become apparent that are worth noting. These include the occurrence of intrusive audible beeps from the wands as observational codes are scanned, natural lighting interfering with codes being scanned successfully, and the observer(s) having to look down at the scan sheet and away from the person being observed. The audible beep limitation was overcome by special programming done for us by Videx that allowed the wand to illuminate a small light-emitting diode (LED) plugged into the download port instead of beeping when the scan was good.

SETTING UP FOR DATA COLLECTION WITH *MOOSES*

Code File

MOOSES allows the user to define a specific code file for a particular research project. This user-defined code file is the cornerstone of the *MOOSES* program; it allows for the flexibility of using the same software package for several different projects by simply choosing the code file that is needed for that particular project. When creating a particular code file, the user will give a label to a code (alphanumeric or special codes based on a function key, which are referred to as *toggles*), enter a brief description of the code, and assign a code type. The types of codes that can be used in designing an observation system are described in the following subsections.

Frequency-Only Codes

Frequency-only codes allow the user to record the simple frequency of an observed event. Duration is not calculated, and these codes do not interrupt the ongoing recording of other behaviors.

Frequency and Duration Codes

This code type should be selected when coding for both frequency and duration of a particular behavior is desired. A unique feature of this type of code is that it allows the user to define a level for each code. Each level represents a class of codes that are considered mutually exclusive. Thus, if several levels of codes are defined, the user can record different topographies of a particular class of behavior while maintaining a continuous record for several different levels. For example, one could compare the frequency and duration of different topographies of aggression (e.g., Level 1) while coding the different types of teacher instruction (e.g., Level 2) observed in a typical class period.

Interval Codes

Interval codes are used to code behaviors on a momentary time schedule (which is defined by the user). Interval codes can be only one digit and are mutually exclusive. Each digit in an interval code is analyzed separately. For example, in the code "15," the first digit represents the level of academic engagement observed in a classroom, where 1 = engaged and 2 = disengaged, and the second digit represents the relative noise level in the room, where 3 = quiet, 4 = moderate, and 5 = loud. Thus, 15 indicates that at a particular interval the child was engaged and the noise level was loud. These data also can be collected concurrently with other, more continuous coding (e.g., teacher interaction).

Collection Program (*GETMDAT*)

Selecting Collect Data from the File menu runs the data collection program *GET-MDAT*. The collection program then reads the MOOSES.CFG file to determine the data path and operation modes settings. The user is then prompted for a file name, the desired header information, and the session duration in minutes. As mentioned above, *GETMDAT* can be run in isolation on laptop computers that might not be able to support the Windows 95 platform. These data files can be uploaded to a more sophisticated machine for later analysis. *GETMDAT* will save at least two and possibly three files. If interval collection is enabled, a file with a .INT extension will be saved containing the interval data. A file with the extension .EVE will hold the events that are entered in the time stream at the arrow prompts. A file with the .TOG extension will contain the toggle data collected using the F1 through F9 function keys. With the exception of interval codes, for which times are not needed, each entry will be put into the file as a code, a comma, and then the time of entry from the beginning of the session. Event files are written to disk at the end of the session, whereas the other data types are written to the disk at the time of entry.

Data File Types

MOOSES creates and uses several types of files to hold data and codes. Table 1 describes the file types and default extensions.

SETTING UP FOR DATA COLLECTION WITH *WANDA*

Like *MOOSES*, *WANDA* uses a code file to tell the program how to treat the scan codes it encounters in the files of scanned codes. The code file format can be created using any standard word processor and consists of a line of information for each scan code being used. Normally, a different code file is made for each scan sheet being used to collect data. Figure 1 shows an example of a scan sheet. The scan sheet can be made using a word processor or drawing program. The bar code is simply typed by choosing the symbology font. Laser printing is preferable to

Table 1. *MOOSES* file types and extensions

File type	Default extension	Description
Event file	.EVE	Standard event file, holds event data recorded by *GETMDAT*
Toggle file	.TOG	Standard toggle file, holds toggle data recorded by *GETMDAT*
Interval file	.INT	Standard interval file, holds interval data recorded by *GETMDAT*
Code file	.COD	Holds a code set for a given project or analysis method
List file	.LST	Holds a list of filenames of one type for use with the list analysis feature

Figure 1.   Sample time wand bar codes.

use of a dot-matrix or ink-jet type of printer. Each line of the code file contains the code itself, a textual description of the code used to label printouts, and a number indicating the code's level. Level is used here to tell the program that codes of the same level are mutually exclusive and exhaustive. This allows multiple levels of duration events to be collected and analyzed. For example, measuring different forms of severe behavior problems exhibited by a child with mental retardation in different environments during a day would require a multilevel coding scheme. Table 2 shows how a coding scheme could be set up.

WANDA can support up to 10 mutually exclusive levels. The program is guided by the Settings menu, in which code levels are durational in nature and other levels are considered for frequency counts only. As a raw scan file is sorted, the codes are checked against the code file to ensure that they are defined in a given code set. Editing of the raw scan file may be required from time to time to correct scanning mistakes. WANDA has a special code called the edit code that can be defined in the Settings menu. If this code is scanned it tells the program to delete the previously scanned code while the sort is being performed. Finally, a code described as a "narrative record" code is used to leave a mark in the raw scan file where more complex editing needs to be done.

ANALYSIS OPTIONS FOR MOOSES AND WANDA

Because of shared similar features, both software application programs are described together. Analysis can be conducted on a single data file or on a list of data files. If one selects a list one can pick the Skip to Pooled check box; if this box is checked, MOOSES will present only the output that is summed over the whole list and will skip output for each individual file in the list. Outputs can be sent to a printer, a spreadsheet file, a database, or a statistical program for further analy-

Table 2.   Example of a simple WANDA coding scheme as entered into a code file

Code	Description	Level
0	No self-injury	1
1	Self-injury (arm)	1
2	Aggression (staff)	2
3	Aggression (peer)	2
4	No aggression	2
10	Dining room	3
11	Living room	3
12	Outside	3
13	Bedroom	3

sis. Data files can be scanned for errors before analyses are conducted, and the user has the ability to recode several individual behaviors to a single class.

Frequency and Duration

This choice provides the frequency and duration of codes in your files. No duration data are output for frequency-only codes. Codes in the same level are mutually exclusive and exhaustive. That is, codes that are in the same level start and end other codes within the same level, and each duration level should contain the total amount of time for the total session.

Interobserver Agreement

Choosing this analysis results in an interobserver agreement report that compares pairs of files from two observers. Two methods are used, one based on a comparison of each second in each file and another that involves generating a time window around the first observer's codes and seeking agreements in the second observer's file. We recommend the first method for comparing duration codes and the second method for frequency-only codes. Each of these methods is described in turn in the following subsections.

Second-by-Second Comparisons

This analysis is done for each mutually exclusive level. It compares each second in the time stream and creates a matrix in which each second is tallied into the proper cell to indicate what code was in effect for each observer. The matrix in Table 3 provides an illustration. This matrix sets up the codes for the first observer across the top and the codes for the second observer down the side. Each second is tallied for the entire 180-second session. Consider code 111. Both observers coded a 111 for 56 seconds; Observer One coded 111 for 12 seconds while Observer Two coded 222; Observer Two coded 111 for 4 seconds while Observer One coded 222, and so on. Note that all of the seconds that agree are down the diagonal of the matrix, where both observers were coding the same code. *MOOSES* calculates Cohen's kappa (Cohen, 1960) and an agreement ratio (agreements divided by total seconds) for this matrix. The program also calculates agreement ratios and kappa for each code. Kappa for each code is obtained by summing the matrix into a simple two-by-two matrix (i.e., 111 versus not 111) and calculating kappa on the smaller matrix.

Time Window Analysis

This analysis works by examining each code in the first observer's file and then examining a time window in the second observer's file for a code that matches. If a match is found, an agreement for that code is tallied. Codes that are not matched are tallied as disagreements. An agreement ratio is then reported for each code

Table 3.   Interobserver agreement matrix

	111	222	333	Total
111	56	4	0	60
222	12	43	5	60
333	0	3	57	60
Total	68	50	62	180

(agreements divided by agreements plus disagreements). This method should be used for codes in the data set for which one is concerned with frequency only and not duration (for more detail see MacLean, Tapp, & Johnson, 1985).

Multilevel Analysis

This analysis provides a report on the number of seconds spent in different codes across different mutually exclusive levels. It works by creating a file that contains a record for each second. This file is referred to as the *matrix* in the dialogue box. The matrix file contains a record for each second of the file being analyzed. The code entered at each level is written to the column of the matrix that represents that level. A new code is formed by concatenating the codes in each column of interest, and the frequencies of these new codes are tallied. The resulting output consists of the number of seconds spent in each of the new codes that are found in the matrix. Duration levels in states of interest can then be compared (e.g., the levels of aggressive behavior when parents are present versus the levels of aggression when parents are absent).

Sequential Analysis

This analysis allows users to examine sequential relationships in the data based on event sequences or time windows. Antecedent (given) codes and consequent (target) codes are defined and selected by the user with a dialogue box in *MOOSES* or a script in *WANDA*. Options that can be set include the number of event lags or the number of seconds of interest and the direction of counting (forward or backward). Several standard statistics are computed for the resulting sequential frequency tables. The event-based method counts the frequency with which a selected code follows other codes at discrete event steps or lags. Consider the two-by-two contingency table shown in Table 4 for a Lag 1 event-based forward sequential analysis.

The "A" cell shows the number of times that both a given and a target code were found. Counting starts at the first event and tallies frequencies according to the questions above the cells. The counter then moves to the next (second) event, and so forth. When the N-minus-lag code is reached, counting stops for that session. For example, the observed probability that a given code was followed by a target code is calculated by $A \div T$, where $T = A + B + C + D$ (the total number in the matrix). The observed conditional probability that a target code occurred when a given code occurred is computed by $A \div (A + B)$, and so forth. Several statistics have been suggested for testing the strength of these sequential relation-

Table 4.   A 2 × 2 contingency for a Lag 1 forward sequential analysis

	The next code was one of the consequent/target codes	The next code was NOT one of the consequent/ target codes
The code was one of the antecedent/given codes (as class) or the given	A	B
The code was NOT one of the antecedent/given codes (as class) or the given	C	D

ships and are computed by *MOOSES* and *WANDA*. The statistics and the associated formulas are shown in Table 5, and descriptions can be found in more detail in "References" (Bakeman, McArthur, & Quera, 1996; Bakeman & Quera, 1995).

The time-based counting method uses the same contingency table and statistics but with a different question being answered for each second of the time stream. A window of x seconds is formed from each occurrence of a given event (x can be changed in the dialogue box). The contingency shown in Table 6 is then formed. With this matrix it is possible to examine the conditional probability of the second (as our unit of analysis) being in the window given that the second contained a target code, or $A \div (A + C)$. In other words, how often did the target happen within the time window? The same statistics are computed for the time-based matrix that were used with the event-based matrix.

Visual Analysis

This analysis provides a visual representation of a time line for the multilevel matrix discussed above. Up to 20 codes can be displayed. The visual analysis requires that the user have a VGA (video graphics adapter) or compatible computer screen.

APPLICATIONS OF *MOOSES*

Most applications of *MOOSES* have been in the study of the social behavior of children and adolescents with emotional and behavioral disorders. These applications have included identifying the antecedents and consequences of aggressive behavior in classrooms for students with emotional and behavioral disorders (Wehby, Symons, & Shores, 1995), describing the classroom interaction patterns of children with or at risk for behavior disorders (Jack et al., 1996; Shores et al., 1993; Wehby, Dodge, Valente, & Conduct Problems Prevention Research Group, 1993), coding the social interactions of children with autism (Dugan et al., 1995; Kamps,

Table 5. Formulas for indexes of sequential association using cell values shown in Tables 4 and 6

Statistic	Formula
Allison Liker's Z	$Total = A + B + C + D$
	$ExpFreq = \dfrac{(A + B)(C + D)}{Total}$
	$PI = \dfrac{A + B}{Total}$
	$ALZ = \dfrac{A - ExpFreq}{)ExpFreq(I - PI)}$
Pearson's r	$\sqrt{\dfrac{ALZ^2}{Total}}$
Yule's Q	$\dfrac{AD - BC}{AD + BC}$
Transformed *kappa*	If $A + B < A + C$, then $MIN = A + B$; otherwise, $MIN = A + C$
	$\dfrac{A - ExpFreq}{MIN - ExpFreq}$

Leonard, Potucek, & Garrision-Harrell, 1995), and studying the effects of high-probability request sequences on the appropriate behavior of students with emotional and behavioral disorders (Davis & Reichle, 1996).

Most of these studies have used *MOOSES* to describe the frequency and duration of social interaction behaviors in classroom settings. Others have used the lag sequential analysis program to report sequences of behavior. For example, Shores et al. (1993) reported the first use of *MOOSES* to describe the social interactions between teachers, aggressive students, and their peers in classroom settings. The general results of this study showed that the majority of interactions in these classrooms could be classified as neutral. Teachers tell a student to do something (*mand*), and it is highly predictable that students will comply, which is typically followed by another teacher mand. Positive teacher consequences for appropriate behavior were seldom observed. Sequential analysis of teacher and student behavior revealed that when an aggressive behavior occurred, the most probable antecedents were some type of peer behavior. The most probable consequences for aggressive/disruptive behavior were also some type of peer behavior (e.g., peer talk, peer aggression, peer negative mand). In a follow-up study with a similar population of students (Wehby et al., 1995), higher observed rates of aggressive behavior allowed for a more thorough sequential analysis of the antecedents and consequences of aggressive behavior. For aggression toward teachers the most frequent antecedent observed was a teacher social command.

STUDIES USING WANDA

Optical bar code readers or time wands have been used in research investigating stereotyped movements in developmental disabilities (Symons & Davis, 1994), in applied psychopharmacology research for severe self-injury (Symons, Fox, & Thompson, 1998), and in studies of classroom and residential academic and social behavior (Eiler, Nelson, Jensen, & Johnson, 1989; M.D. Saunders, Saunders, & Saunders, 1993; R.R. Saunders, Saunders, & Saunders, 1994; see also Chapter 9). A number of these studies have specifically used the *WANDA* software program. Symons and Davis (1994) used *WANDA* and real-time data recording to examine the relation between teacher instructional prompts to task completion and gross motor stereotypies in a student with severe intellectual disabilities and autism. Although prompts appeared to have little effect on the overall rate of task completion, their presence was correlated with lower percentages of stereotyped body

Table 6. A 2 × 2 contingency for a time-based forward sequential analysis

	The second contained one of the consequent/ target codes	The second DID NOT contain one of the consequent/target codes
The current second was in the time window formed by antecedent/given codes	A	B
The current second was NOT in the time window formed by antecedent/given codes	C	D

rocking, hand flapping, and finger flipping during vocational tasks. Elsewhere, *WANDA* was used during an experimental evaluation of a combined behavioral and pharmacological treatment for severe self-injury in an adolescent with intellectual and developmental disabilities (Symons et al., 1998). Reductions in daily rate of self-injury were documented during the medication-alone phase, and further reductions were noted during combined treatment phases. Furthermore, the sequential analysis option of *WANDA* was used to examine sequential dependencies between the occurrence of student self-injury and teaching staff behavior. Specifically, sequential analyses were used to describe the social antecedents and consequences of self-injury during assessment, placebo, drug, behavioral, and combined treatment phases. Under some classroom circumstances significant differences were found between the unconditional and conditional probabilities of self-injury and teacher attention, suggesting that adults were more likely to attend to the student when he or she self-injured. This sequential dependency was equally likely whether the student was being administered placebo or active medication.

CONCLUSIONS

Overall, rapid changes in software and hardware technology have improved our ability to conduct observational work in special education research and applications. The flexibility of innovative computer-assisted programs such as *MOOSES* and *WANDA* permits powerful analyses to be conducted with relative ease. At the user end, decisions can be made regarding data-recording format, type of data, type of analysis, and calculation of interobserver agreement. Although problems remain concerning the conceptual integration of results from different levels of analysis, these difficulties are welcome because they reflect our expanded ability to record and analyze multiple forms of behavior concurrently and consecutively, to preserve time, and to ask fundamental questions about sequence and timing in behavioral streams in applied settings. As this technology continues to improve and is applied to other investigations, difficulties of implementation should be resolved. It is important to note, however, that although advances in hardware and software technologies provide us with greater opportunities to accurately capture behavior, we should resist the temptation to allow the technology to guide the science. Rather, it should be considered another tool with which we can actively conduct our research.

REFERENCES

Bakeman, R., McArthur, D., & Quera, V. (1996). Detecting group differences in sequential association using sampled permutations: Log odds, kappa, and phi compared. *Behavior Research Methods, Instruments, and Computers, 28,* 446–457.

Bakeman, R., & Quera, V. (1995). *Analyzing interaction: Sequential analysis with SDIS and GSEQ.* New York: Cambridge University Press.

Cohen, J. (1960). A coefficient of agreement for nominal scales. *Educational and Psychological Measurement, 20,* 37–46.

Davis, C.A., & Reichle, J. (1996). Variant and invariant high-probability requests: Increasing appropriate behaviors in children with emotional-behavioral disorders. *Journal of Applied Behavior Analysis, 29,* 471–481.

Dugan, E., Kamps, D., Leonard, B., Watkins, N., Rheinberger, A., & Stackhaus, J. (1995). Effects of cooperative learning groups during social studies for students with autism and fourth-grade peers. *Journal of Applied Behavior Analysis, 28,* 175–188.

Eiler, J.M., Nelson, W.W., Jensen, C.C., & Johnson, S.P. (1989). Automated data collection using bar code. *Behavior Research Methods, Instruments, and Computers, 21*, 53–58.

Jack, S.L., Shores, R.E., Denny, R.K., Gunter, P.L., DeBriere, T., & DePaepe, P.A. (1996). An analysis of the relationship of teachers' reported use of classroom management strategies on types of classroom interactions. *Journal of Behavioral Education, 6*(1), 67–87.

Kahng, S., & Iwata, B.A. (1998). Computerized systems for collecting real-time observational data. *Journal of Applied Behavior Analysis, 31*, 253–261.

Kamps, D.M., Leonard, B., Potucek, J., & Garrison-Harrell, L. (1995). Cooperative learning groups in reading: An integration strategy for students with autism and general classroom peers. *Behavioral Disorders, 21*(1), 89–109.

MacLean, W.E., Jr., Tapp, J.T., & Johnson, W.L. (1985). Alternate methods of software for calculating interobserver agreement for continuous observation data. *Journal of Psychopathology and Behavioral Assessment, 7*, 65–73.

Saunders, M.D., Saunders, J.L., & Saunders, R.R. (1993). A program evaluation classroom data collection with bar codes. *Research in Developmental Disabilities, 14*, 1–18.

Saunders, R.R., Saunders, M.D., & Saunders, J.L. (1994). Data collection with bar code technology. In T.I. Thompson & D.B. Gray (Eds.), *Destructive behavior in developmental disabilities: Diagnosis and treatment* (pp. 102–116). Thousand Oaks, CA: Sage Publications.

Shores, R.E., Jack, S.L., Gunter, P.L., Ellis, D.N., DeBriere, T.J., & Wehby, J.H. (1993). Classroom interactions of children with behavior disorders. *Journal of Emotional and Behavioral Disorders, 1*(1), 27–39.

Symons, F.J., & Davis, M. (1994). Instructional conditions and stereotyped behavior: The function of prompts. *Journal of Behavior Therapy and Experimental Psychiatry, 25*, 317–324.

Symons, F.J., Fox, N.D., & Thompson, T. (1998). Functional communication training and naltrexone treatment of self-injurious behavior: An experimental case report. *Journal of Applied Research in Intellectual Disabilities, 11*, 273–292.

Tapp, J., & Symons, F.J. (1995). *WANDA: A bar code observation analysis program* [Unpublished software]. Nashville, TN: Vanderbilt University, John F. Kennedy Center for Research on Human Development.

Tapp, J., Wehby, J.H., & Ellis, D. (1995). A multiple option observation system for experimental studies: MOOSES. *Behavior Research Methods, Instruments, and Computers, 27*(1), 25–31.

Wehby, J.H., Dodge, K.A., Valente, E., & Conduct Problems Prevention Research Group. (1993). School behavior of first grade children identified as at-risk for development of conduct problems. *Behavioral Disorders, 19*(1), 67–78.

Wehby, J.H., Symons, F.J., & Shores, R.E. (1995). A descriptive analysis of aggressive behavior in classrooms for children with emotional and behavioral disorders. *Behavioral Disorders, 20*(2), 87–105.

7

Computer-Assisted Integration of Physiological and Behavioral Measures

Maria L. Boccia and
Jane Elizabeth Roberts

Johnny is sitting in the middle of the floor. The television is on. Suddenly, he starts rocking and flapping his hands. The researcher observing Johnny's behavior codes "stereotypy." How can we interpret this behavior? Is Johnny engaging in stereotypies because he is bored and this provides stimulation that enhances his arousal? Or is he overstimulated by the television program and the familiar, repetitive stereotypy serves to reduce his arousal and calm him down? There is no way to tell from just coding the behavior as stereotypy.

Sometimes, behavioral observation alone is not enough to interpret behavior. Because of the nature of the research question or the limitations associated with interpretation of behavior or other reasons, behavioral observation alone does not always provide enough information to fully understand the nature and underlying mechanisms of behaviors. Physiological measures are often used to supplement, elaborate, or help interpret behavior. *Psychophysiology* is the study of the relations between behavior and physiology. The purpose of this chapter is to provide an overview of the what, how, and why of physiological measures that can be used by researchers studying individuals with developmental disabilities and to outline the various ways in which these measures can be related to behavioral observations. Examples from our own work, using *The Observer* (1996), are described as well to illustrate the utility of combining behavioral and physiological measures.

There is a growing interest among researchers studying developmental disabilities in exploring the utility of physiological measures. Physiological measures can provide convergent information about diagnosis, arousal and hyperarousal, and reactivity. They can provide information about drug effects and the impact of other types of treatment. Because of increasing information regarding the genetic origins of and biological factors involved in developmental disabilities, physiological measures offer the promise of increased understanding of syndrome causes and outcomes.

PHYSIOLOGICAL MEASURES

To some extent the type of physiological measure chosen will depend on the research question and the behavior of interest, as well as on how these measures are conceptually related to one another. Biopsychologists often are most interested in the role of the central nervous system in the regulation of behavior. This typically entails some aspect of autonomic nervous system (ANS) function. The autonomic nervous system is that branch of the central nervous system that regulates internal organs such as the cardiovascular and gastrointestinal systems and hormone-producing glands. The ANS is composed of the parasympathetic nervous system (PNS), which is associated with rest and restoration, and the sympathetic nervous system (SNS), which is associated with mobilization of energy for action. Many of the physiological response systems of interest to biobehavioral researchers are controlled by the ANS (see Table 1).

Hormones such as cortisol or catecholamines have been used frequently in psychophysiological research. These agents have traditionally been assessed through blood samples, which limits their appeal for many researchers working with children with developmental disabilities, but assays have been developed to measure these and other factors in saliva and urine, the collection of which is much less invasive. In fact, one can measure a host of biological factors through these body fluids, including "stress" hormones, catecholamines, steroidal hormones, immunoglobulins, cytokines, drugs, and any other agent that can move from blood vessels into the tissue fluids of the body.

In addition to these chemical measures, cardiovascular measures, including blood pressure, heart rate, vagal tone, heart rate variability and reactivity, and

Table 1. Autonomic nervous system measures typically used in psychophysiological research

Measure	Reflects higher nervous system function	Reflects parasympathetic nervous system function	Reflects sympathetic nervous system function
Hormones	No	Yes, depending on which hormone	Yes, depending on which hormone
Brain imaging	Yes	No	No
Cardiovascular measures	Indirectly through autonomic nervous system	Yes	Yes
Electrodermal measures	Indirectly through autonomic nervous system	No	Yes

pulse ejection time, often are used. Each of these measures requires somewhat different instrumentation and provides slightly different information regarding ANS activity. For example, vagal tone measures provide information about the parasympathetic nervous system, whereas pulse ejection time provides information about the sympathetic nervous system, two different and somewhat complementary branches of the ANS.

Another noninvasive physiological measure that is growing in popularity, and that is often used in conjunction with cardiovascular measures to assess SNS activity, is electrodermal activity or skin conductance measures. The electrical conductivity of the skin can be affected by physical and emotional stimuli because it is controlled by the SNS. Electrodermal activity is monitored by placing electrodes on the skin surface. The measurement of electrodermal activity depends on the fact that electrical conductance is enhanced by perspiration (which is an excellent electrolyte because of the salt content), which is under sympathetic control.

Finally, brain-imaging techniques are becoming increasingly available and are used to study cognitive, emotional, and memory processes. Electroencephalography, including evoked responses and hemispheric lateralization, has been used for decades to examine brain activation and localization of function in a variety of contexts. Positron emission tomography and structural and functional magnetic resonance imaging technologies are expanding the ways that we can look at the brain under various circumstances. There still are severe limitations on what individuals can be asked to do while undergoing these brain-imaging procedures, thus limiting their usefulness for young children or children with developmental delays. It is clear, however, that this is a rapidly developing field in which advances likely will enhance the usefulness of these techniques for research with individuals who have developmental disabilities. All of these brain-imaging techniques require sophisticated and expensive equipment and a high degree of technical and theoretical expertise in both gathering and interpreting the data.

The type of data collected is an important consideration as well. Some of these measures are collected at specific times, whereas others are continuous. For example, salivary or urinary hormones and functional magnetic resonance images are usually collected at specific times during a study, such as before and after manipulation. Heart rate, however, can be collected at the level of each heartbeat or sampled at specified intervals from a few seconds to minutes or hours. The options available for relating behavior to physiology vary as a function of whether the measures (both behavioral and physiological) are point or continuous variables.

Issues in the Use of Physiological Measures

Adding the measurement of physiological parameters to a behavioral research program requires the consideration of a number of factors (Fahrenberg & Myrtek, 1996). There may be significant challenges to the research program, including additional personnel costs; additional equipment costs; additional expertise on the part of the research team; additional demands on the participants, who already may have a significant load placed on them by the behavioral research; and increased complications for data management, analysis, and interpretation. In our own research, the addition of physiological measures such as sleep staging, circadian rhythms, and immunology and endocrinology (for a review, see Reite & Boccia, 1994) required significant increases in all of these areas. Although the expansion of this research program to include these physiological measures greatly enhanced what we were able to learn, it also more than doubled the personnel required to run the studies and significantly complicated the analysis and interpretation of the results. The decision to add physiological measures to a behavioral research program should be made carefully, weighing the added value of the information gained against the real costs of collecting it.

There are important reasons why the addition of physiological measures to behavioral research might be considered. As in the example that opened this chapter, it may clarify the significance of the behavioral data. If heart rate can serve as an indicator of ANS arousal, then simultaneous measurement of heart rate and behavior may illuminate whether the occurrence of stereotypy occurs at times of arousal or depression of ANS activity and whether it is associated with increases or decreases in arousal. Soussignan and Koch (1985), for example, examined this question in typically developing children entering kindergarten and discovered that heart rate declined significantly during stereotypies, relative to heart rate immediately before and after the stereotypies, suggesting an arousal-reducing function in these children.

Physiological measures also may prove to be better predictor variables than behavioral measures. Doussard-Roosevelt, Porges, Scanlon, Alemi, and Scanlon (1997) examined the developmental outcomes of very low birth weight preterm infants. In addition to heart activity measures, including vagal tone, they examined birth weight, gestational age, Apgar scores at 1 and 5 minutes, socioeconomic status, maternal age, and other health-related variables. At 3 years, they obtained measures that reflected behavioral regulation, mental processing, knowledge base, social competence, and motor skills. As is predictable from the existing literature (Hock et al., 1991; Hoy, Bill, & Sykes, 1988; Vohr & Garcia-Coll, 1986), birth weight, medical risk, and socioeconomic status were strong predictors of developmental outcome. However, heart activity measures also were strong predictors of outcome, contributed unique predictive ability to the study, and related to a different set of outcome measures than the other predictor variables. In fact, this measure particularly enhanced the ability to predict developmental difficulties in very low birth weight infants between 1,000 and 1,500 grams, a group likely to receive less attention than extremely low birth weight infants (less than 1,000 grams).

Finally, with increased identification of the genetic and biological origins of developmental disabilities, physiological mechanisms, causes, and correlates are of interest in and of themselves. To understand, for example, how the organization of the brain differs in children with fragile X syndrome as a function of the defect in the *FMRP* gene requires attention to physiological parameters to offer the hope of developing real and effective treatment protocols.

Analyzing Behavior–Physiology Relationships

How one relates physiological measures to behavior depends on the research question. The physiological measure could be used as a dependent variable. Behaviors, personality traits, conditions, or interventions may be the predictor variables of interest, and physiological measures may be the outcome variables. Later in this chapter we describe a study of boys with and without fragile X syndrome in which heart activity measures were the dependent variables and the presence or absence of fragile X syndrome served as the predictor variable.

On the assumption that physiological measures can serve as markers for conditions or individual differences, one can also use them as independent variables. Heart rate, for example, can be used to categorize children as high reactors or low reactors (the degree to which heart rate is elevated in response to stimulation), and this classification can be used as an independent variable in studying responses to stressors. For example, Katz and Gottman (1995) demonstrated that vagal tone measures (reflecting parasympathetic activity) in children predicted their emotional vulnerability to the experience of marital conflict between their parents. They collected information on marital conflict from the parents as well as heart rate data on 5-year-old children and computed the corresponding vagal tone (see discussion later in this chapter). Three years later they obtained teacher ratings on the children's behavior problems in the classroom. They found that children with lower vagal tone exhibited a significantly stronger relationship between the amount of marital hostility displayed by their parents and subsequent externalizing behavior problems. There was no such relationship among children with high vagal tone. The authors concluded that high vagal tone can buffer children from some of the negative effects of marital conflict.

Finally, when both behavior and physiology are continuous variables, one can examine the correlations and patterns of change over time between the two. For example, Hughes, Uhlmann, and Pennebaker (1994) studied skin conductance level (SCL) and heart rate (HR) while participants wrote about different emotional topics. They then correlated SCL and HR with the actual words and phrases that the participants wrote. They found no relationship between HR and the content of the writing. SCL, however, was higher (suggesting increased sympathetic arousal) when participants expressed negative emotions or when they used denial or the passive voice. SCL decreased (suggesting reduced sympathetic arousal) when participants used positive emotions or self-references and at the conclusions of sentences and thoughts.

One of the main attractions of using physiological measures along with behavioral measures is that it provides a convergent measure of what one is interested in documenting. If one is interested in assessing hyperarousal in children with fragile X syndrome one can measure the presence, rate, or frequency of stereotypies or behavior dysregulation. One can also assess HR or SCL and examine physiological arousal as another test of hyperarousal in a different, biological, domain. A physiological measure can confirm and validate the observation that under certain conditions, or in cases of a particular developmental disability, a particular behavior indicates some underlying condition or response.

MONITORING HEART ACTIVITY

Heart activity measures have been of interest to researchers because individual differences can provide information about cardiovascular or other health risks, central nervous system (CNS) dysregulation, and basic personality or temperamental differences in psychological response styles. There are a number of important issues to consider when choosing HR as the physiological index of ANS function. One must understand the nature of the heart activity generated and how the CNS contributes to that activity, as well as how the heart responds uniquely to CNS input. In addition, one must understand how to collect this information and decompose it into the relevant components of interest.

Of particular importance is the fact that the ANS regulates the heartbeat (Sokolov & Cacioppo, 1997). This provides the opportunity to investigate ANS activity via heart signal in a relatively noninvasive way. The ANS regulation of HR is mediated by the sympathetic and parasympathetic nervous systems. Although traditionally it has been assumed that these two systems function reciprocally, it is becoming increasingly clear that the relationship is much more complex and dynamic (Berntson, Cacioppo, & Quigley, 1991). Thus, an increase in HR may reflect sympathetic activation, parasympathetic withdrawal, or a combination of the two. In fact, Sokolov and Cacioppo (1997) demonstrated that a group of "high HR reactors" contained subgroups of each type.

ANS input into HR arrives via the vagal nerve for the PNS and the sympathetic efferents for the SNS. One widely used method of separating the contributions of these two systems is spectral analysis (Mezzacappa, Kindlon, & Earls, 1996). This technique does for the variation in beat-to-beat intervals what a prism does to light: It breaks the variation down into its component parts. The power of the spectrum is the variance in the signal, which can be assessed for various frequency ranges that represent ANS input (see subsequent explanation in this chapter).

There are several cautionary points that must be made about using HR in this way. First is the nature of the information. HR variability is a complex end point representing not only the contribution of the ANS but also the heart's response (especially the pacemaker's) to that input and to other inputs, such as mechanical pressure from breathing, chemical signals, and so forth (Akselrod, 1995). Second are the limitations of the statistical methods. Spectral analysis was developed to analyze complex nonorganic signals and is based on several assumptions that biological signals do not necessarily meet, such as the assumption of stationarity (that the data's mean does not change during the interval of data collection). Consequently, paradigms have been developed that deal with these issues and thus make HR a useful measure for psychophysiological research.

There are a number of systems available for collection of HR data. We use the Mini-Logger 2000 (manufactured by Minimitter, Inc.) in our laboratory. This system uses Polar chest belts to detect R-waves (the largest component of the heart signal and the one typically used in this type of research). The belt is fitted to the child's chest at the base of the sternum and is secured with a snap. No glue or electrolyte is required because the child's own perspiration establishes the contact points. This radio telemetry system eliminates the need for traditional electrodes, which must be glued in place and hence are potentially aversive to young children with or without disabilities. The Mini-Logger 2000 is a small, portable receiver set to the frequency of the Polar belt transmitter; it collects and stores R-wave intervals into files subsequently downloaded to personal computers for analysis. Minimitter software converts the logger data to an ASCII file that can be imported into other programs.

To verify that the Mini-Logger 2000 and Polar chest belt were accurate and reliable instruments for the collection of heart activity data, we collaborated with another laboratory.[1] We used Porges's system (described by Calkins, 1997) and the

_____

[1] We thank Susan Calkins for assisting us with this effort.

Mini-Logger 2000 system simultaneously to evaluate heart activity data from one individual. The data from both systems were compared, and the results indicated that the two systems produced highly concordant results. The mean difference between the interbeat interval (IBI) values generated by the two systems was 3 milliseconds.

Once the data are collected and converted to an ASCII file they can be imported into other software, such as *MXEdit* (1989) or *The Observer*. After collection of the data we edit the files for errors and analyze them by means of spectral analysis. This method can be used to calculate the relative contributions of the sympathetic and parasympathetic systems. For children in the age range that we study, the .24-Hertz to 1.04-Hertz bandwidth represents purely parasympathetic input into the IBI pattern, whereas the .04-Hertz to .24-Hertz bandwidth represents both sympathetic and parasympathetic input. Therefore, an estimate of the sympathetic input into the IBI pattern can be derived by computing the ratio of the power in the .04-Hertz to .24-Hertz range to the power in the .24-Hertz to 1.04-Hertz range.

USING *The Observer* TO INTEGRATE BEHAVIOR AND PHYSIOLOGY

The Observer is a commercially available software package designed to facilitate the direct, on-line collection of behavioral observations either in a live situation or from videotape. We have found it to be an excellent system for our applications in terms of reliability, flexibility, and technical support. This program provides a general purpose system for the collection of user-customized behavioral observation data. As such, it provides sufficient flexibility to be as complicated or as simple as required by the demands of the particular research protocol.

The flexibility of the system derives from the fact that users create their own behavioral coding systems using the main program. *The Observer* is organized in a modular design. There are several program modules that function separately. One module permits the development of a data collection program customized to meet the particular demands of the research project. Thus, factors such as the number of behavior categories, whether they are frequency or duration categories, whether or not all categories or subgroups of categories are mutually exclusive, and how long observations last are under the control of the user. One can design a scoring system as simple or as complex as the context demands. This module creates miniature programs, called configuration files, that can be run independently by transferring to other personal computers or downloading the configuration files to hand-held computers. Thus, in our own laboratory, the main computer on which data analysis and summary is conducted is in one location, and we collect data at multiple observation stations in the laboratory. Once the data collection is complete, the data set is transferred back to the main computer workstation for statistical analysis with another module of *The Observer* or is exported into another software package.

Noldus Information Technology also provides add-on programs that can convert configuration files for use on other machines, many of which are handheld or waterproof models suitable for field workers. Thus, if one is going into classrooms to observe the effects of the mainstreaming of children with developmental delays, one can collect observations conveniently and unobtrusively on a palmtop Psion Workabout and download the results to a desktop personal computer for analysis.

The Observer has a series of hierarchically arranged menus for each program task. The Windows version creates Projects, which permits one to keep multiple experiments on one computer without confusion or interference between them. From the opening menu one may choose to create the observation system (Configuration), collect observations (Event Recording), analyze data (Data Analysis), transfer files to or from handheld computers (Download File and Upload File), or modify where on the floppy disk or hard drive the data go and which computer is being used (System Defaults).

In the Configuration section the user defines all of the details of how data will be collected. One can determine, for example, how long an observation session will last, or choose to leave it open ended, whether one wants to collect data continuously or at specified intervals, and how many individuals one wishes to collect data from simultaneously. The user also defines how many behaviors to observe and organizes these behaviors into classes that can be analyzed as a group. The system also allows the user to define (or not) modifiers for each behavior code. This allows one to add codes to the behaviors to indicate, for example, intensity, location, or social partner. An interesting feature of this system is the ability to define "channels." In this case, separate focal participants can be assigned to particular classes of behavior. This permits one to observe multiple focal participants and reduce the number of keystrokes required to record the observations.

Event recording involves the use of the configuration file created expressly for a particular user's application. In our laboratory we may be running several different projects at any given time, and each of these will have a custom-designed scoring system, all of which run on *The Observer* and do not interfere with each other in any way. Because each experiment has a separate Project in *The Observer*, and the configuration and data files are uniquely associated with each Project, there is no confusion regarding which scoring system (configuration file) was used to collect any particular data set.

There are several features available in the Event Recording component that are especially helpful. There is, for example, a Notepad function that permits one to open a window and record an ad libitum observation or write a note of any sort. These notes and observations are saved with the raw data file and appear on the report for that observation session after analysis. There is also an on-line Help system that informs the user about *The Observer* functions and lists the coding system if the user forgets which keystroke codes which behavior (one also has the option of leaving the codes in a window on the screen during the coding session and using the mouse to enter the codes instead of using keystrokes). Different windows inform the user when the session started, how long it has been running, and which behavior codes have been activated. If the user makes a mistake there is an Edit function that can be activated to correct it. The scoring system can be defined so that the observation session is suspended while this editing occurs and resumes after the editing is complete. The observation can be ended either by reaching the maximum time allowed or by a user-initiated command.

Data analysis with *The Observer* also is flexible. The system permits one to select summary statistics, exploratory graphics display, sequential data presentation, and various formats of output. *The Observer* provides a number of helpful analysis procedures within the Data Analysis module. One can produce basic statistics such as means, standard deviations, and latencies. One can produce report files of these basic statistical analyses that can be printed or displayed for visual inspection. There is also an exploratory graphics feature that produces graphics displays of the data that can be printed. More advanced analyses include lag sequential and nested analyses. Finally, *The Observer* is able to compute inter-observer reliabilities. These analyses can be conducted on one observation at a time or they can be collapsed across several observations (e.g., as in our laboratory when we want to summarize all observations for a week into one observation).

Although *The Observer* can conduct all of these analyses, it is often necessary to conduct other, more complex types of analyses. *The Observer* can export files that permit one to take the data into other programs for analysis, such as spreadsheet programs (e.g., *Excel* [1996], *Lotus 1-2-3* [1999], *Quattro Pro* [1999]), database programs (e.g., *Paradox* [1999]), or statistics programs (e.g., *SAS* [1999], *SPSS* [1999], *Systat* [1999]). In addition, matrices can be produced for import into *MatMan* (1998).

In addition to the base package, which includes all of the features described thus far, Noldus Information Technology produces an optional program module that permits direct interfacing with videotape recordings. The *VTA System* (1996) (*VideoPro* [1998] in the latest version) permits the user to score behavior from a videotape onto which a time code has been written. The user can stop the tape, search backward or forward, and play the tape in slow motion. Because the system reads the time from the videotape rather than from the computer clock, the actual duration of the behavior is preserved. This is an advanced function that is valuable for very fine, moment-by-moment analysis of behavior. This system also can accommodate time-lapse videotape data collection, so that one can monitor behavior continuously around the clock and preserve duration to the resolution of the scale of the time lapse. The latest version, *VideoPro*, adds the additional ability to code digitized video from compact disks. Thus, one can copy the videotape segment to a readable compact disk and then code directly from the compact disk, with the videotape image presented on the computer monitor. This obviates all of the mechanical difficulties that can arise when one uses videotapes, including problems with the quality of the time code stamp and videocassette recorder head quality and cleanliness, that can interfere with the coding process.

The DOS version of *The Observer* (1991) has the additional feature of being able to read external files that contain other types of data. Thus, one can use *The Observer* to integrate behavioral observations collected with the system and continuous physiological data collected simultaneously with another system. Because *The Observer* allows one to use files generated from other systems it provides the greatest flexibility in terms of choice of physiological measure. One is not restricted to what Noldus Information Technology has implemented for physiological assessment. For example, we have used this system both to integrate heart rate and behavior in our research with monkey models of bereavement and to examine the effect of different emotional expressions on hemispheric lateralization via electroencephalography (Boccia, Davis-Goldman, Noldus, O'Leary, & Teale, 1995). In the next section, we describe the application of this system to the study of hyperarousal in boys with fragile X syndrome, in which we use multiple heart rate measures, including raw heart period, vagal tone, and other measures.

HEART RATE AND AROUSAL IN BOYS WITH FRAGILE X SYNDROME

Fragile X syndrome is the primary known cause of hereditary mental retardation (Hagerman & Cronister, 1996). Approximately 85% of males with fragile X syndrome have developmental delays, and virtually all of them have learning difficulties. Behavioral difficulties often constitute the most significant barrier to successful functioning and are cited by parents and educators as their primary concern (Hatton & Bailey, 1997). Common behavioral difficulties include avoidant social interaction, hand biting, body rocking, tactile defensiveness, hyperactivity, autistic-like behavior, impulsivity, stereotypies, poor attention, aggression, and self-injury. Stereotypies in particular are most frequently observed in transitions, interpersonal exchanges, and high-demand performance activities. This has led to the hypothesis that these behaviors result from "hyperarousal."

Individuals with low vagal (parasympathetic) tone have difficulty regulating their behavior, whereas individuals with average or high vagal tone do not have these difficulties (Porges, 1996). This may be related to developmental changes in ANS functioning parallel to behavioral development. As behavior matures and shifts from reflexes and homeostatic functions to behaviors that are more cognitively mediated, there is a subordination and integration of primary reflexive behavior into more complex voluntary behavior. This, Porges suggests, corresponds to a change of balance in the nervous system from more sympathetic to more parasympathetic input.

This study investigated physiological indices of arousal involving heart activity, comparing boys with fragile X syndrome to typically developing peers. The heart activity measures included mean heart period or IBI, vagal tone estimate, and sympathetic tone estimate. These variables were examined while the children participated in an experimental protocol of alternating low and moderate levels of behavioral and cognitive demand.

We expected to find that boys with fragile X syndrome would display a shorter and less variable IBI (corresponding to a higher heart rate) than boys without fragile X syndrome and would exhibit significantly higher sympathetic tone estimates and lower vagal tone estimates than boys without fragile X syndrome. We also expected that there would be significantly different patterns of heart activity measures between the relatively higher-demand and lower-demand phases of the experiment in the two groups of boys.

Methods

Boys with fragile X syndrome were drawn from the Carolina Fragile X Project, which spans a three-state area: North Carolina, South Carolina, and Virginia (Hatton & Bailey, 1997). Children who were taking medication with documented cardiovascular effects were excluded, as were children for whom there was documentation of a known history of cardiovascular disease. Sixty-four boys, half with and half without fragile X syndrome, were studied. We discuss here a subset of 40 of these children for whom data analysis is complete: 20 boys with fragile X syndrome and 20 boys who were typically developing.

The children participated in a 30-minute experimental session that consisted of alternating low-demand "baseline" (watching a videotape) and moderately demanding (completing cognitive tasks) phases. The cognitive tasks were based on subtests from the Stanford-Binet IV (Thorndike, Hagen, & Sattler, 1986) and included verbal (Vocabulary) and nonverbal (Pattern Analysis) tasks. Data on the mental age of the children with fragile X syndrome and the chronological age of the children who were developing typically were used to determine the difficulty level of each test to provide age-appropriate cognitive challenges to each child.

The Mini-Logger 2000 system by Minimitter was used to collect the heart period data. In addition to IBI data, the relative contributions of both the sympathetic and parasympathetic nervous systems on heart activity were assessed by means of spectral analysis. The heart period data were analyzed as described previously, using the software program *MXEdit* developed by Steve Porges.

Videotapes of the experimental sessions were coded using *The Observer*. In addition to coding the experimental phases we coded stereotypies, including motor, verbal, and nonverbal stereotypies, and aggressive acts. *The Observer* was used to analyze experimental phases and behavior concomitant with all heart rate–related variables. All subsequent analyses were completed using *SPSS for Windows* (Release 7.5) (1996). A two (Group) by five (Phase) repeated measures analysis of covariance, with age as a covariate, was performed on the data.

Results

The boys with fragile X syndrome differed from the typically developing boys in a number of ways, including shorter heart period (i.e., faster heart rate), a less active parasympathetic system (lower vagal tone), and different patterns of arousal across the experimental phases. Values of dependent measures for the two groups are presented in Table 2. These values are raw scores, unadjusted for the ages of the children.

We expected that the boys with fragile X syndrome would display a shorter and less variable IBI than the boys without fragile X syndrome. In fact, the boys with fragile X syndrome did display a significantly higher heart rate, reflected in shorter IBI values (Fisher's F ratio $[F][1, 36] = 4.438$, probability $[p] < .05$). There were no differences, however, in measures of variability.

We also expected that the boys with fragile X syndrome would exhibit significantly higher sympathetic tone estimates and lower vagal tone estimates than the boys without fragile X syndrome. There was no significant difference between the two groups of boys for the sympathetic tone estimate. However, there was a significant difference in vagal tone between the boys with fragile X syndrome and the typically developing boys ($F[1, 36] = 7.383$, $p < .01$). The boys with fragile X syndrome had significantly lower vagal tone estimates than the typically developing boys.

Finally, we expected heart activity measures to reflect significantly different patterns between the cognitive tasks and baselines for the two groups of boys. Among the boys with fragile X syndrome a significant effect of Phase was found

Table 2. Mean heart measure values for boys with and without fragile X syndrome (mean plus standard error of the mean)

Study sample	Interbeat interval (IBI)	Vagal tone estimate	Sympathetic tone estimate
Boys with fragile X syndrome	544 (89)	4.84 (1.40)	.46 (.13)
Boys who are developing typically	577 (84)	5.70 (1.24)	.47 (.11)

for sympathetic tone estimates ($F[1, 17] = 3.629$, $p < .01$). Post hoc analyses indicated that the first baseline values differed from the first cognitive task values and that the intermediate baseline values differed from the second cognitive task values. For the boys who were developing typically, no effect of Phase was found for the sympathetic tone estimates.

For vagal tone estimates, there was no significant effect for the boys with fragile X syndrome. For the boys who were developing typically, a significant effect of Phase was found ($F[1, 17] = 5.788$, $p = < .001$). Post hoc analyses indicated that each cognitive task value differed significantly from the adjacent baseline value.

Conclusions

The results of this study support the hypothesis that boys with fragile X syndrome exhibit levels and patterns of physiological arousal that differ from those of their typically developing, chronological age–matched peers. These differences in physiological arousal include shorter heart period (i.e., faster heart rate), a less active parasympathetic system (vagal tone), and different patterns of arousal regulation across the experimental phases.

Although the boys with fragile X syndrome did not show significantly higher sympathetic tone estimates, they did show significantly lower vagal tone estimates. This suggests that the higher level of behavioral and physiological arousal in these children may be attributable more to reduced parasympathetic activity than to enhanced sympathetic activity.

The boys with fragile X syndrome responded with significantly more sympathetic tone during each of the cognitive tasks compared with the immediately preceding baseline. This indicates that the boys with fragile X syndrome responded to cognitive challenge by increasing sympathetic activity. In contrast, the boys without fragile X syndrome did not respond with increased sympathetic activity between any of the phases. Instead, they displayed significant decreases in vagal tone during the cognitive tasks compared with the preceding and subsequent baseline periods.

The results of this study support the hypothesis that boys with fragile X syndrome have significantly higher levels of physiological arousal as measured by heart period. This appears to be attributable to reduced parasympathetic activity, as reflected in lower vagal tone measures, rather than to elevated sympathetic activity. In addition, the boys with fragile X syndrome displayed different patterns of arousal between the phases, modulating their response via sympathetic activity. The typically developing boys, in contrast, responded to the challenge by modulating vagal activity. Because increased vagal tone has been associated with increased behavior regulation (Baumgardner, Reiss, Freund, & Abrams, 1995), these physiological findings of reduced vagal tone and reduced modulation of vagal tone are in agreement with clinical reports of poor behavior regulation in boys with fragile X syndrome. This result highlights how physiological measures can enhance our understanding of children with developmental disabilities and of the significance of behavior.

CONCLUSIONS: DECIDING WHETHER TO USE PHYSIOLOGICAL MEASURES

When deciding whether to include physiological measures in one's research program, a number of issues need to be addressed. Kaloupek and Bremner (1996) listed three misconceptions that should be kept in mind. First, "psychophysiological measures are objective, immune to faking, and capable of providing a direct window on the true psychological state of an individual" (Kaloupek & Bremner, 1996, p. 86). Second, "psychophysiological measures are relatively interchangeable as indicators of arousal" (Kaloupek & Bremner, 1996, p. 86). Third, "there is a constant reciprocal relationship between sympathetic and parasympathetic activity in the autonomic nervous system" (Kaloupek & Bremner, 1996, p. 87). Although it would simplify our work, theoretically and practically, if these statements were true, each is indeed a misconception. Physiological measures present the researcher with all of the complexity and difficulties of assessment and interpretation that behavioral measures do.

The same issues that apply to considerations of behavioral observation research methods apply to physiological methods. One must ask, for example, about reliability and validity. Kamarck (1992) presented an excellent example of taking the principles used in psychometric theory for test development and applying them to the development of a psychophysiological assessment program.

The type and amount of equipment required to collect the particular physiological data must also be considered, in conjunction with the characteristics of the research participants. Some measures can be obtained only with the active cooperation of the participant (such as salivary cortisol). Others can be obtained relatively unobtrusively, with a minimal amount of equipment attached to the participant (e.g., heart rate data collection system described previously). Still others require large and highly specialized pieces of equipment and strictures of participant behavior (e.g., structural magnetic resonance imaging, which requires the individual to remain absolutely still inside a claustrophobia-inducing, loud magnet for long periods of time). All of these factors affect how easy or difficult it will be to collect data about individuals with particular developmental disabilities. One of the advantages of telemetry systems is that they are relatively unobtrusive and simple to use, and once they are in place the individuals being studied are relatively unrestrained in their behavior.

In summary, physiological measures can be a valuable addition to a behavioral research program, as either predictor or outcome variables, and can enhance one's ability to interpret behavioral results. They can be an important source of convergent validation of conclusions based on behavioral results. One must be cautious, however, in deciding to add physiological measures to behavior research. There can be a significant cost associated with the collection of such data, and expertise in the requisite discipline will be required to ensure appropriate understanding of the data and avoidance of errors. Finally, all of the rigor that one puts into behavioral research decisions must also be put into physiological assessments, including concerns about reliability, validity, measurement error, and so on. If conducted properly, however, such measures can be invaluable as a means of enhancing our understanding of phenomena associated with developmental disabilities.

REFERENCES

Akselrod, S. (1995). Components of heart rate variability: Basic studies. In M. Malik & A.J. Camm (Eds.), *Heart rate variability* (pp. 147–163). Armonk, NY: Futura Publishing Co.

Baumgardner, T.L., Reiss, A.L., Freund, L.S., & Abrams, M.T. (1995). Specification of the neurobehavioral phenotype in males with fragile X syndrome. *Pediatrics, 95,* 744–752.

Berntson, G.G., Cacioppo, J.T., & Quigley, K.S. (1991). Autonomic determinism: The modes of autonomic control, the doctrine of autonomic space, and the laws of autonomic constraint. *Psychological Review, 98*, 1–29.

Boccia, M.L., Davis-Goldman, B., Noldus, L.P.J.J., O'Leary, M., & Teale, P. (1995). The integration of physiology (heart rate and EEG) with behavior collected with a computer based observational system. In E. Alleva, A. Fasolo, H.-P. Lipp, L. Nadel, & L. Ricceri (Eds.), *Behavioral brain research in naturalistic and semi-naturalistic settings* (*NATO ASI Series D: Behavioral and Social Sciences, 82*, p. 440). Boston: Kluwer Academic Publishers/NATO Scientific Affairs Division.

Calkins, S.D. (1997). Cardiac vagal tone indices of temperamental reactivity and behavioral regulation in young children. *Developmental Psychobiology, 31*, 125–135.

Doussard-Roosevelt, J.A., Porges, S.W., Scanlon, J.W., Alemi, B., & Scanlon, K.B. (1997). Vagal regulation of heart rate in the prediction of developmental outcome for very low birth weight preterm infants. *Child Development, 68*, 173–186.

Excel [Software]. (1996). Redmond, WA: Microsoft Corp.

Fahrenberg, J., & Myrtek, M. (1996). *Ambulatory assessment: Computer-assisted psychological and psychophysiological methods in monitoring and field studies.* Seattle: Hogrefe & Huber Publishers.

Hagerman, R.J., & Cronister, A. (Eds.). (1996). *Fragile X syndrome: Diagnosis, treatment, and research* (2nd ed.). Baltimore: The Johns Hopkins University Press.

Hatton, D.D., & Bailey, D.B., Jr. (1997). Early intervention for young boys with fragile X syndrome. *National Fragile X Advocate, 2*(3), 14–16.

Hock, M., Horber, J.D., Maloy, M.H., Tyson, J.E., Wright, E., & Wright, L. (1991). Very low birth weight outcomes of the National Institute of Child Health and Human Development Neonatal Network. *Pediatrics, 87*, 587–597.

Hoy, E.A., Bill, J.M., & Sykes, D.H. (1988). Very low birth weight: A long-term developmental impairment? *International Journal of Behavioral Development, 11*, 37–67.

Hughes, C.F., Uhlmann, C., & Pennebaker, J.W. (1994). The body's response to processing emotional trauma: Linking verbal text with autonomic activity. *Journal of Personality, 62*, 565–585.

Kaloupek, D.G., & Bremner, J.D. (1996). Psychophysiological measures and methods in trauma research. In E.B. Carlson (Ed.), *Trauma research methodology* (pp. 82–104). Lutherville, MD: Sidran Press.

Kamarck, T.W. (1992). Recent developments in the study of cardiovascular reactivity: Contributions from psychometric theory and social psychology. *Psychophysiology, 29*, 491–503.

Katz, L.F., & Gottman, J.M. (1995). Vagal tone protects children from marital conflict. *Development and Psychopathology, 7*, 83–92.

Lotus 1-2-3 [Software]. (1999). Cambridge, MA: Lotus Development Corp.

MatMan [Software]. (1998). Wageningen, The Netherlands: Noldus Information Technology.

Mezzacappa, E., Kindlon, D., & Earls, F. (1996). Methodologic issues in the use of heart rate and heart-rate variability in the study of disruptive behavior disorders. In D.M. Stoff & R.B. Cairns (Eds.), *Aggression and violence: Genetic, neurobiological, and biosocial perspectives* (pp. 125–143). Mahwah, NJ: Lawrence Erlbaum Associates.

MXEdit [Software]. (1989). Bethesda, MD: Delta Biometrics.

The Observer for DOS 3.0 [Software]. (1991). Wageningen, The Netherlands: Noldus Information Technology.

The Observer for Windows 3.0 [Software]. (1996). Wageningen, The Netherlands: Noldus Information Technology.

Paradox [Software]. (1999). Ottawa, Ontario, Canada: Corel Corp.

Porges, S.W. (1996). Physiological regulation in high-risk infants: A model for assessment and potential intervention. *Development and Psychopathology, 8*, 43–58.

Quattro Pro [Software]. (1999). Ottawa, Ontario, Canada: Corel Corp.

Reite, M.L., & Boccia, M.L. (1994). Physiological aspects of adult attachment. In M.B. Sperling & W.H. Berman (Eds.), *Attachment in adults: Clinical and developmental perspectives* (pp. 98–127). New York: Guilford Press.

SAS [Software]. (1999). Carey, NC: SAS Institute.

Sokolov, E.N., & Cacioppo, J.T. (1997). Orienting and defensive reflexes: Vector coding the cardiac response. In P.J. Lang, R.F. Simons, & M.T. Balaban (Eds.), *Attention and orienting: Sensory and motivational processes* (pp. 1–22). Mahwah, NJ: Lawrence Erlbaum Associates.

Soussignan, R., & Koch, P. (1985). Rhythmical stereotypies (leg-swinging) associated with reductions in heart-rate in normal school children. *Biological Psychiatry, 21,* 161–167.

SPSS [Software]. (1999). Chicago: SPSS.

SPSS for Windows (release 7.5) [Software]. (1996). Chicago: SPSS.

Systat [Software]. (1999). Chicago: SPSS.

Thorndike, R.L., Hagen, E.P., & Sattler, J.M. (1986). *Stanford-Binet Intelligence Scale* (4th ed.). Itasca, IL: Riverside Publishing Co.

VideoPro [Software]. (1998). Wageningen, The Netherlands: Noldus Information Technology.

Vohr, B.R., & Garcia-Coll, C.T. (1986). Follow-up studies of high-risk low-birth-weight infants. In H.E. Fitzgerald, B.M. Lester, & M.W. Yogman (Eds.), *Theory and research in behavioral pediatrics* (Vol. 4, pp. 1–65). New York: Plenum Press.

VTA System [Software]. (1996). Wageningen, The Netherlands: Noldus Information Technology.

III

Applications in Residential and Community Settings

8

Architecture and Behavior of People with Intellectual Disabilities

Observational Methods and Housing Policy

Travis Thompson,
Mark Egli, and
Julia Robinson

It belonged, somehow, to a new and accursed substance which had come into the structure of life—a structure barren, sterile, and inhuman—designed not for the use of man, but for the blind proliferations of the manswarm, to accommodate the greatest number in the smallest space—to shelter, house, turn out, take in, all the nameless, faceless, mindless atoms of the earth.

Thomas Wolfe (1935, p. 429)

In the mid-1990s, the United Nations (1994) estimated that 600 million people, including many in the United States and Europe, live in inadequate housing. Even in more affluent societies, many families live in poorly designed high-rise public housing projects—multi-unit apartments in dysfunctional buildings that bear little resemblance to what people in those societies would recognize as a home. As part of an effort to improve the quality of life of people with intellectual and other developmental disabilities, most of them have been moved from

This chapter was supported by National Institute of Child Health and Human Development Research Grant Nos. HD 25150 and HD 15052 awarded to the John F. Kennedy Center for Research on Human Development, Vanderbilt University, Nashville, Tennessee.

large, congregate care institutions to community settings alongside community members without disabilities. They live in dwellings, attend school, work at jobs, and participate in leisure activities that are often indistinguishable from those of other members of society. And increasingly, they have the same opportunity to experience substandard housing as many other members of our societies who are less affluent and less powerful than the social norm.

In anticipation of this transition, in the 1980s, we began exploring the nature of community housing and its consequences for people with intellectual disabilities (Robinson, Thompson, Emmons, & Graff, 1984; Thompson, Robinson, Graff, & Ingenmey, 1990). It appeared to us that many of the mistakes that had been made in providing housing for people who were economically deprived, for people who were elderly and infirm, and for battered women and their children were very likely to be repeated in providing housing for people with intellectual disabilities if steps were not taken to avoid those errors. Few societies have been willing to invest sufficiently in community services for people with developmental disabilities to ensure reasonable housing. Much as poverty has taken its toll on members of American society without disabilities, lack of appropriate residential planning for people with intellectual disabilities could lead to similar consequences—namely, housing conditions—that impeded successful transition to socially competent lifestyles.

Although most advocates and experts within the field of intellectual disabilities agree that housing for people with disabilities should resemble typical family dwellings, this change in assumptions about housing for people with developmental disabilities has come about only gradually since the 1970s. This view, which may seem self-evident to most people in the field of intellectual disabilities, has not filtered down to policy makers, government agency personnel, developers, and designers, and it certainly has not been explained to the average citizen. The final design of a residence is the result of many factors: the attitudes and administrative philosophy of the agency, awareness of the range of choices among housing types, assumptions about economy, and perceptions about safety and the way that codes are to be interpreted. Although some design decisions are dictated by specific resident needs, such as accessibility, in most instances regulations or costs are cited as reasons for selecting institutional designs. Economy of scale often is cited as a reason for selecting materials and designs that are not viewed by the public as homelike. In the long run, however, it is more costly to place residents in environments that inhibit competence and promote problem behavior. Each of these consequences has costs above those of housing alone, including costs of additional staffing, costs of property damage, costs of medical treatment incurred by self-injury or aggression toward other residents, and costs of supporting individuals who might otherwise learn skills necessary to obtain jobs.

Observational research designed to evaluate the adequacy of residential living environments for people with intellectual disabilities has been limited. Landesman-Dwyer, Sackett, and Kleinman (1980) studied residential environments using a detailed behavioral observational approach, breaking down broad activity categories into subcodes. Felce, de Kock, and Repp (1986) and Saxby, Thomas, Felce, and de Kock (1986) used an observational approach to assess engagement at home, in the workplace, and in the community. Environmental events as well as social interactions were recorded because they were believed to be relevant to the extent of engagement. Emerson and Hatton (1996) reviewed studies conducted in Great Britain and found that the majority of them used direct behavioral observational methods to measure engagement in activities, but few of them focused specifically on the relation between aspects of the built environment and resident behavior.

Whether a person with intellectual disabilities resides in a semi-independent or supported living arrangement, in a government-licensed residence, or in some other community living model, we have found that the physical features of any residential environment can have a major impact on the way in which those settings are perceived by the resident and by others who interact with the resident (Thompson, Robinson, Dietrich, Farris, & Sinclair, 1996a, 1996b; Thompson et al., 1990). Because a person with intellectual disabilities resides in a building defined as a private home or apartment does not necessarily imply that the residence will be seen as or function as a home. Placing a person with intellectual disabilities in a building labeled as a house in which he or she lives alongside a person without disabilities or a family without a member who has disabilities does not ensure that that individual is residing in a homelike environment if the features of that residence are based on shortsighted cost-cutting measures rather than on long-term programming objectives.

EMPIRICAL INVESTIGATION OF PHYSICAL FEATURES, PERCEIVED HOMELIKENESS, AND RESIDENT BEHAVIOR

In this study, we sought to identify features of residential environments that were associated with meaningful differences in the perceptions of those environments by various viewers, including potential inhabitants, and with differences in the behavior of occupants of those buildings. We used computer-assisted technologies in several ways: 1) to compile information about the physical features of representative rooms and the exteriors of housing for people with intellectual disabilities; and 2) to obtain direct behavioral observations of residents in those buildings, using two different technologies: a) real-time recording using optical bar code readers; and b) recording of behavioral samples obtained from videotape recordings that were later coded by experienced observers using a desktop computer time-locked to a videotape playback device and monitor. We also obtained other information, such as rating scale scores on measures of behavior disorder, program philosophy information, and direct measures of the acoustical properties of the residences in question. In this chapter, we briefly describe each of these procedures and provide representative examples of the data obtained. Finally, we explore some of the implications of the planning of residential housing for people with intellectual disabilities.

Buildings Studied

We conducted studies involving 44 buildings in Minnesota and Tennessee. In Minnesota, we (Thompson et al., 1990) studied 11 buildings: two on the grounds of a large public residential facility, three community residences for people with intellectual disabilities, and six that provided housing for people with no known disability. In the first study, we (Thompson et al., 1996a) examined 20 houses located in cities, small towns, and more rural locations in Tennessee that provided housing specifically for people with intellectual disabilities. In a more recent study

(Egli, Roper, Feurer, & Thompson, 1999), we examined 5 of the same houses from our earlier study and 13 additional houses for people with developmental disabilities located throughout Tennessee, including smaller supported living arrangements.

Architectural Inventory

An architectural inventory was conducted using a measure describing a setting's physical features based on architectural specifications of all of the possible characteristics that theoretically could go into creating such a building. The *Standard Master Specs* of the American Institute of Architects (1987) was used as a reference, although the inventory is not a performance specification but a traditional prescriptive specification that describes physically each door, knob, hinge, lock, and so forth (e.g., material, size, type). This measure was developed to permit the assessment of architectural variables that potentially could be related to the behavior of occupants. The 1,398 items of the inventory were programmed to appear on the screen of the laptop computer sequentially one at a time (e.g., "ceiling height"), and data for each was keyed in (e.g., "8 feet, 6 inches"). The sequence of variables was repeated for each room or hallway. Variables were of two types: categorical (wallpapered versus painted versus exposed brick) and continuous (e.g., room circumference, wall thickness, number of entryways). As each item was entered and stored, the next inventory item automatically appeared on the computer screen. Exterior plot dimensions, the composition and size of the driveway, the composition and size of the entry walkway, and other site features (e.g., shrubs, trees, grass), as well as exterior house information (e.g., awnings, light fixtures, signage), were also obtained. A pool of 1,237 interior variables could be recorded for each of the five rooms, although in practice only a subset of the items were applicable in any given room (e.g., toilets would not be found in kitchens, beds would not be found in bathrooms). The exterior inventory consisted of 161 variables.

Perceived Homelikeness of Buildings

In the two Tennessee studies residences were selected to represent a range of anticipated homelikeness ratings, regions throughout the state, and the age range of people with intellectual disabilities. Residences were neither included nor excluded based on the residents' level of retardation, gender distribution, or presence or absence of behavior problems. Once the residences were selected more detailed information was obtained from each residence's administrator or program director about staff education, years of experience, part-time or full-time employment, and the activities and philosophy of each residence.

Several groups of viewers rated photographic slides of the living room, dining room, hallway, kitchen, bedroom, and bathroom of each of the 44 buildings studied. The raters were given 10 seconds to rate each slide on a five-point Likert scale labeled "homelike" on one end and "institutional" on the opposite end. All studies included young adults with no experience with intellectual disabilities. One study included self-advocates with intellectual disabilities, family members, architects, and administrators of residential programs. Ratings by the various groups of viewers of the degree to which the buildings were seen as homelike were highly correlated, regardless of disability, experience, or professional training.

Behavioral Observations

In the following subsections, we discuss two observational methods that we used to record behavior occurring in a range of architectural settings. Advantages and disadvantages of each method are discussed.

Bar Code Readers   In the first study (Thompson et al., 1996b), direct observations of four residents who had been randomly selected were conducted in each residence: 1) once during a meal or meal-related activity, 2) once during a formally structured training or educational activity, and 3) twice during free time. Observational periods were selected based on the daily schedule within each residence (i.e., when residents were on site and participating in normal activities). Residence staff members were requested to follow their usual routines and asked not to schedule any special activities because of the presence of the observers. Distinctive bar codes represented each room, activity (e.g., meal, instruction), and behavior code category (e.g., resident-to-resident positive interactions). Behavior code categories are shown in Table 1.

At the beginning of each observation period, the observer entered his or her identification number, the observation number, and the participant identification number. The observer then recorded the type of activity occurring and whether staff members were present. Recording was achieved by drawing the lens of the bar code reader across appropriate bar codes printed on a sheet of paper. During the subsequent 10-minute observation period, the individual was observed for 10 seconds, then any of 18 behavior codes were recorded during the subsequent 10 seconds. This sequence was repeated until a 10-minute observation period ended. When each code was scanned, the code identifier and the time to the nearest second were saved to memory in the bar coder. After the observations were completed the data from the bar code readers were downloaded using a serial port to a Macintosh computer. Four hundred observation intervals were associated with each person, yielding a total of 40 minutes observed per person. The number of intervals containing each behavior code was tallied, and the percentage of the total number of intervals containing each code was determined. We then analyzed these data as a function of residential homelikeness.

It became clear that many behavior codes were correlated with variables other than architectural measures. For example, 11 of the 18 behavior codes were significantly correlated with resident IQ scores at the time of admission. Possible associations between staff ratios, program philosophy, and resident characteristics on the one hand, and residential homelikeness on the other hand, may create confounding characteristics when resident outcomes are compared across residential environments. Because it is typically difficult to control for these confounding characteristics in experimental design, statistical control for the impact of these variables may be obtained by the use of hierarchical regression. Hierarchical regression analysis was used to determine if the addition of information about the degree of homelikeness improved our predictions about resident outcomes beyond the improvement afforded by information about preexisting resident and staff characteristics as well as measures of room illumination, noise levels, and program philosophy. The confounding characteristics controlled for in these analyses were 1) preexisting resident characteristics (admission behavior prob-

Table 1.   Observational behavior codes

Behavior code	Observation
A. Person who initiates an action	Target resident, staff member, nontarget resident
B. The room in which the action occurred	Living room, dining room, bedroom, kitchen, bathroom, den, hallway
C. Nonsocial tasks or activities	Household care/maintenance, self-care, use of recreational/leisure materials, property destruction, inappropriate behavior in public (e.g., stripping, soiling themselves), self-injury, repetitive stereotyped behavior
D. Social interactions	Positive social interaction with another resident (e.g., offering assistance), positive social interaction with a staff member (e.g., a positive greeting), negative social interaction with another resident (e.g., complaint, teasing), negative social interaction with a staff member (e.g., saying, "Get out of here"), aggression toward another resident without a social antecedent, aggression toward a staff member without a social antecedent
E. Social consequences of nonsocial tasks or activities and of social interactions	Positive staff response (e.g., saying, "You did a great job!"), negative staff response (e.g., saying, "No, stop that!"), no staff response (i.e., ignoring the resident), positive resident response (e.g., smiling at the resident), negative resident response (e.g., saying, "Leave me alone!"), no resident response (i.e., ignoring the resident), compliance with a staff member's request (e.g., putting away shoes), noncompliance with a staff member's request (e.g., staring away), aggression (verbal or physical) toward another resident, aggression toward a staff member

From Thompson, T., Robinson, J., Dietrich, M., Farris, M., & Sinclair, V. (1996b). Interdependence of architectural features and program variables in community residences for people with mental retardation. *American Journal on Mental Retardation, 101,* 320; reprinted by permission.

lems, admission IQ scores, gender, years in the group home, admission medication, chronological age); 2) staff ratio; 3) residence humidity and noise levels; and 4) program philosophy variables (choice of residence, choice of room, choice of activities, participation in housekeeping).

After controlling for these factors, we found that people living in more homelike residences were more likely to be involved in independent household chores, including participating in meal-related activities or performing individual activities alone. Residential homelikeness was negatively correlated with stereotypic behavior and aggression and was positively correlated with staff-to-resident positive interactions.

Videotaped Observations   Despite showing an influence of residential homelikeness on behavior categories measured during direct observations using a bar code reader, the observations lasted only 40 minutes in each case, and we may not have fully measured the way that residential staff members typically dealt with resident behavior. In the study reported here, we videotaped residents to obtain more extensive behavioral observational samples of resident and staff activity. We then analyzed the tapes of behavior using *PROCODER* (Tapp & Walden, 1993).

We visited 18 homes during the late afternoon and evening on 4 consecutive days, Monday through Thursday. Each day, four or five 10-minute videotape samples were collected for two residents. This yielded a total of 180 minutes of videotape per participant. From this sample we selected a total of eight 10-minute segments for each individual, comprising the first and last 10-minute observation on Tuesday, Wednesday, and Thursday and 10-minute segments obtained during evening meals on 2 of those days.

"Live" observations require that codes be defined and observers be trained before making the observations. Depending on the codes, training observers to implement codes reliably can take as long as a month. Videotapes, on the other hand, can be made before any behavior codes are specified; the people performing the videotaping need only follow a standard videotaping protocol. This advantage was appealing to us because the residences we studied were located throughout Tennessee. It was advantageous to be able to schedule visits to the residences a week at a time and then analyze the videotapes at a later date, when videotaping in all residences was completed.

Videotape observations permit coding of an unlimited number of behavior categories and also allow researchers to introduce new codes at any time and for any segment of tape. While implementing the behavior codes planned for this study (i.e., activity states, stereotypy and maladaptive behavior, social interactions), we observed that some residences were particularly noisy as a result of residents emitting noncommunicative vocalizations. We were curious whether this behavior was more likely to be found in less homelike residences.

We restricted behavior coding to observations occurring in living rooms and dining areas (i.e., public areas in which we had made extensive observations in each home). We accomplished this by using *PROCODER*. Specifically, we identified the range of videotape frame numbers associated with observations occurring in living rooms and dining rooms. These values were recorded in "segment files," and a unique file was associated with each videotape participant. *PROCODER* used the information from the segment files to present only the desired frames to the coder. The tape was presented to the coder 30 seconds at a time. After viewing each 30-second segment, the coder entered one of four codes by typing the appropriate code on the keyboard. The codes indicated whether a loud vocalization, a soft vocalization, both loud and soft vocalizations, or no vocalizations were emitted by any resident during the interval. The code was then assigned to the segment as identified by the frame numbers. We did not include conversation, or any apparent attempt at communication with others, in the vocalization category.

With regard to whether occurrences of noncommunicative vocalization were associated with residential homelikeness, it was necessary to acknowledge that this variable was very likely to be a function of the residents' cognitive abilities. We were encouraged by the partial correlations between homelikeness and the occurrence of any form of vocalization ($r = -.43$, probability [p] $= .08$) and loud vocalization ($r = -.47, p = .05$), controlling for resident IQ scores. Because we had not planned to examine nonvocal communication in this manner, a second visit to the residences would have been required had we not chosen to videotape our observations. In a future study, we plan to examine the effects of both residential homelikeness and residential acoustics on communication by residents.

Perceived Homelikeness and Architectural Features

We think of homelikeness as a natural category in that it is not defined by rules regarding necessary and sufficient features, as are the biological categories of male and female. Rather, we assume that whether a residence is categorized as home-like is determined probabilistically (Rosch & Mervis, 1975). Exemplars of a natural category are more similar, on average, to other members of the category than to exemplars of another category. Thus, a given architectural feature, such as an illuminated exit sign, may appear in exemplars classified as institutional as well as in those categorized as homelike; however, its presence may be more highly correlated with one category than with the other. Hence, the placement of exit signs in an otherwise homelike residence would not necessarily compel observers to categorize the residence as institutional. Nonetheless, we assume that the appearance of such features tends to co-vary with the appearance of other features, and that it is the configurations of such features that are predictive of apparent homelikeness.

Although we found apparent homelikeness to be related to resident behavior, it was necessary, for practical reasons, to identify architectural features that were correlated with homelikeness, even though some of these features had no apparent effect on behavior by themselves. Table 2 lists architectural features that were correlated with perceived homelikeness. Homelikeness was negatively correlated with the number of residents living in the building. Some architectural variables negatively correlated with homelikeness also were related to the number of residents, such as the number of seats (e.g., chairs, sofas), ground floor area, corridor size, and room volume. It is important to note, however, that other variables related to homelikeness were not merely artifacts of size. For example, when ground floor area was held constant by dividing total corridor area by ground floor area, there was a statistically significant correlation with homelikeness (i.e., the greater proportion of floor space devoted to corridors, the less homelike the building

Table 2.   Subset of architectural variables correlating with home-likeness

Ground floor area*	Dining room light fixtures*
Corridor area*	Bathroom light fixtures*
Corridor area (% of ground floor)*	Fire equipment*
Room volume*	U-shaped toilet seat*
Room area*	Stereo components
Live plants	Hallway heating/cooling
Dining room seating furniture*	Bathroom walls
Dining room cabinets	Bathroom heating/cooling
Living room seating furniture*	Linear plants/shrubs (exterior)*
Artwork (in living room, dining room)	Driveway width*
Living room artwork	Total sidewalk length*
Electric power outlets	House-to-driveway sidewalk*
Light fixtures*	Facade height/length

*, negative correlation.

appeared). The number of heating and cooling units might be expected to directly reflect building size and occupancy, but this was not the case in our sample.
Heating and cooling units were negatively correlated with occupancy and ground
floor area and positively correlated with homelikeness. Homelikeness was also
related to specific kinds of furnishings, such as decorative artwork and plants, as
well as to fire equipment and exit signs. These observations suggest that simply
reducing the number of residents in a group home would not influence the relevant architectural features associated with its previous occupancy that continue to
prevent the residence from appearing homelike.

Figure 1 shows floor plans from residences examined in our most recent
study of 18 residences (Egli et al., 1999). Residence A was originally designed for
people with no known disability. As of 1996, it housed five adults with intellectual disabilities. It was the sixth most homelike residence in the study. Residence B,
on the other hand, was designed as a group home for people with intellectual disabilities. Although it originally housed eight people, its occupancy had been
reduced to four before our study. It ranked seventeenth in homelikeness.

Even without any information about the furnishings in these homes, notable
characteristics are apparent about Residence B from the floor plan. It has a long,
rectangular shape often associated with office or educational settings. There is a
high degree of symmetry in the layout of the rooms and little differentiation in the
size and arrangement of the bedrooms. In contrast to Residence A, there is little
physical differentiation between functionally distinct rooms in Residence B (i.e.,
living room, corridor, dining room). Unlike typical residences, Residence B has
separate living quarters for staff members. Furthermore, two rooms designed as
bedrooms were being used as a den and an administrative office. Perhaps the
most notable feature of Residence B is the large undisrupted corridor, permitting
living room occupants to observe residents entering and exiting bedrooms. In this
residence our research staff frequently observed residents running the length of
the corridor. One would expect this undesirable behavior to occur less frequently
in a residence having a corridor layout like that of Residence A. Although it is
commonly believed that residences with fewer occupants are beneficial for people
with intellectual disabilities, reducing occupancy without major architectural
changes is not expected to affect the apparent homelikeness of the residence or its
consequences.

Behavior of Residents in Relation to Homelikeness and Architectural Features
In the following sections, we discuss how a variety of residential architectural features were measured and how their effects on behavior were examined.

Cluster Analysis   In the first study of 20 residences (Thompson et al., 1996a,
1996b), we identified 351 architectural inventory variables that were present sufficiently often to be analyzed statistically. A cluster analysis was conducted to
determine which homes shared the greatest proportion of features in common.
Separate cluster analyses were carried out for living rooms, dining rooms, bedrooms, and bathrooms. Ward's method was used for clustering, and the analyses
were based on squared Euclidean distance measurements. The houses fell into
two broad categories: 1) homes that were renovated older, private, single-family
dwellings (3 homes); and 2) homes built specifically to serve as group homes (17
homes). Subsequent analysis revealed that these two broad categories were ultimately subdivided into five distinguishable clusters.

Cluster 1 included two houses originally built as single-family homes that retained both interior and exterior features from when they functioned as single-family homes. These were rated as being among the more homelike of the houses studied (second and eighth rank). Cluster 2 included only one home built as a single-family home. It appeared homelike on the exterior but had been remodeled on the interior with very institutional features. The overall ranking of this home was thirteenth. Cluster 3 contained two large residences designed to accommodate 12 and 14 residents; they resembled schools or clinics. They were the only two homes in the study that had concrete block walls. These buildings were ranked seventeenth and nineteenth out of 20 for homelikeness. Cluster 4 included 12 houses that were built with U.S. Department of Housing and Urban

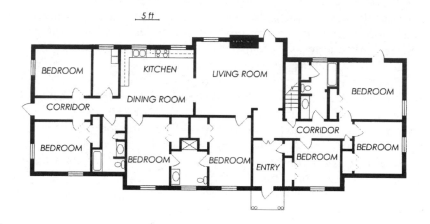

Residence A

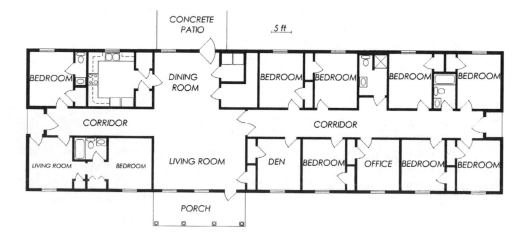

Residence B

Figure 1. Floor plans from residences ranked sixth (Residence A) and seventeenth (Residence B) in homelikeness among the 18 residences studied by Egli et al. (1999).

Development (HUD) funds as group homes to accommodate eight people each. The average rank of these houses was 10.9. Cluster 5 was composed of two houses designed idiosyncratically by architects as group homes (i.e., the plan was used for the building in question only). These homes were ranked first and seventh in homelikeness.

Analysis of the relations between architectural features and the behavior of residents revealed several consistent findings. The behavior of residents in four homes (ranked according to their mean homelikeness ratings as numbers 13, 17, 19, and 20) differed from that of residents in the other 16 homes on a variety of Aberrant Behavior Checklist (Aman, Singh, Stewart, & Field, 1985) and direct observational dimensions. Two of the four buildings in this cluster were institutional-appearing residences for 12 and 14 people. They were constructed throughout of concrete block and brick with vinyl floors and moldings, which were among the more institutional features of all of the houses we studied. One of the buildings in the same physical feature cluster was an eight-person HUD home that included the most institutional interior features of any building studied. The fourth home in this cluster was originally designed as a single-family home, but it had been renovated on the interior using highly institutional lighting, moldings, and floor and wall surface materials.

There were significant differences in resident behavior across clusters of homes based on physical features of a given room type (e.g., dining rooms). The best predictor of maladaptive behavior of group home residents was the combination of physical features of dining rooms, which was associated with significant differences on four of five Aberrant Behavior Checklist scales and eight negative behavior observational codes as well as the degree to which residents were non-involved. It is important to bear in mind that the residential clusters in this analysis were determined strictly by their physical features, not by the perceptions of raters. Analysis of the associations between resident behavior and clusters of physical features not based on subjective responses or subjective impressions of homelikeness provided independent verification of the importance of architectural features on behavior.

Residential Acoustics, Homelikeness, and Behavior   Much of our previous work focused on visually based perceptions of homelikeness. Acoustical features may be important as well. Homes with unusual acoustical properties may inhibit normal conversation, promote undesirable vocalization, or create an aversive ambient environment. One acoustical measure we found that correlated with visual perceptions of homelikeness was room reverberation (Egli et al., 1999). Reverberation measures indicate how long sounds at various frequencies persist in the room. Under typical conditions sound from a direct signal will decrease by 6 decibels with every doubling of distance from the sound source. By contrast, reverberant sounds reflected from a room's surfaces will not decrease inversely with distance but may actually increase and even exceed the intensity of the sound source. Hence, rooms with excessive reverberation tend to be perceived as noisier because of the persistence of sound. This may impair speech comprehension (Finitzo-Hieber & Tillman, 1978).

Room reverberation was defined as the amount of time in seconds required for a decaying sound whose source is no longer present to decrease by 60 decibels below its peak level (Egan, 1988; Knudsen & Harris, 1978). Room reverberation measures were estimated from the decay function resulting from presenting a broad-band, high-intensity sound in an unoccupied room and recording the decay time using a portable dual-channel sound level meter and real-time analyzer (Larson-Davis Laboratories, Model 2900). The sound used was the popping of a balloon. The spectrum of a popped balloon is broad band (i.e., it contains frequency components over a large spectral range), which allows the real-time analyzer to extract narrow frequency bands for further analysis. It also has temporal characteristics that allow a precise estimate of the moment of signal termination.

Sound reverberation in the living rooms and dining rooms had a significant inverse correlation with the perceived homelikeness of these rooms when viewed in photographs (dining room: $r = -.69, p = .001$; living room: $r = -.48, p = .04$) as well as with mean homelikeness scores (dining room: $r = -.74, p = .001$; living room: $r = -.70, p = .001$). These findings suggest that room reverberation time has the potential to combine with other features in these rooms to create an overall impression of institutionality or homelikeness. The extent to which a setting is perceived to be representative of culturally defined norms can influence judgments about whether behavior in the setting conforms to expected standards. The effect that a room's sound reverberation has on an observer's judgment depends on the settings in which comparable reverberation properties typically occur. In our sample approximately half of the living rooms and dining rooms in the less homelike houses had reverberation times resembling those of a lecture hall or cinema.

People with some disabilities (e.g., autism) appear to be especially prone to disturbance by sounds of specific frequencies, particularly persistent repetitive sounds (e.g., Rimland, 1990). In addition, many people with developmental disabilities have communication problems likely to be exacerbated by long reverberation times. Speech intelligibility declines at longer room reverberation times (Finitzo-Hieber & Tillman, 1978). Furthermore, high levels of reverberation disperse sounds from multiple sources throughout the room, resulting in a subjectively noisy environment. As a result, one would expect that individuals with fundamental communication and perceptual problems would be more likely to be confused, frustrated, and agitated in those circumstances.

Agitation is commonly associated with stereotypies. In our study, videotape data were coded for frames containing both mild and severe stereotypy. The percentage of total frames containing these behavior categories was computed. We found a statistically significant relationship between mean room reverberation and severe stereotypy ($r = .45, p < .01$) when controlling for the effects of an individual's IQ score and apparent residential homelikeness.

DESIGN AND PLANNING OF RESIDENTIAL HOUSING FOR PEOPLE WITH INTELLECTUAL DISABILITIES

For many people the goal of community inclusion of individuals with intellectual disabilities in typical residential housing is a philosophical matter, not an empirical concern. It is seen as the right thing to do. Most people assume that it is better to live in any house in a community than in a large congregate care public institution, which may be true. For other people the goal is to save the government, and therefore the taxpayers, money. The latter group hopes that it will cost less in the long run for people with intellectual disabilities to live in normal homes in the community. This combination of advocacy and antitaxation sentiment has provided a powerful political force for change, but it is important to recognize that the two groups' goals are very different.

This becomes a problem when the implementation of the philosophy leads to outcomes that are different from those that the advocates anticipated. The difficulty is that the implications of acting on the philosophy have not been carefully considered. Advocates seeking full community inclusion mean full inclusion in middle-class housing, with middle-class resources and a middle-class lifestyle. They do not mean housing in a depressed area of the city, in substandard housing, and among neighbors engaging in substance abuse and illicit activity. It is safe to assume, however, that there will be continued and perhaps increased pressure to cut funding to community services in most Western nations. Government agencies will be pressured by elected officials to cut corners wherever possible, including support for appropriate residential services.

The problem is further complicated by an apparent lack of awareness by some residential planners of what constitutes a homelike building. Cost cutting nearly always translates into substituting institutional-appearing materials and features for more homelike features. In our most recent study (Egli et al., 1999), there was a trend for homelikeness to be negatively correlated with the age of the home in the 14 homes built specifically for people with developmental disabilities. Nonetheless, three of the nine least homelike residences were built after 1990, suggesting that residential planners continue to neglect features concordant with a homelike environment.

Our research, which has relied almost entirely on computer-assisted observational technology, suggests that far more attention needs to be paid to the nature of residential housing for people with intellectual disabilities. States, provinces, cantons, and other units of government must devise more adequate cost-effective systems to monitor the quality of behavioral and lifestyle outcomes for people with intellectual disabilities in community living arrangements. The computer-assisted technologies described in this chapter and by Felce and Emerson (see Chapter 11) provide useful approaches.

In seeking equality for individuals with intellectual disabilities, we want to make certain which type of equality we have in mind. Equal access to poor housing is no one's goal, but without careful planning that may be the outcome. Owen (1992) suggested that "Every house is a living museum of habitation," meaning that the way of life and daily activities of the previous occupants shape the ways in which a home functions for the new occupants. A house that was designed for and has functioned as a home for a single family more readily conforms to the needs of a new family (including a group composed of several people with developmental disabilities) than a building designed to function as an institution, even if the more institutional building was labeled a house. According to Brand, "Institutional buildings act as if they were designed specifically to prevent change for the organization inside. When forced to change anyway, as they always are, they do so with expensive reluctance and all possible delay" (1994, p. 7). We have the opportunity to make wiser decisions based on observational data, which could not be obtained any other way.

REFERENCES

Aman, M.G., Singh, N.N., Stewart, A.W., & Field, C.J. (1985). The Aberrant Behavior Checklist: A behavior rating scale for the assessment of treatment effects. *American Journal of Mental Deficiency, 89,* 485–491.

American Institute of Architects. (1987). *Standard master specs.* Washington, DC: Author.

Brand, S. (1994). *How buildings learn: What happens after they're built.* New York: Viking Penguin.

Egan, M.D. (1988). *Architectural acoustics.* New York: McGraw-Hill.

Egli, M., Roper, T., Feurer, I., & Thompson, T. (1999). Architectural acoustics in residences for adults with mental retardation and its relation to perceived homelikeness. *American Journal on Mental Retardation, 104,* 53–66.

Emerson, E., & Hatton, C. (1996). Deinstitutionalization in the UK and Ireland: Outcomes for service users. *Journal of Intellectual and Developmental Disability, 21,* 17–37.

Felce, D., de Kock, U., & Repp, A. (1986). An eco-behavioral analysis of small community-based houses and traditional large hospitals for severely and profoundly mentally handicapped adults. *Applied Research in Mental Retardation, 7,* 393–408.

Finitzo-Hieber, T., & Tillman, T.W. (1978). Room acoustics effects on monosyllabic word discrimination ability for normal and hearing impaired children. *Journal of Speech and Hearing Research, 21,* 440–458.

Knudsen, V.O., & Harris, C.M. (1978). *Acoustical designing in architecture.* New York: American Institute of Physics for the Acoustical Society of America.

Landesman-Dwyer, S., Sackett, G.P., & Kleinman, J.S. (1980). Relationship of size to resident and staff behavior in small community residences. *American Journal of Mental Deficiency, 85,* 6–17.

Owen, D. (1992). *The walls around us: The thinking person's guide to how a house works.* New York: Vintage Books.

Rimland, B. (1990). Sound sensitivity in autism. *Autism Research Review International, 4,* 4.

Robinson, J.W., Thompson, T., Emmons, P., & Graff, M. (1984). *Towards an architectural definition of normalization: Design principles for housing severely and profoundly retarded adults.* Minneapolis: University of Minnesota.

Rosch, E., & Mervis, C.B. (1975). Family resemblance studies in the internal structure categories. *Cognitive Psychology, 7,* 573–605.

Saxby, H., Thomas, M., Felce, D., & de Kock, U. (1986). The use of shops, cafés, and public houses by severely and profoundly mentally handicapped adults. *British Journal of Mental Subnormality, 32,* 69–81.

Tapp, J.T., & Walden, T.A. (1993). *PROCODER:* A professional tape control, coding and analysis system for behavioral research using videotape. *Behavior Research Methods, Instruments, and Computers, 25,* 53–56.

Thompson, T., Robinson, J., Dietrich, M., Farris, M., & Sinclair, V. (1996a). Architectural features and perceptions of community residences for people with mental retardation. *American Journal on Mental Retardation, 101,* 292–313.

Thompson, T., Robinson, J., Dietrich, M., Farris, M., & Sinclair, V. (1996b). Interdependence of architectural features and program variables in community residences for people with mental retardation. *American Journal on Mental Retardation, 101,* 315–327.

Thompson, T., Robinson, J., Graff, M., & Ingenmey, R. (1990). Home-like architectural features of residential environments. *American Journal on Mental Retardation, 95,* 328–341.

United Nations, Centre for Human Settlements (Habitat). (1994). *Sustainable human settlements development: Implementing agenda 21.* Nairobi, Kenya: Author.

Wolfe, T. (1935). *Of time and the river: A legend of man's hunger in his youth.* New York: Charles Scribner's Sons.

9

Monitoring Staff and Consumer Behavior in Residential Settings

Richard R. Saunders and
Jay L. Saunders

There are several reasons to monitor behavior: to determine the current dimensions of some behavior (e.g., rate, duration, relation to contextual variables), to detect whether the behavior changes along one or more dimensions across time or changing conditions, to assess for behavioral co-variation, and to assess the relationship between behavioral change and one or more environmental events. In a human services environment, the behaviors most frequently monitored are those of the individuals served (i.e., consumers) and the staff who provide direct supports, such as teachers, job coaches, and residential support staff. In these settings behavior monitoring often is individualized or person specific. Observations of the effects of introducing a behavioral intervention for aggression or prescribing a particular drug for control of self-injury are typical examples of individualized monitoring. Recording students' responses to instruction in matching to sample or teachers' performances in conducting educational planning conferences also are examples. Other chapters in this book address behavior monitoring that corresponds to some of these examples; the discussion of individualized behavior monitoring in this chapter, however, is restricted to monitoring in residential settings. Because residential settings are large and also may provide educational and vocational services, some of the issues and examples we examine overlap with elements discussed in other chapters.

This chapter was supported in part by National Institute of Child Health and Human Development Grant No. 5-P30HD02528 to the Schiefelbusch Institute for Life Span Studies, University of Kansas.

This chapter also discusses group monitoring in residential settings (i.e., observing and recording what individuals in the service setting are doing at a group level and compiling and analyzing the data without regard to the momentary composition of the group observed). The purpose of this type of behavior monitoring is to assess the influences of conditions and condition change that apply generally in the setting. Subsequent chapters will expand on our introduction to this type of monitoring. The results of group monitoring can have interesting implications for practices in individualized monitoring; thus, the two forms are related. A primary goal of this chapter is to introduce our view of that relationship. Because this text is designed to focus on computer-based solutions to behavioral observation and recording, our discussion is based on our experiences with such solutions.

SOME GENERAL TECHNOLOGY-RELATED OBSERVATIONS

Developing effective, efficient, and affordable computerized data collection systems for either type of behavior monitoring in residential settings is a particularly challenging task. The trend toward smaller residential settings distributed throughout communities makes it difficult to place computer equipment and computer-literate staff in each residential location. Because the residential setting generally is not the center of administrative activity, it is often equipped with the poorest-quality computer equipment. Creating multisite networks with the capacity for high-speed data transmission often is prohibitively expensive. Once computer systems are in place, the cost of providing technical support and maintenance is a further complication. Staffing patterns in residential settings also produce special challenges. In residential settings most staff members are not selected on the basis of computer skills or training, because most of them are employed in direct care services. These providers often are assigned in nonoverlapping shifts, which complicates any attempt to maintain continuity of computer equipment use. Moreover, lean staff ratios, which are common, limit the ability of staff to perform less essential tasks regularly, of which data collection may be one.

Two approaches to data collection in residential settings have arisen in response to these problems. One technique is to use external staff to collect data using sampling methods. This technique has several significant advantages. Staff members who observe across residential environments can use centralized computer resources for analysis and reporting. This approach greatly reduces the number of staff members needing specialized training and the number of computers or portable data collection devices (e.g., bar code scanners, personal data assistants, palmtop computers). In general, the cost of developing software for a small number of computer-based data collection tools is relatively inexpensive. This approach is used more often for group monitoring than for individualized behavior monitoring. Organizations often are more willing to require all staff members to dedicate a portion of their day to data collection for individualized monitoring than to assign a few individuals exclusively to the same tasks.

Thus, a second approach to data collection is to substitute computerized tools for the paper-and-pencil data collection methods typically used by direct care staff. Automated data collection systems can improve the accuracy of collected data and greatly reduce the time needed to prepare the data for analysis—that is, collapsing paper-and-pencil records into useful tables and graphs. Systems designed to automate data collection by direct care staff have several requirements, however, that have been difficult to meet. The data collection devices must be highly portable, inexpensive, and very rugged. Furthermore, the system must be easy to learn and require no more time than the paper-and-pencil systems. The greatest impediments to the adoption of these systems are the costs of equipping each on-duty staff person with a data collection device and of developing software that creates an easy-to-learn and easy-to-use system. An indirect benefit of adopting this approach and resolving these problems is that the technology not only permits staff to record the behavior they are observing, but the act of doing so also is automatically recorded, complete with several important parameters. For example, the locations of staff members who are using the recording devices can be captured, along with the exact times of the observations and the identities of the individuals being observed. These data can become integral parts of the facility's group behavior monitoring database and can be used independent of the individualized monitoring system in which they were generated. These data must be used wisely, however, or the staff may reject the system entirely.

CHAPTER ORGANIZATION

Having introduced our topics generally, next we discuss in detail our approach to computer-based individualized monitoring and then group monitoring. In the former we introduce the *Data Collection Assistant (DCA)* (J.L. Saunders, 1999), a software program we developed for settings making the shift from paper-and-pencil methods to computer-assisted methods. In the process of testing *DCA* and other, earlier potential solutions we discovered a number of "system" variables that bear directly on the effectiveness of any individualized monitoring method. Aspects of these variables are important for interpreting and using the results of group monitoring, which we discuss last.

MONITORING INDIVIDUALS: OUTCOME EVALUATION

The most common form of behavior monitoring in residential settings involves observing and recording the behavior of the individuals served and events affecting their behavior. For example, recording the frequency of instances of self-injurious behavior is essential for evaluating the impact of this repertoire, for assessing its functions, and for planning some treatment. Recording the onset and resolution of ear infections in the same individual not only provides an entry in his or her health record but also may contribute to greater understanding of the cause of the self-injury. Such documentation or evidence of data collection is ubiquitous in the clinical records of individuals served in residential facilities.

The second most common form of individualized behavior monitoring involves observing and recording the results of interventions and services described in each consumer's individualized plan, such as a response to treatment of self-injury. Since the 1960s, individualized planning has become a staple of service delivery for people with developmental disabilities. Over time the taxonomy of individualized planning has continued to evolve. Descriptors of this process shifted first from *multidisciplinary* to *interdisciplinary* and then to *transdisciplinary*. This continuum reflected the trend toward a broadening of the planning team and an integration of its efforts. Overlapping this trend was a shift in the labels for the products of the process. *Service plan* gave way to *program plan,* which in turn became *habilitation plan.* In due course *action plan, personal plan,* and *lifestyle plan* became the names for the process in some agencies. These revisions generally reflect an increased emphasis on involving the recipient of the services in the planning process, the purpose being to ensure that the product of planning is not an end in itself but rather describes strategies to enable the individual to achieve his or her personal goals.

An unwavering feature of individualized planning, despite the relabeling of the process and product, has been an insistence that the contents include objective strategies with measurable outcomes. Measurement inevitably leads to observation, data collection or documentation, and data analysis. As a result, nearly every individual employed in the field of developmental disabilities has received some training in data collection methods. This training often involves three distinct elements. First, training often focuses on teaching staff how to state desired outcomes, objectives, or goals objectively, so that progress toward them can be measured. Second, training often addresses the various approaches to measurement suitable to the various forms of objectives. Examples include describing, counting, timing, rating, and sampling. Third, training generally includes suggestions for the actual process of data collection, such as using wrist counters, stopwatches, checklists, scoring sheets, self-graphing tally sheets, and so forth.

This third area of training often engenders the most discussion, because it is the element closest to the implementation of data collection and the one most fraught with problems. Most of these problems arise from one simple fact: The people most likely to be in a position to observe an event are also the people least likely to have their hands free to record it. Consequently, event records frequently are created some time after events occur, and often after multiple events have occurred or after events have occurred for some considerable period. The result is data with suspect accuracy. The more suspicious the validity of the data, the less motivated staff are to organize, review, and make decisions based on the data. Sometimes the data collected receive only the attention necessary to make a plausible presentation to a second party, whose interest in the data rarely exceeds the verification that it exists (e.g., supervisors, accreditation and funding surveyors). Despite these problems, many facilities invest many hours per month in data preparation and organization, and frequently the time invested is that of the most highly paid professional staff. Thus, any method that promotes timely data collection and minimizes postcollection preparation is desirable. Creating such a method has been our goal for more than 2 decades, beginning with an early paper-and-pencil version (R.R. Saunders & Koplik, 1975). As our search began to involve evaluation of computer-assisted possibilities we added qualities to our criteria other than timeliness and automated organization. These included immediate storage and protection of recorded events, long-term storage with easy retrieval, and automated graphic presentation.

Bar Code Technology

After reading a seminal paper on data collection with bar code technology (Eiler, Nelson, Jensen, & Johnson, 1989), we began to explore its potential for application to data collection in residential settings. Early on, we chose Videx equipment because of its low cost, durability, and portability and thus created software to support that equipment. Bar code scanners such as those offered by Videx are suited to behavior monitoring because an observed event can be recorded with the single pass of a scanner over a single bar code. The scanners we used initially were lightweight and no larger than a stack of four or five credit cards. These devices, which now have more memory and other features, are capable of storing several days' worth of monitoring data. The data retained by bar code scanners can be transferred easily to a computer via a communication device, so the data are available for review and analysis moments after a series of observations ends. Another feature of data collected via bar code scanners is that each observation is "stamped" with the date and time when the observation is made. These parameters become fields in the database along with the event recorded. The bar codes to be scanned can be carried as pages on a clipboard or in a folder, placed on small cards that can be carried in a pocket, placed with adhesive on flat surfaces in key locations in the environment, and so forth. Thus, data collection is reduced to a series of simple steps: Grasp the scanner and pass it over a bar code conveniently located nearby.

Additional details regarding data collection, storage, and analysis with bar codes (including interobserver agreement) are available elsewhere (M.D. Saunders, Saunders, & Saunders, 1993; R.R. Saunders, Saunders, & Saunders, 1994). For our purposes it is the easy portability of scanners and their ability to record the time of each scan automatically that makes them desirable as key elements in the system.

Data Collection Assistant

Our preliminary work with bar code technology eventually led to the development of the *Data Collection Assistant*. The *DCA* is an application tool written by the second author of this chapter in Delphi for personal computers operating in the Windows 3.1, 95/98, and NT environments. It was designed to bring the technological advances in bar code systems to bear on programmatic data collection in human service settings. Thus, *DCA* was designed to facilitate data collection in settings where individuals receive support services and where detailed evaluations of the outcome of those services are desired.

Operational Overview of DCA   Historically, in educational, habilitation, and treatment service delivery, the results of a variety of assessments of an individual's status, skills, preferences, and needs are used as the basis for planning. In the course of the planning, priorities are identified and services are targeted for those priorities. The convention in educational and social services is to refer to these services as *supports* and to the array of services generically as a system of supports. The array of supports identified as needed may include assistive technology, personal instruction, medical treatment, nursing services, opportunities for expression of choice and preference, opportunities to display existing competencies, and opportunities for social integration and interaction. *DCA*, as a system-of-supports tool, enters the picture when the planning has been completed and implementation of the supports is imminent. At this time, the service agency usually begins preparing to monitor implementation of the supports and to evaluate their effects. *DCA* is used to create a file or record of the individual being served that includes a detailed description of each support, a tracking form for each support with scannable bar codes as the tracking input medium (as opposed to pencil and paper), and a computer storage area for the results of the tracking. After the uploading of any tracking information from the bar code scanner to the computer, *DCA* can present the tracking data to the user in graphic and printed report formats immediately.

Using DCA   Using *DCA* involves the general steps described in the subsections that follow.

Setting terminology preferences   The user determines how *DCA* will refer to individuals, their supports, and their plans on the screen and in reports and graphs. Depending on the actual language preferences indicated, each user's referents (e.g., individuals, consumers, people) may be different from those of other users.

Creating individual descriptors   The user indicates several different ways in which individuals will be described in a report or on a tracking form (e.g., gender, date of birth, residence, case manager assigned) and enters the wording of those descriptors in multiple-choice pull-down menus for later use. The user also indicates which descriptors will be printed on which documents.

Creating lists of individuals   The user enters the name of each individual to be tracked and enters the descriptors applicable to each name entered (with the multiple-choice pull-down windows created as described above).

Creating lists of observers   The user creates one or more lists of individuals who will actually scan the bar codes on the tracking forms. The user enters the names of these people into the appropriate lists. *DCA* assigns each person a unique bar code so that all collected data can be identified by the collecting agent.

Creating and labeling support formats   Although the contents of each support are nearly always individualized and unique, the elements of a support may be the same as those of other supports for the same individual or for other individuals. Thus, for efficiency, the user creates support formats or templates. The user selects character, numeric, date, and text elements and their labels for each format created. Subsequently, when a new support is to be created, the user chooses an existing format, applies it to the new support, and enters the contents of each element (e.g., training instructions, name of instructor, implementation date) in the format. The contents of the support format are later added to the bar code tracking form before printing. Figure 1 shows a *DCA* screen in which a support format is being created.

Creating lists of reasons data were not collected   Reasons why a support is not implemented or why its implementation is not recorded may vary from agency to agency and from situation to situation. If the user desires that observers be able to classify why data were not collected when data collection was scheduled, the user can create a list of reasons. *DCA* assigns a unique bar code to each reason, and these bar codes may be added to tracking forms at the user's discretion.

Creating individualized supports   When a new, individualized support is to be created, the user must name or label the support (e.g., Making Change for a Dollar), select the support format to be applied from the list of formats already created, and select the data collection method to be used from a multiple-choice list (e.g., count, prompt hierarchy, yes/no). The user next enters the contents of each element in the support format chosen. This process is facilitated by using multiple-choice pull-down windows containing many commonly used words or phrases. The user then selects, from another multiple-choice list, the desired print format for the bar code tracking form. From another multiple-choice list the user classifies the support by type (e.g., instruction, medical treatment, environmental adaptation). Finally, the user adds the bar codes for reasons why data were not collected, if this option is desired. Figure 2 shows an example of an individualized support enabled for bar code data collection.

Printing bar code tracking forms   The user prints the tracking forms on a laser printer for use by the observers. The user also should protect the tracking forms with clear plastic or Mylar covers to prolong the life not only of the forms but also of the clear lenses of the bar code scanners to be used.

Putting bar code scanners in service   DCA supports data collection with Videx bar code scanners. The user programs the scanner with *DCA* in a one-step process. *DCA* then keeps track of which scanners are in use, their programming status, and their most recent uploading of collected data. Each bar code contains the name of the individual served, the support, the details of the support, and the observed outcome.

Collecting data and uploading   The user distributes the scanners and bar code tracking forms to individuals on the lists of observers. After some period of scanning bar codes, the scanners are returned to the host computer for uploading of the collected data (requiring 1–3 minutes per scanner). The collected data are now available for viewing as graphs or reports. In earlier versions of Videx scanners, battery charging between uses was required. The newer scanners are powered by replaceable AA batteries.

Creating graphs   The user creates graphs of collected data for one support at a time. The graphs may consist of multiple data series if the support contained more than one event observed and recorded. When multiple events have been recorded they also may be collapsed into a single data series for graphing. The user speci-

Independent Dressing

Use	Type	Element Title		Print Element On			Multiple Choice	
				Forms	Reports	Admin		
☑	Character	Setting	▼	☑	☑	☑	☐	Edit
☑	Character	Days To Implement	▼	☑	☑	☑	☐	Edit
☑	Character	QMRP	▼	☑	☑	☑	☐	Edit
☐	Character		▼	☐	☐	☐	☐	Edit
☐	Character		▼	☐	☐	☐	☐	Edit
☐	Character		▼	☐	☐	☐	☐	Edit
☑	Date	Date Effective	▼	☑	☑	☑		
☐	Date		▼	☐	☐	☐		
☐	Numeric		▼	☐	☐	☐		
☑	Text	Materials	▼	☑	☑	☑		
☑	Text	Instructions	▼	☑	☑	☑		
☐	Text		▼	☐	☐	☐		
☐	Text		▼	☐	☐	☐		

✓ OK   ✗ Cancel   Reset   ? Help

Figure 1.   A sample screen from the *Data Collection Assistant* program. The screen shows the elements to be included in a skill acquisition program.

fies the inclusive dates of data from the series with on-screen calendars. The graphing editor, with on-screen help files, enables the user to create and display the completed figure in a variety of possible formats, such as pie charts, bar graphs, and line graphs.

Creating reports   The user has several options for creating reports. The user may create a report on one support for a single individual, or reports may be generated for clusters of individuals or supports in a simple operation. Clusters include reports for all supports for one individual, all supports for all individuals, or all supports for a group of individuals defined by a common personal descrip-

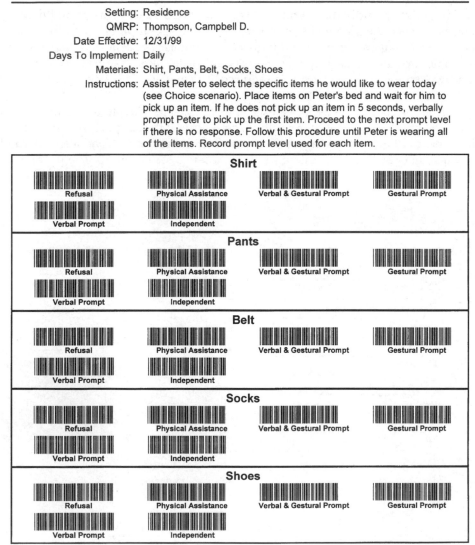

Figure 2.   A bar code–based data sheet for a dressing program conducted with training based on a Prompt Hierarchy.

tor (e.g., service coordinator, qualified mental retardation professional, residence). Clusters also may include all supports of a particular type (e.g., medical treatment) for one, some, or all individuals or all supports generated with a particular support format for one, some, or all individuals. The user specifies the inclusive dates of data for the reports from the series with on-screen calendars. The user selects from a multiple-choice list whether the data in the reports are to be collapsed as daily, weekly, biweekly, monthly, or user-defined entries. *DCA* also prints special administrative summaries of the current supports for each individual for review and further planning.

Overview of Data Collection Formats   *DCA* was designed to support the most common forms of data collection in use in human service settings. Thus, the following formats are available.

Yes/No   With the Yes/No data collection format the user scans a bar code representing "Yes" or a bar code representing "No" in response to a question printed on the data collection form. When Yes/No is selected as the format, the collected data may be viewed in reports or graphs as data series of the number or percentage of "Yes" or "No" answers per time period specified (e.g., day, week, month). The Yes/No data collection format may be used to collect data on a support (e.g., instructional program, physical therapy, application of adaptive equipment) for which a yes or no answer to a single question produces the documentation desired. For example, the question may be as simple as, "Was the scheduled physical therapy session provided?" This documentation method is an example of how to collect data on general outcomes such as attendance, participation, service delivery, and so forth.

The Yes/No data collection format also may be used to collect data on a support for which the answers to several independent questions are related but not necessarily sequential. For example, regarding a support involving physical therapy the questions could ask whether the individual 1) rolled from a supine to a prone position without assistance, 2) sat unassisted on the mat for 30 seconds, and 3) protectively extended arms when rolled on a large ball. This is an example of how to collect data on several desirable outcomes or objectives that are intended to be the result of a single service provided to the individual.

In addition, the Yes/No data collection format may be used to collect data on a support for which the answers to several questions produce documentation on a series of steps that usually occur in the same order from day to day. For example, for a support involving monitoring activities of daily living, the questions could ask whether the individual 1) dressed for the day, 2) put his or her pajamas away, 3) made the bed, 4) combed his or her hair, 5) washed his or her face, and 6) brushed his or her teeth. This is an example of how to collect data on whether earlier positive outcomes achieved through some support, such as individualized instruction, continue to be maintained.

Finally, the Yes/No data collection format may be used to collect data on a support for which the answers to several questions produce documentation on a series of even more tightly connected behaviors that constitute a single routine. For example, a support involving instruction in activities of daily living could include 1) obtaining a plate, 2) obtaining a jar of peanut butter, 3) obtaining a loaf of bread, 4) opening the loaf of bread, and 5) removing two slices of bread, and so forth, to complete making a sandwich. This is an example of how to collect data on the independent development of all of the steps in a sequence or chain of behaviors that make up a single daily routine. With this format for data collection the results can be viewed in graphs or reports as a single data series or collapsed into one data series across all steps.

Keypad   With the Keypad format, the user scans a series of bar codes representing the digits 0–9 until the desired number is created (e.g., 32) and then scans a bar code to acknowledge that the number created is correct and is to be accepted (e.g., Enter). When Keypad is selected as the format the collected data may be viewed in reports or graphs as data series from the sum of keypad entries or the average of keypad entries. The Keypad data collection format may be used to collect data on a support for which a single numeric or quantitative entry produces the documentation desired. For example, in a positive behavioral support the following might be sufficient: "How many points earned?" This documentation method is an example of how to collect data on outcomes that are open ended in terms of what the results may be (i.e., outcomes for which there is no expected or maximum value). The Keypad data collection format also may be used to collect data on a support for which several numeric or quantitative entries produce the documentation desired. For example, the monitoring of activities of daily living described above could be scored with a keypad entry to indicate the number of seconds needed to complete each step after the completion of the preceding step (i.e., response latency).

Count   With the Count format, the user scans a bar code representing "Increment" whenever an event printed on the data collection form occurs (or "Decrement" to correct a recording error). When Count is selected as the format the collected data may be viewed in reports or graphs as data series of total events. Thus, the Count method of data collection is most suitable for documenting each time an event occurs, particularly under conditions in which the number of opportunities for the event to occur is open ended (i.e., the number is likely to be different from day to day). An example application of the Count method is the documentation of a symptom or side effect associated with a disorder that might be responsive to a pharmacological intervention.

Duration   With the Duration format the user scans a bar code representing "Start Clock" to begin the calculation of the duration of an event printed on the data collection form and then scans a bar code representing "Stop Clock" to signal the end of the event. When Duration is selected as the format the collected data may be viewed in reports or graphs as 1) total number of events observed, 2) total duration of the events, and 3) average duration of the observed events. An example of duration recording from a residential situation could be the time spent in different leisure activities and the frequency of change in the activity measured. With the Duration method the duration of each event or episode is calculated by *DCA* by subtracting the time the clock was stopped from the time the clock was started. A tabulation of the number of clock starts for each activity yields the count for these events or episodes. The Duration data collection method in *DCA* is not a mutually exclusive duration system, i.e., more than one clock may be in use at any given moment.

Likert Scale   With the Likert Scale format the user scans a bar code representing a value on a numeric scale in response to a question printed on the data collection forms. When Likert Scale is selected as the format the collected data may be viewed in reports or graphs as 1) sum of ratings; 2) average of ratings; and 3) percentage of ratings equal to, less than, or more than some scale value. The

Likert Scale data collection method is included in *DCA* to provide a means of conducting subjective ratings in situations in which the more objective measures described above are not entirely suitable. As with the methods already described, supports using the Likert Scale format may address just one outcome or multiple outcomes. *DCA* permits Likert Scales with up to 11 values (0–10). An example of Likert Scale use could be the rating of an individual's energy level at several times during the day as an assessment of the sedative effects of a drug prescription for psychomotor seizures.

Prompt Hierarchy   With the Prompt Hierarchy format the user scans a bar code that represents the prompt level required to evoke the behavior/step printed on the data collection form. When Prompt Hierarchy is selected as the format the collected data may be viewed in reports or graphs as 1) sum of levels scored; 2) average of levels scored; and 3) percentage of scores equal to, less than, or greater than some level. The Prompt Hierarchy data collection method is included in *DCA* to accommodate a common instructional practice in behavioral training and education settings. Typically, a desired performance is analyzed with respect to its essential components (i.e., *task analysis*). The essential components are assigned the status of "steps" in the completion of the overall performance. Instruction in this performance sometimes addresses all of the steps in the performance during each instructional session (i.e., *total task instruction*). Other teachers prefer to provide instruction in only one step at a time (i.e., *chaining*). Some teachers begin one-step instruction with the last step in the performance (i.e., *backward chaining*), and other teachers begin with the first step (i.e., *forward chaining*). *DCA* permits chains or sequences of up to 25 steps to be included in a single support and, as with the Likert Scale format, *DCA* permits Prompt Hierarchies with up to 11 values (0–10).

Among individuals who use task analyses in preparation for teaching, some prefer to begin instruction with a few key steps. When the performance of those steps has met some criterion, additional steps are added, perhaps one at a time. This approach has been observed being used by individuals who teach by any of the three methods mentioned above (i.e., total task, backward chaining, and forward chaining). To accommodate this practice, *DCA* permits the user first to create a support with all of the steps that ultimately will be taught. Next, the user may turn off (with an on-screen switch) those steps that will be taught later. When the data collection forms are printed, only the steps switched "on" are printed. Subsequently, when performance on these steps meets some criterion, one or more of the new steps may be switched from "off" to "on." New data collection forms printed subsequent to this switching will include the added steps. *DCA* refers to steps that are switched on and off as "active" and "inactive." *DCA* also recognizes a third category, derived from observations of professional practice: "completed." Thus, another option in *DCA* is to turn steps for which all criteria have been met from active status to completed status. In this case completed steps are no longer printed on new data collection forms. The step-completed feature was incorporated so that teachers favoring the backward chaining and forward chaining methods could ensure instruction of the targeted step by creating data collection forms with only that step printed. The practical importance of the step-deactivation/activation/completion feature is that the individuals collecting the data never see steps on the data collection forms for which data should not be collected.

DCA in Applied Settings   *DCA* has been available since only 1997 but is in use in several public schools, community agencies for individuals with developmental disabilities, and institutions. As this book goes to press, comprehensive customer evaluation is incomplete but encouraging. It should be noted, however, that for the users of *DCA*, data collection was already a priority and the shift to bar code technology was only that—a change in technology. For agencies that do not place as high a priority on data collection, a move to data collection with bar code technology may present greater challenges in initial implementation. In addition to possible changes in agency philosophy or emphasis regarding data collection, one of the most routinely raised concerns has been how staff adapt and make the shift from paper-and-pencil methods. At one of the facilities that served as a beta test site (i.e., a location other than the developer's location where the software is tested prior to release), where *DCA* and its predecessors have been in use for several years, staff members were queried about this concern. No one could provide an answer because all staff members had become employed there after the shift to bar code data collection had occurred. The facility had gradually shifted to teaching data collection with this technology as its sole system. Although one case may not be convincing, it can be indicative of the possibility that bar code data collection may be no more difficult to establish in the workplace than the use of previous technological marvels, such as pencils, typewriters, calculators, and word processors.

After the installation of *DCA* in several settings and subsequent extensive use, some additions have been suggested. First, a specialized overnight tracking system is a feature that many residential settings desire. Bar code scanners can be used in very low light conditions, so scanning bar codes in darkened bedrooms does not pose a problem. Residential settings often serve individuals with a variety of presenting conditions that warrant observation during the night. These include pica and other forms of self-injury, seizure activity, sleepwalking, and so forth. Furthermore, any individual who is ill may require some overnight monitoring. Thus, a feature is being developed that allows a rapid review of monitoring from the previous night, both to verify the condition of the individual monitored and to verify that the staff monitored with the frequency scheduled. A second desired feature would be a component designed specifically for conducting functional analyses (Carr, 1977; Iwata, Dorsey, Slifer, Bauman, & Richman, 1994). The primary aspect of data collection during functional analyses that is not supported by *DCA* is the ability to have multiple observers record simultaneously and independently, with the intention of comparing their records for interobserver agreement. We have used this methodology with bar code data collection in research (R.R. Saunders et al., 1994), and it is being readied for inclusion in *DCA*.

Promising Technologies Other than Bar Code Systems

Bar code scanners are portable, rugged, and easy to use. We have adapted them to our data collection needs for these reasons. Data collection forms for bar code scanners can be designed to make data collection easy and fast, another reason we favored this technology. The latest generation of bar code scanners also is very energy efficient, offering months of data collection on a single set of alkaline batteries or several days on rechargeable batteries. Bar code scanners appropriate for residential monitoring cost between $300 and $600, however, a price that many agencies find prohibitive. As alternatives to bar code systems, several other technologies may become or lead to improved alternatives.

iButtons   Dallas Semiconductor released an automated identification tag called the iButton. The iButton is a small battery casing that is similar in design to a watch battery. Inside an aluminum casing is a memory chip that stores a unique identification number. Data are collected by touching a portable data collection device to the iButton. The iButton's serial number, along with the date and time, is recorded by the device. The iButtons were designed primarily for the asset-tracking industry (i.e., inventory control). This technology is promising because iButtons are small, rugged, inconspicuous, and environment-proof. iButtons can be placed on equipment, furniture, and walls both inside and outside the facility. One possible use of this technology is the tracking of staff movement and service delivery during overnight hours. Another application could be to monitor the use of adaptive equipment.

Palmtop Computers   Palmtop computers are more portable and rugged than their laptop counterparts. Developing data collection systems for palmtop computers is relatively easy. The "clamshell" case design combined with small keyboard keys, however, can make data collection difficult for a staff person providing direct services. Thus, the primary advantages of the palmtop computer are also its disadvantages. Furthermore, palmtop computers have small screens, small keyboards, limited computing power, and limited storage capacity.

Personal Data Assistants   After the release of the Apple Newton, a long list of personal data assistants (PDAs) entered the market. The PDA market did not materialize at that time, however, and many models were abandoned. In the intervening years, PDAs have been used primarily by the medical and insurance industries; they cost between $2,000 and $5,000. The PDA market has now rebounded. The revival is primarily the result of the release of the Microsoft Windows CE operating system for portable devices and the introduction of 3-Com's Palm Pilot personal assistant. The cost for the present generation of PDAs is between $200 and $500, and a wide variety of inexpensive models are available. One long-term advantage of this technology is its orientation toward the consumer market, which should lead to decreasing prices in the coming years. New PDAs have stronger processors, more memory, and longer battery life than their predecessors. New programming tools are making software development easier and faster. The PDA market is still evolving rapidly, however, which could leave facilities with discontinued and obsolete equipment in a matter of months or years. Although the technology presents several risks, it offers promise as an affordable data collection technology for residential settings.

Derivative Outcome of Implementing Computer-Based, Individualized Monitoring

The results of using *DCA* or some other computer-based system can appear impressive, with paperless data collection, immediate access to updated tables and graphs, professional-looking reports, and so forth. In fact, it is easy to be too impressed. A potential result is an insidious increase in expectations of how much behavior to monitor and how much data to collect. As with any plan to increase expectations of staff, it is important to know how much time is consumed in doing what they are doing already and how much time is left for doing more. In addressing this issue we have prompted staff and administrators of residential facilities to think of each staff member's work load as analogous to a cup containing water.

Usually in residential settings the correct analogy is a cup already full to the brim; thus, putting any more water in will result in other water flowing out. Adding more water without knowing how full is the cup is dangerous because we have no control over what pours out. Generalizing from water to staff responsibilities, we must know how full each staff member's cup is already to determine how much more we can add or to determine what to remove first. To answer this question, we use two calculation devices developed specifically for this purpose.

One-to-One Tabulator   We created the One-to-One Tabulator to determine the number of minutes each day that an individual consumer will require involvement with one or more staff members on a one-to-one basis. In theory, staff members involved with one individual on a one-to-one basis cannot simultaneously provide effective supports, including general supervision, to any other individuals. The greatest accuracy is achieved with this device if the information is supplied by someone actually observing the routines, events, and programs involving the individual and recording the precise number of staff members involved and the length of their one-to-one involvement with the person with developmental disabilities. If this is not possible, staff members who provide the assistance should be asked for estimates of the average number of staff members and the average amount of one-to-one time required. Supervisors or other treatment team members should review the estimates, however, to ensure that the information provided is realistic and can be verified by direct observation. The actual time recorded or the estimates should be expressed in minutes or fractions of minutes. Examples of one-to-one situations include 1) assisting an individual to complete a routine as independently as possible, 2) completing the routine for a totally dependent individual, 3) providing an intervention specified in the individualized plan, 4) providing training as specified in the plan, and 5) ensuring the privacy and dignity of an individual. Clearly, on a typical day one-to-one examples include both scheduled (contained in a formal plan) and unscheduled situations. Unscheduled does not mean unexpected, however. Waking an individual in the morning, assisting in the toilet, responding to a request for assistance, preventing a self-injurious behavior, and adjusting someone's position in a wheelchair are not necessarily described in any individualized planning document but clearly are anticipated by staff as parts of their daily responsibilities.

Estimates or calculations of duration should take into account only those treatments, interventions, and training programs that are conducted properly. When data collection is a part of these one-to-one supports, its consumption of time should be factored in. Care should be taken also that the length recorded or estimated is only for the portion of the routine, treatment, intervention, or program that requires the one-to-one or greater staffing. The records or estimates should be entered for each individual on a separate One-to-One Tabulator form (Figure 3). The average number of staff members required in each instance of correctly performed one-to-one services should be entered next. Usually, only one staff member is required, but some interventions (e.g., protection from harm), treatments, and lifting situations (e.g., change of position, being lifted into and out of bed, placement on assistive toileting or bathing equipment) may require two, three, or more staff members. Next, the average daily frequency of each event or program should be recorded or estimated without regard to staffing patterns. That is, the estimate should be based on how often the staff should be involved in one-to-one interactions, without regard to the actual number of staff members on duty for a particular day. For each item the duration should be multiplied by the number of staff members needed, and this product should be multiplied by the daily frequency. Finally, these products are totaled to provide the number of one-to-one minutes required by the individual (rounded to the nearest minute).

Staffing Calculator   To estimate the overall staff demand of a one-to-one nature for a group of individuals, the total minutes of one-to-one services (from the One-to-One Tabulator form) for each individual is entered on the Staffing Calculator

Routine Events	Avg. Dur.	X	# Staff	X	Daily Freq.	= Total 1:1 Min.
Arising From Bed:	☐	X	☐	X	☐	= ☐
Routine Toileting:	☐	X	☐	X	☐	= ☐
Dressing/Undressing:	☐	X	☐	X	☐	= ☐
Tooth Brushing:	☐	X	☐	X	☐	= ☐
Grooming:	☐	X	☐	X	☐	= ☐
Face Washing:	☐	X	☐	X	☐	= ☐
Shaving or Makeup:	☐	X	☐	X	☐	= ☐
Hand Washing:	☐	X	☐	X	☐	= ☐
Bathing:	☐	X	☐	X	☐	= ☐
Eating:	☐	X	☐	X	☐	= ☐
Change of Position:	☐	X	☐	X	☐	= ☐

Unscheduled Events

	Avg. Dur.	X	# Staff	X	Daily Freq.	= Total 1:1 Min.
Toilet Accident:	☐	X	☐	X	☐	= ☐
Seizure:	☐	X	☐	X	☐	= ☐
Behavioral Episode:	☐	X	☐	X	☐	= ☐

Other Treatment or Training Programs

	Avg. Dur.	X	# Staff	X	Daily Freq.	= Total 1:1 Min.
Program 1:	☐	X	☐	X	☐	= ☐
Program 2:	☐	X	☐	X	☐	= ☐
Program 3:	☐	X	☐	X	☐	= ☐
Program 4:	☐	X	☐	X	☐	= ☐
Program 5:	☐	X	☐	X	☐	= ☐
Program 6:	☐	X	☐	X	☐	= ☐
Program 7:	☐	X	☐	X	☐	= ☐
Program 8:	☐	X	☐	X	☐	= ☐
Program 9:	☐	X	☐	X	☐	= ☐

Individual's Name:_____   Date:_____   **Total** ☐

Figure 3.   The One-to-One Tabulator form for calculating the total number of minutes one consumer requires of one-to-one attention by staff on an average day.

form (Figure 4). The totals are summed to a new total for the group and divided by 120 (i.e., minutes per hour multiplied by two shifts of personnel) to produce the number of one-to-one hours per 8 hours of time (one worker's shift) that the individuals are likely to be awake (between approximately 6:00 A.M. and 10:00 P.M.). To determine the minimum number of staff members needed on duty to support this one-to-one demand per shift, the number of hours at the top of a column that is larger than the shift total (from the box at the bottom of the form) is located. In this column (e.g., the 24-hour column) the number on the row that corresponds to the number of individuals living in the residence is located next (e.g., if eight persons live in the residence, the row aligned with the box for Individual 8 shows a 4 in the 24-hour column). This number should be subtracted from the number of hours at the top of the column (e.g., 24 − 4 = 20 hours). This subtraction process is an adjustment to account for staff meals and breaks that effectively reduce their consumer contact time from 8 to 7 hours per shift. If the result is as

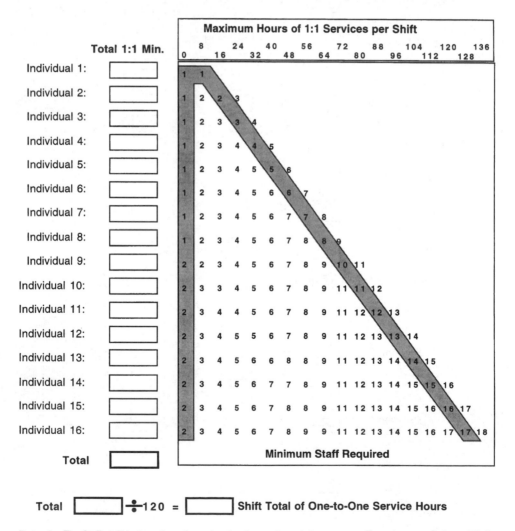

Figure 4. The Staffing Calculator form for estimating the number of direct care staff members needed per shift for the supervision and habilitation services for a group of consumers.

large or larger than the shift total, then the number on the row is the minimum number of staff members required (e.g., 4). If the result is smaller than the shift total, then the number of staff members needed is the number on the row in the next column to the right (e.g., 5, as shown in the 32-hour column).

Generally, when the shift total is as large or nearly as large as the result of subtracting the number on the row from the number of hours at the top of the column, the residence will be staffed at the lower limit required to produce an acceptable program for all individuals. When the shift total is considerably smaller than the result of the subtraction, the opportunity to produce a richer program will be much greater. The shaded areas in Figure 4 indicate staffing levels that actually may be slightly lower than the minimum required but that represent a best fit for the one-to-one data. Staffing at levels slightly less than the numbers shown on the chart does not mean that the staffing will be inadequate. For lower staffing to be acceptable, however, the distribution of one-to-one services must be balanced among individuals and/or the individuals must require minimal or no supervision when not receiving one-to-one services. The possibility that the number on the chart is higher than it needs to be is more likely toward the left end of any row (except in the gray area) and much less likely toward the right end of any row. In general, the staffing numbers on the chart assume that general supervision is always needed and that one staff member should not be expected to provide supervision to more than eight individuals at any time.

Use of the One-to-One Tabulator and the Staffing Calculator enables a determination of whether a particular team or combination of staff members has any time left, on an average day, for more responsibilities, including data collection. Another method of gathering information that administrators and program directors can use for decision making is group monitoring. Usually, group monitoring arises in response to a set of questions different from "How much time remains for more responsibilities?"

MONITORING GROUPS: AGENCY OUTCOME EVALUATION

Behavior monitoring of groups sometimes arises as a function of an agency's interest in whether some new treatment method, teaching tool, specific employee practice, or distribution of employees will result in significant benefits to consumers (Harchik, Sherman, Sheldon, & Strouse, 1992; Ivancic, Reid, Iwata, Faw, & Page, 1981; Page, Iwata, & Reid, 1982; Parsons & Reid, 1993; Parsons, Schepis, Reid, McCarn, & Green, 1987; Risley & Cataldo, 1973; Seys & Duker, 1988, 1993; Sturmey, 1995). In other cases monitoring arises to determine whether more general changes in agency philosophy or policy, usually introduced through staff training, result in changes in the nature of staff–consumer interactions or in consumer outcomes (Bodfish & Konarski, 1992; Doerner, Miltenberger, & Bakken, 1989; Gross, Maguire, Shepard, & Piersel, 1994; Rast & Saunders, 1988; Zarcone, Iwata, Rodgers, & Vollmer, 1993). Monitoring also may arise, however, in response to conclusions by external review groups, certifying bodies, or funding agencies that services must be improved if certain negative consequences are to be avoided (Sulzer-Azaroff, Pollack, Hamad, & Howley, 1998). In this case monitoring may be initiated to prepare a response to negative allegations or to measure success in attempts to address them. Monitoring also may arise as an exploratory tool to detect relationships among variables that would be interesting for further analysis or manipulation (Hile & Walbran, 1991; Seys, Duker, Salemink, & Franken-Wijnhoven, 1998; Vyse & Mulick, 1988; Vyse, Mulick, & Thayer, 1984).

A recent report of behavior monitoring describes a simple case illustration in a large residential facility for people with developmental disabilities (Sulzer-Azaroff et al., 1998). Through a participatory process a planning team decided to monitor consumer engagement (defined objectively) and consumer–staff interactions (across four categories). After training of supervisory staff working in the participating areas (internal monitors) and staff who were to serve as "external" monitors, observations began with paper-and-pencil recording methods. The monitor unsystematically selected one staff member to observe, observed for a few moments, interviewed the staff member observed, shared the results of the observation with respect to engagement and interactions, and transferred the results of the observation to a summary form. On a weekly basis, the data from the observations were summarized for each participating unit (i.e., 25-bed cottage) and reviewed with the staff of the unit at a brief meeting. These meetings also served as opportunities to provide positive feedback on acceptable summary data and to set goals for improvements in the summary data.

Sulzer-Azaroff et al. (1998) reported several results. Once it was fully in effect the monitoring system resulted in about 40–45 observations per week per unit by each set of monitors. The internal monitors consistently recorded higher percentages of staff interacting with consumers than did the external monitors. For the period studied the summary percentages of interactions (from both types of monitors) changed little from week to week, with no trend toward an increase or decrease. Summary data from the external monitors, however, did show some increase in percentages of consumers engaged across the 7-month period of the report. The reported sample of goal setting by a unit, however, revealed no systematic relationship between goals and outcomes. Using the categories of consumer–staff interaction recorded, an analysis revealed no reliable trends in observations of structured activities as the basis for interaction and no reliable trends in the use of reinforcement during interactions.

Sulzer-Azaroff et al. (1998) also reported that at some time after the initiation of the monitoring system a determination of whether activity materials were available for consumer and staff use was added to the recording system. Additions such as this reflect a common component of behavior monitoring systems: the inclusion of measures of outcomes of staff behavior and/or system elements that might affect the primary behaviors being measured. A report by Gross et al. (1994) described an array of these measures, including whether 1) a particular activity was in progress, 2) an activity schedule was present, 3) the activity in progress was the one scheduled, 4) the activity in progress was following some activity-planning guide, 5) the activity plan being implemented had certain characteristics, and 6) the activity related to individualized service plans. In addition, several somewhat more subjective items included whether 1) the number of staff members present was sufficient to accomplish what was scheduled (and what happened that was unscheduled, such as an episode of challenging behavior), 2) the privacy of consumers was protected when necessary, 3) whatever materials present were appropriate to the ages of the consumers, and 4) the activity area was organized for effective training. These additions are similar to those included by Rast and Saunders (1988) in their example, to which they also added measures of 1) consumer appearance, 2) area appearance, 3) appropriateness of the area for the activity in progress, and 4) attention to consumer health needs. Rast and Saunders and Gross et al. also measured, by category, challenging behavior by consumers, how staff responded to challenging behavior, and the degree to which such responses reflected correct implementation of intervention plans.

These more exhaustive monitoring systems share a key characteristic with the system described by Sulzer-Azaroff et al. (1998): The usual observation interval was restricted to about 5 minutes. Thus, these reports describe a "sampling" approach to behavior monitoring intended to generate large numbers of brief but informative observations, or "snapshots" of behavior and its supportive conditions. All of these systems use some form of summarization, collation, or compilation technique to provide periodic (e.g., weekly, monthly) data to be contrasted across time within the observed unit or across units within a period of time or both. The periodic samples of data most often are used as the basis for feedback to the staff member whose behavior is reflected in the samples or to administrators or consultants for their determination of whether some preceding training, restructuring, or other intervention is having the desired effect. In short, behavioral monitoring often arises in response to someone's impression that conditions are not entirely satisfactory and the expectation that with more data the causes and solutions may be found.

Another relatively common feature of reports of behavioral monitoring is the implication that the behavior of staff—particularly staff members who provide the closest supports (i.e., the direct care staff)—is the single most important variable in treatment outcomes or in quality-of-life/treatment conditions. Indeed, Gross et al. (1994) reported that nearly all of the variance in changes in active treatment outcomes that they measured could be accounted for by two variables: 1) frequency of staff interaction and 2) functional aspects of staff interactions.

Recommended Characteristics of Group Monitoring Systems

We have used group behavior monitoring as a cornerstone of our consultative assistance to facilities and agencies desiring to change the outcomes of their services. We prompted these service providers to create teams of employees whose sole purpose was behavior monitoring, data analysis, and data dissemination. These teams were equipped with data collection devices of one type or another, and the members were scheduled to make unannounced observations of consumers and staff on a frequent basis. As a function of our requirements for sufficient data for valid data-driven decision making, the schedule of observations we use has usually resulted in 40–60 observations per month of each consumer and somewhat fewer per individual staff member, because of work schedules. That is, consumers are always present; their lives are of the 24-hour sort. Individual staff members may or may not be present, however, because they ordinarily work only 40 hours per week. It should be noted, of course, that in group monitoring the observation of one consumer is concurrently the observation of other consumers and staff members in the group. Thus, a total of 40–60 observations per month multiplied by the total population of the facility grossly overstates the actual number of observations conducted. In an institution or community program serving 400 individuals, for example, the data stream consists of the products of about 2,500 observations of 5 minutes each per month if the average size of the group observed is 8 individuals. Group size will vary from observation to observation as a function of the settings and activities, such as meals, meal preparation, table games, outdoor play, and so forth. Measures of interobserver agreement should be routine in such systems. Generally, the type of sampling approach described should render agreement of 90% or greater on the variables assessed.

Pandora

Our preferred method of data collection for group behavior monitoring is the use of bar code scanners. Simply described, we create bar code representations of the outcome variables used by Rast and Saunders (1988), Gross et al. (1994), or Sulzer-Azaroff et al. (1998) as examples. (Sulzer-Azaroff et al. also reported that a bar code version of their system had replaced their paper-and-pencil method by the time their report went to press.) An example of an extract from a bar code–based

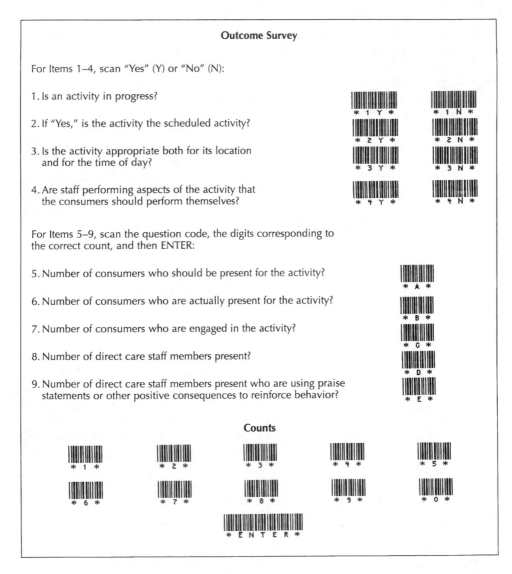

Figure 5. A sample bar code–based recording sheet for a group monitoring program. The sample reflects a yes/no scheme for some questions and an open-ended counting scheme for the remaining questions.

group data collection system is shown in Figure 5. Initially, we created databases to hold the uploaded data from the scanning of such data sheets, and small software programs were created to generate the reports and graphs that were needed for ongoing analysis. In our early experience we worked with the resident computer staff of each facility to create codes, databases, and reports specific to each facility's requirements. Subsequently, the second author of this chapter wrote *Pandora* (J.L. Saunders, 1997), a comprehensive software program in Delphi that creates the same package, individualized for each facility, but without reinventing the software at each facility. The operational details of *Pandora* are similar to those of *DCA* and are available on request.

What Behavior to Monitor and How to Respond to It

Clearly, in group monitoring, as in individual monitoring, one observes and records the behavior(s) one is interested in changing: the dependent variable(s). Often we also observe to determine whether the independent variable(s), such as staff behavior or certain environmental events, is occurring as planned. That is, we observe for indices of treatment fidelity as well as treatment effectiveness. In a closed experimental environment, such as a laboratory, these measures are usually sufficient to provide the data for a complete analysis of behavior–event relationships. This is so in the laboratory environment because impediments to treatment fidelity are few and, when they do arise, they are easily identified and corrected. In the applied environment these characteristics are not present. Impediments to treatment fidelity are common and numerous, their identification is not easy, and eradication may be elusive. To deal with this situation, effective use of group monitoring data may require additional data of another sort and different approaches to analysis (R.R. Saunders & Saunders, 1994).

For example, when administrators review observations of less-than-acceptable performances of direct support staff, retraining, monitoring, and feedback are often considered to be the preferred tools by which to effect change. When the performances of the staff meet expectations, however, but the outcomes for consumers fall short of expectations, administrators generally next look at the quality or appropriateness of the individualized interventions as a potential source of variance. When we restrict our analyses of outcomes in residential facilities to these variables—staff competence and intervention quality—we may engender a cycle of revised intervention plans, staff retraining, and performance monitoring to drive improvement. But if staff competence and intervention quality constitute only a fraction of the variance in program outcome, what else could be responsible?

The results of our experience are shown in Figure 6. In this figure, the performances of groups of consumers and their staff on some hypothetical variable observed are plotted according to percentage range. The height of each bar reflects how many groups in the facility performed within each percentage range for each week. Suppose some hypothetical group scored in the 70%–75% range in Week 1 and in the 85%–90% range in Week 2. Many administrators have viewed such changes in performance as indicative of improved staff performance or improved supervision of staff performance. Often, public praise or other awards are given for such observed changes. Usually, however, in Week 3 of observations the score for this group decreases to a lower range, as shown. In our experience, then, most fluctuations in measures of outcomes stem from sources of variance outside the immediate control of the staff members whose performances are measured. Thus, reward or punishment for changes in level of performance usually fails to have the intended effect (Noltz, Boschman, & Tax, 1987).

Using group monitoring data appropriately requires some important assumptions. First, if a new policy, method, or administrative expectation is a variable with sufficient potency to affect staff behavior, it will affect the behavior of most staff members. Thus, the most likely effect on the data is not to move the measured performances of individual groups around within a generally static distribution of such performances but to move the entire distribution in a common direction. Second, variation in the location within the distribution of a particular group, as shown in Figure 6, should be expected because of sources of variance unrelated to the independent variable of momentary interest. Indeed, those groups that routinely change positions in a distribution from one reporting period to the next reflect a "normal" response to the combined effects of all of an agency's policies, staffing methods, treatment expectations, and so forth. Examples of normal variation include shifts attributable to vacations or illness among staff, replacement of experienced staff with new staff, changes in the composition of the consumer group, breakdown of assigned vehicles, and temporary shortage of activity materials.

In contrast, the groups that do not move (show normal variation) are abnormal and bear further investigation and analysis. Such abnormality usually indicates the presence of one or more variables not common to any other group,

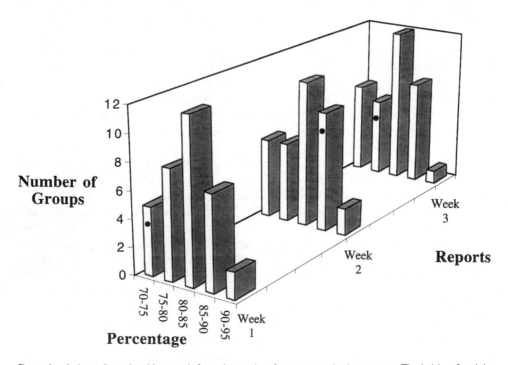

Figure 6.   A three-dimensional bar graph from the results of a group monitoring program. The height of each bar reflects the number of groups scoring within each scoring range on a hypothetical monitoring variable. The black dot on the face of one bar in each week's data reflects the scoring location of one hypothetical group for the 3 weeks.

variables whose influence overrides the influence of in-common variables. A typical example is a supervisor or leader with particularly good or bad characteristics. Another typical example is a grouping of consumers that exceeds the capacities of the assigned staff, despite a staff-to-consumer ratio that is the same as that in every other group. Our application of the One-to-One Tabulator and the Staffing Calculator has frequently revealed this variable and its reverse, a high ratio of staff relative to one-to-one demands. Also likely, particularly in small settings with few consumers and fewer staff members, are staff–consumer incompatibilities. In a comparatively large group home a personality conflict between one staff member and one consumer rarely overrides the influences of other system variables. In a home with two consumers and one staff member, however, the effects are substantial.

One source of variance in group outcomes that is beyond the control of staff—staff coordination—is discussed separately, both because it has the potential for large effects and because it is so common. Although common, this variable is hardly benign.

Staff Coordination

In a relatively small residential unit of eight consumers the average pattern of staffing in the United States is two staff members assigned to be on duty. Administrators know that to have two staff members on duty, three or four must be hired and assigned to that work shift or time period because the mathematics of vacations, illnesses, holidays, and so forth generally create this proportion of "hired" to "on duty." Four staff members hired, however, results (with 5-day work weeks) in six combinations of two staff members each. Thus, each staff member, say Staff Member A, will team with Staff Members B, C, and D every few days. So, all staff members will participate in three different two-member teams. Furthermore, Staff Member A may be senior to Staff Member B, junior to Staff Member C, and on par with Staff Member D, creating three different ways for the two staff members of each of these three teams to coordinate their activities (and there are six two-member teams that must coordinate). If we reverse our view of this arrangement to see it from a consumer's vantage, there may be six permutations of how the consumer is supported (per shift). Our experience is that people with developmental disabilities do not respond well to inconsistencies in positioning, instruction, assistance in eating, and so forth.

To complicate matters even more, if the group of eight consumers is somewhat more difficult to support than most, the number of staff members assigned per shift may be three, requiring the employment of five. That works out to 10 possible combinations of three staff members each to provide support to the consumer, and each staff member will participate in six different three-member teams. Clearly, staffing patterns create a formidable problem. For example, if in the latter setting with three staff members per shift a consumer's positive behavior support plan for self-injury is revised to include new procedures, the person responsible for training the staff on the new procedures faces considerable challenges. If staff members trained on the first day can pass on the training to other staff members, only one training session may be needed. However, if each staff member is to be trained and competency tested before working with the individual consumer, two or three sessions will be required, depending on the assignment rotation. That addresses one shift, but there are two others; in total, up to eight sessions may be required for this one change in just one consumer's support plans.

Staff Utilization

Another variable relevant to behavior monitoring is staff utilization or staff choreography. Direct support staff in residential settings work amid the "forest" of consumers and other staff members. Theirs is not the perspective of a supervisor or staff coordinator with the luxury of observing the interaction of staff and consumers from outside of the forest. We have found that staff benefit from a plan for their behavior with groups of consumers as much as or more than they benefit from the individualized plans for treatment and other supports. The approach of the first author of this chapter to staff choreography or staff team planning is called the *scenario system* because it uses staff "scenarios" as the cornerstone of service delivery (M.D. Saunders, Spradlin, & Saunders, 1987; R.R. Saunders, Rast, & Saunders, 1988).

Scenario System

A scenario is a brief written description of the intended sequence of interactions between staff and the consumers they support. A scenario describes these interactions within a period of time with natural boundaries, such as a meal, a period of leisure, or the time in the workplace between coffee breaks. Each scenario describes the interactions of naturally occurring groups of staff and consumers, such as the residents and staff of a small group home. The scenario depicts the interactions as they "should be," i.e., as envisioned by the employee responsible for what occurs during the period addressed by the scenario. Ideally, what is envisioned should result from an integration of the individual needs of the consumers addressed; general positive practices applicable to the type of consumers supported; and practices derived from the particular agency's published philosophy, policies, and procedures. Scenarios have three purposes: 1) to create an integrated treatment or service plan for small groups of consumers for definable units of time; 2) to create a staff training guide specific to each unit of time; and 3) to create, for outcome evaluation, a "standard" for each unit of time with which the actual performances of the individuals involved can be compared. Because the scenario is written, performance comparisons can be made by any observer who possesses a copy of the scenario.

Adopting the scenario approach results in the creation of volumes of written material, and it is reasonable to ask, Why expend such energy when most agencies are engulfed in paperwork already? And, moreover, why discuss it here? The rationale is that other documents—individualized action/support/habilitation plans, policy and procedure manuals, clinical records, incident reports, and positive behavior support plans—do not provide a picture of what the most ubiquitous products of human services should look like. Those products are consumer behavior, staff behavior, and staff–consumer interaction as they are expressed together under naturally occurring conditions. As in the measurement of any manufactured product, a standard for that product must exist if the quality of the product is to be measured precisely (see Saunders & Saunders, 1994). In residential settings, the presence of staff implies that the consumers require their presence to complete essential daily tasks and preferred activities. Thus, in these settings consumer behavior is dependent on staff behavior. Scenarios provide the standards for staff behavior for the various tasks and activities in which consumers are supported.

In group monitoring in a setting using the scenario system, observers can record the degree of correspondence between the written description of what should be occurring and what is actually occurring. Thus, rather than observers being placed in a position of drawing subjective conclusions about the appropriateness or effectiveness of a group's performance, they can compare it with a standard. These comparisons produce critical data because they force a consideration of whether unacceptable performances reflect staff failure to follow the scenario or whether the scenario outlines performances unattainable by the group. The latter conclusion compels managers to discriminate among possible causes other than poor motivation or work ethic. Alternative causes include incorrect staff ratios, poor supervision, poor program organization, insufficient training, and so forth. In short, written standards provide protection for direct care staff from erroneous inferences from group monitoring data. They also protect management from the usual results of such erroneous inferences, i.e., exposing capable, highly motivated, responsible staff to unfounded negative feedback, unnecessary retraining, or ostensibly motivating pep talks, which often lead to fewer capable, motivated staff members being on the payroll, not more.

Summary
Group monitoring systems should measure staff performances and consumer outcomes with a breakdown by staffing teams, first to calculate how many teams there are, and second to compare the relative effectiveness of individual teams. Furthermore, any monitoring system should assume that performance variability, rather than performance consistency, is the most likely outcome. The problems of staff coordination, which are produced by larger numbers of combinations of staff members, may be exacerbated by overall support demands that stress staff capability to meet those demands, even under the best conditions. Even staffs not plagued by having different members teamed on different days, however, can be beset by support demands that exceed their average capacity to address them. Determining how many staff members are sufficient should be an empirical process. Sufficiency should be measured by 1) a calculation of how much time each consumer requires of staff, and 2) objectively comparing the performance of the consumers and their staff with a standard for group performance. Such comparisons should be made in all settings and activities in which the group participates.

CONCLUSIONS
Residential settings are complex environments in which individuals interact in a continuous stream. Who interacts with whom at any given moment is affected by many variables, and the nature of the interaction is likewise determined by many variables. An expectation that staff in residential settings will record 1) the interactions of the consumers, 2) events affecting the consumers or created by the consumers, and 3) the responses of the consumers to staff behavior is common. Not so common has been an evaluation of how data collection by staff "fits" into the overall array of expectations of residential staff. Thus, the design or redesign of residential staff job descriptions should begin with an evaluation of the system

within which they work. We designed *Pandora* and our staffing measurement tools for such evaluations, and *DCA* was the data collection system that resulted from our evaluations. Our testing of the software also led to an informative set of observations.

The high cost of shifting from paper-and-pencil individualized monitoring to a bar code system requires agencies to have sound rationales for doing so. One such rationale is that many agencies desire to improve the quality and utility of the data collected so that data-based decisions in consumer services are rendered more valid. In addition to qualitative rationales, however, agencies need financial rationales. In designing *DCA* we focused on *not adding* to the work load of direct care staff; reducing their time spent on data collection was never a realistic expectation. Thus, the financial incentive for converting to a bar code system was the reduction in the hours that the higher paid professional staff spent on data organization and preparation. This is an important result in terms of treatment and also because the cost savings realized continue each subsequent year after the conversion. Generally, the professional time gained by a conversion to a bar code system will pay for the conversion in the first year.

In addition to learning about agency rationales for bar code systems, we learned about other aspects of residential facilities. One was the disturbing frequency with which recorded data on individual consumers—computer based or not—failed to show consumer improvement or progress. Similarly, we observed that the most common response to such situations was a series of meetings resulting in revisions to the individual's action plan or habilitation plan. Nevertheless, subsequent consumer improvement or progress rarely resulted from the revisions. Concurrent to these observations we had the opportunity to follow the collection and analysis of group monitoring data in the same programs or facilities. It was from the group monitoring data that solutions to poor progress by individual consumers often began to emerge. That is, system problems were preventing many individually planned services from being particularly effective.

Thus, we offer another rationale for shifting to computer-based individualized monitoring systems: The expensive conversion to a computer-based system leaves little additional cost, if any, for also establishing a comprehensive group monitoring system. Our experience suggests that a group monitoring system is an essential companion to individualized data collection systems, particularly expensive ones. Therefore, when computer-based systems become financially feasible, equipping group monitoring systems should be given as high a priority as equipping individualized monitoring systems. Indeed, we can think of no better use of the professional's time, now released from data preparation, than direct observation of group behavior and collection of group data. Who more than the individuals responsible for designing residential services and supports could benefit from regular direct observation of the results?

REFERENCES

Bodfish, J.W., & Konarski, E.A., Jr. (1992). Reducing problem behaviors in a residential unit using structural analysis and staff management procedures: A preliminary study. *Behavioral Residential Treatment, 7,* 225–234.

Carr, E.G. (1977). The motivation of self-injurious behavior: A review of some hypotheses. *Psychological Bulletin, 84,* 800–816.

Doerner, M., Miltenberger, R.G., & Bakken, J. (1989). The effects of staff self-management on positive social interactions in a group home setting. *Behavioral Residential Treatment, 4*, 313–330.

Eiler, J.M., Nelson, W.W., Jensen, C.C., & Johnson, S.P. (1989). Automated data collection using bar code. *Behavior Research Methods, Instruments, and Computers, 21*, 53–58.

Gross, E.J., Maguire, K.B., Shepard, S.M., & Piersel, W.C. (1994). Development and evaluation of the active treatment client rights checklist. *Research in Developmental Disabilities, 15*, 1–18.

Harchik, A.E., Sherman, J.A., Sheldon, J.B., & Strouse, M.C. (1992). Ongoing consultation as a method of improving performance of staff members in a group home. *Journal of Applied Behavior Analysis, 25*, 599–610.

Hile, M.G., & Walbran, B.B. (1991). Observing staff–resident interactions: What staff do, what residents receive. *Mental Retardation, 29*, 35–41.

Ivancic, M.T., Reid, D.H., Iwata, B.A., Faw, G.D., & Page, T.J. (1981). Evaluating a supervision program for developing and maintaining therapeutic staff–resident interactions during institutional care routines. *Journal of Applied Behavior Analysis, 14*, 95–107.

Iwata, B.A., Dorsey, M.F., Slifer, K.J., Bauman, K.E., & Richman, G.S. (1994). Toward a functional analysis of self-injury. *Journal of Applied Behavior Analysis, 27*, 197–209. (Reprinted from *Analysis and Intervention in Developmental Disabilities, 2*, 3–20, 1982)

Noltz, W.W., Boschman, I., & Tax, S.T. (1987). Reinforcing punishment and extinguishing rewards: On the folly of OBM without SPC. *Journal of Organizational Behavior Management, 9*, 33–46.

Page, T.J., Iwata, B.A., & Reid, D.H. (1982). Pyramidal training: A large-scale application with institutional staff. *Journal of Applied Behavior Analysis, 15*, 335–351.

Parsons, M.B., & Reid, D.H. (1993). Evaluating and improving residential treatment during group leisure situations: A program replication and refinement. *Research in Developmental Disabilities, 14*, 67–85.

Parsons, M.B., Schepis, M.M., Reid, D.H., McCarn, J.E., & Green, C. (1987). Expanding the impact of behavioral staff management: A large-scale, long-term application in schools serving severely handicapped students. *Journal of Applied Behavior Analysis, 20*, 139–150.

Rast, J., & Saunders, R.R. (1988). Quality assurance. In R.R. Saunders, J. Rast, & M.D. Saunders (Eds.), *A handbook for scenario-based active treatment* (pp. 227–262). Parsons: University of Kansas.

Risley, T.R., & Cataldo, A.J. (1973). *Planned activity check: Materials for training observers.* Lawrence, KS: Center for Applied Behavior Analysis.

Saunders, J.L. (1997). *Pandora* [Software]. Overland Park, KS: Bluestem Technologies.

Saunders, J.L. (1999). *Data collection assistant* [Software]. Overland Park, KS: Bluestem Technologies.

Saunders, M.D., Saunders, J.L., & Saunders, R.R. (1993). A program evaluation of classroom data collection with bar codes. *Research in Developmental Disabilities, 14*, 1–18.

Saunders, M.D., Spradlin, J.E., & Saunders, R.R. (1987). A scenario for active treatment. *Mental Health and Retardation Quarterly Digest, 6*, 1–7.

Saunders, R.R., & Koplik, K. (1975). A multi-purpose data sheet for classroom recording and graphing. *AAESPH Review* [Predecessor to *Journal of The Association for Persons with Severe Handicaps*], *1*, 1–8.

Saunders, R.R., Rast, J., & Saunders, M.D. (Eds.). (1988). *A handbook for scenario-based active treatment.* Parsons: University of Kansas Life Span Institute.

Saunders, R.R., & Saunders, J.L. (1994). W. Edwards Deming, quality analysis, and total behavior management. *Behavior Analyst, 17*, 115–125.

Saunders, R.R., Saunders, M.D., & Saunders, J.L. (1994). Data collection with bar code technology. In T.I. Thompson & D.B. Gray (Eds.), *Destructive behavior in developmental disabilities: Diagnosis and treatment* (pp. 102–116). Thousand Oaks, CA: Sage Publications.

Seys, D., & Duker, P. (1988). Effects of staff management on the quality of residential care for mentally retarded individuals. *American Journal on Mental Retardation, 93*, 290–299.

Seys, D., Duker, P., Salemink, W., & Franken-Wijnhoven, J. (1998). Resident behaviors and characteristics as determinants of quality of residential care: An observational study. *Research in Developmental Disabilities, 19*, 261–273.

Seys, D.M., & Duker, P.C. (1993). Staff management procedures and changes in the distribution of nontargeted activities by residential staff members: A secondary analysis. *Behavioral Residential Treatment, 8,* 21–28.

Sturmey, P. (1995). Evaluating and improving residential treatment during group leisure situations: An independent replication. *Behavioral Interventions, 10,* 59–67.

Sulzer-Azaroff, B., Pollack, M.J., Hamad, C., & Howley, T. (1998). Promoting widespread, durable service quality via interlocking contingencies. *Research in Developmental Disabilities, 19,* 39–61.

Vyse, S., Mulick, J.A., & Thayer, B.M. (1984). An ecobehavioral assessment of a special education classroom. *Applied Research in Mental Retardation, 5,* 395–408.

Vyse, S.A., & Mulick, J.A. (1988). Ecobehavioral assessment of a special education classroom: Teacher–student behavioral covariation. *Journal of the Multihandicapped Person, 1,* 201–216.

Zarcone, J.R., Iwata, B.A., Rodgers, T.A., & Vollmer, T.R. (1993). Direct observation of quality of care in residential settings. *Behavioral Residential Treatment, 8,* 97–110.

10

Analyzing and Treating Severe Behavior Problems in People with Developmental Disabilities

Observational Methods Using Computer-Assisted Technology

Frank J. Symons and
William E. MacLean, Jr.

People with mental retardation, autism, and related developmental disabilities who exhibit severe behavior problems are at risk for leading restricted and relatively isolated lives (Meyer, Peck, & Brown, 1991). Aggressive behavior toward others, destroying public and personal property, and severe self-injurious behavior are three of the most damaging, disturbing, and difficult-to-manage classes of severe problem behaviors (Thompson & Gray, 1994). Prevalence estimates notwithstanding, there remains much to be learned about the prevention and treatment of such destructive behavior. The 1991 National Institutes of Health consensus conference on the treatment of destructive behavior in people with disabilities concluded that many of the severe behavior problems exhibited by people with mental retardation are multifaceted and require multiple methods of assessment and treatment. Our ability to assess and treat severe problem behaviors depends, in part, on reliable and accurate measurement. Important advances

This chapter was supported in part by U.S. Public Health Service Grant No. HD 35682 from the National Institute of Child Health and Human Development to the University of North Carolina at Chapel Hill.

also depend on our ability to approach old problems from new perspectives. Innovations in computer-assisted technologies for observational research are providing the basis for change and the promise of novel solutions for severe behavior problems.

One goal of this chapter is to describe the nature of the severe problem behaviors exhibited by many people with mental retardation and related developmental disabilities. A second goal is to discuss how recent developments in observational software and hardware have been applied to assist in the analysis and treatment of these problem behaviors. In this regard we outline general observational strategies used to assess and evaluate treatments for severe behavior problems in people with developmental disabilities. Next we provide specific examples of tactics used in applying computer-assisted technology to assess and treat self-injurious behavior. The use of this powerful technology is then illustrated with a case study. We conclude by considering conceptual, technical, and practical issues related to observational data collected with computer-assisted technology.

SEVERE BEHAVIOR PROBLEMS IN PEOPLE WITH MENTAL RETARDATION AND DEVELOPMENTAL DISABILITIES

The term "severe behavior problems" has emerged as a shorthand description of a variety of behaviors that are difficult to treat and have maladaptive consequences such as bodily harm requiring medical intervention or exclusion from typical social or educational activities (Schroeder, Tessel, Loupe, & Stodgell, 1997). They may be characterized along multiple dimensions, including the behavior's appearance or topography (form), how often it occurs (frequency or rate), how long it lasts (duration), how long before it begins (latency), its severity (intensity), and what happens before or after its occurrence (sequence). There are multiple forms of behaviors considered problematic, including physically aggressive behavior such as hitting others; verbal aggression such as making threats; self-injurious behavior such as head banging, hand biting, and eye gouging; repetitive stereotypic behavior such as hand flapping, body rocking, and hand mouthing; disruptive classroom or work behavior such as impulsive behavior, hyperactivity, and inappropriate vocalizations; and other inappropriate behaviors such as pica, rumination, enuresis, and encopresis (see Bates & Wehman, 1977, for an early review; Konarski, Favell, & Favell, 1992; Schroeder et al., 1997).

Prevalence estimates for severe behavior problems vary depending on the terms and definitions used (e.g., challenging behavior, destructive behavior, autoaggression, stereotypic motor disorder), the populations sampled (e.g., community versus institution, school age versus adult), and the method of measurement used (e.g., direct observation, surveys, questionnaires). Estimates vary, therefore, and range from 10% to 60% of people with mental retardation presenting with some form of severe problem behavior at some time in their lives. In addition, individual factors related to the presence of severe behavior problems include degree of intellectual impairment, history of institutionalization, presence of central nervous system disorders, sensory and communication impairments, and specific environmental contingencies (Davidson et al., 1994; Murphy, 1997; Schroeder et al., 1997). Finally, a growing body of research suggests that some forms or patterns of severe problem behavior may be etiology specific (e.g., the severe biting of the lips and fingers associated with Lesch-Nyhan syndrome).

In this chapter, we consider three of the most problematic categories of severe problem behavior: aggression, property destruction, and self-injurious behavior. *Aggressive behavior* typically refers to the intended infliction of harm or injury on another person. In people with developmental disabilities, aggressive behavior can occur in many forms or topographies, including hitting, biting, choking, kicking, spitting, and hair pulling (Reid & Parsons, 1992). Prevalence estimates vary depending on measurement strategies and certain personal characteristics such as gender (more males are aggressive than females), age (more adolescents and young adults are aggressive than children), and degree of disability (more people with severe cognitive impairments are aggressive than people with less severe cognitive impairments) (see Murphy, 1997, for a comprehensive review; Reid & Parsons, 1992). Aggressive behavior in people with mental retardation and related developmental disabilities (combining physical injury and threat of injury) occurred in 18% of the total population (total sample = 369,277) of one health district in a United Kingdom survey (Harris, 1993). Prevalence rates were twice as high in institutional settings compared with community settings. In the United States estimates of aggressive behavior also suggest lower rates for individuals living in community-based settings than for individuals residing in institutions (Borthwick-Duffy, 1994; Eyman & Call, 1977).

Property destruction is considered a severe problem behavior leading to increased risk for reinstitutionalization or continued institutional placement (National Institutes of Health, 1991). In a statewide population survey of 91,164 individuals receiving services from the California Department of Developmental Services in 1987, Borthwick-Duffy (1994) documented that approximately 7.1% of the sample had serious problems related to property destruction (i.e., serious property destruction within the past year and/or minor property damage on six or more occasions within the past year). Compared with aggression and self-injurious behavior, there is less detailed knowledge available about the personal characteristics and situational variables associated specifically with property destruction exhibited by people with mental retardation and related developmental disabilities.

Self-injurious behavior (SIB) is a highly problematic and damaging behavior with profound implications for a person's health and quality of life. Self-injury increases the risk for restrictive residential placement or a return to institutional placement, social stigmatization, and decreased opportunities to learn (see Symons & Thompson, 1997, for a review). Epidemiological estimates for the prevalence of SIB among people with mental retardation, autism, and related developmental disabilities range from 5% to 60%, depending on the methods used and the populations sampled (Borthwick-Duffy, 1994; Rojahn, 1994). Prevalence estimates for adults with mental retardation suggest that approximately one person in five living in a residential treatment facility engages in some form of self-injury (Thompson & Gray, 1994). Serious health problems are posed by persistent self-injury, including blindness associated with eye poking, subdural hemorrhage from forceful head banging, infections from self-inflicted skin picking, and anorectal disease resulting from rectal picking and digging (Bhargava, Putnam, Kocoshis, Rowe, & Hanchett, 1996; Hellings & Warnock, 1994).

Common to these three classes of problem behavior are reports that treatments are time-intensive, costly, and frequently ineffective in eliminating the behavior (Schroeder, 1991). At best treatment programs must remain in force for extended periods, and then changes in treatment personnel may lead to corruption of established treatment programs and resumption of behavior thought to be under control (Horner & Carr, 1997). Community-based service providers are unlikely to tolerate or accommodate individuals who are aggressive, destroy property, or self-injure, which may lead to continued institutionalization or reinstitutionalization. Moreover, severe behavior problems make it more likely that an individual will be administered psychotropic medication (Aman, 1993), abused (Crosse, Kaye, & Ratnofsky, 1993), and forced to spend time in mechanical or physical restraint (Jacobson & Ackerman, 1993). The seriousness of these problems cannot be overstated, nor can the need for effective and comprehensive interventions. Measurement plays a critical role in our ability to diagnose, assess, and treat severe behavior problems and to monitor short-term and long-term treatment outcomes.

GENERAL STRATEGIES FOR MEASURING
AND OBSERVING SEVERE BEHAVIOR PROBLEMS

A central tenet in our approach to treating severe behavior problems is that intervention plans must be informed by high-quality diagnostic and assessment procedures. In turn, our ability to assess and diagnose accurately the causal factors controlling an identified problem behavior depends, in part, on both conceptual and practical aspects of our measurement system. The primary assessment systems used in research for severe behavior problems in people with mental retardation include both indirect and direct measurement strategies, and their validity is determined by the usefulness of the results for their intended purpose (i.e., treatment research, diagnosis, survey).

Specific measurement strategies for surveying, assessing, and treating severe behavior problems include interviews, rating scales, checklists, and direct observation. These approaches vary in a number of important ways and have strengths appropriate to specific applications. A primary distinction concerns whether the behavior problems are measured indirectly or directly. By *indirect measurement* we refer to instruments specifically relying on subjective reports involving moderate to high levels of inference, such as rating scales, behavioral checklists, self-reports, and teacher/staff reports. By *direct measurement*, we mean the direct observation of behavior with minimal levels of inference. Although the primary distinction between indirect and direct measurement involves the method of data collection, there are attendant implications for both reliability and validity of measurement (Shores, 1988). Simply stated, the more inference required to record the behavior, the less reliable and potentially less valid the measurement system becomes, depending on the uses for which the instrument is intended.

Direct observational methods are typically used when the type of information gained through standardized testing, global rating scale assessments, or questionnaires is not appropriate for the specified purpose of inquiry (Sackett, 1978a, 1978b). For example, if measurement of problem behavior is driven by testing theory that involves the comparison of different groups of individuals with etiology-specific disabilities, then indirect measurement based on parent report may be valid for initial exploratory research (i.e., Do people with Prader-Willi syndrome or Smith-Magenis syndrome self-injure?). Observational measurement strategies may be better suited for subsequent research questions, such as elucidating the nature of the self-injury (How often does it occur? Under what circumstances does it occur?). Indirect measurement strategies that rely on clinician or parental impressions may be less valid because of the potential for biased reporting, inaccurate recall of instances of the behavior, or insensitivity to behavior change. In this chapter we consider only direct observation methods. Readers interested in a comprehensive review of available rating scales and behavior checklists for assessing behavior problems and psychopathology among people with mental retardation should consult Aman (1991).

Additional consideration of the diagnostic or treatment question will lead to a specific choice among observational sampling strategies. Observational data may be obtained by means of live observation, videotape, or film. Observational data can be recorded in real time as a continuous behavior stream or by time-sampling or interval-recording methods (MacLean, 1990). There are advantages and disadvantages associated with each strategy. Interval data collection schemes tend to require less expensive and complex equipment, make fewer demands on the observer relative to continuous recording, and result in higher interobserver agreement values (Sackett, 1978a, 1978b). The disadvantages include a relative insensitivity to low-rate behavior and the possibility of distorting data when modified frequency time sampling is used (Sackett, 1978a, 1978b). By comparison, continuous observation data collection is time-intensive and effort-intensive and typically requires the use of electronic or computer-assisted data recorders, but it provides a potentially rich data record that can support the use of sequential and time series analyses.

After deciding on an observational recording strategy and developing a coding scheme, observers must be trained rigorously in the use of observational methods before data collection begins (MacLean, 1990). After training, the standard index of reliability becomes a coefficient of interobserver agreement. In its simplest form interobserver agreement is based on two or more observers recording the same behavioral code at approximately the same time. This very general strategy becomes easier or more difficult depending on such factors as the type of data collection (interval or continuous), the complexity of the code set, the discriminations that must be made by the observer regarding whether particular behaviors occurred, and the length of the observation period (see Bakeman & Gottman, 1997; MacLean, Tapp, & Johnson, 1985, for more detailed discussions of these issues).

Finally, the unit of analysis (that event that is counted and tallied in observational research) is an important component of observational measurement validity. Deciding on an appropriate unit of analysis is often a conceptual exercise. Measurement of units such as concurrent and simultaneous behavioral sequences has heretofore been difficult and posed practical and technological problems. However, innovations in computer-assisted recording procedures and novel software have developed to the point that observational data can be collected sequentially and concurrent clusters preserved in real time. Behavioral sequences, for example, can be analyzed by comparing the actual number of transitions occurring between sequences of behavior with the number of such transitions that would be expected if the sequences were random. Analyses of this sort help determine whether the observed sequences occurred at or above chance levels. Such information can be extremely useful in increasing our ability to predict the environmental conditions in which certain patterns of severe behavior problems are likely to occur or that are associated with low levels of severe behavior problems. In either instance behavioral interventions can be formulated that create conditions in which severe behavior problems are reduced and more appropriate, adaptive behaviors are reinforced.

FUNCTIONAL ASSESSMENT OF SEVERE BEHAVIOR PROBLEMS

A recurring theme in the literature on severe behavior disorders for the past 25 years has been the recognition that these behaviors may serve a function for the people who exhibit them (e.g., Carr, 1977). For example, the behaviors might lead to positive reinforcement in the form of staff or teacher attention or be motivated by the desire to escape from situational demands. Methods for determining the function of severe behavior problems have followed two pathways, both of which rely, in part, on direct observation.

Functional assessment methods include direct observation, questionnaires, and semistructured behavioral interviews designed to infer function. For example, the Motivation Assessment Scale (MAS) (Durand & Crimmins, 1988, 1992) consists of 16 questions that have the potential to distinguish between the receipt of attention or tangibles, escape, and sensory stimulation as consequences of a target behavior. Similarly, direct observation of problem behavior in naturalistic settings has the potential to identify the presence or absence of co-occurring behaviors that suggest a similar range of possible motivations. Sturmey (1994) published a review of the available questionnaires and interviews purporting to assess the function of aberrant behaviors. He concluded that the available instruments have significant limitations and that additional research would be valuable in establishing their usefulness and efficacy. Duker and Sigafoos (1998) evaluated the MAS and reported that the reliability scores and factor structure varied depending on the index of reliability used and the topography or form of the behavior being evaluated. They suggested that the MAS should be used in conjunction with other assessment approaches that rely on direct observation or experimental analysis to generate and evaluate functional hypotheses.

It is generally thought that the value of functional assessment procedures is in generating hypotheses for intervention. Experimental functional analyses are used to confirm these hypotheses by directly manipulating environmental conditions (Iwata, Dorsey, Slifer, Bauman, & Richman, 1982; Van Houten & Rolider, 1991). Through the use of analog probes, variations in specific problem behaviors indicate their possible function. Data collection in functional analysis studies relies on direct observation because the assessment question is whether specific operationally defined behaviors are more likely to occur in one condition or another. For this reason, global ratings derived from observers are less helpful than frequency counts or duration measures because they may be less sensitive to behavior change. Consider the case in which unique stimulus variables associated with problem behavior might be overlooked during an initial assessment. Carr, Yarbrough, and Langdon (1997) reported on exactly this situation for three different individuals with autism and severe behavior problems (aggression, self-injury, and property destruction). Using direct observation, descriptive functional assessment, and experimental functional analyses, Carr and colleagues demonstrated that contradictory conclusions could be made about variables that maintain problem behavior depending on the presence or absence of unique or idiosyncratic stimuli during functional analysis sessions. For example, rates of problem behavior in the same assessment condition were higher when specific idiosyncratic stimuli were present in the session than when the stimuli were absent (e.g., small objects for one individual, puzzles for the next). For our purposes, these findings are important because they reinforce the need for detailed observation as an integral component in the identification of variables related to severe behavior problems.

COMPUTER-ASSISTED OBSERVATION SYSTEMS AND SEVERE BEHAVIOR PROBLEMS

A number of innovative software and hardware advances have been made in research on the assessment and treatment of severe problem behavior since the appearance of Sackett's seminal two-volume series on observing behavior in people with mental retardation and developmental disabilities (1978a, 1978b). The form, duration, rate, and sequence of stereotypies, aggression, and self-injury have been described and analyzed for school-age children and adults in community living settings and residential treatment facilities. Perhaps the first study to use direct observation and electronic data collection in this area was one on the environmental context of stereotyped behavior in young children (Baumeister, MacLean, Kelly, & Kasari, 1980). Detailed analyses revealed that behaviors covaried with ongoing environmental activity, that multiple stereotypies were functionally interrelated, and that particular teacher behaviors affected the frequency and/or conditional probability of a child's aberrant behavior.

Repp and colleagues developed observational software for palmtop and laptop computers for application in their research on stereotypic responding in a variety of environments (Repp & Deitz, 1990; Repp, Karsh, Van Acker, Felce, & Harman, 1989). Their software, which operates on a microcomputer, allows the user to collect observational data in real time in applied settings. Data may be collected in a variety of ways, including event-only or some combination of event and real-time duration, with both being recorded as either concurrent or mutually exclusive responses. The program is equipped to calculate interobserver agreement for each category of collected data. Utilities exist that allow the user to rearrange behavioral categories (i.e., combine, substitute, edit) for a variety of post hoc statistical analyses. Specifically, the configuration of their data analysis program allows observers to record events and behaviors that occur concurrently with the target behavior. The collected data are subsequently formatted to permit contingency table analysis of temporally proximate conditions or events and their influence on the occurrence of the target behavior (i.e., determining the probability of stereotyped repetitive behavior occurring given the occurrence of another specified behavior or event).

Emerson and colleagues have used computer-assisted technology to directly observe multiple topographies of severe behavior problems in people with mental retardation for the purposes of functional assessment and treatment planning (Emerson et al., 1996; Emerson, Thompson, Reeves, Henderson, & Robertson, 1995). In addition, their work is an example of the application of sequential analytic techniques to observational data. Emerson et al. (1996) used time-based lag sequential analysis to describe multiple forms of problem behavior by five individuals with mental retardation in two different settings. Conditional probabilities and associated z-scores were calculated for each individual to test for significant sequential dependencies. The authors pointed out that counting a time unit (e.g., 1 second) as the target event more than once in the context of time-based sequential analysis introduces noise into the test of the significance of sequential dependencies. In other words, if the target event can recur during the time specified by the lag (e.g., 10 seconds), then there is the possibility of artificially inflating the counts for the base or target variable. Their work also illustrates an interesting graphical technique to display exploratory time-based analysis results (see Chapter 4).

Bakeman and Quera (1995) have developed two related software programs for the purpose of easily and efficiently analyzing sequential observational data. A general standardized format for sequential data (SDIS) has been developed to fill a long-standing void in the sequential analysis of observational data. Specifically, SDIS represents the first real attempt to propose a standard for representation of sequential data. If used widely, such a mechanism would lead to sharing of data and programs with relative ease. Second, Bakeman and Quera have introduced a general-purpose computer program referred to as a generalized sequential querier (GSEQ). Essentially, GSEQ is a general purpose observational data analysis program for sequential data that runs on IBM-compatible personal computers in a DOS environment (see Chapter 18).

Finally, Kahng and Iwata (1998) (see Chapter 3) have reviewed specific computerized systems for collecting direct observational data on severe problem behavior. Fifteen developers and programmers of observational computerized systems were surveyed, and features of each system were reviewed, including the required data collection device, hardware operating system, data collection options, data analysis options, reliability statistics options, and price. As their review indicated, a variety of observational software packages are available, affordable, and applicable for assessment and treatment research in severe behavior problems.

SPECIFIC APPLICATIONS OF COMPUTER-ASSISTED TECHNOLOGY: ASSESSING AND TREATING SELF-INJURIOUS BEHAVIOR

Research conducted by Symons, Fox, and Thompson (1998) has been directed toward the assessment and treatment of SIB in individuals with mental retardation, autism, and related developmental disabilities. A specific aim of this research has been the evaluation of the opiate antagonist naltrexone hydrochloride as a potential treatment for self-injury either alone or combined with conventional behavioral interventions based on a functional assessment. Before medication evaluation, the possible behavioral or social functions of self-injury are assessed with direct observation using real-time recording procedures based on a mutually exclusive and exhaustive recording scheme. In the tradition of functional assessment, hypotheses are generated about possible controlling social variables after staff interviews are conducted and observational data are collected. Detailed staff interviews are conducted using the Functional Analysis Interview (O'Neill, Horner, Albin, Storey, & Sprague, 1997). Observational data are then collected in real time during typical daytime routines. These data are analyzed at two levels. The first level includes rate, duration, and other summary-level statistics for each individual's self-injury. The second level includes sequential analyses that yield observed and expected frequencies as well as conditional probabilities among the behaviors that may reveal possible controlling social variables. In general, SIB is subtyped by probable social function (i.e., attention, escape, tangible, or other).

The observational data are collected by computer-assisted devices such as hand-held Psion Workabout computers or hand-held optical bar code scanners. Interobserver agreement is calculated on a minimum of 25% of observation sessions for any individual during treatment evaluations and on 20% of observation sessions for any individual during assessment conditions. Two primary types of codes are used to record SIB and social interaction. Frequency or event codes simply require that the code be key pressed or scanned the moment the behavior or event occurs. Each time the behavior occurs the appropriate event code key is pressed or the code is scanned. Duration or state codes require the observer to code the behavior at both its onset and its offset.

The coding system is exhaustive, mutually exclusive, and multilevel. This means that there is always something to code (exhaustive) and that only one code can be associated with a particular event (mutually exclusive). Multilevel simply refers to the multiple levels of recording required. For example, SIB codes are one level, teaching staff or peer behaviors are another level, and codes designating the physical and social context are another level. Within each level, codes are mutually exclusive and exhaustive.

CASE EXAMPLE: A DESCRIPTIVE ASSESSMENT OF SELF-INJURIOUS BEHAVIOR USING SEQUENTIAL ANALYSIS

Behavioral research suggests that for some school-age students with disabilities there can be a relation between specific aspects of teacher behavior and the occurrence of severe SIB. Specifically, teacher prompting can increase the probability of SIB in some students with mental retardation and related developmental disabilities. It is not entirely clear, however, what effect the overall instructional or activity context may have on this relation (e.g., one to one versus small group versus large group). Given this consideration, we posed the following research question for a student named Mark with severe SIB: Was Mark more likely to self-injure after teacher prompts during one-to-one activity than after teacher prompts during a group activity?

Participant

Mark was a 12-year-old male student with autism and mental retardation requiring extensive support who exhibited SIB. He attended a self-contained special education classroom in a general education public school. Mark had multiple topographies of self-injury, including head banging, hand biting, head slapping, and leg kicking. Our initial assessment and teacher report suggested that hand biting was the most serious and most prevalent of these forms. Informal observations and teaching staff interviews suggested that Mark's SIB was most likely to occur during the early morning and afternoon classes during periods of teacher instruction.

Procedure

Mark was observed directly on each of 15 days for two 15-minute observation sessions in his classroom. Mutually exclusive and exhaustive data were collected continuously. Two trained observers used handheld optical bar code scanners to record the observation data. Teacher prompts (verbal, gestural, and physical) and self-injury were recorded during daily one-to-one and group teaching activities.

Results

Mark's overall mean rate of SIB was 12 times per minute based on 450 minutes of direct observation. In general, SIB occurred at a higher rate during group activity (mean, 13.3 times per minute) than during one-to-one activity (mean, 10.7 times per minute), although the overall difference was relatively small. This result, however, does not tell us how teacher prompts relate to Mark's self-injury. The total number of prompts was greater in the one-to-one activity condition (mean, 148.1) than in the group activity condition (mean, 89.0) (Figure 1).

Sequential Analysis

To answer our specific question about the relation between teacher prompts and self-injury, we conducted a sequential analysis. In general, this analysis procedure determines whether the probability that one event or behavior leading to another

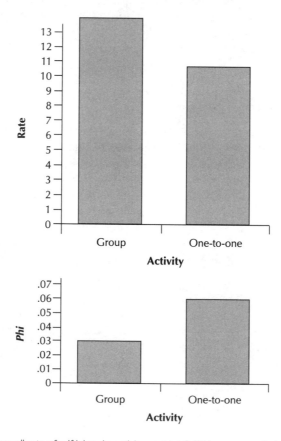

Figure 1.   Top, Mark's overall rate of self-injury by activity context. Self-injury occurred at a higher mean rate during group activity. Bottom, Results of sequential analysis suggesting that self-injury was more likely to follow teacher prompts during one-to-one activity than during group activity.

is significantly different from what would be expected by chance (see Chapters 4, 18, and 19). There are several different indices of sequential association or dependency that can be calculated depending on the specific research question and the nature of the data collected. Because the base rate of self-injury was greater in the group activity condition (mean, 13.3 times per minute) than in the one-to-one activity condition (mean, 10.7 times per minute), transitional probabilities were inappropriate indices of sequential dependency. Because the total number of prompts was greater in the one-to-one activity condition (mean, 148.1) than in the group activity condition (mean, 89.0), a z-score was a poor choice as an index of sequential dependency because it is sensitive to the total number of prompts (i.e., the antecedent variable). Subsequently, a phi coefficient was calculated as an index of sequential dependency for self-injury occurring within 5 seconds of teacher prompting.

Phi is simply a Pearson's correlation coefficient (r) for two dichotomous variables that controls for the total number of coded behaviors (Yoder & Tapp, 1990). A sampled permutation procedure (Bakeman, Robinson, & Quera, 1996) was used to compare the *phi* coefficients as dependent scores and to test the difference between the two activity contexts on the sequential dependency between SIB and teacher prompts. Sampled permutation tests repeatedly shuffle the observed data randomly and compute the mean difference to create an empirical distribution from which postshuffle difference scores can be compared with the observed preshuffle difference score. The mean r for the group activity condition was .03. The mean r for the one-to-one activity condition was .06. The sampled permutation test based on 10,000 shuffles showed the observed mean difference of .03 to be significant (i.e., 95% of the 10,000 chance differences between the means were less than the observed difference between the means). It is likely, therefore, that the observed difference would be repeated in other behavior samples from the same student. Furthermore, there was a stronger and more significant positive sequential dependency between SIB and teacher prompts during one-to-one activities than during group activities. Therefore, despite the higher rate of SIB during group activities, teacher prompts were more likely to result in self-injury during periods of one-to-one activity.

This is an important finding because it has several implications for subsequent analyses and intervention for Mark's self-injury. First, it appears that Mark's SIB is influenced differently by teacher prompts depending on the activity context. Second, it is likely that during one-to-one activity much of Mark's self-injury is negatively reinforced (i.e., self-injury results in escape from teacher prompts). Third, if Mark's self-injury during one-to-one activity is negatively reinforced, then an appropriate intervention can be designed specifically for this situation. The intervention would include at least two components: escape extinction and differential reinforcement of an alternative, appropriate form of behavior. It does not follow, however, that changes in SIB during one-to-one activity would reliably lead to changes in SIB during group activity because it is possible that Mark's SIB during group activity is under the control of different mechanisms. In summary, the use of computer-assisted technology permitted precise assessment of the conditions associated with self-injury that linked directly with treatment planning. Thirty minutes of data collection for 15 days yielded sufficient information to make meaningful statements regarding factors that appeared to influence the moment-to-moment expression of self-injury. Further assessment in the group setting using additional combinations of observational codes would be necessary to determine whether self-injury was influenced by environmental conditions that are subject to manipulation.

SOME REMAINING ISSUES

A number of issues remain in the use of computer-assisted technology to collect observational data for the assessment and treatment of severe behavior problems. First, practical issues related to technical assistance and support are relevant, particularly for users who work outside of university-based programs. With the development and continued refinement of electronic mail, the Internet, and the World Wide Web, some aspects of this problem may diminish. Nevertheless, computer-assisted approaches have unique hardware and software requirements that necessitate specialized technical assistance and support.

An additional practical consideration is time commitment. Although computer-assisted technologies facilitate data entry, storage, and descriptive analyses, there is a significant time commitment required for 1) staff training, 2) program modifications, and 3) analysis. In the first instance, unlike with typical paper-and-pencil recording measures, sufficient time must be devoted to training observers in the acquisition and maintenance of data with potentially complex coding schemes that require manual dexterity and rapid reaction time to navigate keyboards or other data entry devices. In addition, staff time and expertise must be allocated on a continuous basis for program modifications or customizations. Although several programs are prescribed and allow for only minor changes, in many cases there is sufficient program flexibility that familiarity with some minimal level of basic programming can be an asset. As new questions are asked, new code configurations, analysis options, and output parameters may be required. Finally, staff time devoted to analysis and interpretation of computer-collected observational data can be substantial. This is related, in part, to two problems, one preventable and the other unavoidable. First, in some cases the ease with which massive amounts of observational data can be collected by computer-assisted technologies appears to have elevated data collection above asking good research questions, developing specific hypotheses, and planning logical research designs. Thus, it is easy to produce an abundance of observational data in the absence of a clear analytical plan. Stating specific research questions or hypotheses and designing an observation strategy accordingly can prevent many of the logistical problems associated with exploring data sets and trying to find significant results. On the other hand, some research projects require large amounts of observational data, and the time devoted to their analysis and interpretation can be considerable and unavoidable.

There are also concerns that are both practical and conceptual related to low-rate behavior and representative sampling frequency. In the first case, if a target behavior is occurring at very low rates, then recording instances of it is problematic no matter what observational method is being used. Moreover, for those instances that are recorded, the base rate may preclude detection of contingencies among behaviors. There are no absolute practical algorithms to solve practical problems associated with low base rates of behavior. If the behavior is, in fact, problematic, this is a particular difficulty for researchers relying on computer-assisted innovations in real-time data collection and sequential analysis.

Conceptually, low base rates leave one puzzling over the correct interpretation of significant sequential dependencies determined by differences between z-scores, *phi*, and Yule's Q. In some respects problems of this sort appear to be similar to more familiar arguments concerning statistical versus clinical significance. For instance, in the case of Mark described above, despite the fact that there was a statistically significant context-dependent difference between the sequential dependency for teacher prompts and SIB, one wonders whether the difference between the observed rates of roughly 13 and 11 times per minute and the conditional probabilities of .03 and .06 is truly meaningful. On the other hand, such an analysis provides an empirical platform from which to answer the question.

Finally, there remains the question of representative sampling frequency, i.e., how much information is necessary before one can be fairly certain that it is representative. Although not a direct consequence of computer innovations, this problem is more germane now than before because we can now collect more observational data in greater quantities in real time than was possible before.

CONCLUSIONS

Innovations in technology provide much-needed assistance for researchers and practitioners trying to understand and treat the severe behavior problems of people with mental retardation and developmental disabilities. Observational data can be collected in real time with relative ease. Sophisticated analyses can be performed on the temporal relations among multiple classes of behavioral and environmental variables. In turn, these analyses can lead to the development of specific testable hypotheses and the evaluation of individually tailored treatments. The treatments themselves can then be evaluated with the same observational protocol (i.e., behavioral codes, sampling system) used to assess the initial behavior problem, thus ensuring a high degree of sensitivity to any possible behavior change. As individuals with significant disabilities and behavior problems continue to be included in all aspects of community living, continued innovations in computer-assisted observational technology will provide, in part, the basis for change and the promise of novel solutions for severe behavior problems.

REFERENCES

Aman, M.G. (1991). *Assessing psychopathology and behavior problems in persons with mental retardation: A review of available instruments.* Rockville, MD: U.S. Department of Health and Human Services.

Aman, M.G. (1993). Efficacy of psychotropic drugs for reducing self-injurious behavior in developmental disabilities. *Annals of Clinical Psychiatry, 5,* 171–188.

Bakeman, R., & Gottman, J.M. (1997). *Observing interaction: An introduction to sequential analysis* (2nd ed.). New York: Cambridge University Press.

Bakeman, R., & Quera, V. (1995). *Analyzing interaction: Sequential analysis with SDIS and GSEQ.* New York: Cambridge University Press.

Bakeman, R., Robinson, B.F., & Quera, V. (1996). Testing sequential association: Estimating exact *p* values using sampled permutations. *Psychological Methods, 1,* 4–15.

Bates, P., & Wehman, P. (1977). Behavior management with the mentally retarded: An empirical analysis of the research. *Mental Retardation, 15,* 9–12.

Baumeister, A.A., MacLean, W.E., Jr., Kelly, J., & Kasari, C. (1980). Observational studies of retarded children with multiple stereotyped movements. *Journal of Abnormal Child Psychology, 8,* 501–521.

Bhargava, S.A., Putnam, P.E., Kocoshis, S.A., Rowe, M., & Hanchett, J.M. (1996). Rectal bleeding in Prader-Willi syndrome. *Pediatrics, 97,* 265–267.

Borthwick-Duffy, S.A. (1994). Prevalence of destructive behaviors: A study of aggression, self-injury and property destruction. In T. Thompson & D.B. Gray (Eds.), *Destructive behavior in developmental disabilities: Diagnosis and treatment* (pp. 3–23). Thousand Oaks, CA: Sage Publications.

Carr, E.G. (1977). The motivation of self-injurious behavior: A review of some hypotheses. *Psychological Bulletin, 84,* 800–816.

Carr, E.G., Yarbrough, S.C., & Langdon, N.A. (1997). Effects of idiosyncratic stimulus variables on functional analysis outcomes. *Journal of Applied Behavior Analysis, 30,* 673–686.

Crosse, S.B., Kaye, E., & Ratnofsky, A.C. (1993). *A report on the maltreatment of children with disabilities* (Contract No. 105-89-1630). Washington, DC: National Center on Child Abuse and Neglect.

Davidson, P.W., Cain, N.N., Sloane-Reeves, J.E., Speybroech, A.V., Segel, J., Gutkin, J., Quijano, L.E., Kramer, B.M., Porter, B., Shoham, I., & Goldstein, E. (1994). Characteristics of community-based individuals with mental retardation and aggressive behavioral disorders. *American Journal on Mental Retardation, 98,* 704–716.

Duker, P.C., & Sigafoos, J. (1998). The Motivation Assessment Scale: Reliability and construct validity across three topographies of behavior. *Research in Developmental Disabilities, 19,* 131–142.

Durand, V.M., & Crimmins, D.B. (1988). Identifying the variables maintaining self-injurious behavior. *Journal of Autism and Developmental Disorders, 18,* 99–117.

Durand, V.M., & Crimmins, D.B. (1992). *The Motivation Assessment Scale (MAS) administration guide.* Topeka, KS: Monaco & Associates.

Emerson, E., Reeves, D., Thompson, S., Henderson, J., Robertson, J., & Howard, D. (1996). Time-based lag sequential analysis and the functional assessment of challenging behavior. *Journal of Intellectual Disability Research, 40,* 260–274.

Emerson, E., Thompson, S., Reeves, D., Henderson, D., & Robertson, J. (1995). Descriptive analysis of multiple response topographies of challenging behavior across two settings. *Research in Developmental Disabilities, 16,* 301–329.

Eyman, R.K., & Call, T. (1977). Maladaptive behavior and community placement of mentally retarded persons. *American Journal of Mental Deficiency, 82,* 137–144.

Harris, P. (1993). The nature and extent of aggressive behavior amongst people with learning difficulties (mental handicap) in a single health district. *Journal of Intellectual Disability Research, 37,* 221–242.

Hellings, J.A., & Warnock, J.K. (1994). Self-injurious behavior and serotonin in Prader-Willi syndrome. *Psychopharmacology Bulletin, 30,* 245–250.

Horner, R.H., & Carr, E.G. (1997). Behavioral support for students with severe disabilities: Functional assessment and comprehensive intervention. *Journal of Special Education, 31,* 84–104.

Iwata, B.A., Dorsey, M.F., Slifer, K.J., Bauman, K.E., & Richman, G.S. (1982). Toward a functional analysis of self-injury. *Analysis and Intervention in Developmental Disabilities, 2,* 3–20.

Jacobson, J.W., & Ackerman, L.J. (1993). Who is treated using restrictive behavioral procedures? A population perspective. *Research in Developmental Disabilities, 14,* 51–66.

Kahng, S., & Iwata, B.A. (1998). Computerized systems for collecting real-time observational data. *Journal of Applied Behavior Analysis, 31,* 253–261.

Konarski, E.A., Jr., Favell, J.E., & Favell, J.E. (Eds.). (1992). *Manual for the assessment and treatment of the behavior disorders of people with mental retardation.* Morganton, NC: Western Carolina Center Foundation.

MacLean, W.E., Jr. (1990). Issues in the assessment of aberrant behavior among persons with mental retardation. In *Assessment of behavior problems in persons with mental retardation living in the community* (NIH Publication No. 90-1642, pp. 135–145). Bethesda, MD: U.S. Department of Health and Human Services.

MacLean, W.E., Jr., Tapp, J.T., & Johnson, W.L. (1985). Alternate methods of software for calculating interobserver agreement for continuous observation data. *Journal of Psychopathology and Behavioral Assessment, 7,* 65–73.

Meyer, L.H., Peck, C.A., & Brown, L. (Eds.). (1991). *Critical issues in the lives of people with severe disabilities.* Baltimore: Paul H. Brookes Publishing Co.

Murphy, G. (1997). Understanding aggression in people with intellectual disabilities: Lessons from other populations. In N.W. Bray (Ed.), *International review of research of mental retardation* (Vol. 21, pp. 33–68). San Diego: Academic Press.

National Institutes of Health. (1991). *Treatment of destructive behavior in persons with developmental disabilities* (NIH Publication No. 91-2410). Bethesda, MD: U.S. Department of Health and Human Services.

O'Neill, R.E., Horner, R.H., Albin, R.W., Storey, K., & Sprague, J.R. (1997). *Functional assessment and program development for problem behavior: A practical handbook* (2nd ed.). Pacific Grove, CA: Brooks/Cole.

Reid, D.H., & Parsons, M.B. (1992). Aggression. In E.A. Konarski, Jr., J.E. Favell, & J.E. Favell (Eds.), *Manual for the assessment and treatment of the behavior disorders of people with mental retardation* (Tab BD3, pp. 1–7). Morganton, NC: Western Carolina Center Foundation.

Repp, A.C., & Deitz, D.E.D. (1990). Using an ecobehavioral analysis to determine a taxonomy for stereotyped responding. In S.R. Schroeder (Ed.), *Ecobehavioral analysis and developmental disabilities: The twenty-first century* (pp. 122–140). New York: Springer-Verlag New York.

Repp, A.C., Karsh, K.G., Van Acker, R., Felce, D., & Harman, M.L. (1989). A computer-based system for collecting and analyzing observational data. *Journal of Special Education Technology, 9,* 207–217.

Rojahn, J. (1994). Epidemiology and topographic taxonomy of self-injurious behavior. In T. Thompson & D.B. Gray (Eds.), *Destructive behavior in developmental disabilities: Diagnosis and treatment* (pp. 49–67). Thousand Oaks, CA: Sage Publications.

Sackett, G.P. (Ed.). (1978a). *Observing behavior: Vol. I. Theory and applications in mental retardation.* Baltimore: University Park Press.

Sackett, G.P. (Ed.). (1978b). *Observing behavior: Vol. II. Data collection and analysis methods.* Baltimore: University Park Press.

Schroeder, S.R. (1991). Self-injury and stereotypy. In J.L. Matson & J.A. Mulick (Eds.), *Handbook of mental retardation* (2nd ed., pp. 382–396). New York: Pergamon Press.

Schroeder, S.R., Tessel, R.E., Loupe, P.S., & Stodgell, C.J. (1997). Severe behavior problems among people with developmental disabilities. In W.E. MacLean, Jr. (Ed.), *Ellis' handbook of mental deficiency, psychological theory and research* (3rd ed., pp. 439–464). Mahwah, NJ: Lawrence Erlbaum Associates.

Shores, R.E. (1988). Highlighting analysis in applied behavior analysis: Designing and analyzing single subject research. In R.B. Rutherford, Jr., & J.W. Maag (Eds.), *Monograph in Behavioral Disorders, 11,* 144–155.

Sturmey, P. (1994). Assessing the functions of aberrant behaviors: A review of psychometric instruments. *Journal of Autism and Developmental Disorders, 24,* 293–304.

Symons, F.J., Fox, N.D., & Thompson, T. (1998). Functional communication training and naltrexone treatment of self-injurious behavior: An experimental case report. *Journal of Applied Research in Intellectual Disabilities, 10,* 1–20.

Symons, F.J., & Thompson, T. (1997). A review of self-injurious behavior and pain in persons with developmental disabilities. In N.W. Bray (Ed.), *International Review of Research in Mental Retardation* (Vol. 21, pp. 69–112). San Diego: Academic Press.

Thompson, T., & Gray, D.B. (Eds.). (1994). *Destructive behavior in developmental disabilities: Diagnosis and treatment.* Thousand Oaks, CA: Sage Publications.

Van Houten, R., & Rolider, A. (1991). Applied behavior analysis. In J.L. Matson & J.A. Mulick (Eds.), *Handbook of mental retardation* (2nd ed., pp. 569–585). New York: Pergamon Press.

Yoder, P.J., & Tapp, J.T. (1990). SATS: Sequential analysis of transcripts system. *Behavioral Research Methods, Instruments, and Computers, 22,* 339–343.

11

Observational Methods in Assessment of Quality of Life

David Felce and
Eric Emerson

Diary of a week-end: A Saturday for Christopher

At 7:30 A.M.: Christopher was sitting in his wheelchair and a day-nurse was feeding him his hot breakfast. . . . Christopher could not see what was on his plate. . . . He finished his breakfast at a quarter to eight, and then until 8:30 he sat and waited for a nurse to take him to the bathroom. He did not have anything on his wheelchair table-tray, although at one point another child gave him a broken wind-up toy and he smiled; the toy fell to the floor as he put his hand on it, and a nurse picked it up as she passed down the ward and put it back on his tray; but five minutes later it fell down again and then remained on the floor.

At 8:30 A.M.: Christopher was wheeled into the bathroom and lifted onto the wooden "potty-chair" (the commode). . . . Christopher sat in the potty-chair until 9 o'clock. Nobody spoke to him.

At 9:00 A.M.: Christopher was wheeled back into the ward and put on his cot, where he had his trousers put on, and his shoes and socks. Then he was lifted into his wheelchair and taken back to the bathroom, this time to have his face washed. He went back to the ward at 9:30 and was pushed into the little hobbies room for ten minutes as the ward was being swept.

From 9:40 A.M. until 12:05 P.M.: Christopher sat in his wheelchair by the piano at one end of the ward. He had nothing on his chair-tray. He was given a drink just before 11 o'clock. Then for a few minutes after drinks, another child went up to him and "wrestled" with him: this made him laugh and he waved his arms and got very excited. The same child then fetched him three torn playing cards, put them on his tray for a few minutes and then ran off with them again. Christopher spent two hours and twenty-five minutes in this same spot . . . during that time none of the ward staff spoke to him or put anything on his tray.

From 12:05 until 12:30 P.M.: Christopher was being fed his lunch. . . . The nurse did not sign to him or speak to him as she fed him. After he had been fed, he remained still sitting in the same place until 1 o'clock.

At 1:00 P.M.: Christopher was taken to the bathroom, toileted . . . washed and put into his pyjamas.

At 1:30 P.M.: Christopher . . . was pushed back to the ward and placed near the piano again.

From 1:30 until 4:15 P.M.: Christopher sat in the same place, by the piano. He had nothing to do and was not moved about the ward at all. Nobody spoke to him or signed to him. During this 2¾-hour period of sitting in one place with nothing to do, three children made a procession with their wheelchairs one behind the other and "marched" down the ward between the beds. Christopher, who all the time watched the children intently, laughed at the procession and waved his arms with pleasure. . . .

At 4:15 P.M.: It was supper time. Christopher was fed by a nurse who stood in front of him with the plate held up high; he could not see what was on the plate. . . . No nurse was seen to speak to Christopher at any time during supper.

At 5 P.M.: Christopher was taken to the toilet and then washed.

By 5:25 P.M.: He was lying in his cot.

From 5:25 until 7:00 P.M.: Christopher was lying in his cot watching the other children. Nobody gave him anything to do, nor communicated with him in any way.

At 7:00 P.M.: Lights were put out after the children had been given a last drink. (Oswin, 1973, pp. 81–83)

Maureen Oswin's closely observed account of the details of one person's day is a very powerful portrayal of neglect. However, the quoted passage provides no information on Christopher's state of mind or any feelings of satisfaction or dissatisfaction he might have had with the quality of his life. Instead, it gives an objective account of his actual behavior or "lifestyle." Yet it still seems to constitute a rich commentary. Understanding why this might be so is vital to appreciating the role that observational methods can play in quality-of-life assessment.

Quality of life was embraced in the 1990s as a concept of central importance to the debate about the effectiveness of services for people with developmental disabilities. The challenge of how to capture it has been increasingly taken up within service evaluation and research. Such interest is part of a wider view that quality of life is a relevant outcome for health and social policies and practices more generally (e.g., Orley & Kuyken, 1994; Renwick, Brown, & Nagler, 1996; Schalock, 1996a). However, despite its frequent use in academic and common speech, the concept remains ill-defined and contentious (Hatton, 1998).

Generally, the term is used to encompass the breadth of lived experience. In keeping with this, most commentators agree that quality of life is a multidimensional construct that must reflect different important domains of life (e.g., Campbell, Converse, & Rodgers, 1976; Cummins, 1997; Felce, 1997; Parmenter, 1988; Schalock, 1996b). Quality of life is often taken to encompass such diverse areas as personal well-being; health; psychological or emotional state; social affiliation and belonging; material circumstances and security; personal development and identity; self-determination; and contribution or role at home, in school or at the workplace, and in the community. There remains, however, a continuing debate concerning the significance, in conceptualizing and operationalizing quality of life, of objective descriptions of life conditions compared with the appraisal of the person's subjective satisfaction with his or her life. This debate in many ways reflects two distinct traditions within the quality-of-life literature (cf. Emerson, 1985; Zautra & Goodhart, 1979). The dominant approach among people who work with individuals with developmental disabilities has been the measurement of the quality of life as experienced by individuals. An alternative and quite distinct approach has as its primary focus the measurement of the quality of life available within populations, communities, or groups of people.

The former (individualistic) approach, which recognizes that the same life conditions are likely to be experienced differently by different people, has tended to conclude that the individual's perspective or subjective experience must constitute the primary focus of quality-of-life assessment (e.g., Taylor & Bogdan, 1996). However, adopting personal satisfaction as the ultimate arbiter of opportunity and experience is not as straightforward as it might seem (Felce, 1997; Felce & Perry, 1995; Hatton, 1998). The primacy of personal satisfaction as a measure of the life conditions a person experiences rests on the implicit assumption that subjective well-being reflects such conditions. However, as Edgerton (1990, 1996) has pointed out, there is an increasingly convincing body of longitudinal research that testifies to the intrapersonal stability of subjective well-being despite changing circumstances. As individuals adapt to circumstances and events, statements of satisfaction with life may be for the most part independent of the person's experience, deriving rather from personality, disposition, or temperament (Costa & McCrae, 1988; Costa, McCrae, & Zonderman, 1987; Diener, Sandvik, Pavot, & Fujita, 1992; Suh, Diener, & Fujita, 1996).

So there is an apparent paradox in the individualistic approach to quality-of-life assessment. The importance of individual self-determination and individual differences means that no objective standards of quality of life can be set. Yet, individual expressions of satisfaction may not reflect consensus views regarding the wider, multidimensional concept of quality of life. Edgerton (1996) concluded by urging a decoupling of the objective standards of quality from the subjective experience of well-being. Taking a population-based perspective, he argued that every effort should be made "to ensure that persons with mental retardation have access to better housing, health care, recreational activities, employment and everything else that an enlightened society can provide its citizens" (1996, p. 88). However, people should be individually free to choose between encountered options and to strive for satisfaction in life in their own ways, even though some of them inevitably will be more successful than others.

The distinction between individual-level and population-level assessment is one to which Felce (1997) also alludes. Personal values and self-determination in line with preferences are critical at an individual level. However, if quality-of-life assessment is operationalized at the aggregate population level, objective indicators for a defined group of interest may be compared with total population norms and ranges to establish the social equity of a group's circumstances. The distribution of a lifestyle characteristic, such as an index of health, or income, or activity level, will be influenced by many factors, among them personal values and choices. The distribution, therefore, contains variance attributable to the differences between individuals and the self-determination they exercise. If one assumes that the choices made by the population subgroup are representative of those made by the population as a whole, then comparison of the respective subgroup and total population distributions not only takes account of preferences but also reveals differences not attributable to the personal choices that people make. Moreover, one can use the burgeoning literature on the desires and preferences of people expressed through self-advocacy and consultation to test whether such an assumption might be warranted. For example, on the basis of the solicited views of people with developmental disabilities (Audit Commission/Social Services Inspectorate Wales, 1993) it is unlikely that personal choice explains their low representation in the work force, their relative state of poverty, or their low level of age-peer friendships. The use of objective measures (or social indicators) at a population level may provide a powerful measure of distributive justice by reflecting how life conditions affect the realized lifestyles of people to whom social policies are directed.

The direct observation of the lifestyle experienced by members of a defined group, of course, could provide an important social indicator within such a population-based approach. By contrasting the typical situation for people with developmental disabilities to that for people in the society as a whole one can explore the social equity of people's circumstances and whether environmental conditions support a lifestyle typical of the reference population. We subscribe to the view made by many quality-of-life commentators that the basic components of quality of life are those things that are common to all people and to the human condition and that they are the same for people with or without disabilities or any other particular characteristic (Brown, Renwick, & Nagler, 1996; Cummins, 1997; Felce, 1997; Schalock, 1996b). We also subscribe to the view that conceptualizations of quality of life may best be seen as a framework for measurement (Felce, 1997) or as an organizing concept (Schalock, 1996b) that can benefit from methodological pluralism (Heal & Seligman, 1996). A single measure or measurement approach may not adequately address the quality-of-life concept but may illuminate a particular aspect of it and make a contribution to its assessment in combination with other indicators.

Returning to "A Saturday for Christopher," the description is powerful because it touches important aspects of the human condition. Except for that small minority of individuals who choose the contemplative life, interaction with the environment characterizes people's existence unless they are traumatized, ill, chronically depressed or withdrawn, or in some other way incapacitated. Curiosity or an innate inclination to interact with the environment may have become integral to the human condition because of its survival value. Moreover, selection on a different time scale is also implied by socialization. Although cultures tolerate enormous variety in individual behavior, they typically shape conformity among citizens to certain norms. Such norms may be age and/or environment specific. For example, expectations about the nature of activity and what constitutes a conducive environment may differ for a toddler or an adolescent and for a church or a pub. However, the existence of expectations points to the fact that members of societies have a sense of what is culturally typical. Quality of life is a culturally bound concept, and there is a level of departure from the typical, such as that conveyed in the description of Christopher's Saturday, that can be recognized as such. If an identifiable class of people are shown to have life conditions and experiences that vary significantly from the typical, then the likelihood is that a sizable proportion of those individuals have a quality-of-life problem.

OBSERVATIONAL QUALITY-OF-LIFE INDICATORS

Given a growing consensus on the domain structure of quality of life, we now explore how observational methods might play a particular role. Drawing together contributions from the developed world, Schalock (1996b) listed eight core quality-of-life domains: emotional well-being, interpersonal relationships, material well-being, personal development, physical well-being, self-determination, social inclusion, and rights. Although some of these relate to observable activity (see below), the majority of quality-of-life concerns listed and their associated exemplary indicators are states of existence, circumstances that have developed over time or that have a sense of enduring beyond the immediate activity or concern of the moment. In this, they conform to the notion of accomplishment used by Gilbert (1978) and, in commenting on the goals of services for people with developmental disabilities, by O'Brien (1987). Examples from each domain include:

- Emotional well-being
  a. Spirituality
  b. Freedom from stress
  c. Contentment

- Interpersonal relationships
  a. Intimacy
  b. Affection
  c. Family
  d. Friendships
  e. Supports

- Material well-being
  a. Ownership
  b. Financial security
  c. Employment
  d. Possessions

- Personal development
  a. Skills
  b. Competence
  c. Advancement

- Physical well-being
  a. Health
  b. Nutrition

- Self-determination
  a. Autonomy
  b. Choices
  c. Personal control
  d. Self-direction

- Social inclusion
  a. Acceptance
  b. Status
  c. Roles
- Rights
  a. Privacy
  b. Access
  c. Ownership
  d. Civic responsibilities

   The concern of Gilbert and Gilbert (1992) is to emphasize behavior that leads to accomplishment. Not all behavior or activity of the moment is equally valued or valuable. A concern for outcome points one toward promoting behaviors that lead to or build accomplishment. The accomplishments listed by O'Brien (1987) have a similar preoccupation with conditions of living that are enduring. Community presence, community participation, competence, status and respect, and choice and rights refer to people having tenure within their communities; a variety of ongoing relationships with other people; a range of experiences, skills, and capabilities; a social reputation; and a degree of ability to exercise control over the course of life.
   Activity that can be observed is a more transient affair. However, neither Gilbert nor O'Brien suggested that accomplishment can be gained by any route other than the pursuit of everyday activities. For Gilbert behavior is one side of the performance equation; not all behavior may lead to accomplishment, but all accomplishments stem from or rest on behavior. Similarly, O'Brien includes a consideration of participation in valued activity within the definition and discussion of all five accomplishments. Accomplishment cannot be attained in a vacuum; it is gained or conferred as a result of one's participation in everyday life. It is the longer-term consequence of repeated social interaction or other forms of engagement in activity. Interaction and engagement thus could be seen as fundamental building blocks of human existence. Although not capturing the qualitative nuance of many quality-of-life abstractions, they are centrally concerned with how people spend their time. Fidler (1996) maintains that well-being results from participation in personally relevant activities whose meaning derives from self-care and maintenance, societal contribution, interpersonal engagement, or intrinsic gratification. Although motivation cannot be observed directly, the initiation, nature, and extent of participation in activity can be. Table 1 lists exemplary indicators amenable to direct observation classified by Schalock (1996b).

QUANTIFYING ENGAGEMENT IN ACTIVITY

The principal dimensions of engagement in activity are extent (time spent) and quality. Quality includes the nature of the activity (e.g., social interaction, leisure, household) and other salient aspects such as whether it was self-initiated (i.e., voluntary). Secondary dimensions include variety, pacing, and blocking. From consideration of these dimensions it becomes possible to determine how "busy" people are, the distribution of their time across specific classes of activities, the variety of activities in which they participate, and how their time is organized (e.g., the pacing of activity/inactivity).

The most flexible method for constructing an ecological record is time-anchored qualitative description, using the full breadth and subtlety of language to describe events, such as in the example from Oswin's research (1973) quoted above. However, there are advantages to summarizing large amounts of data and comparing data across situations if behavior is coded in some standard way and its duration is measured systematically. Coding schemes and category definitions in principle can reflect more or less precise distinctions in the quality of different forms of activity, together with cultural age-group and setting expectations, depending on the complexity of what can be achieved in practice. Time-sampling procedures have made multiple-category observation in the natural environment feasible, and small, portable computers have permitted real-time data capture on the same basis (see Chapters 3 and 4).

Clearly, observational categories and definitions can vary. For example, Felce, de Kock, and Repp (1986); Beyer, Kilsby, and Willson (1995); and Saxby, Thomas, Felce, and de Kock (1986) used different definitions of the underlying concept to observe engagement in the home, workplace, and community, respectively. The principal aim is to obtain a descriptive record of how people spend time. Engagement in activity is typically defined as participating in a social activity or getting ready for, doing, or clearing away one of a range of constructive or functional pursuits such as personal (self-care) activity, domestic (household) activity, gardening, leisure activity, or educational activity (see Felce et al., 1986). Other categories we normally use include challenging behavior (e.g., aggression, self-injury, destructiveness, stereotypy) and disengagement (e.g., passivity, aimless walking, unpurposeful activity). Environmental conditions and events experienced by the person being observed can be recorded at the same time. Thus, social interaction can be recorded and the reciprocity of the relationship established. Moreover, the observation of social contact received from others encompasses staff, caregiver, or supporter activity. This, in conjunction with observation of the

Table 1.   Observable indicators of quality of life

Dimension	Exemplary indicator	Observational measure
Interpersonal relationships	Interactions	Extent of social activity
		Quality and reciprocity of social activity
Personal development	Purposeful activity	Social, domestic, self-care, work, community, educational, and leisure activities
Physical well-being	Recreation	Leisure activity
	Activities of daily living	Domestic, self-care, and community activities
Social inclusion	Roles at work	Work activity
		Interaction with colleagues
	Roles in the community	Community activities
		Interaction with citizens

Source: Schalock (1996b).

person's engagement in activity, can determine the initiation and level of independence of activity.

The availability of portable computers has considerably simplified the acquisition of the type of ecological record we want to capture; we have used Psion Series 3 palmtop devices in our work (see Chapter 4). A typical study uses the activity categories described above to provide an exhaustive record of the behavior of the person with developmental disabilities being observed and a number of codes that relate to the attention he or she receives from staff. These codes might consist of all forms of verbal, gestural, or physical contact made to the person divided into two categories: assistance with activity (e.g., instruction, prompting, demonstration, guidance) and other forms of attention (e.g., conversation). Codes are then allocated to the QWERTY keyboard of the palmtop computer in a pattern that helps the observer. For example, we use the right side of the keyboard for codes concerned with the behavior of the person with developmental disabilities and the left side for codes relating to the staff attention that the person receives. We use the top line of letters for constructive engagement codes (e.g., Y = social, U = personal, I = domestic, O = leisure, P = other), the middle line for challenging behavior (e.g., H = stereotypy, J = aggression, K = self-injury, L = destruction, ; = other), and the bottom line for disengagement (e.g., M = disengaged). The letter keys A and D might then be chosen for the two staff attention codes for assistance and other contact. In practice, labels denoting the code names may be stuck to the keys, but the codes will be distinguished by their allocated letter keys in the analysis and data tabulation.

The first-level analysis produces a record for each code of the number of onsets (i.e., frequency of occurrence), the rate (i.e., frequency divided by total time), the cumulative duration of occurrence, and the percentage duration of

Resident ID	HL				Resident		HL		
Setting	House 1				Setting		House 1		
Session	Pre 1				Session		Post 1		
Serial code	HL111				Serial code		HL121		
Session time	1440				Session time		1850		
Code	Freq	Rpm	Dur	% time	Code	Freq	Rpm	Dur	% time
Y	12	.50	190	13.2	Y	22	.71	500	27.0
U	7	.29	226	15.7	U	8	.26	264	14.3
I	1	.04	34	2.4	I	8	.26	418	22.6
O	2	.08	58	4.0	O	1	.03	61	3.3
P	0	.00	0	0.0	P	0	.00	0	0.0
H	15	.62	504	35.0	H	7	.23	320	17.3
J	0	.00	0	0.0	J	0	.00	0	0.0
K	0	.00	0	0.0	K	0	.00	0	0.0
L	0	.00	0	0.0	L	0	.00	0	0.0
;	8	.33	263	18.3	;	2	.06	168	9.1
M	16	.67	646	44.9	M	12	.39	494	26.7
A	1	.04	10	0.1	A	15	.50	111	6.0
D	12	.50	143	9.9	D	15	.50	407	22.0

Figure 1.   Example observational output.

occurrence (i.e., cumulative duration divided by total time). Two observation session records are shown in Figure 1, the first taken before a staff training intervention and the second after. These records use the observational categories and codes described above. Resident H.L. was twice as engaged in social interaction (Code Y) in the second session. Other constructive but nonsocial forms of engagement (Codes U, I, O, and P) also increased. These were defined as mutually exclusive and therefore can be summed. Resident H.L. spent 22.1% of her time engaged in nonsocial activities before the staff training and 40.2% after, the main change coming from increased participation in domestic activities (Code I). Stereotypic movements (Code H) were the main form of inappropriate behavior in both sessions, occurring to some extent in conjunction with inappropriate vocalizations (included within Code ;). However, both occurred less in the second session than in the first. Increased participation in constructive pursuits in the second session is also reflected in a lower occurrence of disengagement (Code M). Note that the resident behavior codes sum to more than 100% because social and nonsocial engagement categories can overlap, as can social engagement and stereotypic movements. The staff training intervention had an effect on the total extent of staff attention that H.L. received, increasing from 10% to 28%, and on the proportion given in the form of assistance, increasing from virtually nil to more than one fifth of all contact.

ILLUSTRATIVE RESEARCH

In the following sections we illustrate the application of observational methods to determining the quality of life of adults with developmental disabilities.

Social Activity

Landesman-Dwyer, Stein, and Sackett (1978) and Landesman-Dwyer, Sackett, and Kleinman (1980) studied 20 group residential settings using a detailed observational measure involving several major activity categories, each broken down into constituent codes. The category *general social activities* constituted 12 activity codes: affection and courting, intimate contact, approving or rewarding, receiving approval or rewards, assisting, defending/protecting, being defended/protected/consoled, sharing resources, teasing and joking, initiating social interaction-general, responding to social interaction-general, and mutual general social interaction. *Negative social activities* constituted five codes: disapproving or punishing, receiving disapproval or punishment, competition or aggression, receiving competition or aggression, and other (to be specified). Secondary coding schemes covered the nature of any physical or gestural communication, the nature of any verbal communication, and whether assistance was needed or received. Time spent socially engaged and the effect of resident characteristics and resident group size on such activity were reported. Patterns of affiliation and friendship also were reported by Landesman-Dwyer, Berkson, and Romer (1979). In a subsequent study, Landesman (1987) described the use of a similar measure to evaluate the redevelopment of and resettlement from a large institution. In this study a further distinction was made in the nature of social activity between *general social interaction* and *special affiliative behavior*.

Perry and Felce (1994) also observationally measured the extent of engagement in social activity as part of an assessment of the quality of life in 15 community residences in South Wales. Social engagement was defined as a two-way process in which the person in question was either making a social overture to someone else who was attending to him or her or attending to someone else who was making a social overture. The extent of social contact received from other people also was measured. The results illustrate the range of social activity found between settings and the difference in social responsiveness between people who were more or less able. For example, more able residents were engaged in two-way social interaction, on average, about three fifths of the time that they received social contact, whereas such interaction occurred only about one fifth of the time for less able residents.

Purposeful Activity in the Home

Direct observation of the extent of engagement in activity has been the most frequently used outcome measure in British deinstitutionalization research since 1980 (Emerson & Hatton, 1994). In an updated review Hatton and Emerson (1996) considered 118 publications reporting the findings of 70 separate British research studies since the same year. Seventy-seven publications based on 47 studies provided evidence of the participation of residents in everyday activities. The majority of these publications (44 of 77) and studies (27 of 47) concerned directly observed engagement in activity.

The definition of engagement has been used with sufficient consistency across studies to allow for a collation of results (Emerson & Hatton, 1994). With averages weighted for numbers of participants, people in small community residences spent 48% of their time engaged in constructive activities, people in larger community hostels and units spent 25% of their time engaged, and people in hospitals spent 14% of their time engaged. This analysis reinforces the findings of individual studies, the majority of which were in favor of small community residences. However, it also shows that people with developmental disabilities still lead lives that are typically constrained in terms of constructive occupation compared with more general experience. The situation may have improved in the progressive move away from the institutional regimens described by Oswin (1973) and encapsulated by the low level of engagement found in hospitals by Emerson and Hatton, but the full occupation that characterizes the lives of others is still not typical for more than a few individuals with developmental disabilities.

Such concern is accentuated by the wide variation in resident engagement found in service models. Engagement levels in the studies reviewed by Emerson and Hatton (1994) varied from 8% to 74% in community residences, from 6% to 54% in community hostels and units, and from 2% to 23% in hospitals. In a descriptive study of 15 small community residences Felce and Perry (1995) demonstrated that variation in engagement levels (range, 13%–88%; mean, 49%) was highly correlated with scores on the Adaptive Behavior Scale (Nihira, Foster, Shellhaus, & Leland, 1974), a result consistent with findings from other studies (Felce et al., 1986, 1998). Felce et al. (1986), Felce (1996), Emerson et al. (1993), and Jones et al. (1999) also found an association between engagement levels and the level of assistance that people with more severe disabilities receive.

A particular aspect of the categorization of purposeful activity described above is that it highlights the extent to which residents with developmental disabilities control their own household lives, with or without support. The emphasis given to the homelike character of the residence in the replacement of institutional services presumably reflects an expectation that residents would be afforded access to the functional activities of everyday life. Seeing to one's own needs, albeit with support if necessary, is part of assuming an adult role. The study by Felce and Perry (1995) showed that such participation was virtually nonexistent for residents in the four houses for the least able residents and that it occupied about 25% of the time in the three houses in which the most able residents lived. Engagement in domestic activity overall averaged 13% of the time and was significantly related to resident ability. However, the contrast between these results and those from an earlier demonstration project serving equally disabled residents (Felce, 1996) shows that such a dependent role is not inevitable. Increased participation can be supported when staff decrease the extent to which they do household activities for residents and increase the level of assistance they give to residents to do the same activities themselves. This has been demonstrated by an experimental evaluation of staff training (Jones et al., 1999).

Participation and Roles in the Workplace

Integration in the workplace and productivity are two principal concerns to which direct observation has been applied in employment research. Chadsey-Rusch, Gonzalez, Tines, and Johnson (1989) took a narrative record of the social interactions of eight pairs of workers with and without disabilities who had worked in the same job for similar lengths of time. Each interaction was subsequently coded according to who was the initiator and the receiver of the interaction, if the receiver responded to the initiator, whether it was related to the work task or not, and its purpose. The latter was described by one of 11 possibilities: to direct, question, criticize, praise, offer assistance, request assistance, be polite, greet, tease/joke, inform, or get attention. Storey and Horner (1991) also observed the social interactions of workers with disabilities to assess their social integration in the workplace. In this case the purpose was to determine whether different employment contexts (individual placements, enclave arrangements, and work crews) gave rise to different levels of integration. Interaction categories included receiving assistance, requesting assistance, providing assistance, receiving instruction, providing instruction, receiving social amenities, providing social amenities, receiving compliments, providing compliments, receiving teasing, providing teasing, receiving criticism, providing criticism, work conversation, and personal conversation. They also observed engagement in work as a measure of productivity.

Beyer et al. (1995) compared the work engagement and social interactions of workers with and without disabilities using observational definitions that were derived from those used by Chadsey-Rusch et al. (1989) and Storey and Horner (1991). Engagement at work was defined as on-task, off-task appropriate (i.e., a socially acceptable behavior outside of doing the job), off-task inappropriate, and disengaged. Interactions were coded as direction, question, criticism, praise, offering assistance, requesting assistance, being polite, greeting, teasing or joking, gaining attention, general conversation, or other. The authors found that there was no significant difference between workers with and without disabilities in the percentage of time spent engaged in activity overall (87% and 88%), although workers with disabilities spent significantly more time doing the job and workers without disabilities spent significantly more time off-task. Overall, workers with disabilities initiated significantly fewer interactions and received fewer interactions from other people than workers without disabilities. However, there were no significant differences between the two groups of workers in the frequency of interaction and to whom people talked when job coaches were absent. When present, job coaches became the main focus of interaction for supported workers, and the content of interaction differed. Workers without disabilities more frequently directed others, teased and joked, and were involved in general conversations, whereas workers with disabilities more frequently received praise and greetings.

Participation in the Community

There has been considerable interest in the extent to which people with developmental disabilities are integrated into community life, particularly as a consequence of service reforms designed to promote such integration. Many studies have examined the frequency of community activities undertaken by people with developmental disabilities as a key indicator (e.g., Burchard, Hasazi, Gordon, & Yoe, 1991; de Kock, Saxby, Thomas, & Felce, 1988). However, it has been widely recognized that physical presence in the community is a necessary but not a sufficient condition for social integration (Bellamy, Newton, LeBaron, & Horner, 1990). This awareness has reinforced the research interest in friendship networks and time spent with friends and significant others (Howe, Horner, & Newton, 1998; Todd, Evans, & Beyer, 1990). However, there have been few observational studies of the role and activity of people with developmental disabilities when undertaking community activities or when with friends and associates, despite the fact that active participation and interaction on the part of the person with disabilities is integral to the notion of integration.

One such study of the engagement in the community of people with severe or profound developmental disabilities was conducted by Saxby and colleagues (1986). This study was designed to address the question of whether the role of the person with developmental disabilities was an active one involving participation in the substantive activities of the community setting or whether it constituted passively accompanying staff. It involved observing 10 people going shopping six times each and going out for a meal or a drink in a café or pub three times each. Two broad categories of engagement in activity were defined: *substantive*, i.e., participation as demonstrated by some motor activity relevant to the setting in question (e.g., in shops, pushing a cart, picking up purchases, offering money; in cafés or pubs, ordering, consuming food, drinking, smoking), and *interaction*, i.e., appropriate speech, gesture, or touch as a means of communicating with another person or observable signs of attention to another person addressing the participant in question. Within the latter category, interactions were distinguished as being with 1) an accompanying person with developmental disabilities, 2) accompanying staff, or 3) a member of the public. Substantive occupation occurred, on average, 29% of the time while shopping and 36% of the time while in cafés or pubs. Interaction with members of the public was low, about 2% of the time, and was similar between the two types of settings. Interaction with other members of the household party occurred 6% of the time while shopping and 11% of the time while in cafés or pubs. Constructive engagement and the level of interactions within the home for the same people were found to be higher in another study (Felce et al., 1986). Therefore, their roles as active participants were not realized as well in the community as in the home.

CONCLUSIONS

The central concern of direct observation is with people's interaction with their material and social worlds. The research described goes some way toward demonstrating the application of systematic direct observation of social interaction and more general engagement in activity to quality-of-life assessment and, thereby, setting an agenda to understand and improve the important living conditions on which opportunities for people with pervasive disabilities depend. The extract from Maureen Oswin's seminal study (1973) with which this chapter began illustrates the nature of life when opportunities to engage in social and nonsocial activities are not present. Such descriptions are echoed in the low levels of measured engagement commonly found in institutional settings. The concern, then, has been with the design of supportive environments that provide and realize opportunities for more diverse engagement in activity.

The extent of the problem varies across people. Several studies have consistently demonstrated a relationship between the extent of engagement in activity and the independent skills of the person, at least when the level of assistance received from staff was low. This is an obvious result but one that is frequently overlooked when the design of residential services is discussed. What staff or other supporters do when supposedly enabling people with disabilities to participate in ordinary living is an important issue. The nature of the support and its extensiveness need to be differentiated across settings according to the degree of disability of the individuals served. The degree of support, however, is not necessarily closely determined by the factors that have received the most interest in the process of reform, such as the physical characteristics of the setting and the numbers and characteristics of staff members. It is perhaps not surprising, but it is still salutary in policy terms, that the provision of small, decent, homelike, architecturally typical, well-staffed, and managerially autonomous community homes does not guarantee a typical or even adequate quality of life for residents. It is also salutary to find repeated evidence from a number of our own studies (e.g., Felce et al., 1998; Hatton, Emerson, Robertson, Henderson, & Cooper, 1995) that investment in staff alone does not enhance quality of care and quality of life.

Observation in the workplace has delineated the similarities and differences in the roles of people with developmental disabilities and colleagues without disabilities. An immediate concern has been with job retention, initially addressing productivity and then sufficient conformity to social norms. But productivity and social integration also can be interpreted from the perspective of the worker with disabilities, as part of the felt experience. Workers with disabilities appear to be constructively occupied in the workplace much of the time. However, their social relationships with colleagues are not entirely reciprocal. In particular, the presence of job coaches constitutes a barrier to social relationships with other people in the workplace. The emphasis on developing more natural forms of support stems from these findings. In a much more restricted way, the one observational study reviewed of people with developmental disabilities undertaking activities in the community broached similar issues. It is a line of research deserving of greater attention.

Finally, we return to the assignment for objective measurement in quality-of-life assessment we discussed initially, namely, to establish the similarity or difference of a subgroup and the society as a whole at a population level. Clearly, this calls for similar measurement across representative general population samples to establish normative or typical levels and distributions. Some of the studies, notably those of supported employment, have compared people with and without disabilities in similar environments and thereby have produced normative data. However, how the general population behaves at home or in the community has not been observed extensively, and it is only assumed that people generally organize their lives to be constructively occupied. That this assumption might be valid is at least suggested by the finding of a strong correlation between adaptive behavior scores and engagement in activity. People with developmental disabilities with good independent skills apparently choose to engage in activity most of the time (Felce & Perry, 1995). The impact of living with a more severe disability, therefore, may be seen in the time people spend not engaged in activity. The adequacy of service support may be assessed in terms of how well it helps people with more severe disabilities overcome such barriers. Direct observation of engagement and disengagement provides a sensitive measure. Even with the inclusive definitions of engagement used here, the measure still has utility because only the most able among the individuals we have researched approximate the fully engaged life that we believe most of us have and, indeed, take for granted. People with greater disabilities lead lives with fewer opportunities and unfulfilled potential, even in the better services that we have observed.

REFERENCES

Audit Commission/Social Services Inspectorate Wales. (1993). *Learning disabilities, quality and the All Wales Strategy: Enabling service users to set the agenda.* Cardiff, United Kingdom: Welsh Office.

Bellamy, G.T., Newton, J.S., LeBaron, N.M., & Horner, R.H. (1990). Quality of lifestyle outcomes: A challenge for residential programs. In R.L. Schalock (Ed.), *Quality of life: Perspectives and issues* (pp. 127–137). Washington, DC: American Association on Mental Retardation.

Beyer, S., Kilsby, M., & Willson, C. (1995). Interaction and engagement of workers in supported employment: A British comparison between workers with and without learning disabilities. *Mental Handicap Research, 8,* 137–155.

Brown, I., Renwick, R., & Nagler, M. (1996). The centrality of quality of life in health promotion and rehabilitation. In R. Renwick, I. Brown, & M. Nagler (Eds.), *Quality of life in health promotion and rehabilitation: Conceptual approaches, issues, and applications* (pp. 3–13). Thousand Oaks, CA: Sage Publications.

Burchard, S.N., Hasazi, J.S., Gordon, L.R., & Yoe, J. (1991). An examination of lifestyles and adjustment in three community residential alternatives. *Research in Developmental Disabilities, 12,* 127–142.

Campbell, A., Converse, P.E., & Rodgers, W.L. (1976). *The quality of American life: Perceptions, evaluation and satisfactions.* New York: Russell Sage Foundation.

Chadsey-Rusch, J., Gonzalez, P., Tines, J., & Johnson, J.R. (1989). Social ecology of the workplace: Contextual variables affecting social interaction of employees with and without mental retardation. *American Journal on Mental Retardation, 94,* 141–151.

Costa, P.T., Jr., & McCrae, R.R. (1988). Personality in adulthood: A six-year longitudinal study of self-reports and spouse ratings on the NEO Personality Inventory. *Journal of Personality and Social Psychology, 54,* 853–863.

Costa, P.T., Jr., McCrae, R.R., & Zonderman, A.B. (1987). Environmental and dispositional influences on wellbeing: Longitudinal follow-up of an American national sample. *British Journal of Psychology, 78,* 299–306.

Cummins, R.A. (1997). Assessing quality of life. In R.I. Brown (Ed.), *Quality of life for people with disabilities: Models, research, and practice* (2nd ed., pp. 116–150). Cheltenham, United Kingdom: Stanley Thornes Publishers.

de Kock, U., Saxby, H., Thomas, M., & Felce, D. (1988). Community and family contact: An evaluation of small community homes for severely and profoundly mentally handicapped adults. *Mental Handicap Research, 1,* 127–140.

Diener, E., Sandvik, E., Pavot, W., & Fujita, F. (1992). Extraversion and subjective well-being in a US national probability sample. *Journal of Research in Psychology, 26,* 205–215.

Edgerton, R.B. (1990). Quality of life from a longitudinal research perspective. In R.L. Schalock (Ed.), *Quality of life: Perspectives and issues* (pp. 149–160). Washington, DC: American Association on Mental Retardation.

Edgerton, R.B. (1996). A longitudinal-ethnographic research perspective on quality of life. In R.L. Schalock (Ed.), *Quality of life: Vol. I. Conceptualization and measurement* (pp. 83–90). Washington, DC: American Association on Mental Retardation.

Emerson, E. (1985). Evaluating the impact of deinstitutionalization on the lives of mentally retarded people. *American Journal of Mental Deficiency, 90,* 277–288.

Emerson, E., Cooper, J., Hatton, C., Beecham, J., Hallam, A., Knapp, M., & Cambridge, P. (1993). *An evaluation of the quality and costs of residential further education services provided by SENSE-Midlands.* Manchester, United Kingdom: University of Manchester, Hester Adrian Research Centre.

Emerson, E., & Hatton, C. (1994). *Moving out: The impact of relocation from hospital to community on the quality of life of people with learning disabilities.* London: Her Majesty's Stationery Office.

Felce, D. (1996). The quality of support for ordinary living: Staff:resident interactions and resident activity. In J. Mansell & K. Ericcson (Eds.), *Deinstitutionalization and community living: Intellectual disability services in Britain, Scandinavia, and the USA* (pp. 117–133). London: Chapman and Hall.

Felce, D. (1997). Defining and applying the concept of quality of life. *Journal of Intellectual Disability Research, 41,* 126–143.

Felce, D., de Kock, U., & Repp, A. (1986). An ecobehavioral analysis of small community-based houses and traditional large hospitals for severely and profoundly mentally handicapped adults. *Applied Research in Mental Retardation, 7,* 393–408.

Felce, D., Lowe, K., Perry, J., Baxter, H., Jones, E., Hallam, A., & Beecham, J. (1998). Service support to people with severe intellectual disabilities and the most severe challenging behaviours in Wales: Processes, outcomes and costs. *Journal of Intellectual Disability Research, 42,* 390–408.

Felce, D., & Perry, J. (1995). The extent of support for ordinary living provided in staffed housing: The relationship between staffing levels, resident dependency, staff:resident interactions and resident activity patterns. *Social Science and Medicine, 40,* 799–810.

Fidler, G. (1996). Lifestyle performance: From profile to conceptual model. *American Journal of Occupational Therapy, 50,* 139–147.

Gilbert, T.F. (1978). *Human competence: Engineering worthy performance.* New York: McGraw-Hill.

Gilbert, T.F., & Gilbert, M.B. (1992). Potential contributions of performance science to education. *Journal of Applied Behavior Analysis, 25,* 43–49.

Hatton, C. (1998). Whose quality of life is it anyway? Some problems with the emerging quality of life consensus. *Mental Retardation, 36,* 104–115.

Hatton, C., & Emerson, E. (1996). *Residential provision for people with learning disabilities: A research review.* Manchester: University of Manchester, Hester Adrian Research Centre.

Hatton, C., Emerson, E., Robertson, J., Henderson, D., & Cooper, J. (1995). *An evaluation of the quality and costs of services for adults with severe learning disabilities and sensory impairments.* Manchester, United Kingdom: University of Manchester, Hester Adrian Research Centre.

Heal, L.W., & Seligman, C.K. (1996). Methodological issues in quality of life measurement. In R.L. Schalock (Ed.), *Quality of life: Vol. I. Conceptualization and measurement* (pp. 91–104). Washington, DC: American Association on Mental Retardation.

Howe, J., Horner, R.H., & Newton, J.S. (1998). Comparison of supported living and traditional residential services in the state of Oregon. *Mental Retardation, 36,* 1–11.

Jones, E., Perry, J., Lowe, K., Felce, D., Toogood, S., Dunstan, F., Allen, D., & Pagler, J. (1999). Opportunity and the promotion of activity among adults with severe learning disabilities living in community housing: The impact of training staff in active support. *Journal of Intellectual Disability Research, 43,* 164–178.

Landesman, S. (1987). The changing structure and function of institutions: A search for optimal group care environments. In S. Landesman, P.M. Vietze, & M.J. Begab (Eds.), *Living environments and mental retardation* (pp. 79–126). Washington, DC: American Association on Mental Retardation.

Landesman-Dwyer, S., Berkson, G.B., & Romer, D. (1979). Affiliation and friendship of mentally retarded residents in group homes. *American Journal of Mental Deficiency, 83,* 571–580.

Landesman-Dwyer, S., Sackett, G.P., & Kleinman, J.A. (1980). Small community residences: The relationship of size to resident and staff behavior. *American Journal of Mental Deficiency, 85,* 6–18.

Landesman-Dwyer, S., Stein, J.G., & Sackett, G.P. (1978). A behavioral and ecological study of group homes. In G.P. Sackett (Ed.), *Observing behavior: Vol. I. Theory and application in mental retardation* (pp. 349–377). Baltimore: University Park Press.

Nihira, K., Foster, R., Shellhaus, M., & Leland, H. (1974). *AAMD Adaptive Behavior Scale.* Washington, DC: American Association on Mental Deficiency.

O'Brien, J. (1987). A guide to life-style planning: Using *The Activities Catalog* to integrate services and natural support systems. In B. Wilcox & G.T. Bellamy (Eds.), *A comprehensive guide to* The Activities Catalog: An alternative curriculum for youth and adults with severe disabilities (pp. 175–189). Baltimore: Paul H. Brookes Publishing Co.

Orley, J., & Kuyken, W. (Eds.). (1994). *Quality of life assessment: International perspectives.* New York: Springer-Verlag New York.

Oswin, M. (1973). *The empty hours: A study of the week-end life of handicapped children in institutions.* London: Penguin Books Ltd.

Parmenter, T.R. (1988). An analysis of the dimensions of quality of life for people with physical disabilities. In R.I. Brown (Ed.), *Rehabilitation education series: Vol. 3. Quality of life for handicapped people* (pp. 7–36). London: Croom Helm.

Perry, J., & Felce, D. (1994). Outcomes of ordinary housing services in Wales: Objective indicators. *Mental Handicap Research, 7,* 286–311.

Renwick, R., Brown, I., & Nagler, M. (1996). *Quality of life in health promotion and rehabilitation: Conceptual approaches, issues, and applications.* Thousand Oaks, CA: Sage Publications.

Saxby, H., Thomas, M., Felce, D., & de Kock, U. (1986). The use of shops, cafés and public houses by severely and profoundly mentally handicapped adults. *British Journal of Mental Subnormality, 32,* 69–81.

Schalock, R.L. (Ed.). (1996a). *Quality of life: Vol. I. Conceptualization and measurement.* Washington, DC: American Association on Mental Retardation.

Schalock, R.L. (1996b). Reconsidering the conceptualization and measurement of quality of life. In R.L. Schalock (Ed.), *Quality of life: Vol. I. Conceptualization and measurement* (pp. 123–139). Washington, DC: American Association on Mental Retardation.

Storey, K., & Horner, R.H. (1991). Social interactions in three supported employment options: A comparative analysis. *Journal of Applied Behavior Analysis, 24,* 349–360.

Suh, E., Diener, E., & Fujita, F. (1996). Events and subjective well-being: Only recent events matter. *Journal of Personality and Social Psychology, 70,* 1091–1102.

Taylor, S.J., & Bogdan, R. (1996). Quality of life and the individual perspective. In R.L. Schalock (Ed.), *Quality of life: Vol. I. Conceptualization and measurement* (pp. 11–22). Washington, DC: American Association on Mental Retardation.

Todd, S., Evans, G., & Beyer, S. (1990). More recognised than known: The social visibility and attachment of people with developmental disabilities. *Australia and New Zealand Journal of Developmental Disabilities, 16,* 207–218.

Zautra, A.J., & Goodhart, D. (1979). Quality of life indicators: A review of the literature. *Community Mental Health Review, 4,* 1–10.

IV

Applications in Education and Families

12

Observing Complex
Adult–Child Interactions

Computer-Supported Coding, Analysis, and Graphing

Ann P. Kaiser,
Jon Tapp,
Ned A. Solomon,
Elizabeth M. Delaney,
Sara S. Ezell,
Peggy P. Hester, and
Terry B. Hancock

Collecting, managing, and analyzing complex data is a challenge for language intervention researchers. Language is composed of discrete units of meaning (e.g., morphemes, words) that are linked together to represent relational meanings (expressed by sentences). Sentences, and multiword utterances approximating sentences, have both linguistic structure and social meanings. Particular forms of language used by speakers (e.g., comments, expansions, instructions) present or respond to specific behavioral demands by others (e.g., questions, models, instructions). Because interactions between conversational partners are of special

The development of the programs described in this chapter was supported by the National Institute of Child Health and Human Development (Grant No. 9OYM0002) and the National Institute of Mental Health (Grant No. R01MH54629).

interest to language intervention researchers, the language and behavior of two individuals is coded concurrently. In our language intervention research systematic changes in the linguistic and social behavioral dimensions of both parent and child language use in conversational contexts are the focus. Measurement of systematic change requires precise, reliable measurement of the specific aspects of language form and use and rapid analysis of data to examine trends in these measures during intervention.

Both the complexity of the language system and the need to analyze language from multiple perspectives within a single study influence the selection and use of data collection and analysis systems. The requisite features of such systems are: 1) the system must be able to encode language data at three levels concurrently: linguistic form, behavior of the individual, and interactions among individuals; 2) the system must be able to provide rapid and accurate analysis of data for all three levels; 3) the system must be able to encode and analyze language and behavior for two speakers in ongoing interactions; and 4) the system must be able to interface with secondary data analysis methods that will be used to summarize data, display data graphically for individuals, and analyze data for groups of participants.

Computer technology and the development of data entry, summary, and analysis programs have advanced language intervention research by streamlining all aspects of data collection and preparation. The flexibility, reliability, and speed with which data can be entered, summarized, and analyzed using this technology allow researchers to collect larger samples of data and to use the data that have been collected in more than one analysis, without recoding and reentry. These features, in turn, increase both the reliability of data analysis and the efficiency of the process. Automatic systems for counting, summarizing, and computing reliability free research assistants to complete coding and transcription tasks that require human decision making rather than spending time on routine counting and calculations. Finally, increasing the precision and efficiency of data analysis allows the researcher to focus on higher-level graphic analyses for single-subject design studies, statistical analyses of data in group designs, and interpreting the outcomes of those analyses.

The benefits for intervention researchers using single-subject designs are especially important. In single-subject designs common to applied behavior analysis (Kazdin, 1982), data from baseline and intervention sessions are summarized and graphed for visual inspection. Intervention research conducted within an applied behavior analysis framework requires frequent observation sessions within relatively brief periods of time. For example, several parent-training sessions may be conducted during a week. Research implementation decisions and evaluation of treatment efficacy are based on visual inspection of the levels and trends depicted in data displayed graphically. Single-subject designs are well suited for investigations of language intervention; however, the feasibility of such designs has traditionally been constrained by the demands of complex coding of language data, summarization of data, and preparation of graphs for visual inspection. The development of computer-based entry and analysis programs such as those described in this chapter increases the feasibility of single-subject designs by reducing the time required for these tasks. Although such efficiencies are notable in any case, the contributions in the area of language intervention are particularly noteworthy because they increase the scope of experimental analysis of behavior that can be undertaken.

OVERVIEW

This chapter describes a computer-supported system for coding and analyzing complex behavioral data collected in studies of language intervention. The composite system, *KIDTALKER* (Tapp, Kaiser, Solomon, Delaney, & Ezell, 1999), was developed to support a longitudinal program of research focusing on parent-implemented language interventions for children at risk for and with identified language disabilities. The chapter is organized into three sections: 1) an overview of the research program, 2) a description of the *KIDTALKER* software system, and 3) directions for future development of related systems to support language intervention research.

MILIEU TEACHING RESEARCH PROGRAM

Milieu Teaching is a naturalistic, conversation-based approach to teaching children new communication skills in the context of everyday interactions with adults (Hart & Rogers-Warren, 1978). Since 1983 the Milieu Teaching Group at Vanderbilt University has been engaged in research to improve language and communication skills for preschool-age children who are at risk for school failure and children with identified disabilities (see Kaiser, Lambert, Hancock, & Hester, 1998, for a review of this research). Our initial studies focused on demonstrations of the effectiveness of Milieu Teaching procedures implemented by therapists and teachers using primarily single-subject designs. Subsequent studies have investigated applications of Milieu Teaching by parents (e.g., Alpert & Kaiser, 1992; Delaney & Kaiser, 1998; Hemmeter & Kaiser, 1994) and implementation of Milieu Teaching with multiple partners (Hester & Kaiser, in press). We have compared a range of approaches to naturalistic language intervention using group designs (Yoder, Kaiser, & Alpert, 1991; Yoder et al., 1995). These comparison-of-treatment studies continue as we seek to determine the most effective combination of therapist-implemented and parent-implemented treatments to facilitate language development in children with significant language delays (Kaiser et al., 1998).

Our work also examines the effect of multicomponent naturalistic interventions to promote communication development and positive social behavior on at-risk children enrolled in Head Start and other low-income child care centers (Kaiser & Hester, 1997). The hallmark of this program of research is its focus on early intervention in the context of everyday adult–child interactions. Typically, we collect data during play interactions involving children and their caregivers. Videotaping is used to collect samples of interactions in child care centers, clinic play rooms, and homes. A typical videotaped sample of an adult–child interaction to be analyzed is 15–30 minutes in length, includes a child and an adult engaged in play and conversation, and yields 300–800 utterances and instances of nonverbal behavior.

Over time, our program of research has evolved to 1) include larger numbers of child participants, as required by group designs in comparison-of-treatment and prevention studies (e.g., 90–180 children per study); 2) incorporate repeated measures across settings, time, and conversational partners, as needed to analyze the generalized, maintained, and long-term effects of treatments; and 3) use more complex systems to code communicative interactions, reflecting changes in our conceptual understanding of the process of communication and our broadening interests in the relationship between language and social behavior. For example, our ongoing study of a multicomponent intervention to promote communication development and prevent problems in social behavior (Kaiser & Hester, 1997) involves 180 children and their parents. The study is longitudinal; each family is observed six times during a 3-year period. One half of the sample is randomly assigned to treatment, which includes direct intervention with the child and intervention to teach parents to implement language and behavior support strategies. These two portions of the multicomponent intervention use single-subject research designs and require collection of more than 50 data points in child care and home settings. Each observational session is coded for adult behavior (parent or therapist) and child behavior. The linguistic complexity of adult and child language as measured by mean length of utterance and number of different words, language teaching by the adult and functional language use by the child, and aspects of social behavior for both the adult and child are coded for each session. The three levels of measurement (linguistic, functional, and social behavior) correspond to the goals of the intervention: increasing child language complexity, teaching the child new forms of and functions for language, and improving positive social behavior during adult–child interactions. Therapist-implemented and parent-implemented portions of the intervention occur separately but concurrently. Data for each intervention session are used in making decisions about procedures and targets for the next sessions in both portions of the intervention. Rapid coding and analysis of data are essential because intervention sessions with children and families are conducted two to four times each week. Approximately 30 children and their families participate concurrently in the intervention phase of the study. Longitudinal follow-up observations are conducted in the families' homes for 2 years after the intensive intervention. To ensure a high level of reliability in data coding, reliability checks are conducted by having two observers code approximately 20% of the observation data. Reliability samples are distributed across participants, conditions, settings, and primary observers. Reliability is monitored for each child's data on an ongoing basis. Retraining of observers and independent recoding of selected data are initiated if reliability checks indicate less than 80% reliability on target measures.

KIDTALKER: COMPUTER SOFTWARE FOR CODING, ANALYZING, AND SUMMARIZING DYADIC INTERACTIONS

The *KIDTALKER* software was designed to allow accurate, rapid, and multilevel coding of linguistic and behavioral data collected from videotapes of adult–child interactions. The software consists of existing language analysis programs and new programs specifically created for our language intervention research. Our conceptual assumptions about the nature of adult–child communication and the goals of intervention are reflected in the software's focus on individual utterances as the primary unit of analysis; the specific categories and definitions used to code utterances; the structural analysis of teaching episodes or sequences of adult–child behavior; and the conventions for counting, summarizing, and presenting data. The software is described in terms of its current application; however, several generations of closely related systems preceded the system described

Table 1.   Components of the *KIDTALKER* system

Component	Description
SALT software: Transcript entry	Transcriptions of child and adult utterances are entered following *SALT* protocol for segmentation and punctuation.
SALT software: Code entry	Codes for individual child and adult utterances and selected nonverbal behaviors are entered using *SALT* protocol.
Summary program: KIDTALK.EXE	Coded data are counted by category and episode; frequencies, percentages, and correct and incorrect episodes are calculated. Data are calculated for child and adult.
SALT software: Linguistic analysis	Linguistic analysis is run separately for adult and child utterances already transcribed and entered. Mean length of utterance, diversity of vocabulary, and other measures are reported for both speakers.
New vocabulary analysis: VOCAB.EXE	Novel word roots are identified in each sample. These words are compared with the individual child's list of all words to identify first occurrences of new words. A list of new words and a frequency count of new words is saved. The child's list of words is modified to include newly identified words in each session.
Reliability analysis: *SALTRELY*	Data coded independently by two observers are compared for each utterance and for sequences of behavior in episodes. Percentages of agreement are calculated for individual behaviors and categories of behavior. Data are compiled into a reliability summary for the session.

here. Our intention was to develop a framework for a dynamic system that could be adapted to fit emergent issues and questions in our program of research. Thus, the core system has been adapted for use in several studies by changing the codes, summary programs, and format output resulting from the software.

An overview of the *KIDTALKER* system is contained in Table 1. Each component of the system is described below. Examples illustrating each component are included with the descriptions. Technical requirements for the system are described briefly. Table 2 provides a summary of the steps in data collection, coding, summarization, analysis, and graphing.

Systematic Analysis of Language Transcripts (SALT): Transcribing, Entering, and Analyzing Linguistic Data

SALT[1] (Miller & Chapman, 1996) is a set of computer programs created to analyze language samples from one or more speakers during communicative interactions. *SALT* allows clinicians and researchers to transcribe language samples into a format for studying several components of language, including lexical, syntactic, and semantic categories. For our research purposes *SALT* is used to compute mean length of utterance, frequency of utterances of one to six or more words, lists and

---

[1]*SALT* was developed by Jon F. Miller and Robin S. Chapman at The Waisman Center at the University of Wisconsin–Madison. Single-user and site-licensed versions are available from the software's originators. *SALT 5.0* is a Windows-compatible format and includes extensive options for data analysis that are not described here.

Table 2.   Sequence of data coding and analysis

1. Collect videotaped sample of adult–child interaction
2. Transcribe utterances from videotapes using *SALT* protocol
3. Verify transcription by a second observer
4. Code adult and child data from videotapes and transcripts using *SALT* protocol
5. Run linguistic analysis using *SALT* protocol
6. Run summary program
7. Run new vocabulary program
8. Run reliability program (20% of samples)
9. Import data of Lotus *Freelance* graphics program for display
10. Import data to individual child database for further analysis
11. Import reliability data to reliability database

frequencies of word roots and bound morphemes, and categorization of different parts of speech used in and missing from an individual's language sample. Most important, *SALT* provides a medium for affixing a specific set of linguistic and behavioral codes to individual lines of dialogue. This coding of individual utterances is the core of our behavioral observation system (Delaney, Ezell, Solomon, Hancock, & Kaiser, 1997). An overview of the codes is given in Table 3.

Figure 1 shows a few lines of a coded transcript file. The first character in each line is a code that identifies the speaker (i.e., "c" for child, "a" for adult). The first characters also are used to denote comment lines with special characters (i.e., "+") that are informational but are ignored by the linguistic and code analysis program. The second character is always a space, followed by the transcription of the actual text or dialogue (i.e., "give me the ball"). Codes are entered in the *SALT* format by placing them in square brackets before the ending punctuation in a particular line. For example, in Figure 1 the first adult utterance was coded [yq], denoting a yes/no question. The first child utterance was coded [cmr], denoting a "responsive child comment" or a comment by the child in response to a question

```
 1    $ Child, Adult (speaker identification line)
 2    + ID: .001
 3    + CHILD NAME: Turner
 4    + SEX: male
 5    + SESSION: Baseline #1
 6    + SITE: Kennedy Center
 7    + ADULT: Mom
 8    + DOE: (date of event) 10/30/99
 9    + TRANSCRIBER: AP
10    + DOT: (date of transcription) 10/30/99
11    + VERIFIER: NAS
12    + DOV: (date of verification/coding) 10/30/99
13    − 12:31 (starting time of session)
14    a are you ready to start [yq]? (an adult yes-or-no question)
15    c yes [cmr]. (a child comment in response to a question)
16    a I have two ball/s [dt]. (an adult descriptive talk)
17    a the blue ball is go/ing down [dt]. (an adult descriptive talk)
18    c that was fast [cmi]! (a child-initiated comment)
19    a it/'s fast/er than the yellow ball [mex]! (an adult meaning expansion)
20    c yay, mine win/ning the race [cmi]! (a child-initiated comment)
21    a yours won the race [lex]. (an adult lexical expansion)
```

Figure 1.   Sample *SALT* transcript with bracketed codes.

Table 3.   Overview of *KIDTALKER* behavioral codes

Adult behaviors	Codes	Child behaviors	Codes	Miscellaneous	Codes
Descriptive talk	[DT]	Initiated utterance	[-i]	Off-camera	+[OC]
Other	[O]	Response to prompt	[-r]	Pause	=(P)
Yes-or-no question	[YQ]	Spontaneous imitation	[-s]	Transition	+[transition]
Request for clarification	[REC]	Comment	[CM]	End of transition	+[endtransition]
Model	[MO]	Question	[Q]	Trainer teaching	+[TT]
Test mand	[TM]	Request	[R]	Trainer praise	+[TP]
Real mand	[RM]	Child verbal negative	[CVN]	Trainer neutral	+[TN]
Nonverbal command	[NVC]	Child physical negative	[CPN]		
Indirect command	[IC]	Compliance	[C]		
Direct command	[DC]	Noncompliance	[NC]		
Adult behavioral response	[ABR]	Accurate	[A]		
Nonverbal imitation	[I]	Not accurate	[NA]		
Verbal mapping	[VM]	Child behavioral response	[CBR]		
Correction	[COR]	Nonverbal request	[NVR]		
Reflective statement	[RF]	Nonverbal behavior	[NVB]		
Repeat	[RE]	Child no time	[CNT]		
Linguistic expansion	[LEX]	Appropriate no response	+[CANR]		
Meaning expansion	[MEX]	Unintelligible	[CX]		
Physical follow-through	[PFT]				
Verbal follow-through	[VFT]				
Physical praise	[PP]				
Unlabeled praise	[UP]				
Labeled praise	[LP]				
Adult physical negative	[APN]				
Adult verbal negative	[AVN]				
Not following child's lead	[FL]				
Adult no time	[ANT]				
Adult no response	;[PANR]				
Adult unintelligible	[AX]				

or a behavioral or linguistic prompt by the adult. The Code Summary function of *SALT* provides the frequency counts for individual codes. Because codes are printed adjacent to utterances, it is relatively easy to check for coding errors by reviewing the transcript.

Transcription and Coding in SALT   The first step in the analysis of a language sample is the transcription of a videotaped session of a parent–child or trainer–child communicative interaction. Research assistants, trained in using the *SALT* program and the specific *SALT* rules for typing words and utterances, transcribe speaker utterances from videotapes of the session. The transcription of a 10-minute session takes approximately 30–120 minutes, depending on the number of verbalizations, the quality of the recording, and, most important, the intelligibility of the speakers. To ensure the reliability of the transcription, each transcript is reviewed by a second transcriber while watching the videotape. This review is used to verify the transcription and to check the format to determine if the *SALT* transcription rules were followed. After the transcription has been verified a coder affixes the behavior codes to each line of dialogue. In some cases, nonverbal communicative behaviors, such as nonverbal requests or commands and physical positives and negatives, also are coded. Ten-minute transcripts can take 45–180 minutes to code, depending on the number of verbalizations, the number of nonverbal behaviors being observed, and the complexity of behavior sequences. For example, parent–child baseline sessions occurring before the parent has been taught systematic language support strategies are more time consuming to code because behavioral sequences do not follow a predictable pattern. There may be many incomplete or partially correct attempts at Milieu Teaching episodes. To determine the reliability, two coders independently code 20% of the sessions for each adult–child dyad. Coding by the two individuals for these reliability sessions is compared using the *SALTRELY* (Tapp et al., 1999) program (part of the *KIDTALKER* software package) described below.

Coded data are used to quantify the use of specific intervention strategies, to determine the accuracy of the implementation of the intervention strategies, to quantify sequences of adult–child behavior, and to measure the effects of the intervention on child language use. Data from individual sessions are used immediately when implementing single-subject designs. Coded data influence treatment decisions and form the basis for feedback and coaching provided to each adult–child dyad and for the evaluation of the effects of the interventions on both adult and child. Summaries of coded data also are used in group designs to make more general statements about the effectiveness of intervention on a larger population of children and adults.

System Advantages and Limitations   There are several advantages to using the current *SALT* programs for transcribing, coding, and analyzing data. Before *SALT*'s updated versions became available, transcribing and coding required several additional steps, resulting in more time spent on each phase of data entry and coding. Initially, language transcription and coding were done in standard orthographic form. The transcriber then typed the session into a word-processing program, and this file was later transferred into *SALT* for further analysis. In some cases it took more than 10 hours to compile the necessary information for graphing or providing feedback to intervention participants. With the updated versions a session can be transcribed, coded, summarized, and graphed in less than 3 hours.

There are a few limitations imposed by this highly efficient system. The need to stay within the utterance-driven structure of coding limits certain types of coding. Valuable measures of context, extensive nonverbal behavior, and relationships among nonverbal behaviors are difficult to code in this format. Data are not coded for exact time or duration, as with the *PROCODER* system (Tapp & Walden, 1993). Although two codes can be connected to a single utterance, specific routines must be written to analyze multicoded utterances. The slower, handwritten coding and summary process was sometimes useful because extensive contact with the data ensured that the coder was very familiar with the adult–child interactions and allowed insight into the qualitative aspects of these interactions. Nonetheless, given the large number of participants in our studies (more than 800) and the period of data collection for each participant (18–36 months), we believe that the streamlined coding system adequately captures the variables that are important in answering our research questions.

Data Summary Program (KIDTALK.EXE)

SALT is an efficient system for determining the frequency of particular parts of speech and types of utterances, but it is incapable of counting dyadic sequences from the transcript (i.e., the caregiver says X and then the child says Y). To capture sequences of behavior we initially developed a summary sheet on which sequences could be tallied by a research assistant. Completing the summary sheet by hand was a time-consuming process, required precise counting and several different calculations, and was subject to numerous errors. With minor modifications of our coding procedure we were able to create a computer program to count sequences of variables. An example of a summary sheet is shown in Figure 2. This program was especially helpful in determining correct and incorrect Milieu Teaching episodes, child compliance with adult instructions, and adult use of opportunities to expand child utterances. These sequences are central to our intervention; thus, development of the program was a key step in tailoring existing *SALT* software to our research.

KIDTALK.EXE (part of the *KIDTALKER* software package) was designed using *Microsoft Visual Basic 6.0* (Microsoft, 1999). The program operates by asking the user to select a transcript to analyze. The transcript is then processed and a summary containing 1) frequency counts for individual behaviors (e.g., number of adult expansions), 2) percentages for components of categories of behaviors (e.g., percentage of adult expansions at child target level), 3) occurrences of sequences of behavior (e.g., number of Milieu Teaching episodes), and 4) percentage calculations for sequences (e.g., percentage of correct Milieu Teaching episodes) is output. The summary is sent directly to a spreadsheet program (*Microsoft Excel* [Microsoft, 1998]). The output file created by KIDTALK.EXE (Tapp et al., 1999) is an ASCII file with the label for each variable followed by a comma, followed by the value for the variable. The program provides more than 50 variables in its output and sends the file directly to the spreadsheet program without user intervention. The summarization process that took at least 1 hour to complete by hand takes just a few seconds with the summary program. The data provided are accurate and easily moved into a graphing program to be displayed for visual analysis by participant, or they can be fed automatically into a group data set for statistical analysis at the group level. Moving of summarized data is accomplished by using macros developed for *Excel*.

Reliability Program (SALTRELY.EXE)

Accurate coding of language transcripts is extremely important in language intervention research. As a general rule we assess interrater agreement in 20% of ses-

---

Behavior episodes

Number of indirect command episodes	9
Number of correct indirect command episodes	4
Percentage of correct indirect command episodes	.44
Number of direct command episodes	9
Number of correct episodes	2
Percentage of correct direct command episodes	.22
Total number of all command episodes	18
Total number of correct episodes	6
Percentage correct	.33

Parent feedback to child

Frequency of responsive feedback	61
Number of opportunities for feedback	75
Percentage of responsive feedback	.81

Figure 2.   Sample *KIDTALKER* summary sheet.

sions. When we are training new coders we complete reliability checks more often to determine the new coders' progress toward criterion levels of reliability for coding. To determine reliability we developed a program in *Microsoft Visual Basic 6.0* to compare the coding of the same transcription by two coders. The program, SALTRELY.EXE, accomplishes this by asking the user to select the two files to be compared. The two files are read in, and the first character and appended codes are compared for each line of the transcript. If the same code is appended to a given utterance in each coder's file, an agreement for that code is tallied. If only one coder's record contains the given code, a disagreement for that code is tallied. The agreements and disagreements for each code category are sent to a comma-separated file (i.e., a text file of data values separated by commas), which is subsequently sent to a spreadsheet for display and further analysis. The program uses a code file that is created with a text editor and contains all of the individual codes that are to be checked. The code file can be edited as codes change, but it is generally not altered during a study. An example of an intercoder agreement summary is shown in Figure 3. The program takes only a few seconds to process a pair of transcript files and is easy to use. Before the development of *SALTRELY*, scoring reliability and summarizing reliability data required more than 1 hour for each assessment of interrater agreement. Errors in scoring, counting, and calculation were likely but often were not detected.

SALTRELY allows tracking of progress toward criterion reliability for an individual coder, management of systematic assessments of reliability for an adult–child dyad, and development of a database containing reliability data for each category of coded behavior. Because *SALTRELY* automatically enters reliability data into a database when reliability checks are completed, the user is prepared for later summaries of reliability estimates across children, adults, settings, and measures when the results of studies are reported. This secondary feature of the reliability program increases both the precision and the efficiency of presentation of reliability data.

New Vocabulary Analysis Program (VOCAB)

Vocabulary growth is a variable of interest as an index of child development and to determine how intervention affects the number of new words a child uses across time. Vocabulary growth is described by determining the novel words used across language-sampling sessions. Novel vocabulary is difficult to determine because each word must be compared with the child's existing (previously produced and observed) vocabulary. The child's base of existing vocabulary must be updated after each session. *VOCAB* (Tapp et al., 1999) is the novel vocabulary analysis program for the *KIDTALKER* system. The first time the system is run it stores all of the words found in the child lines of the *SALT* transcript in a new vocabulary file for that child. In this program bracketed codes are ignored and only the transcription of child lines is considered. On subsequent runs the program determines the number of new words used by the child and provides a list of these new words. This number of novel words per session is then used as a single but significant measure indicating the growth of the child's vocabulary. By plotting a cumulative record of the child's new words we can estimate vocabulary growth and determine the effects of intervention on vocabulary. Figure 4 shows a graph of one child's vocabulary data.

File 1	File 2	Code	Freq 1	Freq 2	Dis 1	Dis 2	Agree	A/(A + D)
T5.001	RELYT5.001	[yq]	3	3	0	0	3	1.0
T5.001	RELYT5.001	[mex]	11	6	5	0	6	.545455
T5.001	RELYT5.001	[dt]	33	34	2	3	31	.939394
T5.001	RELYT5.001	[lp]	10	10	0	0	10	1.0

Figure 3. Sample *KIDTALKER* reliability session sheet. (Codes: [yq] yes-or-no questions; [mex], meaning expansion; [dt], descriptive talk; [lp], labeled praise. Column heading abbreviations: Freq 1 and Freq 2, frequency of behavior recorded by Coder 1 and Coder 2, respectively; Dis 1 and Dis 2, disagreements for Coder 1 and Coder 2, respectively; Agree, total number of agreements between Coder 1 and Coder 2; A/(A + D), percentage agreement.)

187

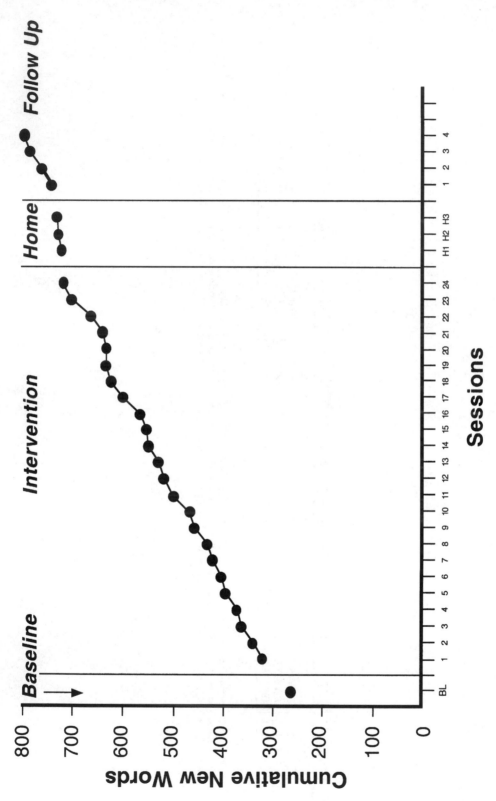

Figure 4.   Cumulative vocabulary growth for one child.

Linkages and Importing Data for Further Analysis

Because all of our programs and analyses are based on the same *SALT*-formatted language transcript and output into *Excel*-compatible text files, we have been able to integrate complex analyses into a general system to be used in several related studies. Without these computer programs the feedback to interventionists and adult participants would be less precise and less frequent. As a result, interventions would take longer and would be far less efficient. Our own software development for special tasks, along with the flexibility of modern spreadsheet programs such as *Excel*, greatly increases the accuracy of the data. We are able to more easily manage the complex transcription and coding aspect of our research. We automate a percentage of the work using these related programs, which saves large amounts of personnel time. We regularly use the system to provide almost immediate feedback to our interventionists, who train caregivers in the intervention procedures. In addition, we can easily integrate these data with data from standardized tests (e.g., Child Behavior Checklist [Achenbach, 1991], Preschool Language Scale [Zimmerman, Steiner, & Pond, 1992]) for statistical analysis using *SAS* (SAS, 1999) and *SPSS* (SPSS, 1999).

TECHNICAL AND TRAINING REQUIREMENTS FOR THE *KIDTALKER* SYSTEM

All of the programs described here were developed to run on an IBM-compatible computer using Windows 95 (or a more recent version). Some of the software (*VOCAB* and *SALT*) can be run using DOS or Windows 95/98/NT. A minimum suggested system would consist of a Pentium processor (100 megahertz or more), 16 megabytes of random access memory, a 1-gigabyte hard drive (or larger), and a monitor. Although it is not required, we recommend that users have a spreadsheet program (such as *Excel*) available for management of the data.

FUTURE DEVELOPMENT OF *KIDTALKER*

Several tasks remain in the development of a comprehensive data collection and management system: 1) development of a more efficient graphics interface to facilitate rapid graphing of data, 2) revision of the new vocabulary analysis function to allow tracking of categories of new vocabulary, 3) development of an adult vocabulary program to serve as a basis for comparing adult and child vocabulary within and across sessions, and 4) design of systems that allow concurrent coding with two different coding protocols to serve as a basis for integrated behavioral analyses. We use a Lotus *Freelance* (Lotus, 1999) program for individual and multiple baseline graphs. Data are imported by "pasting" from the *Excel* spreadsheet summaries. Although this process is relatively straightforward and produces high-quality graphs, we would prefer an automatic transfer of data into a graphics program requiring minimal user responses to produce the 15–20 graphs used to monitor session-by-session data in less time.

Development of new vocabulary analysis programs requires a high level of programming expertise and is expected to be time consuming. As our research focus has shifted toward vocabulary as a key measure, we expect to begin the development of these second-generation vocabulary analysis programs in the near future. A long-term goal is the development of software to interface data coded with two separate coding protocols. For example, in an intervention study designed to increase peer talk we coded baseline, intervention, and generalization session tapes to examine changes in levels of child play. We are interested in concurrent assessment of the content of child utterances and the complexity of play. A time-based coding system or an alternative program for linking data is needed for this level of integrated behavioral analysis.

CONCLUSIONS

The development of an integrated set of software components has greatly increased the efficiency, reliability, and flexibility of data collection by our research team. The use of existing *SALT* programs as a basis for the *KIDTALKER* system has capitalized on the development efforts of other language researchers. Although the *SALT* programs allow for the introduction of specific codes and the selection of linguistic measures unique to a research project, additional programs were developed in our center to increase the efficiency of summarizing categorical and sequence data, to streamline reliability calculations, and to import data for graphic display and statistical analysis. In addition, one new data analysis program was developed to assess changes in children's vocabulary over time. The development of this program expanded the range of measures that could be used to track the effects of the intervention on a session-by-session basis and introduced a new strategy for estimating the development of children's language use over time.

The use of the *KIDTALKER* system has reduced the time required for transcription, coding, data entry, and assessment of interrater reliability for a single session by approximately 6 hours. Additional time savings are realized in graphing and statistical analyses because data are imported from existing summaries rather than reentered. Although greater precision in counting and calculation also has been obtained by automating these functions, it is difficult to estimate the magnitude of change. The obvious benefit of this system for the single-subject researcher is the increased ability to process data rapidly for decision making. Three other benefits are less obvious. First, the summarization and direct entry of observational data into a comprehensive database containing data for many different adult–child dyads allows flexible analyses at the group level. For example, we can select baseline observational data for all children diagnosed with autism and create a description of their rates of more than 30 different communicative behaviors with their parents before intervention. New data can be added as more children with autism participate in our research, and our ongoing description of this group of children can be updated. Second, use of the *KIDTALKER* system has allowed us to develop a systematic coder-training program with criterion performance measures for each step of the transcription and coding process. The tasks and the steps used to complete each task are described precisely in a coder manual. Assessment of the reliability of transcription and coding can be accomplished quickly and easily; therefore, objective feedback on coder performance can be provided to accelerate the training process. Third, the system is flexible in terms of content. The core program functions can be used with research-specific coding systems to address new questions. For example, we have conducted research on an intervention to increase peer-to-peer conversations in a play context (Craig & Kaiser, 1998). Using the program format of the *KIDTALKER* summary and reliability programs, adaptations to accommodate new categories of codes and new sequences of codes for two speakers were made to produce specific programs for the peer data.

In contrast to the time savings resulting from the use of the system, the development time for new components of the system was relatively modest. Close and continued collaboration between the researcher and the program developer has been essential. For this project the programmer needed substantive knowledge of the research questions and general observational methodology as well as some knowledge of the linguistic features and social behavioral functions of language. Several members of the research team provided task analyses for components of the programs, tested prototype programs by coding and analyzing data, and provided error analyses during the development phase. Continued assessment of the functioning of the overall system has allowed us to fine-tune each program and has guided us toward proposed additions and expansions of the system.

The hallmark of observational research is precise, reliable data. The development and application of the *KIDTALKER* system for coding interactions between adults and children has allowed us to meet the standards of this type of behavioral research with a high degree of efficiency. In turn, efficiency in collecting, coding, and summarizing data allows the research team to focus on the implementation of the intervention, the analysis of outcomes, and the development of new research questions based on the data collected.

REFERENCES

Achenbach, T.M. (1991). *Manual for the Child Behavior Checklist and 1991 profile*. Burlington, VT: University of Vermont Department of Psychiatry.

Alpert, C.L., & Kaiser, A.P. (1992). Training parents as milieu language teaching. *Journal of Early Intervention, 16*, 31–52.

Craig, L., & Kaiser, A.P. (1998, March). *The effects of increased social communications skills on play quality and duration*. Poster session presented at the 31st Annual Gatlinburg Conference on Research and Theory in Mental Retardation and Developmental Disabilities, Charleston, SC.

Delaney, E.M., Ezell, S.S., Solomon, N.A., Hancock, T.B., & Kaiser, A.P. (1997). *The behavior-language code: A protocol for coding adult and child behaviors*. Unpublished manuscript, Vanderbilt University, Nashville.

Delaney, E.M., & Kaiser, A.P. (1998). *Training parents who are poor to be responsive to child language and to effectively manage noncompliant behaviors*. Paper presented at the annual meeting of the American Association on Mental Retardation, San Diego.

Hart, B.M., & Rogers-Warren, A.K. (1978). A milieu approach to teaching language. In R.L. Schiefelbusch (Ed.), *Language intervention series: Vol. II. Language intervention strategies* (pp. 193–235). Baltimore: University Park Press.

Hemmeter, M.L., & Kaiser, A.P. (1994). Enhanced milieu teaching: Effects of parent-implemented language intervention. *Journal of Early Intervention, 18*, 269–289.

Hester, P.P., & Kaiser, A.P. (in press). The generalized effects of naturalistic language teaching with multiple partners on children's social communicative interactions. *Journal of Early Intervention*.

Kaiser, A.P., & Hester, P.P. (1997). Prevention of conduct disorders through early intervention: A social-communicative perspective. *Behavioral Disorders, 22*, 117–130.

Kaiser, A.P., Lambert, W., Hancock, T., & Hester, P.P. (1998). *Differential outcomes of naturalistic language intervention*. Paper presented at the 31st Annual Gatlinburg Conference on Research and Theory in Mental Retardation and Developmental Disabilities, Charleston, SC.

Kazdin, A.E. (1982). *Single-case research designs: Methods for clinical and applied settings*. New York: Oxford University Press.

Lotus Development Corp. (1999). *Freelance* [Software]. Cambridge, MA: Author.

Microsoft Corp. (1998). *Excel* [Software]. Redmond, WA: Author.

Microsoft Corp. (1999). *Visual Basic 6.0* [Software]. Redmond, WA: Author.

Miller, J.F., & Chapman, R.S. (1996). *SALT: Systematic Analysis of Language Transcripts* (version 4.0) [Software]. Madison: University of Wisconsin, The Waisman Center, Language Analysis Laboratory.

SAS. (1999). *Statistical analysis system* [Software]. Cary, NC: Author.

SPSS. (1999). *Statistical package for social sciences.* [Software]. Chicago: Author.

Tapp, J., Kaiser, A.P., Solomon, N.A., Delaney, E.M., & Ezell, S.A. (1999). *KIDTALKER: A multilevel software program for coding, entering, and analyzing linguistic and behavioral data* [Software]. Nashville, TN: Vanderbilt University, John F. Kennedy Center for Research on Human Development.

Tapp, J., & Walden, T.A. (1993). *PROCODER:* A professional tape control, coding, and analysis system for behavioral research using videotape. *Behavior Research Methods, Instruments, and Computers, 25,* 53–56.

Yoder, P.J., Kaiser, A.P., & Alpert, C.L. (1991). An exploratory study of the interaction between language teaching methods and child characteristics. *Journal of Speech and Hearing Research, 34,* 155–167.

Yoder, P.J., Kaiser, A.P., Goldstein, H., Alpert, C., Mousetis, L., Kaczmarek, L., & Fischer, R. (1995). A comparison of milieu teaching and responsive interaction in classroom applications. *Journal of Early Intervention, 19,* 218–242.

Zimmerman, I.L., Steiner, V., & Pond, R.E. (1992). *Preschool Language Scale–3 (PLS–3).* San Antonio, TX: The Psychological Corporation.

13

Approaches to Understanding the Ecology of Early Childhood Environments for Children with Disabilities

Samuel L. Odom,
Paddy C. Favazza,
William H. Brown, and
Eva M. Horn

The mandate of public education in the United States has broadened substantially since the early 1990s. No longer does the kindergarten through high school, "one size fits all" model respond to the needs of the diverse population of the United States. One example of this expansion is the provision of services for preschool children with disabilities by public school systems (Odom & Kaiser, 1997). These children may attend classes within the public schools or a range of other inclusive programs in community-based child care or Head Start centers.

Classrooms for young children with (or without) disabilities are complex, dynamic environments. Many features of such class environments affect children's behavior and ultimately their development. For example, the nature of the activities planned, the size of groups, the composition of peers within the group, and the teacher's behavior all have the potential to create learning opportunities for young children or, conversely, to create an environment that does not foster development. Understanding the ecology of such classroom environments

Final preparation of this chapter was supported by Grant No. HO24K960001 (Early Childhood Research Institute on Inclusion), and the research reported was supported by Grant No. HO24B10108 (Project BLEND), both from the U.S. Department of Education.

requires the use of comprehensive observational systems (as one source of infor-mation) that can assess the individual variables or characteristics of the environ-ments and also allow examination of the relationships that exist among classroom variables and child behavior.

Ecobehavioral assessment is one observational approach that captures informa-tion about characteristics of classroom environments and their interrelationships. It has been defined as an "effort to assess environment-behavior interaction . . . and the ecological contexts of student behavior" (Greenwood, Carta, Kamps, & Arreaga-Mayer, 1990, p. 36). Such assessment generates information about fea-tures of classrooms that allow children to engage in behaviors associated with learning and development. The purpose of this chapter is to examine the ecobe-havioral assessment research that has been conducted in early childhood settings for children with and without disabilities. We begin with a brief overview of the history of classroom programs for young children with disabilities, review the ori-gins of ecobehavioral analysis research, describe the application of ecobehavioral assessment to programs for young children with and without disabilities, and conclude with the presentation of data from an ecobehavioral assessment study in inclusive and noninclusive early childhood programs.

PROGRAMS FOR YOUNG CHILDREN WITH DISABILITIES

Early childhood programs for children with disabilities began to appear in the late 1960s. With the enactment of the Handicapped Children's Early Education Act of 1968 (PL 90-538), funds were provided for the development of model demonstra-tion programs as well as for state implementation grants that supported early childhood services (Swan, 1980). In 1975, the Education for All Handicapped Children Act (PL 94-142) provided incentives for states to provide services to preschool-age children with disabilities. The reenactment of this law in the Education of the Handicapped Act Amendments of 1986 (PL 99-457) created a mandate for states to provide services (by 1991) to children with disabilities as young as 3 years of age and also provided incentives for states to create early intervention programs for infants and toddlers with disabilities. Subsequent laws and reenactments have continued to provide support for such programs for infants and young children with disabilities and have increasingly encouraged agencies to provide such services in inclusive environments (i.e., programs con-taining children with and without disabilities). The specific features of programs for young children vary substantially, and understanding how such features relate to children's behavior is critical to building effective programs. As mentioned pre-viously, one approach to gathering such information is through the assessment of the classroom ecology. One method for collecting such information is ecobehav-ioral assessment.

ECOBEHAVIORAL ASSESSMENT

The roots of ecobehavioral assessment lie in ecological psychology, behavior analysis, and the interbehavioral psychology of J.R. Kantor (Morris & Midgley, 1990). From these theoretical perspectives ecobehavioral researchers have created observational systems that accurately measure both the static aspects (e.g., room arrangement, activity materials) and the dynamic aspects (e.g., teacher behavior) of the classroom ecology as well as the behavior of individual children (Carta, Sainato, & Greenwood, 1988). The relationships among the two aspects of the classroom ecology and children's behavior are the focus of ecobehavioral analysis. Of particular interest in much classroom research has been the identification of features of the classroom ecology that might serve as setting events for desirable child behavior or behavior that may lead to learning (Fox, 1990).

For the purposes of our discussion, we define ecobehavioral assessment approaches as direct observational techniques that provide information about structural (e.g., activities, group organization, group composition) and dynamic (e.g., teacher behavior, peer behavior) features of the classroom ecology as well as the behavior of children, adults, and/or peers in the classroom. We differentiate between *ecobehavioral assessment,* which refers to the procedures involved in collecting data on ecological features of classroom environments, and *ecobehavioral analysis,* which examines the relationships among variables. Although some authors have proposed that functional analysis of co-varying variables is an essential aspect of ecobehavioral analysis (Morris & Midgley, 1990), most ecobehavioral studies in early childhood programs have examined only the co-varying relationships of classroom variables and thus are descriptive in nature.

ECOBEHAVIORAL OBSERVATIONAL ASSESSMENT SYSTEMS FOR EARLY CHILDHOOD ENVIRONMENTS

Several of the ecobehavioral observational systems used in early childhood environments are based on previous work in elementary school settings. Coding systems such as the Code for Instructional Structure and Student Academic Response (CISSAR), developed by Greenwood and colleagues (Greenwood, Delquadri, Stanley, Terry, & Hall, 1985), have set the standard for how ecobehavioral data might be collected and analyzed efficiently. Another chapter in this book describes such instrumentation for use with elementary school–age children (see Chapter 15), so the description in this chapter is limited to observational systems designed to collect information in programs for children younger than age 6 years.

Described below are observational systems that have been used in ecobehavioral research conducted in early childhood programs for young children with disabilities. The key features of these systems are listed in Table 1. These systems have several characteristics in common. First, they tend to contain a relatively large number of behavioral categories that are grouped within ecological and social variables. Second, the systems use either momentary time-sampling or interval-sampling procedures rather than the more accurate event recording. The use of these sampling procedures is necessitated by the large number of categories that observers are required to memorize and use in their data collection; event recording with such a large number of categories would be quite difficult. Third, all of the systems collect data directly in the classroom rather than through videotapes. Because of the need to capture information related to the ecology of the classroom and the dynamic quality of some of the variables, videotapes may not have a large enough visual field for the observer and possibly could be reactive. Fourth, all authors have conducted interobserver agreement checks on their systems and have demonstrated that the observers were within the range generally judged to be acceptable (Hartmann & Wood, 1990).

Table 1. Direct observational systems that assess dimensions of the classroom ecology

Name	Type of system	Mode	Variables (behavioral categories in parentheses)
ESCAPE: Ecobehavioral System for Complex Assessment of Preschool Environments (Carta, Greenwood, & Atwater, 1985)	15-second momentary time sample; behaviors divided into four groups and cycled through once per minute	C	Ecological variables: Designated Activities (14), Activity Initiator (4), Materials (12), Location (9), Grouping (5), Composition (7) Teacher subcategories: Teacher Definition (8), Teacher Behavior (10), Teacher Focus (5), Target Behaviors (10), Competing Behavior (6), Verbal Behavior (5)
ACCESS: Assessment Code/Checklist for Evaluation of Survival Skills (Atwater, Carta, & Schwartz, 1989)	10-second intervals	P+P	Activity (3), Group Location (5), Group Size (3), Content of Group Instruction (12), Materials (4), Teaching Format (8), Teacher Focus (2), Prompts (5), Feedback (3), Engagement in Activities (6), Response to Prompts (4), Asking for Assistance (1)
CASPER I: Code for Active Student Participation and Engagement–Revised (Favazza & Odom, 1993)	30-second momentary time sample	P+P C	Activity (8), Initiator (5), Student Behavior (13), Student Social Behavior (4), Teacher Behavior (6), Group Arrangement (7), Group Composition (7)
CASPER II: Code for Active Student Participation and Engagement–Revised–II (Brown, Odom, Holcombe, & Youngquist, 1995)	30-second time sample	C	Activity (15), Initiator (5), Child Behavior (12), Child Social Behavior (8), Adult Behavior (6), Group Arrangement (7), Peer Group Composition (7)
Kontos, Moore, and Giorgetti (1998)	Momentary time sample/scan sample	P+P	Teacher Involvement (6), Interaction with Objects (5), Interaction with Peers (5), Activities (9), Social Context (5)
McCormick, Noonan, and Heck (1998)	Discontinuous 10-second observe/10-second record interval	P+P	Adult Engagement (3), Peer Engagement (3), Activity Engagement (3), Activity Type (2), Structure (2), Size (3), Teacher Behavior (7)

C, computer; P+P, paper and pencil.

Ecobehavioral System for Complex Assessment of Preschool Environments (ESCAPE)

ESCAPE (Carta, Greenwood, & Atwater, 1985) was the first and most widely used ecobehavioral measure developed for preschool children. The expressed purpose of ESCAPE is to describe the range of ecological and social characteristics in preschool environments and the interrelationships among the variables (Carta et al., 1985). Based on the CISSAR model (Stanley & Greenwood, 1981), a system developed for elementary classrooms, ESCAPE has 12 variables each containing between 5 and 14 behavioral categories (a list of behavioral categories appears in Chapter 15). It uses a modified momentary time-sampling system in which the observer records behavioral categories for three variables every 15 seconds. In this way, observers code all variables within 1 minute, and in data analysis the categories coded are considered part of the same 1-minute block. Usually, information is collected for one child in a classroom for periods that range from 2 hours to a full day. Often the longer observational samples are divided into 25- to 30-minute sessions to allow the observer a "rest" period or time to collect more "molar" data using other methodology (e.g., rating scales). Observers collect ESCAPE data with a laptop computer.

Assessment Code/Checklist for Evaluation of Survival Skills (ACCESS)

ACCESS (Atwater, Carta, & Schwartz, 1989) has a slightly different purpose from ESCAPE in that it was designed to provide information about teacher–child interactions during independent work times, group instruction, and transitions in kindergarten environments. Observers collect information on one "index" child for 5 minutes and then go to the next index child in the class until information on all index children has been coded for the day. This system uses a 10-second interval-sampling procedure in which the observer codes information on activity, engagement, and interactions. In addition, information on teaching arrangement, location of materials, and teacher prompting is recorded at the end of each 5-minute sample (Ager & Shapiro, 1995). Observers collect ACCESS data using paper and pencil and then enter the data into a computer database after the observations.

Code for Active Student Participation and Engagement–Revised (CASPER)

CASPER exists in two forms. Based on ESCAPE, CASPER–I (Favazza & Odom, 1993) was developed to assess the classroom ecology of infant and toddler programs. CASPER–II (Brown, Odom, Holcombe, & Youngquist, 1995) was developed subsequently to assess preschool classroom ecologies. Both use the same methodology, but they contain slightly different variables and categories. Both versions of CASPER use a 30-second momentary time-sampling method (i.e., with a 2-second window every 30 seconds representing one moment) in which observers code one category within each variable (e.g., group arrangement, activity, child behavior). A total of $2\frac{1}{2}$–3 hours of data are collected for index or focal children, with data collection being distributed across five or six sessions, usually on different days. Initially with CASPER–I, observers used paper-and-pencil methods to collect data, but a computer program (*Intman*, developed by Jon Tapp) was adapted and is now used in CASPER–I and CASPER–II data collection.

Kontos, Moore, and Giorgetti System

The system developed by Kontos, Moore, and Giorgetti (1998) was designed to collect information about young children's participation in free play activities in inclusive preschool classes and the factors that are related to competence in peer interaction and activity material use. The system used a form of momentary time sampling in which data collectors observed an index child for a 2-second "moment" and recorded categorical information during approximately 15 seconds after the observation. The observers also used a scan technique in which they moved on to the next index child after the first data collection interval. Fifty observational samples were collected for all children across a 2-day period. The variables included teacher involvement, interaction with objects, interaction with peers, activities, and social context, with the number of behavioral categories ranging from five to nine. Observers used paper and pencil to collect the data.

McCormick, Noonan, and Heck System

The system developed by McCormick, Noonan, and Heck (1998) provides information about the nature of activities, characteristics of teachers' behaviors, and children's engagement in inclusive preschool environments. Variables included adult engagement, peer engagement, activity engagement, activity type, structure, size, and teacher behavior, with the number of categories in these variables ranging from three to seven. Data collectors observed a child or teacher for 10 seconds and recorded their observations during the subsequent 10 seconds. Like the system of Kontos et al. (1998), this system used a scan technique in which the observer collected data on one index child for one observation, moved on to the next index child, and started again with the first child after data on all index children had been collected. It differed in that observers collected data on teachers separately, with their observations being part of the scan (e.g., the order might be Child 1, Child 2, Child 3, Teacher 1, Child 4). Fifteen observations per child and 10 observations per teacher were collected in one sample. Observers used paper and pencil to record the data.

Computer-Based Data Collection Systems

Although the ecobehavioral assessment systems just described vary in their use of computerized instrumentation, the use of laptop computers has been essential for some systems. Both ESCAPE and CASPER have extensive variables and category lists. Coding the range of variables is demanding for observers, and, to some extent, laptop computers have eased this data-recording task. Another important advantage of computerized data collection for these systems is the ease of data entry into a central database and immediate analysis of interobserver agreement. CASPER–I first used paper and pencil for data collection but then converted to a computer-based observational system. The computerized system allowed electronic transfer into the database rather than requiring a staff member to transfer the observations from paper to the database. This conversion resulted in an estimated 75% savings in staff time for data entry and management. Also, it is likely that there was less error in the data transfer with the computerized system.

USING ECOBEHAVIORAL ANALYSIS TO EXAMINE
ECOLOGICAL FEATURES OF EARLY CHILDHOOD CLASSROOMS

Ecobehavioral analysis of early childhood classrooms for children with disabilities is a relatively young field. Studies first appeared in the late 1980s and have addressed a range of issues. In this review we grouped this research conceptually into studies of the general features of early childhood special education, studies related to transition, and studies of inclusion at the early childhood level.

Classroom Features of Early Childhood Programs

Carta and colleagues (1988) at the Juniper Gardens Children's Project conducted the first ecobehavioral studies of early childhood special education classrooms. Using ESCAPE they described activities and child behaviors occurring across four preschool environments. Their analysis illustrated how children's engagement varied across different activities in the classroom. Other studies (Carta & Greenwood, 1989; Carta, Greenwood, & Robinson, 1987) demonstrated how the level of engagement in individual activities could be compared with the base rate of engagement across activities. These three studies found that children with disabilities in special education environments were occupied most often by play, preacademic, snack, and transition activities. Children spent a high proportion of their time attending to the teacher, and active engagement varied across children and activities. Together, these studies document the use of an ecobehavioral observational approach as an effective method for assessing the quality of early childhood classroom environments.

To examine the different activities and behaviors of young children with disabilities in special education classes and children who are developing typically in general early childhood programs, Odom, Skellenger, and Ostrosky (2000) used ESCAPE to collect information on 50 children in 10 early childhood special education classes and 50 children who were developing typically and who were enrolled in 10 programs accredited by the National Association for the Education of Young Children. They found that children in special education classes participated in significantly more preacademic activities and that children in early childhood education classes participated in more play activities. Teacher-initiated activity occurred significantly more often in special education classes, and child-initiated activity occurred more often in early childhood classes. Overall, active engagement did not differ in either type of class, but for both types of classes engagement occurred significantly more often in child-initiated than in adult-initiated activities. This study revealed substantial differences between preschool children's experiences in special education and general early childhood classes.

Other investigators have examined more specific features of the classroom ecology using ESCAPE. To determine the relationship between teachers' schedules and activities occurring in the classroom, Ostrosky, Skellenger, Odom, McConnell, and Peterson (1994) compared teachers' reports of their schedules in their classes and the observed designated activities occurring in the classes. This analysis revealed a discrepancy between the reported and observed times that activities occurred, which Ostrosky et al. attributed to teachers not including identified transition time in their schedules and to the necessary variations caused by unplanned events. To determine the use of recommended practices for promoting language development, Schwartz, Carta, and Grant (1996) used ESCAPE and a recommended practice checklist to observe 59 children with disabilities in 26 classrooms. They found that classrooms with relatively high implementation of recommended language intervention had more active child engagement, more play and music activities, less transition time, more pretend play, and more story-time. Also, children in the high-implementation classrooms made more progress on language assessments than children in the low-implementation classrooms.

Children's involvement in social interaction with peers has been of particular interest in early childhood special education (Guralnick & Neville, 1997). To determine the class environments that offer opportunities for children to interact with their peers, Odom, Peterson, McConnell, and Ostrosky (1990) used ESCAPE to observe 94 children with disabilities in special education classes and 33 children who were developing typically in preschool classes. They found that children who were developing typically engaged in significantly more verbal behavior with peers than children with disabilities. In a subsequent analysis they found that both groups of children engaged in peer interaction most often when the designated activity was play and the child behavior was pretend. To analyze further the variables affecting peer interaction, Sontag (1997) used ESCAPE to observe 16 children with disabilities in special education and inclusive preschool environments. Although not finding substantial differences across environments, Sontag did find that verbal behavior to peers occurred significantly more often than the base rate when teachers provided prompts and children were in small groups. In inclusive environments only, verbal behavior to peers occurred significantly more often when children were engaged in pretend play.

Transition

The transition of children with disabilities from preschool to kindergarten classrooms is a particular concern for many professionals and parents (Bruder & Chandler, 1996). Several researchers have used ecobehavioral analysis to assist in the transition process. Carta, Atwater, Schwartz, and Miller (1990) used ESCAPE to assess special education classrooms in which children with disabilities were enrolled and kindergarten classrooms in which they would enroll the next year. In kindergarten classes children spent more time (relative to children in special education classes) in large-group activities, transition (i.e., movement between activities in the class), and class business (i.e., teacher discussing the daily schedule or giving directions to the whole class). Children in preschool special education classes spent relatively more time in play. To provide more information about specific behaviors that appeared to be important in kindergarten classes, Carta et al. (1990) used ACCESS to evaluate the effects of a classroom survival skills intervention. Data from two children with disabilities, followed in a single-case design, revealed that teacher prompting decreased to near zero percent when children with disabilities moved to kindergarten environments. Although engagement declined as well, it was comparable to that of children who were developing typically enrolled in the same classroom.

To facilitate the transition of children from Head Start programs to general kindergarten classes, Ager and Shapiro (1995) used both ESCAPE and ACCESS to gather information about the two classroom environments. They used a "template-matching" approach (Hoier, McConnell, & Palley, 1987) to determine the discrepancy between the skills needed in the Head Start and the kindergarten classes. Using this information the authors designed an intervention in which the

Head Start teachers reorganized their classrooms to be more like kindergarten classrooms. The change led to more successful performance in kindergarten by many of the children in the intervention classrooms (relative to children in a non-treatment control group).

Preschool Inclusion

A primary movement in early childhood special education has been to place children with disabilities in general early childhood education environments with children who are developing typically. Several investigators have used ecobehavioral methods to assess the classroom ecologies of inclusive environments. To examine the experience of children in inclusive preschool environments, Kontos et al. (1998) observed 40 children with disabilities and 66 children who were developing typically during free play periods. Children with disabilities engaged in more art and manipulative activities, whereas children who were developing typically engaged in more computer and dramatic play activities. Children with disabilities engaged in less high-level social play with peers and more low-level play with objects. Taking the analysis one step further, these authors analyzed the correlates of competent peer and object play. Children with and without disabilities who were engaged in competent peer and object play were more likely to be with a child or a group of children and were less likely to be in an environment with a teacher alone or in a group with a teacher and other children. In a study using nearly identical methodology with only children who were developing typically, Kontos and Wilcox-Herzog (1997) found similar results.

In a study of co-teaching in Head Start classes that included children with disabilities, McCormick et al. (1998) observed 23 children with disabilities and 23 children who were developing typically. They found that engagement in class activities was not significantly different for children with and without disabilities. Placement in small groups appeared to lead to greater engagement for all children. Teacher cohesion (i.e., the extent to which teachers used the same types of teaching behaviors) was also related to engagement. Like Kontos et al. (1998), McCormick and colleagues found that the more the teacher interacts with a child, the less likely that child is to interact with peers. Sontag (1997) found the opposite result. These differences are probably attributable to Sontag using a specific "adult support" measure and the other authors measuring interaction at a more molar level.

Extending the investigation of preschool inclusion to a national sample, Brown, Odom, Li, and Zercher (in press) observed 80 children with disabilities and 32 children who were developing typically and enrolled in 16 inclusive preschool programs at four regional sites. Using CASPER–II, children were observed in activities throughout the day. These authors found that children with disabilities and children who were developing typically participated in very similar activities and child behaviors. There was no difference in engagement between groups. The authors constructed a social integration index from categories in the group composition variables and found that the majority of the time, children with disabilities were in groups with children who were developing typically. Also, adults in the classroom directed significantly more support behavior toward children with disabilities than toward children who were developing typically.

COMPARISON OF INCLUSIVE AND NONINCLUSIVE PLACEMENTS FOR CHILDREN WITH AND WITHOUT DISABILITIES

Although a range of studies have examined variables related to inclusion, with the exception of Sontag (1997) researchers generally have not directly compared the classroom ecologies of inclusive environments and noninclusive settings for children with disabilities and children who are developing typically. Moreover, most investigations have examined only preschool classrooms, and there is very little information about inclusive early intervention environments for children younger than age 3. In this section we describe two ecobehavioral analysis studies (Odom, Cronin, Youngquist, Horn, & Brown, 1994). The specific purpose of these studies was to examine the different classroom ecologies for infants and toddlers in different types of inclusive and noninclusive environments. These studies are presented to extend the understanding of inclusive early intervention environments and to provide an illustration of data generated by ecobehavioral analysis methods.

Environments

These studies took place in inclusive and segregated early intervention classes and in nonintegrated general child care classes (i.e., children with disabilities were not enrolled in these classes). In Study 1 (Year 1 study) children with disabilities were enrolled in a segregated early intervention class (eight students with disabilities and two teachers), a team-teaching inclusive class (eight students who were developing typically, four students with disabilities, one early childhood teacher, and one special education teacher), and a community-based inclusive program with an itinerant teacher providing consultation (an average of 12 students who were developing typically, one or two students with disabilities, two early childhood teachers, and one itinerant teacher for 1 or 2 hours per week). The reader is referred to Odom et al. (1999) for a description of these two forms of inclusion. In addition, data were collected for children who were developing typically and enrolled in early childhood education classes that did not enroll children with disabilities. For the community-based inclusive and general child care environments, children were observed in center-based programs, family group child care, and parents' day-out programs. The numerical breakdown is given in Tables 2(a) and 2(b). In Study 2, children with disabilities were enrolled in segregated early intervention programs or community-based inclusive programs. Children who were developing typically all were enrolled in early childhood education classes that did not enroll children with disabilities.

Participants

Thirty-four children with disabilities and 13 children who were developing typically participated in the Study 1 observations. The average age of the children in these groups ranged from 17.6 months for the community-based inclusive program to 28.2 months for the reverse mainstream program. In Study 2, 24 children with disabilities and 8 children who were developing typically participated. Children with disabilities in both studies met the Tennessee criteria for receiving early intervention services: To qualify for services a child must have a 25% delay in two developmental areas or a 40% delay in one area. Specific information on the participants is given in Tables 2(a) and 2(b).

Table 2(a). Study I child demographics

Study I	Segregated	Team-teaching inclusive	Community-based inclusive	Regular child care	Total (N)
Average age (in months)	25.3	28.2	17.64	24.4	
Age range (in months)	(16–33)	(20–35)	(7–32)	(11–33)	
Boys	6	7	3	7	
Girls	6	4	8	6	
Total sample	12	11	11	13	47
		FH = 3	FH = 3		
		CB = 6	CB = 9		
		PDO = 2	PDO = 1		

FH = family child care, CB = center-based child care, PDO = parents' day out.

Procedure

CASPER–I was used to collect ecobehavioral data for all children. As noted previously, CASPER–I is a momentary time sample observational system in which observers record information on a range of variables every 30 seconds. The variables and the categories within each variable are listed in Table 3. Specific operational definitions may be obtained from the first author. In these studies, observers collected five 30-minute samples of data for each child. During Study 1, observers collected information by paper and pencil and relied on a tape recorder for the cue to observe the focal child. These data were then manually entered into a computer database after the session. The summer after Study 1 was conducted CASPER–I was converted to a computerized system, which the observers used in Study 2.

Interobserver agreement was determined for 20% of the observations. Interobserver agreement was calculated by dividing the number of intervals on which observers scored the same category within a variable by 60 (the total number of intervals in the session) and multiplying by 100. Observers were trained to a minimum agreement level of 80% for each variable (collapsed across categories) before the studies began. For Study 1 and Study 2, respectively, the interobserver agreement averaged across behavioral categories within variables and the corresponding ranges were: Activity, 95% (83%–100%) and 95% (80%–100%); Initiator, 97% (94%–100%) and 96% (90%–100%); Student Behavior, 75% (64%–96%) and

Table 2(b). Study 2 child demographics

Study 2	Segregated	Team-teaching inclusive	Community-based inclusive	Regular child care	Total (N)
Average age (in months)	30.9		22.25	20.6	
Age range (in months)	(24–33)		(8–32)	(11–38)	
Boys	3		12	4	
Girls	5		4	4	
Total sample	8		16	8	32
			CB = 16	CB = 8	

CB = center-based child care.

Table 3. Study I mean percentages of observations across categories and levels of significance

Observation	Segregated (S)	Team-teaching inclusive (T)	Community-based inclusive (C)	Regular child care (R)	Probability	Post hoc
Activity						
Transition	12.5	15	10.3	13		
Gross Motor	23.8	26.4	23.3	24.3		
Book/Story	4.4	3.5	4.6	5.9		
Art	3.1	5.9	1.3	2.3		
Pretend-Play	1.1	2.1	0.4	2.1		
Large Block	0.11	0	0	0.66		
Sensory	10.5	11.5	1.4	4.6	.001	T > C, T > R
Manipulative Play	14.4	13.1	30.7	18.9	.019	S > C, S > R; C > S, T, R
Music/Dance	3.4	2.7	5.9	1.5		
Snack/Meals	18.3	11.9	16.3	16.7		
Self-Care	5.3	4.4	1.7	3.9	.008	S > C, T > C; R > C
Preacademic	0	0	0	0		
Circle Time	2.3	3	2.5	4.1		
Cannot Tell	0.02	0.09	0.46	0.31	.03	S, T, R > C
Initiator						
Adult	60.2	40.8	65.9	41.4	.03	C > T, R
Focal Child	39.8	56.4	33.5	58.6		
Peer Who is Developing Typically	0	0	0	0		
Peer Who is Experiencing Developmental Delays	0	0	0	0		
Student Behavior						
Academic	0	0	0	0		
Pretend-Play	0.3	1	0.3	0.6		
Manipulative	23.3	26.5	29.6	22.9		
Gross Motor	24.8	29.8	18	29.3		
Sing/Dance	1.9	0.68	0.78	0.72		
Self-Care	16.6	10.8	11.6	11.3		
Cleanup	0.57	0.95	0.12	0.43	.03	T > C

					p	Comparison
Books	4.5	1.2	0.93	1.9		
Observes Other Child	6.8	8.4	8.2	9.4		
Observes Teacher	14.6	10.8	16.1	12.9		
Focused Attention	2.7	1.4	1.9	4.1		
None	6.7	8.1	12.2	5.8		
Cannot Tell	0.08	0.34	0.15	0.1		
Engagement						
Engaged	69.1	71.1	61.2	68.3		
Disengaged	30.8	28.6	38.6	31.6		
Cannot Tell	0.05	0.3	0.18	0.1		
Teacher Behavior						
Support	11.7	9.8	7.9	6.1	.045	S > R
Approval	4	7.1	4.2	3.9		
Comment	9.1	6.9	8.6	7.5		
Group Direction	5.3	4.4	8.2	5.5		
None	69.9	71.7	71	76.9		
Cannot Tell	0.05	0.15	0.06	0.06		
Social Behavior						
To Teacher	9.5	11.2	7.6	9.9	.0001	R > S, T, C
To Peer	1.1	2.1	1.8	5.9		
Group Arrangement						
Solitary	20.5	28.2	27	26.7		
One-to-One	11.3	13.8	9.7	6.6		
Small Group	5.7	6.9	8.5	7.9		
Small Group with Adult	20.5	14	25.6	15.5		
Large Group	.2	2	2.1	1.9		
Large Group with Adult	41.9	33.2	35.1	45.4		
Group Composition						
All with Delays	61.4	9	8.9	0	.0001	S > T, C, R
Majority with Delays	5	12.2	.4	0	.0001	T > S, C, R
Equal	1.4	9.3	8	0	.0001	T, C > S, R
Majority without Delays	.7	27.5	49.7	0	.0001	C > S, T, R
All without Delays	0	0	.25	70.8	.0001	S > T, R
No Group	31.5	42	32.6	29.2		R > S, T, C

Table 4. Study 2 mean percentages of observations across categories and levels of significance

Observation	Segregated (S)	Community-based inclusive (C)	Regular child care (R)	Probability	Post hoc
Activity					
Transition	12.2	17.2	9.4	.04	C > R, S > R
Gross Motor	6.8	20.8	19.0		
Book/Story	18.8	24.4	30.3		
Art	4.3	3.1	0.1		
Pretend-Play	4.3	1.5	3.58		
Large Block	0.2	.06	0		
Sensory	4.7	1.3	7.1		
Manipulative Play	6.4	3.79	16.3	.006	R > C, R > S
Music/Dance	5.1	2.2	1.9		
Snack/Meals	21.9	19.1	7.2	.04	S > R, C > R
Self-Care	3.9	3.7	2.8		
Cleanup	3.9	1.7	1.3		
Preacademic	.8	.3	.3		
Circle Time	5.9	.35	.1	.0002	S > R, S > B
Initiator					
Adult	66.8	74.1	76.24		
Focal Child	32.8	24.8	23.7		
Peer Who is Developing Typically	0	.21	.04		
Student Behaviors					
Academic	4.17	2.17	3.6		
Pretend-Play	1.69	0.4	0.2		
Manipulative	26.0	30.9	32.2		
Gross Motor	8.7	19.2	21.5		
Sing/Dance	3.4	1.2	0.9	.05	S > R, S > C
Self-Care	10.0	3.7	4.0	.04	S > C, S > R

Engagement

				p	Comparison
Engaged	59.4	61.4	72.6		
Nonengaged	40.6	39.6	27.4		
Cleanup	.9	.23	.17		
Books	4.6	2.0	10.1	.003	R > S, R > C
Observes Peers	8.5	6.8	6.6		
Observes Teacher	16.1	13.7	12.4		
Focused Attention	5.9	11.94	4.03	.0003	C > R, C > N

Group Composition

All with Delays	61.9	1.84	0	.00001	S > R, S > C
Majority with Delays	8.6	1.47	0	.02	S > R, S > C
Equal	.05	.3	0		
Majority without Delays	0	3.8	0		
All without Delays	0	65.7	94.7	.00001	R > S, C > S, R > C
No Group	28.9	25.4	1.8	.001	S > R, C > R

Teacher Behavior

Support	25.11	16.1	19.4	.0001	S > R, S > B
Approval	2.3	.3	.3	.0005	S > B, S > R
Comment	8.8	1.5	2.6	.0004	S > R, S > B
Group Direction	9.8	2.2	1.5		

Social Behavior

To Teacher	26.1	13.7	19.3	.01	S > B
To Peer	4.1	4.3	5.6		

Group Arrangement

Solitary	19.6	21.7	4.2	.013	C > R, S > R
One-to-One	13.28	5.6	1.0	.0007	S > R, S > C
Small Group	4.7	9.0	0.9	.008	C > R
Small Group with Adult	21.4	7.2	3.4	.0001	S > R, S > C
Large Group	.1	9.7	.7	.005	C > S, C > R
Large Group with Adult	40.4	46.8	90.0	.001	R > C, R > S

92% (81%–100%); Social Behavior, 75% (64%–96%) and 93% (89%–100%); Adult Behavior, 76% (61%–91%) and 94% (84%–100%); Group Arrangement, 76% (57%–90%) and 96% (87%–100%); and Group Composition, 85% (72%–100%) and 91% (75%–99%).

Results

The data collected for this study are presented in Table 3 for Study 1 and in Table 4 for Study 2. Univariate analyses of variance were performed for each category, and the Duncan post hoc analysis was used when significant differences across groups were identified. Results are presented by variable.

Activity   Across classes and studies, the activities that occurred most frequently tended to be Gross Motor, Snack, and Transition. Manipulative Play occurred relatively frequently in the classes observed in Study 1, and Books occurred more frequently in Study 2 classes. Manipulative Play occurred significantly more often in the community-based inclusive classes than in the other classes during Study 1, whereas Sensory Play occurred significantly more often in the segregated and team-teaching inclusive classes. In Study 2, Snack/Meals occurred significantly less frequently in the general child care classes than in the other classes, and Circle Time occurred significantly more frequently in the segregated early intervention classes than in the other classes. Also, Transition occurred significantly less often in the general child care classes than in the other classes.

Initiator   In both studies, adult-initiated activities occurred more often than child-initiated activities, although this difference was most pronounced in Study 2. During Study 1, there were differences across classrooms, with the segregated early intervention and community-based inclusive programs having significantly more adult-initiated activities than the team-teaching inclusive and typical child care programs. This trend did not continue in Study 2.

Child Behavior   Children's behavior was similar across classes and years of the study. Children tended to engage in Manipulative Play, Gross Motor, and Self-Care (in the first study) most frequently. In Study 1, Cleanup behavior occurred more often in the team-teaching inclusive classes than in the community-based inclusive classes. In Study 2, Sing/Dance and Self-Care occurred significantly more often in the segregated classes than in the other two classes, and Books occurred more often in the typical child care classes.

Engagement is a composite measure of active student behaviors and is often construed as a measure of the quality of an early childhood environment (McWilliam & Bailey, 1992). Although there were no significant differences in overall engagement in Study 1, children in the community-based inclusive classes appeared to be slightly less engaged than children in the other three class environments. In Study 2, again, significant differences did not occur, but children in the community-based inclusive environments were slightly more engaged than children in the segregated environments, with both groups appearing to be less engaged than the children without delays in general child care environments.

Children in both classes and across both years spent a considerable amount of time observing peers or teachers or focusing attention on the task. In Study 2, children in the community-based inclusive classes engaged in significantly more focused attention than children in the other two classes.

Social Behavior   In Study 1, children engaged in very similar percentages of social behavior directed to teachers, whereas in Study 2, children in the segregated program directed more social behavior to teachers than children in the community-based inclusive programs. Social behavior directed to peers occurred relatively infrequently, although in Study 1, children without delays in the general child care environments engaged in significantly more peer social interaction than children in the other environments.

Teacher Behavior   Support and Comment were the most frequent teacher behaviors across classes and years. In Study 1, Support occurred significantly more often in the segregated than in the general child care environments. In Study 2, Approval, Comment, and Group Direction occurred significantly more often in the segregated environments than in the other environments.

Group Arrangement   In Study 1, few differences existed among classes for group arrangement, with Solitary, Small Group with Adult, and Large Group with Adult occurring most often across groups. In Study 2, Solitary occurred significantly less frequently in the general child care classes than in the other two environments. Children in the segregated classes were in One-to-One instruction and Small Group with Adult significantly more often than children in the two other types of classes. Children in the community-based inclusive environments were more often in Small Group or Large Group than children in the two other environments, and children in the general child care environments were significantly more often in Large Group with Adult than children in the two other types of environments.

Group Composition   The group composition measure illustrates the different classroom makeups. In both studies, this measurement varied in predictable directions, with children in segregated classes being in groups with only children with disabilities, and children in the team-teaching inclusive, community-based inclusive, and general early childhood classes spending most of their time in groups with children who were developing typically.

Engagement and Activity Initiator   Of particular interest in early childhood education is the relationship between activity initiator and engagement. Specifically, one might ask whether children are more often engaged when they initiate activities or when teachers are the activity initiators and whether this relationship differs for children with and without disabilities. To examine these questions we calculated conditional probabilities for engagement given either adult or child initiation of activities. These conditional probabilities are shown in Figure 1. For seven of the eight ecological environments assessed across the two studies, the conditional probabilities for engagement in child-initiated activities were substantially higher than those for engagement in adult-initiated activities. This trend was found for children with and without disabilities.

Discussion

Several conclusions may be drawn from these data. In Study 1, two forms of inclusion were examined, and they produced slightly different results. The team-teaching model produced slightly higher levels of engagement, and the community-based inclusive model produced more focused attention. These data support the proposition that "inclusion" actually consists of several different models that may have different effects for children (Odom et al., 1999).

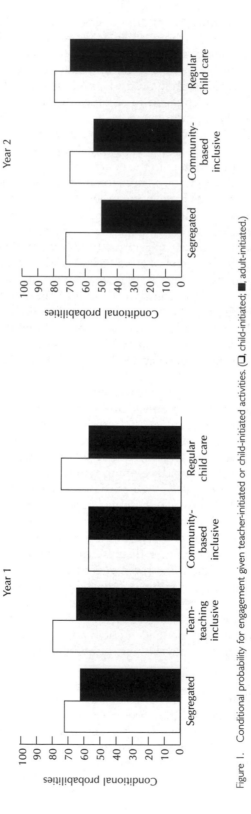

Figure 1. Conditional probability for engagement given teacher-initiated or child-initiated activities. (□, child-initiated; ■, adult-initiated.)

210

Teacher support appeared to occur more frequently in the segregated environments. This may have been attributable to the smaller teacher–child ratio or to the specific curriculum followed. Similarly, teacher-initiated activities occurred more frequently in the segregated environments and, somewhat surprisingly, also in the community-based inclusive environments in Study 1. Perhaps the consultation provided by the itinerant teacher in the community-based programs affected the teachers' perception of the children with disabilities in the class, resulting in the teachers giving more direction to those children. With older children, Brown et al. (in press) also found relatively high levels of adult support for children with disabilities in community-based environments.

The relationship between activity initiator and engagement revealed that when infants and toddlers initiated activities, they were more frequently engaged than when adults initiated the activities. Odom et al. (2000) found a similar relationship in early childhood special education and typical early childhood preschool programs. This study extends their finding to infants and toddlers in classroom environments. These results are consistent with the theory that child-initiated activities may be beneficial for supporting the engagement of young children in early childhood classroom environments.

This study did not reveal any clear advantages of segregated environments over either of the inclusive environments studied. The finding of comparable effects at the behavioral level is similar to the comparable developmental outcomes reported by Bruder and Staff (1998) for infants and toddlers in inclusive and segregated environments. Given that placement in inclusive environments is based on legal and ethical rationales as well as a developmental rationale (Bricker, 1978), a finding of comparable effects for inclusive and segregated programs might bolster support for the inclusive placements.

A Note on Computerized Observational Systems   These studies allowed a somewhat "natural experiment" in which the use of a paper-and-pencil version and a computerized version of the same coding system could be compared. When the computerized system was used in Study 2 the observer agreement percentages were higher than in Study 1 for 68% of the categories. The average agreement across categories was 83% (standard deviation = 14.56%) for Study 1 and 94% (standard deviation = 6.4%) for Study 2. It is possible that having a computer to cue the observer rather than a tape recorder, having a keyboard to enter the data rather than a code sheet and clipboard, and having immediate access to interobserver agreement data after a training and reliability session rather than at a later time after manual calculations may have led to higher levels of interobserver agreement. As stated previously, the data entry into a central database was also considerably eased by the use of a computer to collect data. However, the differences in interobserver agreement also could be attributed to different observers (although the same procedures were used to train the observers in both years) and to differences in the children being observed (although the general developmental levels of the children were similar in both years).

CONCLUSIONS

Advances in computer technology since the 1980s have allowed the development and use of sophisticated observational systems. These systems have been used productively to examine ecological variables within classrooms and to analyze the relationships among those variables. Their application to early childhood environments is increasing and should grow in the future. With this growth in observational technology may come the capacity to use more sophisticated data collection methods and analyses, such as conditional probability analysis. Future analyses might examine the relationship between certain teacher behavior and the engagement of young children, the proximity of peers who were developing typically and the participation of children with disabilities in social interaction, and children's choice of activity areas given adult or child initiation of activities.

The studies described in this chapter used a global measure of engagement. Given the central role of engagement in understanding children's learning in classroom environments, the development of more refined variable categories for assessing engagement may be the next step in this program of research. McWilliam and Bailey (1995) conducted a more precise analysis of the engagement of young children than had occurred previously, but these measures have not been merged into an ecobehavioral system. Such an addition to the available observational systems may prove useful. Finally, moving from the description of engagement to the functional analysis of ecological variables and engagement will be an important future step in this program of research and a major contribution to the field.

REFERENCES

Ager, C.L., & Shapiro, E.S. (1995). Template matching as a strategy for assessment of and intervention for preschool students with disabilities. *Topics in Early Childhood Special Education, 15,* 187–218.

Atwater, J.B., Carta, J.J., & Schwartz, I.S. (1989). *Assessment code/checklist for the evaluation of survival skills: ACCESS.* Kansas City: University of Kansas, Juniper Gardens Children's Project.

Bricker, D.D. (1978). A rationale for the integration of handicapped and nonhandicapped preschool children. In M.J. Guralnick (Ed.), *Early intervention and the integration of handicapped and nonhandicapped children* (pp. 3–26). Baltimore: University Park Press.

Brown, W.H., Odom, S.L., Holcombe, A., & Youngquist, G. (1995). *CASPER II: Code for active student participation and engagement revised. Training manual for observers.* Nashville, TN: Vanderbilt University, John F. Kennedy Center for Research on Human Development.

Brown, W.H., Odom, S.L., Li, S., & Zercher, C. (in press). Ecobehavioral assessment in inclusive early childhood programs: A portrait of preschool inclusion. *Journal of Special Education.*

Bruder, M.B., & Chandler, L. (1996). Transition. In S.L. Odom & M.E. McLean (Eds.), *Early intervention/early childhood special education: Recommended practices* (pp. 287–308). Austin, TX: PRO-ED.

Bruder, M.B., & Staff, I. (1998). A comparison of effects of type of classroom and service characteristics on toddlers with disabilities. *Topics in Early Childhood Special Education, 18,* 26–37.

Carta, J.J., Atwater, J.B., Schwartz, I.S., & Miller, P.A. (1990). Applications of ecobehavioral analysis to the study of transitions across early education. *Education and Treatment of Children, 13,* 298–315.

Carta, J.J., & Greenwood, C.R. (1989). Establishing the integrity of the independent variable in early intervention programs. *Early Education and Development, 4,* 127–140.

Carta, J.J., Greenwood, C.R., & Atwater, J.B. (1985). *Ecobehavioral system for the complex assessment of preschool environments: ESCAPE. Observational system manual.* Kansas City, KS: University of Kansas, Juniper Gardens Children's Project.

Carta, J.J., Greenwood, C.R., & Robinson, S. (1987). Application of an eco-behavioral approach to the evaluation of early intervention programs. In R.J. Prinz (Ed.), *Advances in behavioral assessment of children and families: A research annual* (Vol. 3, pp. 123–155). Greenwich, CT: JAI Press.

Carta, J.J., Sainato, D.M., & Greenwood, C.R. (1988). Advances in the ecological assessment of classroom instruction for young children with handicaps. In S.L. Odom & M.B. Karnes (Eds.), *Early intervention for infants and young children with handicaps: An empirical base* (pp. 217–239). Baltimore: Paul H. Brookes Publishing Co.

Education for All Handicapped Children Act of 1975, PL 94-142, 20 U.S.C. §§ 1400 *et seq.*

Education of the Handicapped Act Amendments of 1986, PL 99-457, 20 U.S.C. §§ 1400 *et seq.*

Favazza, P.C., & Odom, S.L. (1993). *CASPER: Code for active student participation and engagement revised. Training manual for observers.* Nashville, TN: Vanderbilt University, John F. Kennedy Center for Research on Human Development.

Fox, J.J. (1990). Ecology, environmental arrangement, and setting events: An interbehavioral perspective on organizing settings for behavioral development. *Education and Treatment of Children, 13,* 364–373.

Greenwood, C.R., Carta, J.J., Kamps, D., & Arreaga-Mayer, C. (1990). Ecobehavioral analysis of classroom instruction. In S.R. Schroeder (Ed.), *Ecobehavioral analysis and developmental disabilities: The twenty-first century* (pp. 33–63). New York: Springer-Verlag New York.

Greenwood, C.R., Delquadri, J.C., Stanley, S.O., Terry, B., & Hall, R.V. (1985). Assessment of eco-behavioral interaction in school settings. *Behavioral Assessment, 7,* 331–347.

Guralnick, M.J., & Neville, B. (1997). Designing early intervention programs to promote children's social competence. In M.J. Guralnick (Ed.), *The effectiveness of early intervention* (pp. 579–610). Baltimore: Paul H. Brookes Publishing Co.

Handicapped Children's Early Education Act of 1968, PL 90-538, 20 U.S.C. §§ 621 *et seq.*

Hartmann, D.P., & Wood, D.D. (1990). Observational methods. In A.S. Bellack, M. Hersen, & A.E. Kazdin (Eds.), *International handbook of behavior modification and therapy* (2nd ed., pp. 107–138). New York: Plenum Press.

Hoier, T.S., McConnell, S., & Pallay, A.G. (1987). Observational assessment for planning and evaluating educational transitions: An initial analysis of template matching. *Behavioral Assessment, 9,* 5–19.

Kontos, S., Moore, D., & Giorgetti, K. (1998). The ecology of inclusion. *Topics in Early Childhood Special Education, 18,* 38–48.

Kontos, S., & Wilcox-Herzog, A. (1997). Influences on children's competence in early childhood classrooms. *Early Childhood Research Quarterly, 12,* 247–262.

McCormick, L., Noonan, M.J., & Heck, R. (1998). Variables affecting engagement in inclusive preschool classrooms. *Journal of Early Intervention, 21,* 160–176.

McWilliam, R.A., & Bailey, D.B., Jr. (1992). Promoting engagement and mastery. In D.B. Bailey, Jr., & M. Wolery (Eds.), *Teaching infants and preschoolers with disabilities* (2nd ed., pp. 229–255). Upper Saddle River, NJ: Merrill.

McWilliam, R.A., & Bailey, D.B., Jr. (1995). Effects of classroom social structure and disability on engagement. *Topics in Early Childhood Special Education, 15,* 123–147.

Morris, E.K., & Midgley, B.D. (1990). Some historical and conceptual foundations of ecobehavioral analysis. In S.R. Schroeder (Ed.), *Ecobehavioral analysis and developmental disabilities: The twenty-first century* (pp. 1–32). New York: Springer-Verlag New York.

Odom, S.L., Cronin, P.F., Youngquist, G., Horn, E.M., & Brown, W.H. (1994, May). *Ecobehavioral analysis of four early childhood education settings for infants and toddlers with and without developmental delays.* Paper presented at the annual meeting of the Association for Behavior Analysis, Atlanta, GA.

Odom, S.L., Horn, E.M., Marquart, J., Hanson, M.J., Wolfberg, P., Beckman, P.J., Lieber, J., Li, S., Schwartz, I., Janko, S., & Sandall, S. (1999). On the forms of inclusion: Organizational structure and individualized service delivery models. *Journal of Early Intervention, 22,* 185–199.

Odom, S.L., & Kaiser, A.P. (1997). Prevention and early intervention during early childhood: Theoretical and empirical bases for research. In W.E. MacLean, Jr. (Ed.), *Ellis' handbook of mental deficiency, psychology theory, and research* (3rd ed., pp. 137–173). Mahwah, NJ: Lawrence Erlbaum Associates.

Odom, S.L., Peterson, C., McConnell, S.R., & Ostrosky, M. (1990). Ecobehavioral analysis of early education/specialized classroom settings and peer social interaction. *Education and Treatment of Children, 13,* 316–330.

Odom, S.L., Skellenger, A., & Ostrosky, M. (2000). *Ecobehavioral analysis of early childhood special education and early childhood education classes.* Manuscript submitted for publication.

Ostrosky, M.M., Skellenger, A.C., Odom, S.L., McConnell, S.R., & Peterson, C. (1994). Teachers' schedules and actual time spent in activities in preschool special education classes. *Journal of Early Intervention, 18,* 25–33.

Schwartz, I.S., Carta, J.J., & Grant, S. (1996). Examining the use of recommended language intervention practices in early childhood special education classrooms. *Topics in Early Childhood Special Education, 16,* 251–272.

Sontag, J.C. (1997). Contextual factors influencing the sociability of preschool children with disabilities in integrated and segregated classrooms. *Exceptional Children, 63,* 389–404.

Stanley, S.O., & Greenwood, C.R. (1981). *CISSAR: Code for instructional structure and student academic response: Observer's manual.* Kansas City, KS: University of Kansas, Juniper Gardens Children's Project.

Swan, W.W. (1980). The Handicapped Children's Early Education Program. *Exceptional Children, 47,* 12–16.

14

Analysis of Early Communication and Language Intervention Practices Using Observational Technology

JaneDiane Smith,
Jon Tapp, and
Steven F. Warren

Since the late 1970s, great advances have been made in the methods and measures researchers use to analyze early communication and language development and intervention effects in children with developmental delays (Miller, 1996). Yet the technologies that researchers apply to actually collect these data generally have not advanced beyond the ubiquitous use of tape recording and videotaping (Cole, Dale, & Thal, 1996; Dale, 1978). For the most part behavioral researchers still capture the data they intend to analyze just as they did before the advent and wide dissemination of microtechnologies. Once recorded, these audiotapes and videotapes are typically subjected to hours of painstaking coding.

Given the complex nature of language acquisition and use, the time and resources spent in analysis of audiotapes and videotapes is understandable. The use of an increasing array of linguistic and pragmatic analysis programs (e.g., *Systematic Analysis of Language Transcripts* [*SALT*]; Miller & Chapman, 1997) can speed the classification and analysis of data once it has been transformed (i.e., transcribed and coded), but the laborious collection and initial coding process will remain state of the art for many types of communication and language research for the foreseeable future. Nevertheless, there are some types of questions for which on-line observational technologies can make data collection substantially easier and less expensive and that facilitate a more comprehensive array of statistical analyses. These are questions for which the units of analysis are not explicitly linguistic or phonemic in nature but that instead can be codified as an observable set of discrete behaviors. The purpose of this chapter is to describe one such application: the use of optical bar code readers to collect data on the types of language input that children with communication delays receive in various early intervention contexts.

ASSESSING COMMUNICATION AND LANGUAGE INTERVENTION PRACTICES

Infants and toddlers at risk for disabilities frequently experience delays in communication and/or language development. The effects of unremediated delays on social and cognitive development are well documented. Consequently, a variety of intervention practices have been recommended to promote communication and language development in young children with disabilities (Warren & Reichle, 1992; Wetherby, Warren, & Reichle, 1998). Although empirical validation of the effectiveness of such practices is well documented, few descriptive data exist on the extent to which the recommended communication and language intervention practices are implemented in early intervention settings.

Teacher use of recommended communication and language intervention practices with infants and toddlers with disabilities was the focus of an investigation by Smith and Warren (1998). The primary purpose of the study was to determine the extent to which specific communication and language intervention practices were actually being implemented across types of early intervention programs (e.g., integrated, inclusive) and classroom activities (e.g., free play, snack). In an effort to obtain a small but representative sample in which to study the implementation of recommended practices in early intervention settings for children younger than 3 years, Smith and Warren conducted observations in four integrated center-based early intervention programs and four inclusive community-based child care programs.

Communicative interactions were observed between the lead teacher and all children in each classroom during four activities: free play, group, snack- or mealtime, and structured activities (e.g., art, sensory tables). Data were collected for eight categories of recommended communication and language intervention practices: Prompts (e.g., following a child's lead, redirect), Models (active and passive), Linguistic Mapping, Recasting, Imitation, Teacher Talk, Acknowledgment, and No Occurrence. Coding definitions were developed by adapting and synthesizing information from the recommended practices literature (Goldstein, Kaczmarek, & Hepting, 1996) and from two earlier studies that evaluated recommended language intervention practices in preschool children with disabilities (Roberts, Bailey, & Nychka, 1991; Schwartz, Carta, & Grant, 1996). Definitions for these categories are provided in Table 1. Teacher behaviors were coded for occurrence and whether the behavior was directed at a child with disabilities (e.g., target), at a typically developing child (e.g., peer), or at both. To expedite data collection, management, and analysis, a software program was developed for use with a commercially available optical bar code reader to run on personal computers (*WandaPC*[1]) (Tapp & Smith, 1998).

---

[1]Questions or comments regarding the *WandaPC* software can be sent via e-mail to Chapter 14 co-author Jon Tapp at jon.tapp@vanderbilt.edu.

Table 1.   Categories and definitions of recommended communication and language intervention practices

Category	Definition	Example
Prompting communication (Prompt/following the child's lead)	Following the child's attentional lead, the teacher asks a question or delivers a statement to which the child is requested to make a verbal or nonverbal response.	"What is this?" "Tell me what you want."
Prompting communication (Prompt/redirects child's focus of attention or behavior)	The teacher redirects the child's focus of attention or behavior by asking a question or delivering a statement to which the child is requested to make a response.	The child is walking away from the snack table, and the teacher asks, "Do you want a snack this morning?"
Modeling communication (Model/active)	The teacher provides a demonstration of a desired verbal or nonverbal response.	The teacher says, "Say cookie," and gives the child at least 3 seconds to respond.
Modeling communication (Model/passive)	The teacher provides a series of models in rapid succession without providing an opportunity for the child to respond.	The teacher says, "Cracker, say cracker, want cracker," in rapid succession with no opportunity for the child to respond.
Linguistic mapping (Map)	Immediately following the child's communicative act, the teacher provides a descriptive label or states the core meaning for the act.	Child: [Looks at ball and points.] Teacher: "Ball."
Recasting (Recast)	The teacher provides a verbalization that significantly expands or elaborates on the intent of the child's original verbal response.	Child: "Pour rice." Teacher: "Let's pour the rice in the bowl."
Imitation (Imit)	The teacher immediately imitates the child's vocalization.	Child: "Fish." Teacher: "Fish."
Teacher talk (Talk)	The teacher provides verbal statements to a specific child or to a group of children that have a mean length utterance longer than three words.	"It's time to clean up and get ready for snack."
Acknowledgment (Ack)	The teacher verbally acknowledges the child's communicative behavior with or without explicit feedback.	Child: "More juice." Teacher: "Good, you asked for more juice." or Child: "Read story." Teacher: "Okay."
No occurrence	The behaviors as described in this table did not occur during the observation interval.	

WANDAPC: STEP BY STEP

Next, the *WandaPC* (Tapp & Smith, 1998) program is described in step-by-step detail, beginning with a description of the software itself and the necessary hardware to run the program. Information is also presented pertaining to the logistics of creating bar code sheets and code files. Recommendations for managing the TimeWands are presented, as are guidelines for sorting the raw data. Finally, data analysis capabilities of the *WandaPC* program are described.

Software Description

To facilitate collection of interval data for this project a software program was developed to sort, manage, and count codes entered by the scanning of bar codes using Videx TimeWand bar code readers. *WandaPC* is designed to deal with interval-based data for which the observation is done using alternating observe and record periods. The duration of these periods can be customized easily because the end of each interval is determined by an "interval end" code in the data stream. For this study we used a portable audiotape cassette player to cue the observers to observe and then record. The observe duration was 10 seconds and the record duration was 5 seconds. We programmed a computer to make a tape using a digitally recorded voice that said "observe" and then "record" at the proper times. At the end of each recording period, a special code was scanned to indicate the end of that particular interval.

WandaPC sorts scanned codes into files that consist of single observation sessions of interval-by-interval data from the raw scan data files that are downloaded from the bar code readers. In addition, the program performs interobserver agreement analysis and determines percentage of interval counts on the sorted session files. The output from these counting analyses is then loaded into an *Excel* spreadsheet and further analyzed using a statistical analysis software package (e.g., *SPSS* [SPSS, Inc., 1990]).

Hardware Requirements

The *WandaPC* program requires an IBM-compatible personal computer with Windows 3.1 (or later version). At least 4 megabytes of random access memory and 5 megabytes of free hard drive space are required to run the program. At least two Videx TimeWand bar code readers, a downloader/charger cradle, and the download software used with the readers are required. The bar code readers, related hardware, and software are available from Videx (http://www.videx.com). Although it is not essential, a laser-quality printer should be used if possible to print bar code sheets for use in observation sessions because lower-quality printers produce bar codes that often scan poorly.

Bar Code Sheets

Bar code sheets can be made with any word processor for Windows using the Code 3 of 9 bar code font supplied with the TimeWands. The font is selected as any font is chosen; codes are then typed using that font. Care must be taken to ensure that the bar codes are not too small to scan reliably or too large to fit on one page. We created two sheets, one for header information (e.g., observation site numbers, primary and reliability observer, activities) and a second for the codes to be scanned during each observation period (e.g., teacher behavior codes).

Examples of our bar code scan sheets are shown in Figure 1 (header information) and Figure 2 (teacher behavior codes).

Code File

To check codes and determine the order in which analyses are output, a code file must be created containing the same codes that are on the scan sheet, followed by a short description of each code used to label the program's output. The code file is a "text-only" file that can be created using Notepad or any editor utility that can save text-only files. The code file used in this study is shown in Figure 3. The first line of the code file (in this case, "19") indicates to the program the number of codes it is to read in; each subsequent line consists of the code, a comma, and a description of the code in quotation marks.

Managing the TimeWands

Bar code symbology refers to the way in which bars are arranged in a bar code to be recognized and converted to characters. Examples of symbologies include Universal Product Code (a symbology commonly used in supermarkets), Code-A Bar (another commonly used bar code), and Code 3 of 9 symbology. The TimeWands were programmed with the standard application and the Auto 128 symbology, which allows the reader to recognize many different types of bar code

Site

SITE1

SITE2

SITE3

SITE4

SITE5

SITE6

SITE7

SITE8

Primary Observer

P01

P02

P03

Reliability Observer

R01

R02

R03

Activity

FRPLAY

SNACK

GROUP

ART

Figure 1. Teacher strategies file header scan sheet.

||||||||||||||||||||||||||||
START

Maps

||||||||||||||||||||||||||||
EDIT

Prompts

||||||||||||||||||||
TM

Talk

||||||||||||||||||
TL

||||||||||||||||||||
PM

||||||||||||||||||
TT

||||||||||||||||||
TR

Recasts

||||||||||||||||||
PT

||||||||||||||||||
PL

Acks

||||||||||||||||||
PR

||||||||||||||||||
TRC

||||||||||||||||||
TAK

||||||||||||||||||
PRC

||||||||||||||||||
PAK

Models

Imits

||||||||||||||||||
TA

Nothing

||||||||||||||||||
TP

||||||||||||||||||
TI

||||||||||||||||||
NOT

||||||||||||||||||
PA

||||||||||||||||||
PI

Interval End

||||||||||||||||||
INT

||||||||||||||||||
PP

End

||||||||||||||||||
END

Figure 2.   Teacher strategies interval codes scan sheet for recommended communication and language intervention codes.

```
19
TL,"Target L Prompt"
TR,"Target R Prompt"
PL,"Peer L Prompt"
PR,"Peer R Prompt"
TA,"Target A Model"
TP,"Target P Model"
PA,"Peer A Model"
PP,"Peer P Model"
TM,"Target Map"
PM,"Peer Map"
TRC,"Target Recast"
PRC,"Peer Recast"
TI,"Target Imit"
PI,"Peer Imit"
TT,"Target Talk"
PT,"Peer Talk"
TAK,"Target Ack"
PAK,"Peer Ack"
NOT,"Nothing Happened"
```

Figure 3.   The *WandaPC* code file used by Smith and Warren (1998).

symbologies and efficiently use the TimeWands' full 128 kilobytes of memory. The TimeWand bar code readers scan and store codes that can be downloaded later to the host personal computer and stored in a file by the TimeWand II *Application Builder* for Windows (Videx, 1997) software. *Application Builder* permits programming of the TimeWands to provide prompts to the user on the liquid crystal display screen. This prompting takes up memory in the TimeWands and was not necessary for our purposes. Because we wanted to maximize the memory available for data we did not use the Application feature of the bar code readers and instead used the Standard Application, which presents a "scan any code" prompt at all times.

The battery in the TimeWands lasts for 8–10 hours of continual use. Normal, noncontinuous use typically results in data being retained for several days without recharging of the bar code reader's batteries. Recharging is accomplished by plugging the reader (i.e., the TimeWand) into the downloader/charger provided by the manufacturer. Data need to be downloaded from the TimeWand to the computer before the memory of the reader becomes full. Management of the data files was most effective if we downloaded and charged the TimeWands daily. This allowed us to arrange data files into directories by day for easier tracking.

Sorting the Raw Data

To start an observation session, the observer(s) scanned the pertinent header information used for labeling data, then scanned "START." This code tells the program to start arranging data into intervals. *WandaPC* sorts the raw scan data file into single files for each session. The header information is used to name the single-session files. Raw files can be sorted either one at a time or an entire directory at a time. Examples of a raw scan file and the resulting sorted session file are shown in Figures 4 and 5, respectively. All of the header scans are provided in the first line of the session file. The remainder of the session file contains a row of codes scanned in each record interval.

Descriptions of Analyses

Once several sessions of frequency/percentage of intervals data are sent to a data file, they can be exported to *SPSS* (SPSS, Inc., 1990) for analysis. *WandaPC* also performs two types of analysis: interobserver agreement and frequency/percentage of intervals analysis. Analyses are run by selecting them from the standard pull-down menu on the *WandaPC*'s menu bar. Output is provided as a text file opened with Notepad or in the form of a file that can be opened with a spreadsheet program.

For interobserver agreement, the program asks the user for the first session file, then the file to compare it with. The first file is read, and for every code each interval is examined in each file for the presence or absence of the code. The presence of the code is tallied for each interval for each file. A two-by-two matrix is created for each code, and the values and agreement statistics, including Cohen's *kappa* (Cohen, 1960), are provided in the output. Figure 6 shows how codes are tallied into a two-by-two matrix.

H 19980331155032 00 JANE	19980331101629 00 INT	19980331102047 00 TP
19980331100911 00 SITE3	19980331101641 00 NOT	19980331102048 00 INT
19980331100913 00 P01	19980331101641 00 INT	19980331102101 00 TL
19980331100914 00 SNACK	19980331101659 00 PT	19980331102102 00 INT
19980331101251 00 START	19980331101700 00 INT	19980331102117 00 TM
19980331101300 00 TL	19980331101714 00 TA	19980331102118 00 INT
19980331101302 00 TA	19980331101717 00 INT	19980331102142 00 NOT
19980331101303 00 INT	19980331101726 00 PI	19980331102143 00 INT
19980331101315 00 TP	19980331101730 00 TL	19980331102147 00 PL
19980331101316 00 INT	19980331101731 00 INT	19980331102148 00 INT 1
19980331101330 00 TT	19980331101747 00 TA	19980331102204 00 NOT
19980331101331 00 INT	19980331101750 00 INT	19980331102205 00 INT
19980331101343 00 TL	19980331101800 00 TP	19980331102217 00 NOT
19980331101345 00 INT	19980331101801 00 INT	19980331102218 00 INT
19980331101358 00 TT	19980331101814 00 TA	19980331102231 00 NOT
19980331101404 00 INT	19980331101816 00 INT	19980331102232 00 INT
19980331101413 00 TL	19980331101830 00 TL	19980331102246 00 TL
19980331101414 00 INT	19980331101831 00 TM	19980331102248 00 INT
19980331101430 00 PT	19980331101833 00 TA	19980331102302 00 TM
19980331101431 00 INT	19980331101846 00 TA	19980331102312 00 EDIT
19980331101444 00 PA	19980331101849 00 TP	19980331102313 00 TRC
19980331101444 00 INT	19980331101852 00 INT	19980331102315 00 INT
19980331101457 00 TL	19980331101902 00 TA	19980331102331 00 NOT
19980331101500 00 TP	19980331101903 00 INT	19980331102332 00 INT
19980331101503 00 PP	19980331101915 00 TA	19980331102346 00 NOT
19980331101504 00 INT	19980331101915 00 TP	19980331102347 00 INT
19980331101519 00 TP	19980331101916 00 INT	19980331102402 00 TL
19980331101520 00 INT	19980331101930 00 NOT	19980331102405 00 TP
19980331101529 00 TT	19980331101930 00 INT	19980331102406 00 INT
19980331101529 00 PT	19980331101945 00 PT	19980331102418 00 NOT
19980331101530 00 INT	19980331101947 00 INT	19980331102419 00 INT
19980331101541 00 PL	19980331101959 00 TT	19980331102432 00 TT
19980331101543 00 INT	19980331102001 00 TP	19980331102437 00 INT
19980331101556 00 PL	19980331102002 00 INT	19980331102448 00 TT
19980331101558 00 PI	19980331102016 00 TL	19980331102451 00 TA
19980331101559 00 INT	19980331102017 00 INT	19980331102452 00 INT
19980331101614 00 PL	19980331102030 00 PL	19980331102512 00 TT
19980331101615 00 INT	19980331102033 00 PP	19980331102513 00 INT
19980331101628 00 TP	19980331102034 00 INT	19980331102523 00 END

Figure 4.   Sample raw scan data file.

JANE SITE3 P01 SNACK 03/31/1998 10:12:51   TA/
TL/TA/   TA/TP/
TP/   NOT/
TT/   PT/
TL/   TT/TP/
TT/   TL/
TL/   PL/PP/
PT/   TP/
PA/   TL/
TL/TP/PP/   TM/
TP/   NOT/
TT/PT/   PL/
PL/   NOT/
PL/PI/   NOT/
PL/   NOT/
TP/   TL/
NOT/   TRC/
PT/   NOT/
TA/   NOT/
PI/TL/   TL/TP/
TA/   NOT/
TP/   TT/
TA/   TT/TA/
TL/TM/   TT/
TA/TP/   END/

Figure 5.   Single-session file obtained from the raw scan file in Figure 4.

Cohen's *kappa* (Cohen, 1960) evaluates interobserver reliability. However, because of the low frequency with which specific recommended communication and language intervention practices (e.g., linguistic mapping, recasting, imitation) occurred in this study, the generalizability approach (Cronbach, Gleser, Nanda, & Rajaratnam, 1972) was used to calculate interobserver reliability. Information obtained from a *kappa* matrix was used to calculate generalizability (intraclass) coefficients between observers across observation sessions by activity. Reliability data were obtained on 31% of the observations. Generalizability coefficients were acceptable and ranged from .85 to 1.0.

The frequency/percentage analysis calculates the number of times each code occurs in the session. The output file provides the frequency and percentage of intervals for each code in each session. These data can be output for a whole directory of files and imported into a spreadsheet format for further analysis.

Cell A: Total number of intervals in which code X is present in both files.	Cell B: Total number of intervals in which code X is present in first file only.
Cell C: Total number of intervals in which code X is present in second file only.	Cell D: Total number of intervals in which code X is not present in either file.

Figure 6.   Sample interobserver agreement tally.

TEACHERS' USE OF RECOMMENDED PRACTICES

The percentage of time that teachers were observed implementing recommended communication and language intervention strategies varied according to the specific strategies being observed (e.g., prompts, models, recasts). For children with disabilities, use of strategies ranged from a high of 46% (e.g., teacher talk in center-based programs) to a low of 0% (e.g., recasting and linguistic mapping in community-based programs). For typically developing peers, the range was also from 46% (e.g., teacher talk in community-based programs) to 0% (e.g., linguistic mapping and recasting in both center-based and community-based programs). Because of the low frequency with which various strategies occurred (e.g., linguistic mapping, recasting), categories were collapsed to represent passive and active communication and language intervention strategies. *Passive strategies* (e.g., prompts following a child's lead, passive models, teacher talk) tend to support the use of a child's existing communication and language skills, whereas *active strategies* (e.g., active models, linguistic mapping, imitation, recasts) are recommended to teach new and/or higher-level skills. The data also indicated that passive communication and language intervention strategies occurred more frequently than active strategies regardless of program type (e.g., center-based, community-based), as shown in Figure 7.

We also examined differences in the use of strategies between types of programs (i.e., centered based, community based) and activities (i.e., free play, group, snacktime/mealtime, structured). For this analysis, categories represented strategies implemented with all children (i.e., with and without disabilities). Nested analyses of variance (ANOVAs) indicated a significant effect for activity (Fisher's F ratio [F](24, 64) = 7.01, probability [p] < .000) for the passive communication and language intervention strategies and signifi-cant effects for program type (F(1, 64) = 20.29, p < .000), site within program (F(6, 64) = 4.28, p < .001), and activity within site within program (F(24, 64) = 1.71, p < .046) for the active communication and language intervention strategies. Center-based programs were observed implementing active language strategies significantly more often than community-based programs. Implementation of these active communication and language intervention practices also varied significantly by individual site and type of activity observed.

The results of this preliminary study suggest that the percentage of time that teachers implement recommended communication and language intervention strategies may be low to moderate regardless of program orientation (i.e., integrated versus inclusive). The implementation of active language intervention strategies with young children with disabilities occurred infrequently (e.g., 12% of the time in center-based programs, 3% of the time in community-based programs). Despite these low levels of implementation, significant effects were identified for program type. Center-based programs were observed implementing active strategies significantly more often than community-based programs. Possible explanations for the differences in implementation between center-based and community-based programs include factors such as teacher knowledge, training, and education and the specific language needs of the children enrolled in the programs. This analysis was limited to just eight programs. Thus, we view these results as strictly preliminary. Future research with a large sample of programs is

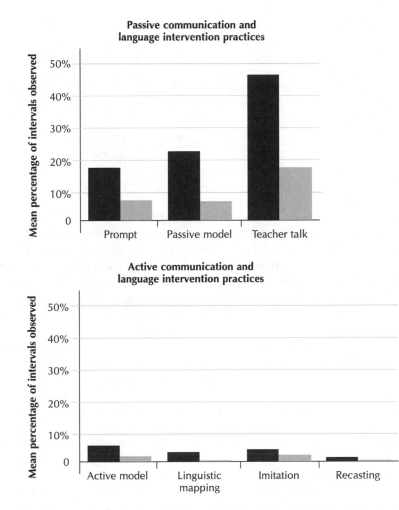

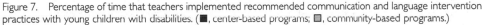

Figure 7. Percentage of time that teachers implemented recommended communication and language intervention practices with young children with disabilities. (■, center-based programs; ▨, community-based programs.)

necessary to verify the differences in implementation between program type, individual sites, and activities.

DISCUSSION

The use of systematic computer-assisted behavior observation technologies such as those described here is uncommon in the early intervention literature. Nevertheless, this technology can be a useful, cost-effective tool for researchers and practitioners interested in behavior that can be coded on-line into discrete categories. Many types of behavior relevant to communication and language development and intervention meet this requirement (e.g., child communicative interactions).

In our application, the optical bar code reader technology offered several advantages. The Videx TimeWand system is easy to use and efficient. It can be used to collect, manage, and analyze a relatively large amount of data. Previously, interobserver reliability data were calculated by hand. Each observation session required approximately 1 hour to count, tabulate, and calculate individual code reliability. Similar time investments were required to calculate frequency data. Using the TimeWand technology, interobserver agreement and frequency data for each session were calculated in approximately 10 minutes, including the time required to download, sort, and analyze the data. We estimate that we saved at least 100 hours of data management and analysis time by using the TimeWand technology in the course of 2 months of data collection. Because the data were exported to a spreadsheet and subsequently to *SPSS* (SPSS, Inc., 1990) for further analysis, human error in calculation also was eliminated. Additional advantages associated with the TimeWands are their compact and lightweight design, which makes them portable and easy to use, and the minimal amount of maintenance and upkeep required.

One limitation of optical bar code readers is that the user cannot observe and record at the same moment, which makes second-to-second real-time recording impossible. An interval observation system (e.g., observe-record-observe-record) must be used. A major limitation specific to the TimeWand technology is the precision with which data needs to be downloaded from the wands. If data are inadvertently downloaded into the wrong file, existing data are replaced with the new data and the existing data become irretrievable. Another major limitation is that TimeWands cannot be used in bright sunlight because it confuses the laser readers. Additional minor disadvantages include the audible cues emitted from the TimeWand and the daily logistics of transporting and maintaining the equipment. An audible beep indicates when a bar code has been properly scanned and stored in the TimeWand. For some children, the beep from the TimeWand and the audiotape cues may be distracting initially (this feature can be disabled by the manufacturer). Occasionally, bar codes may be scanned improperly and repeat scans required. Finally, maintaining the equipment requires recharging the TimeWands regularly as well as carrying additional batteries and an adapter for the audiotape cassette player.

The advantages of the TimeWand typically far outweigh the minor disadvantages inherent in this technology. This observation technology may be useful for many researchers interested in early intervention practices. In our case, the use of TimeWand technology allowed us to collect and analyze data on early language intervention practices in several different contexts much more efficiently and cheaper than traditional methods.

REFERENCES

Cohen, J. (1960). A coefficient of agreement for nominal scales. *Educational and Psychological Measurement, 20*, 37–46.

Cole, K.N., Dale, P.S., & Thal, D.J. (Eds.). (1996). *Communication and language intervention series: Vol. 6. Assessment of communication and language.* Baltimore: Paul H. Brookes Publishing Co.

Cronbach, L.J., Gleser, G.C., Nanda, H., & Rajaratnam, N. (1972). *The dependability of behavioral measurements: Theory of generalizability for scores and profiles.* New York: John Wiley & Sons.

Dale, P.S. (1978). What does observing language mean? In G.P. Sackett (Ed.), *Observing behavior: Vol. 1. Theory and applications in mental retardation* (pp. 219–238). Baltimore: University Park Press.

Goldstein, H., Kaczmarek, L.A., & Hepting, N.H. (1996). Indicators of quality in communi-cation intervention. In S.L. Odom & M.E. McLean (Eds.), *Early intervention/early childhood special education: Recommended practices* (pp. 197–221). Austin, TX: PRO-ED.

Miller, J.F. (1996). Progress in assessing, describing, and defining child language disorder. In K.N. Cole, P.S. Dale, & D.J. Thal (Eds.), *Communication and language intervention series: Vol. 6. Assessment of communication and language* (pp. 309–324). Baltimore: Paul H. Brookes Publishing Co.

Miller, J.F., & Chapman, R.S. (1997). *SALT: Systematic Analysis of Language Transcripts (Windows version 4.1): User's manual.* Madison: University of Wisconsin–Madison, The Waisman Center, Language Analysis Laboratory.

Roberts, J.E., Bailey, D.B., & Nychka, H.B. (1991). Teachers' use of strategies to facilitate the communication of preschool children with disabilities. *Journal of Early Intervention, 15,* 358–376.

Schwartz, I.S., Carta, J.J., & Grant, S. (1996). Examining the use of recommended language intervention practices in early childhood special education classrooms. *Topics in Early Childhood Special Education, 16,* 251–272.

Smith, J., & Warren, S.F. (1998). *Teachers' use of recommended strategies to facilitate communica-tion and language development in young children with disabilities.* Unpublished manuscript, Vanderbilt University, Nashville, TN.

SPSS, Inc. (1990). *SPSS Statistical Data Analysis* [Software]. Chicago: Author.

Tapp, J.T., & Smith, J. (1998). *WandaPC: Software for analysis of bar code data* [Unpublished software]. Nashville, TN: Vanderbilt University, John F. Kennedy Center for Research on Human Development.

Videx, Inc. (1997). *TimeWand II Application Builder for Windows* [Software]. Corvallis, OR: Author.

Warren, S.F., & Reichle, J. (Eds.). (1992). *Communication and language intervention series: Vol. 1. Causes and effects in communication and language intervention.* Baltimore: Paul H. Brookes Publishing Co.

Wetherby, A.M., Warren, S.F., & Reichle, J. (Eds.). (1998). *Communication and language inter-vention series: Vol. 7. Transitions in prelinguistic communication.* Baltimore: Paul H. Brookes Publishing Co.

15

Ecobehavioral Assessment Systems Software (EBASS)

A System for Observation in Education Settings

Charles R. Greenwood,
Judith J. Carta, and
Harriett Dawson

In this chapter, we discuss a line of research and a family of computer-assisted observational instruments designed to inform the development and validation of effective educational environments for children with and without developmental disabilities. The observational instruments are the product of a 35-year effort to improve the social and academic achievements of children at risk for developmental retardation and early school failure through home-based, community-based, and school-based interventions at the Juniper Gardens Children's Project in Kansas City, Kansas (Greenwood et al., 1992). These instruments for preschool (Ecobehavioral System for Complex Assessment of Preschool Environments [ESCAPE]), general education (Code for Instructional Structure and Student Aca-

This chapter was supported by the National Institute of Child Health and Human Development and the Office of Special Education and Rehabilitative Services, U.S. Department of Education (Grant Nos. HD03144, H180B00005, H023C50111, and H023G50012). Additional support was provided by the Kansas Center for Mental Retardation and Developmental Disabilities (Grant No. HD02528).

The comments made in this chapter are those of the authors and do not reflect in any way the views of the funding agencies. *EBASS* product and pricing information can be obtained at the Juniper Gardens Children's Project World Wide Web site: http://www.lsi.ukans.edu/jg/jgcpindx.htm.

demic Response [CISSAR]), and general and special education (Mainstream-CISSAR [MS-CISSAR]) classroom settings are available for use on portable note-book computers using *Ecobehavioral Assessment Systems Software* (*EBASS*) (Green-wood, Carta, Kamps, & Delquadri, 1997). These instruments measure a range of classroom environmental events and teacher and student behaviors, and they have been used in an increasingly large number of descriptive and intervention-oriented research studies (e.g., Greenwood, 1996; Greenwood, Carta, Kamps, & Arreaga-Mayer, 1990).

POVERTY AND DEVELOPMENTAL DISABILITIES

Children living in poverty are at increased risk for developmental delay(s) (Brooks-Gunn & Duncan, 1997). For example, developmental delay is the most common form of mental retardation, and it is thought to be attributable to the toxic effects of unstimulating, underresourced, noncaring, adversive, and abusive environmental factors rather than to organic factors (e.g., Baumeister, Kupstas, & Klindworth, 1990). In the lives of children in poverty, these environments are those of the home, community, and school. Because parents are the first teachers of children, the quality of parenting is a factor in the risk for and the prevention of developmental delays.

Children living in poverty are more likely to have only one primary caregiver in the home. The parents of children in poverty are more likely to be unemployed, underemployed, and undereducated. The parents of children in poverty are known to interact less often with their children, to not respond to their children's initiations to interact, and to terminate interactions with their children more often (e.g., Hart & Risley, 1995). Children in poverty are more likely to be exposed to drugs, alcohol, and violence. Children in poverty who have multiple and cumulative risk factors in their lives (single caregiver plus undereducated caregiver plus very low income plus large family) have normatively lower developmental outcomes (e.g., Carta et al., 1997; Sameroff, 1990).

Children in poverty are less likely to have access to child care programs in their communities, and when they are available programs in impoverished communities are more likely to be of lower quality, reflecting the limited resources available to support them. This is similarly true for preschool and elementary schools in impoverished communities. For example, children in elementary schools in impoverished communities were reported to be less engaged in academic responding during classroom instruction because of less than optimal instructional practices and teacher behaviors compared with children in nonimpoverished settings (Greenwood, Hart, Walker, & Risley, 1994). Even with massive federal government efforts to support and improve educational programs and services in impoverished areas, educational facilities and services often are characterized by less than current and optimal facilities, program features, curricula, instructional practices, and technologies. Consequently, children in urban impoverished areas are more likely to manifest developmental delays, and they are less prepared socially and academically for school.

PROSPECTS FOR PREVENTION

The issue at hand is prevention of the lifelong effects of poor instruction for all children, particularly those living in poverty. The subject matter of concern is the effect of classroom instruction on the behavioral development of young children with and without disabilities. Of particular interest is a student's engagement in highly desirable and relevant behaviors appropriate to the preschool and the elementary school classroom. Also of interest is a student's engagement in less desirable task management and competing inappropriate behaviors. Another concern is the effectiveness of classroom contexts, the instructional arrangements, and teacher behaviors intended to promote students' academic and social responding.

With *EBASS*, classroom instruction and student behavior are defined by the momentary interactions between salient features of the classroom ecology, teacher behavior, and student behavior. Data obtained from recording of these interactions may be used to inform many important research questions related to schooling and children's progress in school. With these instruments questions related to specific instructional interventions and their accelerative effects on student reading and writing (academic responding) or their decelerative effects on student aggression, disruption, and self-stimulation (competing inappropriate behavior) can be addressed. Other questions that can be examined using these instruments are questions related to the quantity and quality of teacher behavior (e.g., questioning, talking, prompting, approval) and questions related to the quantity and quality of classroom ecological arrangements (e.g., grouping of students, materials used, activities). In addition, these instruments support questions regarding how student performance is affected by specific changes in classroom ecology and teacher behavior.

INSTRUCTION AND STUDENT BEHAVIOR DEFINED

Classroom instruction and student behavior in traditional education research have been considered separate constructs and typically have been measured by separate protocols. For example, the school-based research of ecological psychologists looked primarily at classroom architecture, instructional arrangements, and teacher behavior (Gump, 1977). Similarly, the early school-based work of applied behavior analysts focused primarily on measuring student behavior (Morris & Midgley, 1990; Risley, 1977). How they became integrated in our instruments is an interesting aspect of the development of observational research methods.

Early school-based intervention efforts at the Juniper Gardens Children's Project focused on improving the academic behavior and outcomes of inner-city students. Initial studies focused on teaching classroom teachers to use positive reinforcement for increased attention, productivity, and levels of accuracy and to reduce the frequency of off-task and acting-out inappropriate behavior (e.g., Hall, Lund, & Jackson, 1968). Needed for this work were methods of classroom observation that monitored in real time the stream of student behavior and the behavior of the teacher before, during, and after the teacher began to use the new positive reinforcement procedures. Hall and colleagues used a paper-and-pencil, 10-second-interval time-sampling procedure that tracked student study and nonstudy behavior, teacher approval, and teacher proximity within 3 feet of the student. The data from each observation were used to calculate the percentage occurrence of study/nonstudy student behavior, teacher proximity, and teacher approval. Also relevant in the data record was the concurrence of student study behavior, teacher proximity, and approval in one interval as evidence of a teacher's contingent use of the positive reinforcement procedure.

What followed from research using this form of observational measurement was validation of classroom teachers' application of reinforcement principles (Hall et al., 1968). An important finding was that what students did during daily lessons co-varied with how they performed on measures of academic productivity and progress. Later research (Greenwood et al., 1992) examined the effects of manipulating other units of classroom instruction, such as antecedent events and functional situations within classroom instruction. *Antecedent events* were improvements made in classroom environments that encouraged the academic and social skills of students. For example, patterns of supervision, schedules, activities, routines, pacing, and materials were selected that signaled that related patterns of desired behaviors would be reinforced. Where they did not signal reinforcement, discriminations were learned and desired behavior was made more frequent. As antecedents and reinforcement came to be used for different behaviors and in different subject areas, work began to focus on situational factors that differentially affected stimulus control (i.e., *functional situational factors*).

This work sought to understand how further improvements in educational environments improved the performance of students. Because this work required information about changes in classroom ecological events, such as the materials used by the student, the focus of the teacher, and the seating arrangement, the earlier instruments of Hall and colleagues were modified. This work also required information about specific student behaviors (e.g., reading aloud) and teacher behaviors (e.g., nonverbal prompting), so the breadth and specificity of the taxonomy was expanded. The results of this work demonstrated that the use of specific instructions and materials (e.g., readers versus worksheets) often increased student engagement in active, academic responding (e.g., reading aloud) and that their duration affected the cumulative minutes of engagement in that behavior (Greenwood et al., 1992).

This work was termed *ecobehavioral* because it brought together assessment of both the environment and behavior within the same observational taxonomies and protocols:

> The interaction between the child and the environment is continuous, reciprocal, and interdependent. We cannot analyze a child without reference to an environment, nor is it possible to analyze an environment without reference to a child. The two form an inseparable unit consisting of an interrelated set of variables, or an interactional field. (Bijou, 1993, p. 29)

> The goal of *ecobehavioral assessment* is to display the co-variation of and the dependencies between behavior and its ecological contexts, past and present. . . . The goal of *ecobehavioral analysis*, like behavior analysis, is the determination of functional relationships between independent and dependent variables (Morris & Midgley, 1990). However, the assessment of ecological factors greatly extends the power of such analysis. Rather than ruling out the effects of contextual factors as in traditional behavioral assessment, contextual factors are represented in the data record and in the research design. (Greenwood, Carta, & Atwater, 1991, p. 60)

With our first ecobehavioral instrument, CISSAR (Greenwood, Delquadri, & Hall, 1984), it became possible to undertake descriptive studies of children in and out of impoverished schools and to examine how teachers' use of positive reinforcement, antecedents, and functional situational factors differed with respect to student engagement in academic responding during instruction and its relationship to measures of student academic progress (Greenwood, Delquadri, & Hall, 1989; Greenwood et al., 1984).

One outcome of this work indicated that children in schools in impoverished areas were engaged .4 hours less per day or 364 cumulative hours less after 5 years of elementary school compared with children in nonimpoverished schools (Greenwood, Hart, et al., 1994). Teacher behavior and use of materials during instruction in impoverished schools functioned in ways that actually decelerated student academic responding. This work led to a number of intervention studies in which a strategy designed to increase student engagement was developed and validated with individuals, with small experimental and control groups, and in a controlled, longitudinal study (see reviews by Greenwood, 1996).

Because the results of this work supported functional relationships between forms of instruction based on the use of consequences, antecedents, and functional situational factors (e.g., Greenwood, 1991, 1997; Greenwood et al., 1989) and improved student behavior and academic achievement in students at risk, the observation instruments soon were applied to students with disabilities and special needs (e.g., Ysseldyke, Thurlow, Mecklenburg, Graden, & Algozzine, 1984). The development of new instruments based on the established ecobehavioral framework (i.e., ESCAPE; Carta, Greenwood, & Robinson, 1987) also followed. Carta and Greenwood (1985) described the need in early childhood special education for measures capable of assessing more than just student behavior and skill development. They argued for the representation of teacher and preschool ecological factors in the design of and the monitoring of progress in intervention programs. Carta et al. (1987) reported validation results for their preschool ecobehavioral observation instrument, ESCAPE. And, for the first time, an ecobehavioral observation instrument was developed as a software application for use on portable laptop computers. ESCAPE data were entered directly on the keyboard, and observation files were uploaded to a desktop personal computer for storage and data analysis. Soon thereafter, the earlier CISSAR paper-and-pencil recording system also was developed for use on laptop computers.

The advent of mainstreaming and the inclusion of children with disabilities in the general education classroom provided the impetus to revise CISSAR to include ecological features of special education for children educated in both general and special education settings. The product of this effort was MS-CISSAR (Kamps, Greenwood, & Leonard, 1991).

CISSAR, MS-CISSAR, and ESCAPE continued to be used in research on the education and treatment of children in urban general education settings (CISSAR), mainstream special education settings (MS-CISSAR), and preschool early intervention and special education settings (ESCAPE). Because of the custom software developed for each instrument and the practical limitations of existing portable computer technology at the time (no floppy disk drives or hard drives), the use of these instruments remained limited to researchers and research applications. With a grant from the Office of Special Education and Rehabilitative Services, U.S. Department of Education, in 1992, the opportunity arose to develop a software system for notebook computers with both floppy disk drives and hard drives and sufficient memory to afford greater functionality for researchers as well as access by school psychologists, special education interventionists, and other school practitioners. This effort produced *EBASS*.

ECOBEHAVIORAL CONSTRUCTS OF INSTRUCTION

Three theoretical constructs organize and operationalize our ecobehavioral class-room observation taxonomies: *student behavior, teacher behavior,* and *classroom ecology.* According to ecological and behavioral theories, interactions and transactions between and among student behavior, teacher behavior, and classroom ecological arrangements are the putative units of analysis in research on the classroom instructional system. In terms of Bronfenbrenner's multilevel ecological theory (Bronfenbrenner, 1979), student behavior, teacher behavior, and classroom ecological arrangements form a unit, with student behavior at the most micro level, teacher behavior at the middle level, and ecological arrangements at the most macro level. Interactions follow from one level to the next. In terms of behavioral theory, classroom ecology–teacher behavior events, student behavior, and class-room ecology–teacher behaviors operate within Skinner's (1953) three-term con-tingency (antecedent-behavior-consequence interactions) and the higher-order contingencies resulting from these interactions to form setting events and other functional situational factors (e.g., four-term and five-term contingencies). Regardless of the theoretical framework, however, it was evident that change in these events was the phenomenon of importance. For example, a change in an eco-logical factor was followed by a change in student behavior, and that change in student behavior was followed by a change in teacher behavior, which perhaps was followed by another change in ecological factors, reflecting both bidirection-al and multidirectional influences among these constructs as teachers sought to teach their students.

OPERATIONALIZED CLASSROOM CONSTRUCTS

To operationalize a classroom instructional system in these terms, specific tax-onomies of behaviors and events were organized at the most macro level by three categories representing the following theoretical constructions: Ecology, Teacher Behavior, and Student Behavior.

Ecology

Ecological events in a classroom context are those of architecture, arrangement, and materials that act to structure the activities and behavior of students and teachers during classroom instruction.

Teacher

Teacher events in a classroom context include those that identify the person acting as the immediate instructor, the teacher's location relative to the student, and aspects of the teacher's behavior and its focus on particular students. Teachers may be certified adults, peer tutors, or grandparent volunteers, and their behav-ior may be verbal or nonverbal in nature and it may be approving, disapproving, or neutral.

Student

Student events in a classroom context are those that identify the student being observed and the behavior of that student over time. Student behaviors may be verbal or nonverbal, and they may be appropriately active, appropriately passive, or inappropriate.

OPERATIONAL DEFINITIONS

Although organized by ecology, teacher, and student behavior, the operational definitions in each *EBASS* instrument are highly specific to the setting (preschool versus elementary school classroom), to the expected teacher behaviors in that setting (incidental teaching behaviors versus direct instruction), and to the desired student behaviors (target behaviors versus specific academic responding).

ESCAPE Ecobehavioral Taxonomy

ESCAPE contains 92 events in all, organized into six Ecology, three Teacher, and three Student subcategories. As can be seen in Figure 1, Ecology is divided into Designated Activity, Activity Initiator, Materials, Location, Grouping, and Composition (the ratio of children with and without disabilities) subcategories. In the Designated Activity subcategory, which is the subject of instruction, events such as snacking, playing, preacademic activities, and fine motor activities reflect the preschool curricula, as do the events in the other Ecology subcategories (e.g., clean-up).

Teacher is divided into three subcategories: Teacher Definition, Teacher Behavior, and Teacher Focus. Teacher Definition identifies the teacher (e.g., a student teacher), his or her behavior, and its focus on the target of the observation, other students, or the target student plus other students. Student is divided into three subcategories: Target Behaviors, Verbal Behaviors, and Competing Behaviors. The Target Behaviors subcategory includes engaged behaviors such as academic work, pretending, and manipulating. The Verbal Behaviors subcategory includes talking to a teacher, undirected talk, talking to a peer, and the absence of talk. The Competing Behavior subcategory includes off-task, self-stimulation, and acting-out behaviors (see Figure 1).

CISSAR Ecobehavioral Taxonomy

CISSAR contains 55 events in three Ecology, two Teacher, and three Student subcategories. As can be seen in Figure 2, Ecology is divided into three subcategories: Activity, Task, and Structure. Teacher is divided into two subcategories: Teacher Position and Teacher Behavior. Student is divided into three composite subcategories: Academic Responses (seven behaviors), Task Management (four behaviors), and Competing Responses (seven behaviors).

As expected, developmental expectations and environmental differences are reflected in the nature of CISSAR activities, program features, curricula, and student behaviors. Preschoolers are involved in playing, snacking, and preacademic activities, whereas elementary grade students are involved in reading, spelling, mathematics, and other basic academic skills activities. Similarly, the behavioral goals and expectations also differ between preschool and elementary settings, as reflected in the two taxonomies. Active engagement in the preschool setting is focused on target behaviors such as learning to talk about academic work, pretend play, manipulating, and motor activities, among other behaviors. In the elementary school setting engagement is focused on behaviors such as writing, reading, and talking about academic topics. For example, learning to talk to teachers and peers is an important goal in preschool, and talking about academic subject matter is an important goal in elementary school. Similarly, in preschool, academic work, pretend play, self-care, and attention are important; in the elementary school classroom, writing, reading, and asking/answering questions are impor-

ECOLOGY

STUDENT BEHAVIORS

TARGET BEHAVIORS
1. ACAWORK
2. PRETENDING
3. MANIPULAT
4. GRSSMOTOR
5. SNG/RECIT
6. SELFCARE
7. TRANSIT
8. ATTENTION
9. NONE
10. CN'TTELL

VERBAL BEHAVIORS
1. NOTALK
2. TOTEACHER
3. UNDIRECTED
4. TOPEER
5. CN'TTELL

COMPETING BEHAVIORS
1. NONE
2. OFFTASK
3. SELF-STIM
4. ACTINGOUT
5. CN'TTELL

TEACHER BEHAVIORS

TEACHER DEFINITION
1. AIDE/PARA
2. TEACHER
3. ANCILLARY
4. VOLUNTEER
5. STUDNTTCH
6. SUBSTITUT
7. NOSTAFF
8. CN'TTELL

TEACHER FOCUS
1. NONE
2. OTHER
3. TARG+OTH
4. TARGET
5. CN'TTELL

TEACHER BEHAVIOR
1. PHYSASST
2. GEST/SIGN
3. APPROVAL
4. DISAPPROV
5. VERBPRMPT
6. VERBINSTR
7. READ/SING
8. DISCUSS
9. NORESPONS
10. CN'TTELL

ACTIVITY INITIATOR
1. TEACHER
2. CHILD
3. NONE
4. CN'TTELL

DESIGNATED ACTIVITY
1. SNACK
2. PLAY
3. TRANSIT
4. PREACADEM
5. FINEMOTOR
6. MUS/RECIT
7. CLEANUP
8. CLASSBUS
9. STORY
10. SELFCARE
11. GRSSMOTOR
12. TIMEOUT
13. LANGPROG
14. CN'TTELL

MATERIALS
1. NONE
2. FOODPRE
3. INSTRCTNL
4. MANIPULAT
5. ART/WRTNG
6. PRETNDTOY
7. LARGMOTOR
8. STRYBOOK
9. AUDIOVISU
10. BATHROOM
11. OTHER
12. CN'TTELL

LOCATION
1. ATTABLE
2. ONFLOOR
3. UNDEFINED
4. ONEQUIPMT
5. INLINE
6. INCHAIR
7. CN'TTELL

GROUPING
1. SMALLGRP
2. LARGEGRP
3. ONEONONE
4. SOLITARY
5. CN'TTELL

COMPOSITION
1. ALLDISABL
2. NONE
3. ALLNONDIS
4. MORDISABL
5. MORNONDIS
6. EQUAL
7. CN'TTELL

J A G C P

Figure I. The assessment taxonomy for ESCAPE organized by specific events within subcategories within Student, Teacher, and Ecology categories. ESCAPE is designed for preschool and kindergarten general and special education classroom settings.

BEHAVIOR

STUDENT BEHAVIORS

ACADEMIC RESPONSES
1. WRITING
2. PLAYACA
3. READALOUD
4. RDSILENT
5. TALKACA
6. ANSACAQST
7. ASKACAQST

COMPETING RESPONSES
13. DISRUPT
14. PLAYINAPP
15. TASKINAPP
16. TALKINAPP
17. LOCINAPP
18. LOOKARND
19. SELF-STIM

TASK MANAGEMENT
8. ATTNDTASK
9. RAISEHND
10. LOOKMTRLS
11. MOVES
12. PLAYAPP

TEACHER BEHAVIORS

TEACHER POSITION
1. INFRONT
2. ATDESK
3. AMONGSTUD
4. SIDE
5. BACK
6. OUT

TEACHER BEHAVIOR
1. NORESP
2. TEACHING
3. OTHERTALK
4. APPROVAL
5. DISAPPROV

ECOLOGY

ACTIVITY
1. READING
2. MATH
3. SPELLING
4. HNDWRTNG
5. LANGUAGE
6. SCIENCE
7. SOCSTUD
8. ARTS/CRFT
9. FREETIME
10. BUSMGMNT
11. TRANSIT
12. CNTTELL

TASK
1. READERS
2. WORKBOOKS
3. WORKSHEET
4. PAPER&PEN
5. LSTNLECT
6. OTHMEDIA
7. TCH/STDIS
8. FETCH/PUT

STRUCTURE
1. ENTIRGRP
2. SMALLGRP
3. INDIV

Figure 2. The assessment taxonomy for CISSAR organized by specific events within subcategories within Student, Teacher, and Ecology categories. CISSAR is designed for elementary general education classroom settings.

237

tant. Competing inappropriate behaviors are very similar in both settings: off-task behaviors, looking around, acting out, disrupting, and so forth (see Figures 2 and 3).

MS-CISSAR Ecobehavioral Taxonomy

MS-CISSAR contains 101 events in five Ecology, five Teacher, and three Student subcategories. As can be seen in Figure 3, MS-CISSAR adds a number of new events to the CISSAR taxonomy. For example, the Setting subcategory enables recording of the site in which instruction occurs, including special and general education classrooms. Activities expected in special education programs at the elementary school level have been added to the Activity subcategory. For example, in addition to reading, spelling, and mathematics, prevocation, daily living, and self-care activities are included.

Compared with CISSAR, the Teacher Behaviors subcategories have been expanded from 5 to 15 to better describe teacher events and their relationship to student behavior. In MS-CISSAR peer tutors may be recorded as the teacher, and questioning, commanding, and talking by the teacher may be recorded as academic, management, or discipline-related events. Student subcategories were modified only slightly in MS-CISSAR. Noteworthy in MS-CISSAR compared with CISSAR is the ability to record the co-occurrence of academic, task management, and competing behaviors in the same interval. This is helpful in the assessment of children with moderate to severe behavior problems.

In summary, the three instruments in *EBASS* share the same conceptual framework and organization by ecology, teacher, and student events and lend themselves to analyses that are both descriptive and functional with respect to the promotion of student behavior. They differ with respect to developmental age, program features, curricula, and emphasis as appropriate to the instructional programs they represent.

WHY OBSERVE STUDENT BEHAVIOR AND ITS INSTRUCTIONAL CONTEXTS?

There are several excellent reasons for systematically observing student behavior and its instructional contexts. These include assessment for diagnostic purposes, planning interventions, evaluating and monitoring treatment progress, and testing theory in research.

Assessment/Diagnostic Purposes

Student classroom behavior is assessed for a number of purposes. In the case of referral to special education services, a number of questions may be asked about a child's behavior problems and inappropriate behavior. Assessments may be conducted to screen for and identify frequent or intense problem behaviors (e.g., disruption, aggression, noncompliance, looking around) and low levels of desired academic behaviors (e.g., reading aloud, academic talk, attention). Assessment data may be used as a basis for prereferral interventions or as part of the process of developing an individualized education program to guide the provision of special education services. *EBASS* data also can be used in the development of local school behavior norms and criteria for making treatment decisions (Greenwood, Peterson, & Sideridis, 1995).

Another kind of assessment supported by the instruments in *EBASS* is concerned with program placement or the transition of students from one program to another (e.g., from preschool to kindergarten). Using the ESCAPE instrument,

STUDENT BEHAVIORS

ACADEMIC RESPONSES
1. WRITING
2. TSKPARTIC
3. READALOUD
4. RDSILENT
5. TALKACA
6. NOACARSP

COMPETING RESPONSES
1. AGRESSION
2. DISRUPT
3. TALKINAPP
4. LOOKARND
5. NONCOMPLY
6. SELF-STIM
7. SELFABUSE
8. NOINAPPRO

TASK MANAGEMENT
1. RAISEHAND
2. PLAYAPPRO
3. MANIPMTL
4. MOVE
5. TALKMGMNT
6. ATTENTION
7. NOMGMNT

TEACHER BEHAVIORS

TEACHER BEHAVIOR
1. QUESTACA
2. QUESTMGMT
3. QSTDSCPLN
4. CMNDACA
5. CMNDMGMNT
6. CMDDSCPLN
7. TALKACA
8. TALKMGMNT
9. TALKDSCPLN
10. TLKNONACA
11. NONVBPRMT
12. ATTENTION
13. READALOUD
14. SING
15. NORESPONS

TEACHER FOCUS
1. TARGET
2. TARGT+OTH
3. NOONE
4. OTHER

TEACHER POSITION
1. INFRONT
2. ATDESK
3. OUTOFROOM
4. SIDE
5. BACK

TEACHER APPROVAL
1. APPROVAL
2. DISAPPROV
3. NEITHER

TEACHER DEFINITION
1. REGULAR
2. SPECIALED
3. AIDE/PARA
4. STUDNTTCH
5. VOLUNTEER
6. RELATDSRV
7. SUBSTITUT
8. PEERTUTOR
9. NOSTAFF

ECOLOGY

ACTIVITY
1. READING
2. MATH
3. SPELLING
4. HNDWRTNG
5. LANGUAGE
6. SCIENCE
7. SOCSTUD
8. PREVOCAT
9. GRSSMOTOR
10. DAILYLIV
11. SELF-CARE
12. ARTS/CRFT
13. FREETIME
14. BUSMGMNT
15. TRANSIT
16. MUSIC
17. TIMEOUT
18. NOACTVTY
19. CN'TTELL
20. OTHER

SETTING
1. REGLARCLS
2. SPECIALED
3. RESRCERM
4. CHAFT1LAB
5. LIBRARY
6. MUSICRM
7. ARTROOM
8. THERAPYFM
9. HALL
10. AUDITORI
11. OTHER

TASK
1. READERS
2. WORKBOOKS
3. WORKSHEET
4. PAPER&PEN
5. LSTNLECT
6. OTHMEDIA
7. DISCUSSN
8. FETCH/PUT
9. NOTASK

PHYSICAL ARRANGEMENT
1. ENTIREGRP
2. DIVIDEGRP
3. INDIVIDUAL

INSTRUCTIONAL GROUPING
1. WHOLECLSS
2. SMALLGRP
3. ONEONONE
4. INDEPNDNT
5. NOINSTRCT

Figure 3. The assessment taxonomy for MS-CISSAR organized by specific events within subcategories within Student, Teacher, and Ecology categories. MS-CISSAR is designed for programs that include both general and special education classroom settings.

Agar and Shapiro (1995) conducted a best-match comparison between students with disabilities and their preschool programs and several kindergarten programs that were potential receiving sites. The objective was to find a kindergarten with behavioral, teacher, and ecological program features matching those in the preschool program. Template matching is based on the theory that children will be most successful in classrooms in which their behavior and its contexts are similar to those they already know (Cone & Hoier, 1986).

Intervention Planning

After initial assessment results are compiled, it is not uncommon for *EBASS* data to be used in intervention planning. Given information about specific behaviors, plans may focus on behavior reduction (e.g., looking around, inappropriate locale) or behavior acceleration (e.g., task participation, academic talk) within some specific contexts (e.g., reading period). Given information about the occurrence of specific behaviors in specific classroom contexts, a treatment plan also may be informed by evidence of function between classroom contexts and behavior. For example, disruptive behavior may occur twice as often during reading instruction as during daily living instruction. Further examination of the behavioral functions within reading and daily living may suggest a means of altering reading instruction to reduce disruptive behavior relatively quickly. Similar functional analyses may suggest strategies for increasing desired behaviors and may lead to a test of these hypotheses.

Treatment Evaluation and Progress Monitoring

With the onset of intervention, *EBASS* data can be useful in monitoring progress and in further testing of the functional relationship before and after treatment. Repeated observations of the student in the contexts of interest provide data on behavior change and instructional information on the success or failure of the intervention. Such information supports the goal of altering, improving, or revising the intervention strategy as needed. For example, Carta, Atwater, Schwartz, and Miller (1990) reported reductions in time lost to within-classroom transitions using this information.

Testing Theory

EBASS data have been used in a number of studies to test hypotheses related to mechanisms of effective classroom instruction and special education treatment (e.g., Greenwood, Delquadri, Stanley, Terry, & Hall, 1985). For example, in a longitudinal study we used structural equation modeling to fit three theoretical models to CISSAR data and increases in academic achievement. A major theoretical issue was the role played by students' engaged behavior. The results indicated that compared with models that posited direct effects of instruction and student engagement on increases in achievement, the best fit was achieved by a model that posited that student engagement mediated the relationship between instruction, defined by classroom contexts and teacher behavior, and achievement (Greenwood, 1996; Greenwood, Terry, Marquis, & Walker, 1994).

Hypotheses concerning increased student engagement in academic responding as a result of a classwide peer-tutoring intervention in reading, spelling, and mathematics were tested in a longitudinal, experimentally controlled study of increased student achievement. The results indicated that compared with a control group that did not receive classwide peer tutoring, student engagement increased significantly (Greenwood, 1991), and these increases co-varied with significantly improved levels of achievement on standardized test measures of reading, language, and mathematics (Greenwood et al., 1989).

In the 1980s, a number of studies were completed testing hypothesized differences in general versus special education classroom programs for students with mild disabilities (i.e., learning disabilities, behavior disorders, mild mental retardation) and between special education delivered in special education classrooms and special education delivered in general education classrooms. CISSAR and MS-CISSAR instruments enabled researchers to compare these programs in terms of differences in student and teacher behavior and differences in contexts. Thurlow, Ysseldyke, Graden, and Algozzine (1984) reported finding no differences in student academic responding in five different service delivery arrangements (ranging from full-time placement in regular classrooms to full-time placement in self-contained special education classrooms). Similarly, there were no differences in the time that students were engaged in task management or competing inappropriate behaviors. Overall, academic responding time averaged only 45 minutes per school day, with no differences among program arrangements. These and other findings raised serious questions about the uniqueness of categorical special education services and their impact on student behavior.

A number of studies tested hypotheses concerning the effects of alternative special educational practices (Greenwood, 1996). Using MS-CISSAR and other formative evaluation measures of student progress in the curriculum, Marston, Deno, Kim, Diment, and Rogers (1995) compared the outcomes produced by different approaches to reading instruction (e.g., computer-assisted instruction, direct instruction, effective teaching, peer tutoring, reciprocal teaching). They reported that direct instruction, computer-assisted instruction, and reciprocal teaching were the most effective practices for accelerating student academic growth. In each practice teacher behavior and student behavior differences were related in ways unique to that practice. For example, reciprocal teaching, which focuses on questioning and discussing, produced the highest proportion of teacher time spent talking and questioning rather than managing student reading, which was the dominant use of time in direct instruction. CISSAR data appeared to reflect the fidelity of implementation of each practice.

A number of studies of the education and treatment of children with severe disabilities attending school full time in the general education classroom have sought to identify service delivery and classroom contexts that best promote student engagement. Logan, Bakeman, and Keefe (1997) observed 29 students with moderate, severe, and profound intellectual disabilities using MS-CISSAR. The results indicated that one-to-one, small-group, and independent work arrangements were associated with the highest levels of engaged behaviors, extending earlier findings for children at risk (Cooper & Speece, 1990; Greenwood et al., 1989) and children with mild disabilities (Friedman, Cancelli, & Yoshida, 1988) to children with severe disabilities.

EBASS TECHNOLOGY

The CISSAR, MS-CISSAR, and ESCAPE instruments are supported by a software system designed for use on portable notebook computers (Greenwood, Carta, Kamps, Terry, & Delquadri, 1994; Greenwood, Peterson, & Sideridis, 1995). *EBASS*

(Version 3.0) is a user-friendly, multifunction computer program that supports the collection and analysis of data using these instruments (Greenwood, Carta, et al., 1994). Unlike earlier software that supported data collection only, *EBASS* has observer training, interobserver agreement, data management, and data analysis features integrated in the same software system. The added benefit of portable computer technology lies in the ability it gives the observer to conduct an observation session directly on the computer, eliminating the later data entry step common in the processing of paper-and-pencil records. Another advantage is the availability of printouts or screen displays of results immediately after an observation. With *EBASS*, school practitioners have access to these instruments in a form both feasible and acceptable for use in local school districts.

EBASS comes with a tutorial disk and a data collection program disk. The tutorial disk is used in the self-instructional process of learning a taxonomy and its event definitions. The program provides mastery feedback on the use of event definitions and reliability feedback on efforts to calibrate an observer's record with that of a videotaped coding test. The program disk contains the data collection software and sample data from each instrument so that one can learn to use the data analysis tools discussed below. A technical manual provides the necessary information for installing and setting up the software to run on either IBM-compatible or Macintosh portable computers (Greenwood & Hou, 1995). The program requires 398 kilobytes of disk space and may be run on a portable computer with at least one 1.44-megabyte floppy disk drive. Given the size of the hard drives on portable computers in the late 1990s, a program of this size fits very comfortably. The recommended setup puts the program on the computer's hard drive. The tutorial program, however, is designed to run only from the floppy disk drive. *EBASS* can be set up to run in Windows or DOS. To run *EBASS* on a Macintosh computer, personal computer emulation software is required (e.g., *Soft PC* [Insignia Solutions, 1999]).

Collected data may be stored in directories (folders) on the hard drive, or, if the computer is used by multiple observers, as is often the case with school psychologists sharing the same computer, data may be written to the floppy disk drive and the disk removed from the computer when work is completed. This is a recommended practice to protect the confidentiality of collected data because it prevents unauthorized access to the information.

The practitioner's manual provides the information needed to direct learning of each of the instruments as well as documentation for each instrument, including taxonomy; definition information; and technical information on development, validity, and reliability (Greenwood et al., 1997). Learning to use one instrument with the practitioner's manual typically takes 2 weeks.

Tutorial Component

The tutorial component contains two functions: learning instrument definitions and instrument calibration. Observers learn instrument definitions and data entry by selecting the instrument they desire to learn. Each instrument is organized in three levels of increasing difficulty: 1) student events only; 2) teacher and student events; and 3) ecological, teacher, and student events. The user selects the level of difficulty and responds to a series of exercises requiring him or her to read a short scenario and then key in the correct event. The event entered by the user is evaluated by the program and, if it is correct, the next scenario is presented. If the event is in error the program presents the event and its definition along with the correct event and its definition for review. The user is then returned to the recording view and allowed to retry the entry. This response is corrected again if necessary. To advance to the next difficulty level, an overall 90% level of accuracy (no lower than 85% per subcategory) must be achieved. At the end of the tutorial session the user's accuracy level is displayed and advice is given about the need for further study or advancement to the next level is recommended. After completing the third level the user is ready to conduct live practice observations and to attempt calibration.

Calibration is a test of coding accuracy. The user qualifies as trained by conducting a timed observation while viewing the *EBASS* calibration video for the instrument being learned. The video prompts the user to set up and then begin the observation. At the end of the calibration attempt the program reports the percentage of agreement, the *kappa* agreement statistic, and event-by-event disagreement information. The user is certified as calibrated if 90% agreement is reached.

Data Collection Component

The main menu selections in the *EBASS* data collection component are Data Collection, Data Reliability, Data Analysis, Data Export, and Data Management.

Data Collection   The Data Collection function allows the user to select the instrument to be used (e.g., ESCAPE) and, after providing a file name for storing the information, cues the observer to start the observation and begin data entry. The software presents the observer with a screen containing a checklist of event categories and event choices. The observer selects and enters the specific event that was witnessed, after which the software presents the next checklist. New screens (one per interval) are announced by an audible *bleep*. The volume of this sound may be adjusted as desired or the sound may be disabled. New data entry checklists are presented to the observer every 10, 15, or 20 seconds for CISSAR, ESCAPE, or MS-CISSAR, respectively.

Observers enter data using only four keys. The space bar (thumb) is used to scroll through choice options. Thus, observers do not need to be sophisticated keyboard users. Because all other keys on the keyboard are inactive during data collection, the program accepts only legal entries should other keys be hit accidentally. Observers may use either hand for data entry. Before and immediately after a data collection session the software provides the observer with a text box for writing notes and comments related to the observation. These notes are linked to the data file and may be printed out with the data at a later time.

Several other choices and options are available for setting up an observation. The instruments in *EBASS* are standardized, and all *EBASS* users collect data on the same events using the same taxonomy and definitions. Because *EBASS* is not an authoring system, it does not allow users to modify sampling methods, events, definitions, or timing patterns. However, it does allow downsizing of the standard taxonomy. In MS-CISSAR, for example, the user may decide to record only child behavior. The downsizing tool prompts the user for the categories and/or subcategories to be eliminated from the observation and creates the desired taxonomy to be used, which is a subset of the larger taxonomy.

EBASS provides a display of all files (one user's caseload) contained in a specific folder. If the goal is to collect more data on a child observed previously, the user selects one of the child's completed files and the program sets up a new observation using the same taxonomy, full or downsized, that was used previously. This is a great time saver, and it ensures continuity in the data collected for the same child from one session to the next.

Data Reliability   The Data Reliability function supports the analysis of interobserver agreement. The usual procedure of two observers recording the behavior of the same student simultaneously is followed. One observer is designated to prompt the other to start and stop his or her observations to equalize the time observed by each. The data of one observer are written to a floppy disk, which is then read on the other observer's computer so the two files can be compared interval by interval for analysis of agreement. The software prompts for both files and then completes the analysis. Calculated are the percentage of agreement and the *kappa* statistic (see Hollenbeck, 1978), overall and by subcategory. An additional display of event disagreements within subcategories is provided to help observers identify and rule out differences in their understanding of event definitions and to reach consistent application of the instrument's definitions.

Data Analysis   The Data Analysis function supports analysis and display of the collected data. A range of tools are available, including simple percentage of occurrence for each event within each subcategory (e.g., the percentage of time spent using worksheets in the CISSAR Task subcategory of the Ecology category; see Figure 2). When applied to a single observation file, this analysis provides a description of the ecological, teacher, and student events profiled as percentages that sum to 100% within each subcategory. To compute the percentage of occurrence as a summary of all observations collected for a student, a group of students, or a group of observations (e.g., baseline versus treatment), the user simply "tags" the specific files to be pooled within a single analysis. Thus, the user has wide flexibility in computing percentages of occurrences of interest by observation, by sets of observations for a student, or by sets of observations within and across groups of students.

The Conditional Probability function allows the user to examine the probability of a specific student behavior given the temporal correlation with specific situations defined by classroom ecology and/or teacher behavior (Allison & Liker, 1982). These analyses may be used in functional analyses of problem behaviors and behavior reduction interventions as well as in interventions designed to increase low-probability behaviors in some students, particularly academic responding (e.g., reading aloud). The Conditional Probability function enables the user to examine natural classroom situational functions that either accelerate or decelerate student behaviors of interest. After the observation file(s) to be used in the analysis is selected, the program prompts for the situations and student behaviors to be used. A table of descriptive and inferential statistics (*t*-tests) is displayed, along with a graphic representing the accelerative or decelerative effects (the conditional probability of the student's behavior) of specific classroom situations relative to the unconditional probability of the student's behavior.

The Profile Comparison function provides a means of comparing the similarity (or difference) in two profiles. For example, the user may wish to compare two students' behavioral profiles within the Academic Responses subcategory or the profiles of teacher behaviors in an existing placement and in a potential placement setting. After the necessary observations of students and/or classrooms are conducted the program prompts for the "target student or classroom" data and for the "index student or classroom" data. Thereafter, the program provides a table and a graphic display of the percentage of occurrence of the two profiles and a profile of differences. A similarity statistic, the Euclidean distance or D-statistic (Nunnally & Bernstein, 1994), is computed as a means of statistically evaluating similarities and dissimilarities in the profiles. When profiles are identical, the D-statistic is equal to zero; for profiles that are increasingly dissimilar, the D-statistic is larger.

Profile analyses are most useful in making "normative" peer comparisons between a student referred for behavior problems and a typical peer in similar situations. The differences between the one student's competing inappropriate behavior and the behavior of the typical peer may reflect the extent to which the target student exceeds typical expectations in similar classroom situations and conditions. This normative peer analysis may be extended by using the "tagging" tool to include a group of typical children in a range of typical classroom situations. In this case the target peer's behavior is compared with that of a number of typical peers for dissimilarity and with that of a number of students previously referred for behavior problems for similarity. The tool also may be used to profile changes in student behavior or classroom ecology resulting from intervention (as in simple AB design comparisons, where A = before intervention and B = after intervention). By pooling data before and during interaction, results can be used quickly to identify important areas of change.

The Trend function enables the user to prepare a time series plot of events selected for graphing. The tagging tool is used to mark the set of observation files to be used in the analysis. The user then selects the variable to be plotted and the medium of display (on screen, printed out, or saved in a file for later use in a report). The Trend tool plots only one variable at a time. More sophisticated graphs and charts can be made by exporting the data to *SPSS* (SPSS Inc., 1998–1999) and using the *SPSS* charting tools.

The Engagement function enables the user to examine the momentary variation and stability in student engagement in academic responding. Two charts are produced displaying engagement per minute of observation: One displays the onset and offset of engagement, and the other displays a trajectory of cumulative minutes of engagement. In response to the theoretical and empirical support of the importance of student engagement in academic responding, these displays identify moments and periods during classroom instruction when engagement is on or off and support formation of hypotheses concerning the instructional conditions responsible for these performance outcomes.

Exporting Data to Other Applications   The Data Export function supports the need to create data sets from the observations collected in *EBASS* for use in larger research and evaluation efforts. After the files to be exported are tagged the program writes case-based records to a file in which each record is composed of name, date, instrument, and percentages of occurrences of all events by category in the instrument. This data set may be read by the *SPSS* statistical package and combined with other data sets and databases for use in statistical reports and analyses.

Managing the Data   The Data Management function supports routine needs to copy, move, delete, rename, or print out raw data. These tools support backing up data sets, moving data off the machine or to other folders or disks, and changing naming conventions. In some applications viewing the raw data is very important. The Data Management tool allows one to print the raw data, as contained in original *EBASS* file formats or in a transcribed version, displayed interval by interval in temporal order as it was collected. In summary, the *EBASS* package combines several technologies and forms of media: computer software, video for training and simulating observations, and text-based manuals to support self-instruction in its use.

Observational Strategies Used

CISSAR, MS-CISSAR, and ESCAPE use momentary time sampling as the basis for recording of events (Powell, Martindale, & Kulp, 1975). Of the time-sampling methods, momentary time sampling has proven the most accurate in comparisons with event and duration recording (Ary, 1984; Powell, 1984; Powell et al., 1975). An advantage of time sampling is that it reduces the observer's work load (i.e., complexity) (Dorsey, Nelson, & Hayes, 1986) and therefore results in high interobserver reliability in complex, multievent taxonomies. In momentary time sampling, observers only record events occurring at specific times; they do not have to monitor the onset and offset of events (Sackett, 1978). This was important in the original design of these instruments because we wanted to train community residents as well as graduate students to use them in our research.

To record multiple-event streams (ecology, teacher, and student) we interweaved the sampling of each event in subsequent intervals. For example, in MS-CISSAR, ecology, teacher, and student events are recorded in the first, second, and third 20-second intervals, respectively. This same ecology, teacher, and student sampling cycle is then repeated in each 60 seconds of recording thereafter. A similar approach is used in ESCAPE but with 15-second intervals. In this case, however, ecological events are sampled in the first two intervals, with teacher and student events sampled in intervals three and four in each 60-second recording cycle. The original CISSAR uses a one-to-six ratio of ecology to teacher and student event recording based on 10-second-interval momentary sampling. One ecological interval is recorded for every six teacher and student event samples.

The records produced by these sampling schemes contain the observed values for an instrument's ecological, teacher, and student event categories. In MS-CISSAR and ESCAPE there is one such record produced for each minute of recording; in CISSAR one record is produced for every 70 seconds of recording. Matrices are produced (see, e.g., Castellan, 1979), and analyses of percentage of occurrence are based on calculations in each column (percentage of occurrence equals 100 times [frequency of each event divided by total records]). For conditional probabilities the frequencies of specific student behaviors given specific ecological and teacher events are of interest. Given the conditions of interest specified by the user, the records in the data matrix are partitioned to form ecobehavioral joint events from which zero-order conditional and unconditional probabilities are computed using the procedures described by Allison and Liker (1982). Zero-order probabilities reflect concurrent temporal relationships between events. Lagged sequential conditional probabilities are not computed in *EBASS*.

CONCLUSIONS AND CRITICAL ANALYSIS

The discussion next turns to the implications of *EBASS*, an observational methodology for education environments. Specifically, it examines the assumptions and shortcomings of *EBASS* and considers remaining and future theoretical and practical issues.

Assumptions and Shortcomings

The instruments described in this chapter were designed specifically to enable a student's classroom behavior to be analyzed in traditional ways, using percentage of occurrence and change over time as a function of intervention. They also were designed to yield descriptive information on the classroom situations (ecology and teacher) temporally related to student behavior. They are specifically intended to enable estimation of the probability of student behavior given specific classroom situations as defined by ecological and teacher events. These last two features enable the description and generation of hypotheses concerning functional relationships for testing in subsequent experimental research.

To achieve these capabilities sufficient data must be collected on a target student and on temporally related ecology and teacher behavior. As operationalized in these instruments ecology and teacher events are recorded with reference to the target student observed repeatedly over time. In practical terms, this means that considerable time and resources are invested in observing one student so that the matrix of information generated is of sufficient size that conditional probability analyses can be considered stable and derived relationships can be considered representative. This focus on a single student may present some difficulties for scientists and practitioners interested in representing other units. Some researchers may wish to represent the class or the teacher, rather than an individual student, in the context of the classroom ecology. As a result, they may find that the instruments in *EBASS* are not focused on the individuals or sampling events they wish to study. Thus, other instruments will be needed.

Because of the use of momentary time sampling with rotation through ecology, teacher, and student event streams, some temporal distance is placed between student behavior, teacher behavior, and classroom ecology, thus introducing a degree of inaccuracy. These distances are on the order of one or two intervals in MS-CISSAR and ESCAPE and up to 60 seconds in CISSAR. If an observer could reliably track the onset and offset of all 101 MS-CISSAR events simultaneously in real time this problem would not exist. The real effect of this problem is not clear. Theoretically, momentary time sampling is an accurate event estimator. If this is true it also should be an accurate joint event estimator, which is important to the accuracy of conditional probabilities. This, of course, remains to be demonstrated. Some analyses that we completed on the stability of conditional probability relationships in derivation and replication samples using the CISSAR instrument have shown good results (Greenwood, Delquadri, Stanley, Terry, & Hall, 1985, 1986). In addition, changes have occurred in conditional probability relationships in comparisons of baseline and treatment conditions, supporting theoretically predictable changes in these relationships (Greenwood, Schulte, Kohler, Dinwiddie, & Carta, 1986). Taken together, these findings support the utility and validity of these analyses; however, more research is needed on this issue.

Remaining and Future Theoretical Issues

The instruments in *EBASS* provide an interesting and important means of examining how to represent classroom ecology, teacher behavior, and student behavior in a direct observation method with both breadth and depth. Using *EBASS* instruments, research progress has been made in a number of subfields of education and special education, demonstrating how measurement of these variables can be used to better evaluate and educate young children with and without disabilities in impoverished and nonimpoverished schools. In early childhood special education (Carta & Greenwood, 1985), for example, one sees the increasing use of these instruments in original research as well as in new work that has replicated and extended earlier work in inner-city schools. How this technology can be used to produce more effective educational programs, such as classwide peer tutoring, and to increase understanding of the mechanisms by which instructional situational factors accelerate learning and decelerate behavior problems remains to be addressed in future research.

Remaining and Future Practical Issues

Some of the most interesting practical issues regarding *EBASS* information concern the extent to which school psychologists and classroom teachers use it to inform decisions about altering teaching and the design and monitoring of interventions. The program has been purchased by more than 105 people in public schools and university research settings, including five in foreign countries and territories. *EBASS* also has been distributed to 18 graduate training programs for school psychologists around the country for use in their assessment courses.

The most effective use of *EBASS* information in the public schools has been made by school psychologists in support of decision making relative to students with behavior problems receiving special education services under individualized education programs. Much less use has been made by classroom teachers in efforts to alter their instructional practices. This is not surprising because *EBASS* was not intended to be used by teachers, although its information is highly related to instructional effectiveness. Teachers must rely on colleagues charged with evaluating and improving teaching to provide *EBASS* information. With the advent of low-cost portable computers and educational reforms focused on improving student outcomes in local schools, models of teacher consultation, coaching, collaboration, and professional development in the use of *EBASS* information are likely to increase.

The *EBASS* technology described in this chapter represents a major reduction in the barriers that have hindered the use of computer-based observation methods. Farrell (1991) reported that lack of time and training, lack of computer skills, lack of relevant applications, and the low quality of existing software constrained use. Our own 1990 national survey of school psychologists (Greenwood et al., 1995) revealed similar concerns. Eighty-two percent of school psychologists surveyed reported that they conducted classroom observations; however, few reported using portable computers to conduct these observations. Barriers to the use of all forms of observational assessment not mentioned previously included the time needed for reliability checks, the informal design of most observational instruments, and the limited technical and standardization data supporting adequacy. We believe that *EBASS* and many of the other instruments supported by computer and information technology described in this volume have dramatically reduced these barriers. Efforts are under way to upgrade the *EBASS* software and to include additional ecobehavioral instruments, including one for bilingual and English as a second language programs (*ESCRIBE* [Arreaga-Mayer, Tapia, &

Carta, 1993]) and one for very young children in home and child care (*CIRCLE* [Atwater, Montagna, Creighton, Williams, & Hou, 1993]) settings.

In conclusion, *EBASS* and its instruments represent a system with significant potential for use in improving the education and treatment of children in schools. How it will be brought up to wide-scale use to affect the schooling of children with and without disabilities in impoverished schools and how it will be improved for future research remain to be seen.

REFERENCES

Agar, C.L., & Shapiro, E. (1995). Template matching as a strategy for assessment of and intervention for preschool children with disabilities. *Topics in Early Childhood Special Education, 15(2),* 187–218.

Allison, P.D., & Liker, J.K. (1982). Analyzing sequential categorical data on dyadic interaction: A comment on Gottman. *Psychological Bulletin, 91,* 393–403.

Arreaga-Mayer, C., Tapia, Y., & Carta, J.J. (1993). *Ecobehavioral System for the Complex Recording of Interactional Bilingual Environments (ESCRIBE): Observer's manual.* Kansas City: University of Kansas, Juniper Gardens Children's Project.

Ary, D. (1984). Mathematical explanation of error in duration recording using partial interval, whole interval, and momentary time sampling. *Behavioral Assessment, 6,* 221–228.

Atwater, J.B., Montagna, D., Creighton, M., Williams, R., & Hou, S. (1993). *Code for Interactive Recording of Caregiving and Learning Environments (CIRCLE).* Kansas City: University of Kansas, Juniper Gardens Children's Project, Early Childhood Research Institute on Substance Abuse.

Baumeister, A.A., Kupstas, F., & Klindworth, L.M. (1990). New morbidity: Implications for prevention of children's disabilities. *Exceptionality, 1,* 1–16.

Bijou, S.W. (1993). *Behavior analysis of child development* (2nd rev. ed.). Reno, NV: Context Press.

Bronfenbrenner, U. (1979). *The ecology of human development: Experiments by nature and design.* Cambridge, MA: Harvard University Press.

Brooks-Gunn, J., & Duncan, G.J. (1997). The effects of poverty on children. *The Future of Children, 7(2),* 55–71 [Report issued by the Center for the Future of Children, The David and Lucile Packard Foundation, Los Altos, CA].

Carta, J.J., Atwater, J.B., Schwartz, I.S., & Miller, P.A. (1990). Applications of ecobehavioral analysis to the study of transitions across early education. *Education and Treatment of Children, 13,* 298–315.

Carta, J.J., & Greenwood, C.R. (1985). Ecobehavioral assessment: A methodology for examining the evaluation of early intervention programs. *Topics in Early Childhood Special Education, 5,* 88–104.

Carta, J.J., Greenwood, C.R., & Robinson, S. (1987). Application of an eco-behavioral approach to the evaluation of early intervention programs. In R.J. Prinz (Ed.), *Advances in behavioral assessment of children and families: A research annual* (Vol. 3, pp. 123–155). Greenwich, CT: JAI Press.

Carta, J.J., McConnell, S.R., McEvoy, M.A., Greenwood, C.R., Atwater, J.B., Baggett, K., & Williams, R. (1997). Developmental outcomes associated with "in utero" exposure to alcohol and other drugs. In M.R. Haack (Ed.), *Drug dependent mothers and their children: Issues in public policy and public health* (pp. 64–90). New York: Springer Publishing Co.

Castellan, N.J. (1979). The analysis of behavioral sequences. In R.B. Cairns (Ed.), *The analysis of social interactions: Methods, issues, and illustrations* (pp. 81–116). Mahwah, NJ: Lawrence Erlbaum Associates.

Cone, J., & Hoier, T.S. (1986). Assessing children: The radical behavioral perspective. In R.J. Prinz (Ed.), *Advances in behavioral assessment of children and families: A research annual* (Vol. 2, pp. 1–27). Greenwich, CT: JAI Press.

Cooper, D.H., & Speece, D.L. (1990). Instructional correlates of students' academic responses: Comparisons between at-risk and control students. *Early Education and Development, 4,* 279–299.

Dorsey, B.L., Nelson, R., & Hayes, S.C. (1986). The effects of code complexity and of behavioral frequency on observer accuracy and interobserver agreement. *Behavioral Assessment, 8*, 349–363.

Farrell, A.D. (1991). Computers and behavioral assessment: Current applications, future possibilities, and obstacles to routine use. *Behavioral Assessment, 13*, 159–180.

Friedman, D.L., Cancelli, A.A., & Yoshida, R.K (1988). Academic engagement of elementary students with learning disabilities. *Journal of School Psychology, 26*, 327–340.

Greenwood, C.R. (1991). A longitudinal analysis of time, engagement, and academic achievement in at-risk vs. non-risk students. *Exceptional Children, 57*, 521–535.

Greenwood, C.R. (1996). Research on the practices and behavior of effective teachers at the Juniper Gardens Children's Project: Implications for the education of diverse learners. In D.L. Speece & B.K. Keogh (Eds.), *Research on classroom ecologies: Implications for inclusion of children with learning disabilities* (pp. 39–67). Mahwah, NJ: Lawrence Erlbaum Associates.

Greenwood, C.R. (1997). Classwide peer tutoring. *Behavior and Social Issues, 7*, 11–18.

Greenwood, C.R., Carta, J.J., & Atwater, J.J. (1991). Ecobehavioral analysis in the classroom: Review and implications. *Journal of Behavioral Education, 1*, 59–77.

Greenwood, C.R., Carta, J.J., Hart, B., Kamps, D., Terry, B., Arreaga-Mayer, C., Atwater, J., Walker, D., Risley, T., & Delquadri, J. (1992). Out of the laboratory and into the community: 26 years of applied behavior analysis at the Juniper Gardens Children's Project. *American Psychologist, 47*, 1464–1474.

Greenwood, C.R., Carta, J.J., Kamps, D., & Arreaga-Mayer, C. (1990). Ecobehavioral analysis of classroom instruction. In S.R. Schroeder (Ed.), *Ecobehavioral analysis and developmental disabilities: The twenty-first century* (pp. 33–63). New York: Springer-Verlag New York.

Greenwood, C.R., Carta, J.J., Kamps, D., & Delquadri, J. (1997). *Ecobehavioral Assessment Systems Software (EBASS Version 3.0): Practitioner's manual.* Kansas City: University of Kansas, Juniper Gardens Children's Project.

Greenwood, C.R., Carta, J.J., Kamps, D., Terry, B., & Delquadri, J. (1994). Development and validation of standard classroom observation systems for school practitioners: Ecobehavioral Assessment Systems Software (EBASS). *Exceptional Children, 61*, 197–210.

Greenwood, C.R., Delquadri, J.C., & Hall, R.V. (1984). Opportunity to respond and student academic performance. In W.L. Heward, T. Heron, D. Hill, & J. Trap-Porter (Eds.), *Focus on behavior analysis in education* (pp. 58–88). Upper Saddle River, NJ: Merrill.

Greenwood, C.R., Delquadri, J.C., & Hall, R.V. (1989). Longitudinal effects of classwide peer tutoring. *Journal of Educational Psychology, 81*, 371–383.

Greenwood, C.R., Delquadri, J., Stanley, S.O., Terry, B., & Hall, R.V. (1985). Assessment of eco-behavioral interaction in school settings. *Behavioral Assessment, 7*, 331–347.

Greenwood, C.R., Delquadri, J., Stanley, S.O., Terry, B., & Hall, R.V. (1986). Observational assessment of ecobehavioral interaction during academic instruction. In S.E. Newstead, S.H. Irvine, & P.L. Dann (Eds.), *Human assessment: Cognition and motivation* (pp. 319–340). Dordrecht, The Netherlands: Martinus Nijhoff.

Greenwood, C.R., Hart, B., Walker, D., & Risley, T.R. (1994). The opportunity to respond revisited: A behavioral theory of developmental retardation and its prevention. In R. Gardner III, D.M. Sainato, J.O. Cooper, T.E. Heron, W.L. Heward, J.W. Eshleman, & T.A. Grossi (Eds.), *Behavior analysis in education: Focus on measurably superior instruction* (pp. 213–223). Pacific Grove, CA: Brooks/Cole.

Greenwood, C.R., & Hou, L.S. (1995). *Ecobehavioral Assessment Systems Software (EBASS Version 3.0): Technical manual/readme first.* Kansas City: Juniper Gardens Children's Project, University of Kansas.

Greenwood, C.R., Peterson, P., & Sideridis, G. (1995). Conceptual, methodological, and technological advances in classroom observational assessment. *Diagnostique, 20*, 73–100.

Greenwood, C.R., Schulte, D., Kohler, F.W., Dinwiddie, G.I., & Carta, J.J. (1986). Assessment and analysis of ecobehavioral interaction in school settings. In R.J. Prinz (Ed.), *Advances in behavioral assessment of children and families: A research annual* (Vol. 2, pp. 69–98). Greenwich, CT: JAI Press.

Greenwood, C.R., Terry, B., Marquis, J., & Walker, D. (1994). Confirming a performance-based instructional model. *School Psychology Review, 23*, 625–668.

Gump, P.V. (1977). Ecological psychologists: Critics and contributors to behavior analysis. In A. Rogers-Warren & S.F. Warren (Eds.), *Ecological perspectives in behavior analysis: Proceedings of the Kansas Conference on Ecology and Behavior Analysis* (pp. 133–147). Baltimore: University Park Press.

Hall, R.V., Lund, D., & Jackson, D. (1968). Effects of teacher attention on study behavior. *Journal of Applied Behavior Analysis, 1,* 1–12.

Hart, B., & Risley, T.R. (1995). *Meaningful differences in the everyday experience of young American children.* Baltimore: Paul H. Brookes Publishing Co.

Hollenbeck, A.R. (1978). Problems of reliability in observational research. In G.P. Sackett (Ed.), *Observing behavior: Vol. II. Data collection and analysis methods* (pp. 46–62). Baltimore: University Park Press.

Insignia Solutions. (1999). *Universal SoftPC/SoftWindows98 for Macintosh.* Fremont, CA: Author.

Kamps, D., Greenwood, C.R., & Leonard, B. (1991). Ecobehavioral assessment in classrooms serving children with autism and developmental disabilities. In R.J. Prinz (Ed.), *Advances in behavioral assessment of children and families: A research annual* (Vol. 5, pp. 203–237). London: Jessica Kingsley Publishers.

Logan, K.R., Bakeman, R., & Keefe, E.B. (1997). Effects of instructional variables on engaged behavior of students with disabilities in general education classrooms. *Exceptional Children, 63,* 481–498.

Marston, D., Deno, S.L., Kim, D., Diment, K., & Rogers, D. (1995). Comparison of reading intervention approaches for students with mild disabilities. *Exceptional Children, 62,* 20–37.

Morris, E.K., & Midgley, B.D. (1990). Some historical and conceptual foundations of ecobehavioral analysis. In S.R. Schroeder (Ed.), *Ecobehavioral analysis and developmental disabilities: The twenty-first century* (pp. 1–32). New York: Springer Publishing Co.

Nunnally, J.C., & Bernstein, I.H. (1994). *Psychometric theory* (3rd ed.) (McGraw-Hill series in social psychology). New York: McGraw-Hill.

Powell, J. (1984). On the misrepresentation of realities by a widely practiced direct observation procedure: Partial interval (one-zero) sampling. *Behavioral Assessment, 6,* 209–219.

Powell, J., Martindale, A., & Kulp, S. (1975). An evaluation of time-sampling measures of behavior. *Journal of Applied Behavior Analysis, 8,* 463–470.

Risley, T.R. (1977). The ecology of applied behavior analysis. In A. Rogers-Warren & S.F. Warren (Eds.), *Ecological perspectives in behavior analysis: Proceedings of the Kansas Conference on Ecology and Behavior Analysis* (pp. 149–163). Baltimore: University Park Press.

Sackett, G.P. (1978). Measurement in observational research. In G.P. Sackett (Ed.), *Observing behavior: Vol. II. Data collection and analysis methods* (pp. 25–43). Baltimore: University Park Press.

Sameroff, A.J. (1990). Neo-environmental perspectives on developmental theory. In R.M. Hodapp, J.A. Burack, & E. Zigler (Eds.), *Issues in the developmental approach to mental retardation* (pp. 93–113). New York: Cambridge University Press.

Skinner, B.F. (1953). *Science and human behavior.* New York: Macmillan.

SPSS Inc. (1998–1999). *SPSS for Windows: Real Stats Real Easy (Release 9.0.0)* [Software]. Chicago: Author.

Thurlow, M.L., Ysseldyke, J.E., Graden, J., & Algozzine, B. (1984). Opportunity to learn for LD students receiving different levels of special education services. *Learning Disabilities Quarterly, 7,* 55–67.

Ysseldyke, J.E., Thurlow, M.L., Mecklenburg, C., Graden, J., & Algozzine, B. (1984). Changes in academic engaged time as a function of assessment and special education intervention. *Special Services in the Schools, 1,* 31–43.

16

Social Interaction in High School and Supported Employment Settings

Observational Research Application and Issues

Carolyn Hughes,
Michael S. Rodi, and
Sarah Walsh Lorden

A defining feature of inclusive education and supported employment is the amount and quality of time that individuals with disabilities and their general education peers spend with each other (Rehabilitation Act Amendments of 1992 [PL 102-569]; Haring, 1991). Indeed, peers have been identified as valuable sources of support for both students and employees in promoting task performance, social interaction, and social relationships (Hughes, Killian, & Fischer, 1996). In addition, benefits to peers such as increased self-esteem and appreciation of individual differences have been reported (Peck, Donaldson, & Pezzoli, 1990).

PREVIOUS OBSERVATIONAL RESEARCH

To know the extent to which high-quality, supportive interactions are occurring in high school and work environments, systematic observational research must be conducted. Throughout the 1980s and early 1990s, primarily paper-and-pencil observational methods were used to observe social interaction in vivo. Researchers during that time compared the social interaction patterns of individuals with mental retardation and their co-workers in employment settings (e.g., Chadsey-Rusch, Gonzalez, Tines, & Johnson, 1989; Ferguson, McDonnell, & Drew,

1993; Parent, Kregel, Metzler, & Twardzik, 1992). Using direct observation these investigators identified social behaviors that differed between employees with mental retardation and their co-workers. For example, Chadsey-Rusch et al. found that typical workers engaged in more teasing and joking and talked more about social topics than work-related topics than employees with mental retardation. Ferguson et al. reported that typical employees gave more directions, initiated more conversations, and asked more questions than employees with mental retardation. This research also showed that employees with mental retardation and their co-workers rarely interacted with each other.

CURRENT OBSERVATIONAL RESEARCH

Although an extensive literature exists describing social interaction patterns in employment settings, the observational methods used have been written narratives, interval recording, or behavior checklists (Hughes, Kim, & Hwang, 1998). Measures have not been recorded in real time—as can be done using computer-assisted technology—which limits findings related to the rate and the percentage of time that target behaviors occur. In addition, an extensive literature search revealed no published studies of critical social behaviors in high school settings (Hughes, Kim, et al., 1998). Thus, we have no information on the social interaction patterns between high school students with disabilities and their general education peers. The purpose of this chapter, therefore, is to describe our computer-assisted observational research program, which investigates informal social interactions that are typical of a high school lunchroom in which students with disabilities and general education students are physically integrated (Hughes, Lorden, et al., 1998; Hughes, Rodi, et al., in press). The focus of this research is 1) to extend the literature on social interaction that has been conducted in employment settings by using computer-assisted technology in a high school setting, 2) to compare the social behavior of students with disabilities and their general education peers, and 3) to determine the extent to which students with mental retardation interact with their general education peers.

EXTENDING THE RESEARCH BASE

Our observational research program, which investigates social interaction between people with disabilities and their typical peers, departs from previous studies in several ways. First, unlike in the employment studies (e.g., Chadsey-Rusch et al., 1989; Ferguson et al., 1993), we based our behavioral coding system on extensive observations in the actual setting rather than using preestablished categories derived from the employment literature. These preliminary observations allowed us to identify potentially important topographies of social interaction in a high school lunchroom setting. Second, whereas in previous research behaviors were recorded via a continuous paper-and-pencil narrative in 1-minute intervals and coded later in another setting, we coded behaviors in vivo in real time on a second-by-second basis using laptop computers. Our recording system allowed us to collect data on both rate and percentage of time that target behaviors occurred during observations. Third, our computer-assisted observational recording system allowed us to calculate interobserver agreement on a second-by-second basis per behavior per participant per session as a *kappa* coefficient, which incorporates the occurrence and nonoccurrence of target behaviors corrected for chance agreement (Cohen, 1960). In contrast, in the previous studies interobserver agreement was reported only as one overall rating of similarity between raters' narrative recordings per session. Fourth, rather than target work-related social interaction, we focused on an everyday leisure skill—engaging in casual conversations while eating lunch—and established a normative rate and topography for this behavior based on a typical high school population. Fifth, unlike in the studies already cited and other investigations (e.g., English, Goldstein, Shafer, & Kaczmarek, 1997), our technology allowed us to record individuals' affect, appropriateness of interaction, level of attending to a conversational partner, participation in a group activity or game, and topic of conversation. Sixth, ours is one of the few studies in which target behaviors of a nondisabled population were observed in situ to establish goals before intervention (i.e., social comparison; Kazdin, 1982).

The remainder of this chapter describes the methods we used to observe the social interaction patterns of students with mental retardation requiring limited or extensive support and their general education peers in a high school lunchroom. (More detailed descriptions are found in reports by Hughes, Lorden, et al. [1998] and Hughes, Rodi, et al. [in press].) In addition, we report findings and implications of our research. Recommendations are then made for future research and practice, the limitations of the technology are discussed, and concluding suggestions are made for the field.

APPLICATION OF OBSERVATIONAL RESEARCH TECHNOLOGY

The following subsections describe the method used in our observational research. In addition, findings of our investigation are reported.

Method

The description of our research methodology includes the setting, the target behaviors, and the participants involved in our investigation. Our computer-assisted observational methods are also discussed.

Setting   To identify potentially relevant target behaviors related to social interaction we first conducted direct observations of student social interactions in the lunchroom of a large urban high school with 2,700 students that offered courses in academic and vocational preparation. The student population was 58% Caucasian; 40% African American; and 2% Asian American, Native American, and other ethnic groups. The high school served general education students as well as students with disabilities (e.g., mental retardation, autism, learning or behavior disorders; number in subsample [n] = 325). Students with disabilities were served in partially mainstreamed, self-contained, or resource room classes. All general and special education students ate lunch in unassigned seating in one of two large lunchrooms, in which all observations of student social interaction were conducted.

Target Behaviors   Preliminary observation indicated that although general and special education students ate in proximity of each other, virtually no social interaction occurred between members of the two groups. This observation prompted us to investigate how the interactions of the two groups differed, reasoning that if students with disabilities displayed social behaviors that approximated those of their general education peers, social interaction between individuals in the two groups might increase (Haring, 1991). Therefore, we nominated potential target behaviors by informally observing 320 general education students and 39 students with mental retardation requiring limited or extensive support. Twice weekly for 2 months, we observed and recorded sequentially in narrative form all verbal and nonverbal responses typically given by each of the students and the social context in which the responses occurred, using the students' naturally occurring lunch groups as the unit of analysis. (Lunch groups varied little from session to session.) From these observations, we identified 97 behaviors and 33 conversational topics that occurred during conversational interactions. We then used the constant-comparison method (Lincoln & Guba, 1985) to group the listed behaviors and topics by their apparent function into conversational interaction categories that emerged as we examined the data (e.g., attending to social focal point, talking about peers). The process resulted in a list of 9 conversational behavior codes and 10 conversational topic codes. The behavior codes and their definitions are listed in Table 1. Four of the behaviors were event-based measures and five were duration-based measures. The measures incorporated both qualitative (e.g., quality of voice or body language) and quantitative (e.g., rate of initiating or responding) aspects of behavior. In addition, we developed codes that described the social context in which the behaviors occurred (e.g., number and ethnicity of males or females at a table) and the actor and recipient of the behaviors.

Participants   We then applied those 9 behavior and 10 topic codes in observations of two groups of 12 students in the same setting. Students in both groups represented the age, gender, and ethnic composition of the school's student population. Students selected for one group had mental retardation requiring limited ($n = 10$) or extensive support ($n = 2$) and functional communication skills. Twelve general education students who we judged to be socially competent (e.g., they frequently exchanged social bids with their peers) and to engage in conversation often were chosen for the second group. This group's selection criteria were designed to ensure that the target behaviors were performed at a level considered normative and functional within the setting as a means of social comparison with the students with mental retardation (Van Houten, 1979). By comparing the two groups we sought to identify behaviors that discriminated between students with mental retardation and their general education peers that could serve as potential instructional targets (Hawkins, 1991).

Computer-Assisted Observation   For 3 months from 11:00 A.M. to 1:00 P.M. daily we conducted 10 systematic observations of each of the 24 students (i.e., 10 observations of 24 students for a total of 240 observation sessions). Using Compaq Series 2820A laptop computers with 2 megabytes of random access memory, 7.5-inch by 6-inch black-and-white screens, and standard QWERTY keyboard configurations, three trained data collectors observed the targeted students for approximately 20 minutes during each of 10 sessions per student. During each session the students ate lunch in the school lunchroom in unassigned seating in naturally occurring social groups at tables designed to accommodate five to six students. To ensure opportunities for group interaction an observational session was not begun unless the target student sat with at least two other students at a table. Total observation time per student for the 10 observation sessions averaged 2 hours and 50 minutes (standard deviation = 14 minutes).

After obtaining permission from the students at a table to observe them for a 20-minute period, an observer sat approximately 1 meter from the table with the target student in view. All observers were present during all observation sessions; however, they observed different target students at different tables located throughout the lunchroom, except when conducting observations for interobserver reliability analyses, which they did in pairs. Assignment of students to observers was randomized daily.

Observation and Recording Procedures   To measure social interactions we conducted continuous observation using laptop computers with the target student as the unit of analysis. Consequently, only interactions in which the target student participated were scored. Interactions that occurred at the same table but did not involve the target student were not scored.

Because the target student was the unit of analysis the four event-based codes were mutually exclusive (e.g., a target student could not initiate and respond simultaneously or be appropriate and inappropriate at the same time). In addition, the total duration of event behaviors could be collected because the termination of each event was signaled by entering a new code. (If no event code behavior occurred when an event was terminated the code for "no event code occurring" was entered continuously until the onset of an event code behavior.) The actor and the recipient (i.e., target student, peer with mental retardation, general education peer, teacher) of each event-based behavior also were scored, which resulted in a total of 24 event-based behavior code combinations (e.g., "target student initiates appropriately to a peer with mental retardation").

Among the duration-based codes only "positive or neutral affect" and "negative affect" were mutually exclusive (see Table 1). Duration-based codes were scored for the target students only, not for their conversational partners. Event-based and duration-based codes could be scored simultaneously (e.g., "general education peer responds appropriately to target student while attending to and playing a card game and maintaining a positive or neutral affect"), resulting in several hundred possible coding combinations that could be scored at any given second.

Observers recorded data using laptop computers equipped with the *Multiple Option Observation System for Experimental Studies* (*MOOSES*) software program (Tapp, Wehby, & Ellis, 1995), which allows simultaneous recording of event and duration measures based in real time and has been used in investigations of social interaction (e.g., English et al., 1997). (See Chapter 6 for more details about this software.) At the onset of each observation session observers also recorded session start time and the social context within which the behaviors occurred (i.e., number, gender, and ethnicity of peers with mental retardation and general education peers sitting at the target student's table). During the session, they tallied by hand the frequency with which conversational topics were discussed. At the end of each session, observers recorded session stop time and any changes in social context that may have occurred during the course of the session.

Interobserver Agreement   Interobserver agreement was measured on all behavior codes calculated per session per student by having two observers independently score student interactions. For each of the 24 targeted students, 3 sessions were randomly selected from the 10 observation sessions, for a total of 72 interobserver agreement sessions (3 sessions multiplied by 24 students equals 72 sessions, or 30% of the 240 total sessions across students). Point-by-point agreement (Kazdin, 1982) was calculated for both event and duration codes using procedures outlined by MacLean, Tapp, and Johnson (1985). Briefly, agreement was comput-

Table 1. Behavior codes

Code	Definition
Event-based	
Initiation/expansion	Verbal or physical behavior directed toward another person that introduces a new topic or expands on an existing topic, introduces new information not related to information from a previous utterance, or is preceded by at least 15 seconds containing no interactive verbal behavior with the same person. Includes communicative gestures such as waving.
Appropriate initiation/expansion	An initiation or expansion is scored as appropriate if volume, tone, and quality of voice, pitch, intensity, intonation, rate, topography, and topic approximate standards established by social comparison with peers without disabilities within the immediate environmental context (e.g., verbal greeting).
Inappropriate initiation/expansion	An initiation or expansion is scored as inappropriate if the volume, tone, and quality of voice, pitch, intensity, intonation, rate, or topic is not consistent with standards established by social comparison with peers without disabilities within the immediate environmental context (e.g., hugging a stranger when meeting versus greeting verbally, talking to self). Topic repetition also is scored as inappropriate (e.g., "What are windows made of?" when spoken continuously).
Communicative response	Verbal or physical behavior in response to an initiation without expanding on a topic or adding new information to a previous utterance. Includes asking for clarification of an initiation and meaningful nonword verbalizations or gestures that serve as acknowledgments or responses, such as "hm-m-m," "uh-huh," shaking head "yes" or "no," smiling, frowning, waving in response, pointing, winking, or shrugging shoulders.
Appropriate response	A response is scored as appropriate if the volume, tone, and quality of voice, pitch, intensity, intonation, rate, topography, and topic approximate standards established by social comparison with peers without disabilities within the immediate environmental context. A response also is scored as appropriate if it is a statement, question, or gesture that is neutral in tone and intent or simply provides information (e.g., "I ate pizza").
Inappropriate response	A response is scored as inappropriate if the participant sighs, moans, yells or shouts, has a negative affect (e.g., "That's dumb"), or is not consistent with standards established by social comparison with peers without disabilities within the immediate environmental context.

Duration-based

Positive or neutral affect

Participant's behavior generally indicates a positive or neutral affect by smiling, laughing, making positive remarks, leaning toward peer when speaking, maintaining a relaxed body position, looking interested in peer; or holding head up when interacting.

Negative affect

Participant's behavior generally indicates a negative affect by frowning, crying, complaining, making negative remarks, looking away from peer when interacting, maintaining poor body or head posture, looking down, or exhibiting an appearance associated with low self-esteem.

Attending to focal person or social focal point

Participant attends to and shifts attention appropriately and promptly to relevant social stimuli in the immediate environment, as indicated by directing face toward social focal point (e.g., participant sitting with a group of peers at a table shifts attention as speakers shift during conversation). Attending is not scored if participant does not attend to or shift attention appropriately and promptly to relevant social stimuli in the immediate environment, as indicated by not directing face toward social focal point (e.g., participant holds fixed gaze away from speaker at table).

Participating in group activity or game

Participant observes or is engaged in activities or games such as card playing, board games, looking at pictures, or other activities engaged in by students without disabilities within the environmental context.

Engaging in socially inappropriate motor behavior

Participant performs a motor behavior that would be considered socially inappropriate compared with the behavior of peers within the immediate environment or that an observer judges to be interfering in the occurrence of social interaction between the participant and peers or teachers (e.g., continuously rocking torso back and forth, covering face with hands, hitting own chin with hand).

259

ed using a 3-second window (plus or minus) around each code in the primary observer's data file. If a match was found in the second observer's data file, an agreement was scored. All unmatched codes were considered to be disagreements. Data files were compared on a second-by-second basis to calculate occurrence agreement values and *kappa* coefficients for both duration-based and event-based codes. *Kappa* coefficients (Cohen, 1960) were calculated per behavior per session per student to represent an agreement measure for the occurrence and nonoccurrence of target behaviors, corrected for chance agreement between observers. Occurrence interobserver agreement estimates, ranges, and *kappa* values were calculated by averaging each student's scores obtained per session per behavior (available upon request). Mean overall agreement ranged from 90% to 99%. Mean *kappa* values ranged from .53 to .95.

Findings

Findings are reported for conversational interactions and conversational topics for both groups of students. In addition, narrative descriptions of the context in which conversations occurred are provided.

Conversational Interactions   As recommended by Bakeman and Gottman (1986), event-based behaviors that occurred fewer than 10 times or duration-based behaviors that occurred for less than 1 minute across all participants and sessions (68 hours of total observation time) were excluded from further analysis because of their low frequency. Measures eliminated because of low frequency were those in which 1) teachers were the performers or recipients of an initiation or response, 2) students with mental retardation initiated or responded to any of approximately 500 general education students present in the lunchroom (or vice versa), and 3) students with mental retardation or their general education peers exhibited a negative affect.

Means, standard deviations, computed values of *t*-tests (*t*), and alpha levels of the remaining social behaviors are listed in Table 2, grouped by the performer and the recipient of each behavior. Because of their negligible frequency, no interactions between students with mental retardation and their general education peers are reported in Table 2. Therefore, all conversational interactions of students in the lunchroom reported in Table 2 occurred among like peers (i.e., either students with mental retardation or general education students). Event-based behaviors are reported as 1) rate of response and 2) percentage of total observation time during which the response occurred. Duration behaviors are reported as percentage of time only.

Of the 20 behaviors measured, 19 were significantly different (see Table 2). Performance on only one of the measures (i.e., percentage of time responding inappropriately by peers) did not reach statistical significance at a conventional level of probability. General education target students initiated appropriately to peers at a mean rate of 3.17 per minute, whereas target students with mental retardation initiated appropriately at a rate of .87 per minute ($t = 8.58$, probability [*p*] $< .001$). Time spent initiating appropriately to peers averaged almost 18% (of a total of 68 hours) for general education target students compared with less than 5% for target students with mental retardation ($t = 9.12$, $p < .001$). Rates and percentages of time responding appropriately also were significantly higher for general education students. For example, general education target students responded appropriately to peers more than twice per minute, whereas target students with mental retardation responded appropriately less than .5 times per minute ($t = 10.10, p < .001$). Target students with mental retardation and general education students also differed significantly on rate and percentage of time initiating and responding inappropriately, although these behaviors occurred infrequently.

With respect to duration-based behaviors, target students with mental retardation and general education students frequently displayed a positive or neutral affect (94.17% and 87.62% of the time for students with mental retardation and general education students, respectively), although mean performance was significantly higher for students with mental retardation ($t = -2.20, p < .05$). General education students attended to the focal situation approximately 89% of the time compared with slightly more than half of the time for students with mental retardation ($t = 5.97, p < .001$). They also engaged in activities or games more than their counterparts with mental retardation (13.46% versus 1.00% of the time; $t = 1.79, p < .1$). Students with mental retardation spent significantly more of their time (24%) engaged in socially inappropriate motor behavior; general education students engaged in these behaviors less than 1% of the time.

Conversational Topics   The conversational topics discussed by students with mental retardation and general education students are shown in Table 3. Students with mental retardation and general education students discussed similar topics, although at different rates. General education students discussed more than twice as many topics, as grouped by topical category, as students with mental retardation. The topical area most frequently discussed by both groups (more than 25% of total topics for each group) was their peers at school, followed by the food they were eating or food in general. General education students discussed school events and after-school and outside-school events more frequently than students with mental retardation. General education students also told jokes and talked about academic school events more frequently than students with mental retardation. Unlike general education students, students with mental retardation never discussed money. Work or employment was discussed infrequently by both groups. Forty-one percent of all conversation of students with mental retardation consisted of repetitive topics (e.g., questions or statements repeated continuously with no response from conversational partners, such as "What's glass made of?" or "Santa Claus is coming") or nondiscernible speech (e.g., grunts, gibberish, speech incomprehensible to observers), compared with 1% for general education students. Chi-square results (chi-square = 233.631, degrees of freedom = 9, $p < .0005$) indicated a relation between the presence or absence of mental retardation and frequency of topic that could not be attributed to chance. For example, general education students discussed peers and social events and joked at a significantly higher frequency than students with mental retardation.

To determine if differences observed between the two groups could have been influenced by the high frequency of repetitive topics or nondiscernible speech reported for students with mental retardation, we conducted additional analyses. We excluded data for all students ($n = 5$) who had 67% or more of their total topics scored as repetitive topics or nondiscernible speech. We then retallied topics for the remaining seven students with mental retardation, each of whom had 33% or less (mean = 20%) of their total topics scored as repetitive topics or nondiscernible speech. As shown in Table 3, frequencies and percentages did not vary much from those of the entire group of 12 students with mental retardation,

Table 2. Conversational interaction between two groups of students in a high school lunchroom

Behavior	General education students		Students with mental retardation		
	M	SD	M	SD	
Event based					
Initiating appropriately					
Rate[a] of initiating appropriately by					
Target student to peer[b]	3.17	.50	.87	.79	8.58****
Peer to target student	2.40	.39	.60	.48	10.14****
Percentage of time[c] initiating appropriately by					
Target student to peer	17.99	2.73	4.80	4.20	9.12****
Peer to target student	11.14	2.36	3.39	2.78	7.36****
Initiating inappropriately					
Rate of initiating inappropriately by					
Target student to peer	.003	.007	.026	.033	−2.30**
Peer to target student	.002	.003	.022	.019	−3.67***
Percentage of time initiating inappropriately by					
Target student to peer	.01	.03	.18	.29	−1.99*
Peer to target student	.02	.05	.29	.53	−1.73*
Communicative responding appropriately					
Rate of responding appropriately by					
Target student to peer	2.17	.38	.48	.44	10.10****
Peer to target student	2.03	.33	.44	.50	9.20****
Percentage of time responding appropriately by					
Target student to peer	6.87	1.35	2.13	1.71	7.55****
Peer to target student	5.77	1.18	1.81	1.92	6.08****

Communicative responding inappropriately

					t
Rate of responding inappropriately by[a]					
Target student to peer	.001	.002	.010	.014	−2.37**
Peer to target student	.002	.003	.013	.021	−1.94*
Percentage of time responding inappropriately by					
Target student to peer	.001	.003	.073	.117	−2.11**
Peer to target student	.018	.049	.107	.190	−1.57
Duration-based[d]					
Percentage of time displaying positive or neutral affect	87.62	8.22	94.17	6.24	−2.20**
Percentage of time attending to focal person or focal social point	89.22	4.04	56.43	18.59	5.97****
Percentage of time engaging in group activity or game	13.46	23.86	1.00	3.45	1.79*
Percentage of time engaging in socially inappropriate motor behavior	.45	.51	24.05	19.09	−4.28****

[a]Per minute.

[b]"Peers" for students with mental retardation refers to other students with mental retardation. "Peers" for general education students refers to other general education students. Social interactions between students with mental retardation and general education students occurred less than .02% of the time ($< .03$ minutes of 68 hours of total observation time) and were dropped from further analysis.

[c]Percentage of total observation time ($n = 68$ hours).

[d]Target students only.

****t-test, degrees of freedom $= 22$, $p < .001$.

***t-test, degrees of freedom $= 22$, $p < .01$.

**t-test, degrees of freedom $= 22$, $p < .05$.

*t-test, degrees of freedom $= 22$, $p < .1$.

Table 3.   Content of topics discussed by two groups of students in a high school setting

Topical category	Frequency		
	General education students	Students with mental retardation	Selected group of students with mental retardation[a]
Peers	124(27)[b]	52(26)	48(35)
Food	68(15)	25(12)	22(16)
School events (social)	65(14)	6(3)	3(2)
After-school and outside-school events	64(13)	14(7)	14(10)
Jokes	63(13)	9(4)	7(5)
School events (academic)	40(9)	4(2)	4(3)
Money	18(4)	0(0)	0(0)
Television, movies, bands, and celebrities	10(2)	7(4)	7(5)
Work and employment	9(2)	2(1)	2(1)
Repetitive topics or nondiscernible speech	3(1)	84(41)	31(23)
Total	464(100)	203(100)	138(100)

[a]Students with mental retardation ($n = 7$) excluding five students who had 67% or more of their total topics scored as repetitive topics or nondiscernible speech.

[b]Percentage of total topics discussed by group across entire observation time ($n = 34$ hours per group).

other than those reported for repetitive topics or nondiscernible speech. Therefore, although a subgroup of students accounted for a large proportion of repetitive topics or nondiscernible speech, the distribution of all other topical categories did not appear to be influenced by these students.

Context of Conversational Interaction   The context in which conversational interactions occurred was recorded narratively. Students with mental retardation and general education students rarely ate at the same table. In addition, although teachers supervised students (e.g., observed them from a standing position or while sitting at a lunch table), they did not sit with them at the same tables. Students with mental retardation typically ate in groups of four (range, three to six), and general education students typically ate in groups of five (range, three to nine). Across all observed students conversational interactions typically included groups rather than dyads of students. General education students were slightly more likely to eat at a table with peers of the same gender and ethnicity than students with mental retardation.

IMPLICATIONS OF THE RESEARCH

Increasing social interaction among students with disabilities and their general education peers is a goal of many educational and employment efforts (Haring, 1991). Our observational research provides a first step toward describing the social interaction patterns that exist between students with mental retardation requiring limited or extensive support and general education students in a high school lunchroom setting. By noting discrepancies in performance between students with mental retardation requiring limited or extensive support and general education students, we identified behaviors such as attending, initiating conversation, and participating in group activities or games that were performed more frequently by general education students when interacting socially. The next step in establishing an empirical basis for selecting instructional targets to promote social interaction among special and general education students would be to teach students to perform the identified social behaviors at levels shown in our study to produce optimal outcomes (e.g., responses) from conversational partners (Van Houten, 1979). Evaluation of the effects of instruction, such as increased lunchtime conversation with peers, would provide an assessment of the functional validity of the targeted skills (Hawkins, 1991).

RECOMMENDATIONS FOR RESEARCH AND PRACTICE

The following conclusions and recommendations are suggested for research and practice. Suggestions include increasing shared experiences of special and general education students, providing social skills instruction, teaching social interaction skills, and designing instructional programs.

Increasing Opportunities for Shared Experiences

First, high school general education students were found to initiate and respond appropriately, attend to conversation, and engage in group activities or games significantly more than students with mental retardation. Although the content of conversation was similar for the two groups, general education students discussed topics at significantly higher rates. For example, they initiated jokes with each other seven times more frequently than students with mental retardation, which is similar to what was found in the workplace (Chadsey-Rusch et al., 1989). We suggest, therefore, that practitioners should target joking, teasing, and conversational topics in addition to measures of frequency when implementing social skills interventions. Although students with mental retardation may not comprehend the subtleties of complex language, such as figures of speech, that constitute some forms of joking, there are many less sophisticated forms of humorous exchanges in which people participate (e.g., laughing when two people say the same thing simultaneously, looking at the "funnies" with a friend, mimicking a television celebrity). In addition, the fact that students with mental retardation rarely joked or discussed social events may relate to a lack of social experiences, suggesting that social skills interventions should provide opportunities for students to participate with their peers in social events and a variety of other everyday experiences. Parent and colleagues (1992) argued that people are more likely to interact and develop relationships with others who perform similar social behaviors and with whom they share interests and activities in common. Fortunately, "peer buddy" programs, in which students with disabilities and their general education peers interact socially in and out of school, are becoming accepted practice in many high schools, allowing these students to have common shared experiences (Hughes et al., 1999).

Providing Social Skills Instruction

Second, negligible social interaction occurred in the lunchroom between the 12 students with mental retardation and any of the approximately 500 general education peers. This finding corroborates research conducted in other settings, such as elementary schools, that indicates that physical integration alone does not produce social integration among people with disabilities and their typical peers (Gresham, 1982). Differences in social performance may contribute to lack of social integration. Social skills instruction that targets the behaviors investigated in this study, such as initiating and responding, may promote the social integration of students with disabilities by modifying their social performance to approximate that of their general education peers. This suggestion is supported by the fact that contextual factors, such as the number of conversational partners and the physical arrangement of the setting, did not differ for students with mental retardation and general education students. This finding supports the argument that differences in the social interaction of the two groups of students may be attributed primarily to differences in performance of the conversational skills targeted in this study, such as percentage of time initiating or attending.

Teaching Informal Social Interaction Skills

Third, we observed students while they were engaged in a leisure-time activity—conversing with each other while eating lunch—and established optimum rates for the performance of this behavior. An everyday leisure conversational skill may be a fruitful instructional target for increasing social integration because of the likelihood that performing the behavior will be reinforced on a regular basis throughout the day. Many environments offer individuals ample opportunity to practice and receive reinforcement for conversing informally with others. Learning to converse informally may be a pivotal skill that allows one to gain access to the naturally occurring reinforcement in an environment, such as when exchanging greetings with a bus driver or talking with other students between classes in the hall (Baer & Wolf, 1970).

Similarly, general education students were found to engage in group activities or games, such as looking at pictures together or playing cards, more frequently than students with mental retardation. Teaching students to play games or operate electronic devices such as computers or radios with their peers has been shown to be an effective means of increasing social interaction (Kennedy & Haring, 1993). Social skills instruction targeting informal conversation may be more effective when provided within a group-activity or game situation.

Designing Instructional Programs

Our recommendations for research and practice are based on the assumption that students with disabilities can acquire critical social behaviors that approximate those of their general education peers, an assumption that has been supported by empirical research (e.g., Hughes et al., 1996). The concept of *partial participation* (Baumgart et al., 1982), in which an individual is expected to engage in an activity only partially, may be relevant to social interaction. Just as most general education students would probably not expect a classmate with English as a second language to comprehend all of the nuances of spoken English, they probably would not expect that their interactions with students with mental retardation requiring limited or extensive support would be just like their interactions with their typical peers. Nevertheless, general education students have reported having high-quality interactions with their peers with mental retardation (e.g., Hughes et al., in press). In addition, although we observed substantial differences between the social performance of students with mental retardation and that of general education students, there also were many similarities. For example, although the frequency of conversational topics differed for the two groups of students, several topics, such as peers, food, and outside-school events, accounted for similar percentages of the total topics. Furthermore, the contexts of conversations, such as the size of the conversational group, were similar for both groups. By designing instructional programs that incorporate approximations between the social interactions of students with mental retardation and those of their general education peers, interventionists may produce more effective and lasting outcomes.

LIMITATIONS OF THE TECHNOLOGY

Several limitations of the observational research technology we used are noted next. These limitations include collapsing behavior codes and failing to assess the functional validity of targeted behaviors.

Collapsing Behavior Codes

First, in developing our observational coding system we observed conversations for 2 months and developed a list of 97 interaction behaviors, which we collapsed into 16 categories and subsequently reduced to 9. We did so because observers found it difficult to reliably record multiple behaviors in vivo. Although the computer allowed them to record social interactions in real time, nuances of interactions (e.g., questions versus comments) were difficult to capture with the noise level and movement typical of a large high school lunchroom with approximately 500 students. In collapsing the targeted behaviors, however, we may have omitted factors from our analysis that are crucial to conversational interaction. For example, no distinctions were made between verbal and nonverbal behavior, behavior that initiated versus maintained conversation, topic initiations versus topic expansions, requests for actions versus questions that obligated verbal replies, or comments about present versus past or future events. Videotaping students' conversations would have allowed a more precise analysis of additional measures that were difficult to score reliably in vivo by allowing us to rescore observations as needed and to take multiple variables into account. However, videotaping naturally occurring groups of students (i.e., typically five or six students per table) who frequently change seats or facial direction may be difficult and even intrusive in the applied setting of a high school lunchroom.

Failing to Assess the Functional Validity of Targeted Behaviors

Second, although several variables were identified as having significant differences, no inferences can be drawn regarding the relative importance of these variables. An experimental analysis of the effects of increases or decreases in the various behaviors on significant social outcomes would reveal much about the relative importance of targeted behaviors (Goldstein, Kaczmarek, Pennington, & Shafer, 1992). In addition, the functional validity (Hawkins, 1991) of the behaviors should be evaluated by determining if increases in target behaviors relate to increases in social interaction and friendships among students with mental retardation and general education students. Future research also should investigate which individuals would benefit most from the social skills instruction suggested by this study. Although targeted skills may be appropriate for many high school students with mental retardation requiring limited or extensive support, some may require an additional or alternative array of skills (e.g., articulation) or experiences (e.g., peer support network). Finally, the skills targeted in this study may be less appropriate for some environmental contexts than others (e.g., employment).

CONCLUSIONS

Since the 1980s, sophisticated methods for conducting observational research have been introduced (e.g., computer-assisted coding of videotaped performance, computer-assisted data collection in vivo). These methods have many benefits, such as real-time recording of multiple behaviors and manipulation of data for sequential analysis of interactions. In addition, they are well suited for use in controlled settings, such as therapeutic clinics and self-contained classrooms. Computer-assisted technology also is a valuable tool in conducting observational research in everyday environments, such as high school lunchrooms, worksites, and community locations. Accommodations must be made for their use in such settings, however, because the presence of even a single observer has been shown to influence performance (Rusch et al., 1984).

However, having the ability to capture social interaction on videotape or the means to collect social interaction data in real time via a computer does not tell a researcher which behaviors are socially important to consider (Hawkins, 1991; Wolf, 1978). For example, computer-assisted technology may allow investigators to identify the probability that responses are more likely to follow questions than comments (Goldstein et al., 1992), but this finding is relevant only if the targeted behaviors are shown to be socially important to participants within a specific environment or if performance of the behaviors relates to favorable outcomes for participants (Hawkins, 1991).

Therefore, we recommend augmenting the use of computers to collect data on social interaction with social validation methods to 1) identify socially important behaviors and 2) determine if the outcomes of programming efforts are considered by participants and important others in an environment to be of an acceptable magnitude to make a difference in their lives. The observational research program described in this chapter is part of a series of studies we are conducting to identify critical social behaviors among high school students and strategies to measure and teach these behaviors. This effort will be a success if, when combined with supportive environments, it increases social acceptance, satisfying interactions, and lasting relationships, which are valued among individuals with mental retardation and their typical peers.

REFERENCES

Baer, D.M., & Wolf, M.M. (1970). The entry into natural communities of reinforcement. In R.E. Ulrich, T.J. Stachnik, & J. Mabry (Eds.), *Control of human behavior: From cure to prevention* (Vol. 2, pp. 319–324). Glenview, IL: Scott Foresman–Addison Wesley.

Bakeman, R., & Gottman, J.M. (1986). *Observing interaction: An introduction to sequential analysis.* New York: Cambridge University Press.

Baumgart, D., Brown, L., Pumpian, I., Nisbet, J., Ford, A., Sweet, M., Messina, R., & Schroeder, J. (1982). Principle of partial participation and individualized adaptations in educational programs for severely handicapped students. *Journal of The Association for the Severely Handicapped, 7,* 17–27.

Chadsey-Rusch, J., Gonzalez, P., Tines, J., & Johnson, J.R. (1989). Social ecology of the workplace: Contextual variables affecting social interactions of employees with and without mental retardation. *American Journal on Mental Retardation, 94,* 141–151.

Cohen, R. (1960). A coefficient of agreement for nominal scales. *Educational and Psychological Measurement, 20,* 37–46.

English, K., Goldstein, H., Shafer, K., & Kaczmarek, L. (1997). Promoting interactions among preschoolers with and without disabilities: Effects of a buddy skills-training program. *Exceptional Children, 63,* 229–243.

Ferguson, B., McDonnell, J., & Drew, C. (1993). Type and frequency of social interaction among workers with and without mental retardation. *American Journal on Mental Retardation, 97,* 530–540.

Goldstein, H., Kaczmarek, L., Pennington, R., & Shafer, K. (1992). Peer-mediated intervention: Attending to, commenting on, and acknowledging the behavior of pre-schoolers with autism. *Journal of Applied Behavior Analysis, 25,* 289–305.

Gresham, F.M. (1982). Misguided mainstreaming: The case for social skills training with handicapped children. *Exceptional Children, 48,* 422–433.

Haring, T.G. (1991). Social relationships. In L.H. Meyer, C.A. Peck, & L. Brown (Eds.), *Critical issues in the lives of people with severe disabilities* (pp. 195–217). Baltimore: Paul H. Brookes Publishing Co.

Hawkins, R.P. (1991). Is social validity what we are interested in? Argument for a functional approach. *Journal of Applied Behavior Analysis, 24,* 205–213.

Hughes, C., Guth, C., Hall, S., Presley, J., Dye, M., & Byers, C. (1999). "They are my best friends": Peer buddies promote inclusion in high school. *Teaching Exceptional Children, 31,* 32–37.

Hughes, C., Killian, D.J., & Fischer, G.M. (1996). Validation and assessment of a conversational interaction intervention. *American Journal on Mental Retardation, 100,* 493–509.

Hughes, C., Kim, J., & Hwang, B. (1998). Assessing social integration in employment settings: Current knowledge and future directions. *American Journal on Mental Retardation, 103,* 173–185.

Hughes, C., Lorden, S.W., Scott, S.V., Hwang, B., Derer, K.R., Rodi, M.S., Pitkin, S.E., & Godshall, J.C. (1998). Identification and validation of critical conversational social skills. *Journal of Applied Behavior Analysis, 31,* 431–446.

Hughes, C., Rodi, M.S., Lorden, S.W., Pitkin, S.E., Derer, K.R., Hwang, B., & Cai, X. (in press). Comparative analysis of social interactions of high school students with and without mental retardation. *American Journal on Mental Retardation.*

Kazdin, A.E. (1982). *Single-case research designs: Methods for clinical and applied settings.* New York: Oxford University Press.

Kennedy, C.H., & Haring, T.G. (1993). Teaching choice making during social interactions to students with profound multiple disabilities. *Journal of Applied Behavior Analysis, 26,* 63-76.

Lincoln, Y.S., & Guba, E.G. (1985). *Naturalistic inquiry.* Thousand Oaks, CA: Sage Publications.

MacLean, W.E., Tapp, J.T., & Johnson, W.L. (1985). Alternate methods and software for calculating interobserver agreement for continuous observation data. *Journal of Psychopathology and Behavioral Assessment, 7,* 65–73.

Parent, W.S., Kregel, J., Metzler, H.M.D., & Twardzik, G. (1992). Social integration in the workplace: An analysis of the interaction activities of workers with mental retardation and their co-workers. *Education and Training in Mental Retardation, 27,* 28–38.

Peck, C.A., Donaldson, J., & Pezzoli, M. (1990). Some benefits nonhandicapped adolescents perceive for themselves from their social relationships with peers who have severe handicaps. *Journal of The Association for Persons with Severe Handicaps, 15,* 241–249.

Rehabilitation Act Amendments of 1992, PL 102-569, 29 U.S.C. §§ 701 *et seq.*

Rusch, F.R., Menchetti, B.M., Crouch, K., Riva, M., Morgan, T., & Agran, M. (1984). Competitive employment: Assessing employee reactivity to naturalistic observation. *Applied Research in Mental Retardation, 5,* 339–351.

Tapp, J.T., Wehby, J.H., & Ellis, D. (1995). A Multiple Option Observation System for Experimental Studies: MOOSES. *Behavior Research Methods, Instruments, and Computers, 27,* 25–31.

Van Houten, R. (1979). Social validation: The evolution of standards of competency for target behaviors. *Journal of Applied Behavior Analysis, 12,* 581–591.

Wolf, M.M. (1978). Social validity: The case for subjective measurement or how applied behavior analysis is finding its heart. *Journal of Applied Behavior Analysis, 11,* 203–214.

17

Computer-Assisted Assessment of Treatment Effects Among Individuals with Developmental Disabilities

Curt A. Sandman,
Paul E. Touchette,
Jason Ly,
Sarah DeBoard Marion, and
Yvonne E.M. Bruinsma

Reliable measurement of the effects of treatments, such as pharmacological interventions, requires a valid tool for the assessment of human behavior. This requirement is critical for individuals with developmental delays, who often have limited verbal communication skills. Among the most common tools for measuring human behavior are questionnaires filled out by patients or other study participants, scales completed by caregivers or professionals, interviews of patients and staff, and scales related to clinical judgment. These tools have been useful with individuals with developmental delays even though they suffer from obvious and inherent weaknesses, such as bias, reliance on memory of events, and ratings of impressions rather than actual behavior. In the worst case response bias, deception, unshared assumptions, and ignorance can invalidate the information collected with these tools. In the best case these tools may only partially measure the constructs or behaviors of interest. The best possible monitoring system would

This chapter was supported by grants from the National Institutes of Child Health and Human Behavior (Grant Nos. HD31571 and HD28202).

provide a continuous record of behavior that would accurately capture behavioral complexity in naturalistic conditions unimpeded by laboratory constraints. Continuous observations can be recorded in laboratory and naturalistic studies of animals and for some measures of human behavior. For instance, cardiac halter monitoring can provide continuous measures of human heart rate for periods of time. Devices for measurement of activity (pedometers) can provide an index of human ambulation. Other devices can provide an index of sleep or of nutritional intake. These devices are very useful and provide a target goal for assessment of behavior. Monitoring of complex, unconstrained human behavior, however, is not easily programmed into an unobtrusive device. Another person, either by analysis of videotape or direct physical observation, is required for assessment of complex human behavior.

There are few successful examples of time-limited continuous or nearly continuous measurement of complex human behavior. Temporal resolution and duration of observation are essential issues in defining continuous data. These issues contribute critically not only to the choice of analytic strategy but also to the procedures chosen for measurement. In other areas of science, such as analysis of electroencephalograms, these problems have been solved. Measurement procedures can include continuous epochs of data, and time series procedures are routinely applied to summarize complex information. Indeed, there are many statistical tools (e.g., power spectral analysis) for describing complex information, but the study of human behavior has lagged behind because of the absence of measurement tools.

When information about complex human behavior is available, fascinating relationships between states and events can be discovered. For instance, in a study by Guess et al. (1993) the probability that one behavioral state would follow another (transitional probability) was described. Dominant states (the state with the longest duration) were characterized, and the rate of change among various states was determined. These findings have profound implications and should be the model for describing behavior.

Other researchers also have conducted analyses of complex behavioral interactions and have contributed to this kind of data analyses, which was introduced and expanded by Bakeman and Gottman (Bakeman & Gottman, 1986; Bakeman & Quera, 1995; Gottman, 1981; Gottman & Roy, 1990). For example, Emerson, Thompson, Reeves, Henderson, and Robertson (1995) conducted extensive descriptive analyses of the conditions under which the challenging behavior of five individuals with mental retardation requiring extensive support might occur and be maintained. These data were collected using videotaping equipment and then organized off-line using a method similar to those reviewed here (McGill, Hewson, & Emerson, 1994). Similarly, Hall and Oliver (1997) provided a means of examining sequential data graphically (normalized and pooled information about conditions preceding, during, and after a given behavior).

These examples represent the growing trend in behavioral analyses to focus on the relationship between co-occurring events and conditions (e.g., environmental, peer). One of the primary reasons that this kind of description and analysis of data is not used by more behavioral researchers is that both data collection and analytic procedures are extremely complicated.

For instance, in the study by Guess et al. (1993) behavior (state) was coded manually on scoring sheets at 5-second intervals with 5 seconds between each observation (for marking the previous interval). The intervals were timed using an audiotape recorder with prerecorded signals to prompt the observers. Incoming observers (relief observers) attached to the tape recorder 2 minutes before coming on-line at 28-minute intervals. At the end of each 42-minute segment, a new time interval tape was inserted into the tape recorder. Reliability estimates were determined by linking two observers to the same tape recorder and synchronizing their observation periods. This description evokes the image of an army of observers routinely wounded by fatigue, in need of periodic relief, with other comrades close by, wired together by a small machine. It is a remarkable achievement that 25 individuals were observed for a total of 3–5 hours each with these cumbersome procedures, and it is not surprising that such procedures are at best uncommon.

Bar code technology is one method of continuous data observation that has been applied by several researchers (Eiler, Nelson, Jensen, & Johnson, 1989; Forney, Leete, & Lindburg, 1991; Saunders, Saunders, & Saunders, 1994). Eiler et al. (1989) used laptop and pocket computers and a portable bar code scanner to record behavioral data in a residential treatment setting for individuals with developmental disabilities. Each target behavior was assigned a bar code label and printed on a one-page entry form. When the individual displayed a behavior, the appropriate corresponding symbol was scanned by the observer. A similar method was used by Forney et al. (1991) for the collection of sequential, focal animal data. These authors reported this method of observation to be an improvement over older methods such as keyboard entry. In addition, the amount of training time was reduced with this method because observers could quickly refer to descriptions of behavior that were printed beside the bar code labels. One problem with this system was that it often required repeated scans of a given label before the code was read (Eiler et al., 1989), so it was difficult to observe multiple target behaviors that occurred in rapid succession. Rapid behaviors were nearly impossible to record accurately when the observer reentered the bar code symbol one, two, or even three times in succession. Even with advances in this technology that have improved the sampling rate (Saunders et al., 1994) a scanning system may be inappropriate for high rates of behavior. Our study involves collecting data in a residence for people with mental retardation requiring pervasive support who display serious self-injurious behavior, and in this quickly changing environment an alternative form of observation has become necessary (Table 1).

One option for collection of continuous data is the use of videotapes for off-line scoring and analysis. We have used this approach and developed a computer-assisted system (*Observational Data Acquisition Program [ODAP]*; Hetrick, Isenhart, Taylor, & Sandman, 1991) for assessment of behavior. Our study (Sandman et al., 1993) of a relatively large number of individuals illustrated the strengths of using direct observations of behavior compared with evaluations of behavior derived from rating scales. This double-blind, crossover study of self-injuring individuals addressed several methodological inconsistencies in previous protocols (see Sandman, 1990/1991, for a summary), including evaluations derived from rating scales (e.g., Campbell, Adams, Small, Tesch, & Curren, 1988; LeBoyer, Bouvard, & Dugas, 1988; Linneman & Walker, 1989; Willemsen-Swinkels, Buitelarr, Nijhof, & Van Engeland, 1995). We compared the use of rating scales with daily, direct observations of behavior over a period of 10 weeks (resulting in

Table I. Observational technologies

General	Method	Type of observation	Populations studied	Ratio of labor to observation	Analysis	Cost
Bar code technology	Automated data collection using bar code (Eiler et al., 1989)	Continuous real-time observation of discrete behaviors	Behavioral monitoring in residential settings for individuals with developmental disabilities	Low (training time is reduced by reduction in memorization of necessary behavioral codes)	None; raw data files are provided to be read by a traditional statistical package	Approximately $800 for two-scanner installation
	A bar code scoring system for behavioral research (Forney et al., 1991)	Collection of sequential focal data (including simultaneous or overlapping behaviors)	Simple and complex interactions between nonhuman primates	Low (time to train observers is low because observers do not have to memorize complex codes)		Contact first author
Videotape	PROCODER (Tapp & Walden, 1993)	Manipulation (coding, marking, and scoring) of videotaped observation	Social referencing in infants with developmental delays	High (approximately 20 hours labor [coding] needed per hour of video observation)	Interobserver agreement for all types of data and Cohen's *kappa* (1960) for some types of data	$450 for program and support (does not include hardware and video equipment)
	C-QUAL (Duncan & Sayre, 1991)	Computer-aided transcription of videotaped action sequences	Face-to-face interaction in child development research	Exact ratio not given, but based on a similar method the ratio would be high	None available; analysis-ready files are created and analysis programs are recommended	Contact first author
	OBSERVE, formally known as Observational Data Acquisition Program (ODAP) (Hetrick et al., 1991)	Continuous real-time observational data (frequency and duration of 10 or fewer coded events)	Behavioral and environmental factors related to self-injurious behavior	Low (data compiled automatically)	None; analysis-ready data files are produced	No charge if floppy disk is provided with request; includes manual
Laptop or palmtop computer	The Observer for Windows (Noldus, Information Technology, 1991)	Continuous time-based and/or event-based real-time observation	Self-injurious behavior in people with pervasive developmental disorders	Low (observers are readily trained)	Interobserver agreement, descriptive statistics, lag sequential analysis	Contact first author
	Multiple Option Observation System for Experimental Studies (MOOSES) (Tapp, Wehby, & Ellis, 1995)	Continuous time-based and/or event-based real-time observation	Classroom interaction of children with behavioral disorders (Conduct Problems Prevention Research Group, 1992; Shores et al., 1993)	Low (not reported but estimate based on similar observation)	Interobserver agreement, Cohen's *kappa*, descriptive statistics, lag sequential analysis	$450 (includes software and manual only)

20–25 hours of observations per individual). Observations of individuals in our study were made from computer-assisted analysis of videotape (Hetrick et al., 1991; described below), neurological examinations, and behavioral rating scales.

Twenty-one individuals with severe/profound neurodevelopmental disabilities completed the entire protocol, including six daily video sessions, 4 days each week for 10 weeks. Self-injurious behavior (SIB) was identified as a major problem for all individuals, none of whom had been successfully treated previously. The 10-week period was divided into 2 weeks of open placebo and 8 weeks of double-blind, placebo-controlled administration of three doses (.5, 1.0, and 2.0 milligrams per kilogram [mg/kg]) of an opiate-blocking agent, naltrexone (NTX). A computerized observational program (Hetrick et al., 1991) was used to record behavior viewed from videotapes. The program permitted automatic measurement of frequency and duration of behavior. At programmed intervals the observer was prompted for ratings of activity and severity of behavior. Interrater reliability was very satisfactory (.81–.96). Approximately 20–25 hours of direct observation were collected for each individual. Three indices of SIB were examined from the videotape record: frequency, duration, and severity. Stereotypy and activity also were evaluated with this system.

In addition to direct observations of behavior, several rating scales were used. The Objective Neurological Examination (Sandman et al., 1993) is tailored for individuals with mental retardation and specifically rates features of mental status, cranial nerves, motor function, cerebellar function, and reflexes. A 15-item adaptation of the Conners' Parent Teacher Questionnaire (Conners, 1969, 1985) has been used in several studies of NTX and SIB (Campbell et al., 1990; Sandman, Barron, & Coman, 1990; Sandman, Barron, Crinella, & Donnelly, 1987) and has been reported to be sensitive to drug effects. The Summation of Maladaptive Expression (Sandman et al., 1993) is a 56-item scale that measures six domains (Isolation, Activity, Agitation, Lethargy, Stereotypy, and Sensory Neglect). The Parent Teacher Questionnaire and the Summation of Maladaptive Expression were completed by the raters at the conclusion of direct observation each day.

The major objective of this project was to determine if treatment with NTX decreased maladaptive behavior, specifically SIB, in a significant number of individuals. Direct observations of behavior strongly suggested that SIB decreased when individuals were administered NTX. In contrast, data collected from the rating scales failed to detect any effect of NTX. Determination of the significant effects of NTX on behavior required an estimate of chance changes in behavior. A modified Monte Carlo forecast was used to determine the probability that a pattern of behavior occurred by chance. Typically, a Monte Carlo simulation is used to generate a sequence of random events (or vectors). An empirical determination of chance fluctuations in SIB was made by contrasting the change in SIB during two temporally adjacent placebo periods. Then, the likelihood of reductions in SIB after NTX was tested by chi-square analysis against the empirical estimate of chance (see Sandman et al., 1993; Sandman, Hetrick, Taylor, & Chicz-DeMet, 1997). With these procedures we tracked the effects of medication on complex human behavior.

The results are presented in Figure 1. This figure shows that the three doses exerted differential effects on SIB. A significant proportion of individuals improved by established criteria after both the 1-mg/kg dose and the 2-mg/kg dose, but improvement in SIB at the lowest dose (.5 mg/kg) failed to achieve sta-

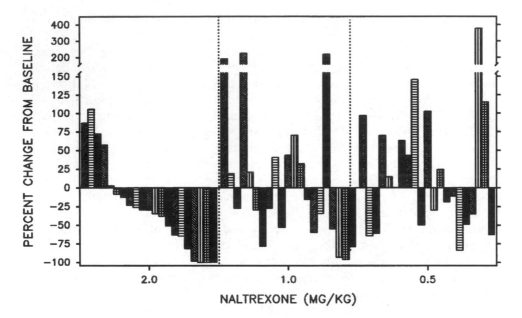

Figure 1.   Changes in self-injurious behavior for three doses of naltrexone expressed as percentage change from placebo baseline. Each histogram represents a single individual, and each individual is represented on each graph in the same location (i.e., the last individual in the 2.0-mg/kg dose panel is also the last individual in the 1.0-mg/kg and .5-mg/kg panels). (From Sandman, C.A., Hetrick, W.P., Taylor, D.V., Barron, J.L., Touchette, P., Lott, I., Crinella, F., & Martinazzi, V. [1993]. Naltrexone reduces self-injury and improves learning. *Experimental and Clinical Psychopharmacology, 1,* 249; reprinted by permission.)

tistical significance. In a subgroup we determined that individuals with the highest change in plasma levels of endogenous opioids after a SIB episode had the most positive response to the highest dose of NTX (Figure 2; Sandman et al., 1997). With these behavioral observations we determined that changes in the hypothalamic-pituitary-adrenal axis after SIB may predict differences in individual patient response to opiate blockers.

The severity of SIB, stereotypy, and patient activity ratings were not influenced by any dose of NTX. The effects of NTX on neurological ratings (the Objective Neurological Examination) were not significant for any of the major neurological dimensions. Analysis of the Parent Teacher Questionnaire and the Summation of Maladaptive Expression indicated that NTX had no significant effects on ratings of behavior (Figure 3). To determine if the scales differentiated response to drug rather than just exposure to different doses, patients with greater than 50% improvement by direct observation after NTX were compared with "nonresponders." This analysis did not change the primary findings. Correlations were not significant among the rating scales and change in SIB at any dose.

The failure to observe changes in ratings of behavior after treatment with NTX is consistent with the findings of an influential study (Willemsen-Swinkels et al., 1995) that examined global ratings of behavior by staff. In that study, a single fixed dose of NTX in patients with autism (11 of them with SIB) was reported to be ineffective according to global ratings of clinical improvement. If we had relied solely on rating scales, even though the scales measured discrete behavioral factors and the data were collected daily, we would have concluded that NTX was

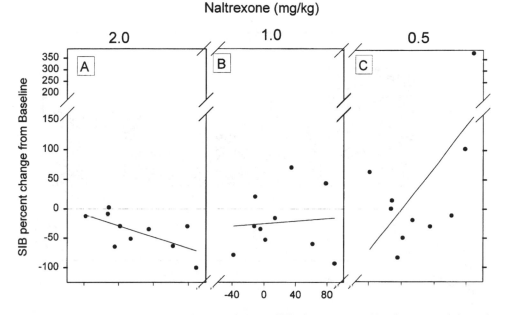

Figure 2.   Relation between change in self-injurious behavior (SIB) after treatment with naltrexone and change in beta-endorphin after SIB. The results indicate that change in beta-endorphin after SIB predicts reduced SIB at the highest (i.e., most effective) dose of naltrexone (A) but not at 1.0 mg/kg (B) or .5 mg/kg (C). (A: $r = -.66$, $p = .038$; B: $r = .086$, $p = .812$; C: $r = .583$, $p = .077$.)

ineffective in improving SIB. However, based on up to 25 hours of direct observations of behavior for each individual it was clear that SIB decreased after administration of NTX.

PROCODER, a software similar to *ODAP*, is an elaborate system that also allows for the off-line manipulation (i.e., coding, marking, scoring) of videotaped observations (see Chapter 5). In addition, it has the ability to conduct limited data analysis, such as interobserver agreement and Cohen's *kappa* (Cohen, 1960). It was designed by Tapp and Walden (1993) at Vanderbilt University's John F. Kennedy Center for Research on Human Development and is used to study complex interactions such as infant social referencing. Sessions are recorded and the resulting videotape is time coded using a tape control system (BCD 4000 or BCD 232c [BCD Associates]) or other time code support system such as the Society of Motion Picture and Television Engineers' time-coding system. This time code can be written to either the audio portion or the video portion of the tape. After the session is time coded, a behavioral coding scheme is developed and stored in an IBM-compatible personal computer that has at least 640 kilobytes (KB) of random access memory (RAM).

PROCODER allows for both interval and event coding. Interval coding requires that the tape be marked by a number of frames, after which a rating code is requested (either in real time or slow motion). Raters enter a code by pressing a key. Analyses of either interval or event data, include frequency and duration of behavior and interobserver agreement. For frequency data, agreement can be calculated by matching coding events with a user-selected time window (in frames). Agreement for interval, duration, and rating data is derived by computing Cohen's *kappa* and an agreement ratio.

(A)

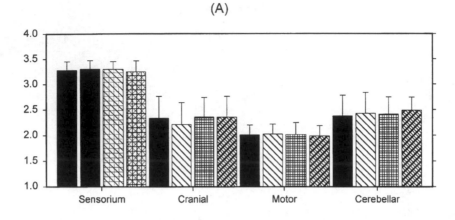

(B)

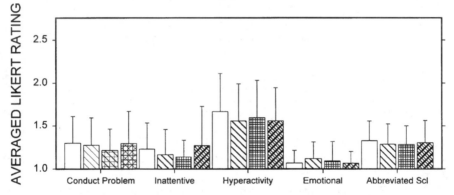

(C)

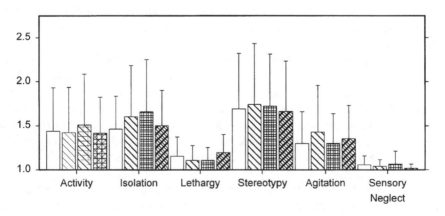

Figure 3. Effects of naltrexone (NTX) on rating of behavior from the Objective Neurological Examination (mean rating for each treatment condition: low rating = impairment) (A), the adapted Conners' Parent Teacher Questionnaire (degree of activity rated on scale of 1–4 for each treatment condition: 1, not at all; 4, very much) (B), and the Summation of Maladaptive Expression (SOME) (mean ratings on scale of 1–5 for each treatment condition: 1, least severe; 5, most severe) (C). NTX Dose (Mg/Kg; ■- PLC ◧- 2.0 ▦- 1.0 ▨- 0.4). (PLC, Placebo.) (From Sandman, C.A., Hetrick, W.P., Taylor, D.V., Barron, J.L., Touchette, P., Lott, I., Crinella, F., & Martinazzi, V. [1993]. Naltrexone reduces self-injury and improves learning. Experimental and Clinical Psychopharmacology, 1, 251; reprinted by permission.)

Walden (1996) used *PROCODER* to determine how well various raters (parents and nonparents) were able to judge social behaviors of children with and without delays. The results showed that looking behavior of children with delays (e.g., child's look at parent's face) was much more difficult for raters to judge (their ratings of these behaviors were slower and less accurate). In addition, raters had less confidence in their judgments of these children. Knieps, Walden, and Baxter (1994) also used this system to code videotaped observations of 11 children with Down syndrome and their matched controls. Child and parental affective expressions were rated on a five-point affectiveness scale. Children with Down syndrome did not differ with respect to lability and intensity of affect; however, children with typical development matched the affect of their parents but the children with Down syndrome did not.

A third system for analyzing videotaped observation is *C-QUAL* (Duncan & Sayre, 1991). This software is similar to *PROCODER* in some ways, but it is used for research on face-to-face interaction that focuses on speech and action sequences. It is an adaptation of *GALATEA* (Futrelle & Potel, 1975; Potel, Sayre, & MacKay, 1980), which has been used to generate animation of animal movements, and it was created to dissect complex human sequential data such as speech. The user creates a pictorial representation of speech from recorded signals. Transcription takes place through careful insertion of codes for behavior between actors (e.g., the eye gaze between two people), which is overlaid on the video image of speech. The observer can control how fast and in what direction to view and transcribe the tape. In addition, speech can be analyzed at any tape speed and in both directions and can be represented in several different forms.

Hardware requirements depend somewhat on the level of analysis needed, and there are no provisions for data analysis. However, the program is designed to produce computer data files ready for analysis. The authors recommend *THEME* (Magnusson, 1989, as cited in Duncan & Sayre, 1991) for this analysis.

There are advantages of videotaped analyses of observational data. As these examples illustrate, detailed analyses can be completed for very complex human behavior. One disadvantage is the cost of the total system. Transcription and video-coding devices must be purchased apart from the software (Tapp & Walden, 1993). A larger disadvantage, however, is the time required to conduct this kind of analysis. For example, it is estimated that with *PROCODER* (Tapp & Walden, 1993) 20 hours of coding time is necessary for every 20 minutes of videotaped observation.

We and others (Boccia et al., 1997; Emerson et al., 1995; Tapp, Wehby, & Ellis, 1995) have exchanged these time-intensive methods for other methods that allow us to obtain larger amounts of continuous observational data with fewer resources. We made the change to an on-line approach for several reasons. First, as mentioned above, the videotape approach is extremely time consuming. For our goal of nearly continuous behavioral samples over many hours (40 hours per individual) this time investment is not practical. Second, the presence of equipment that stores archival information can be very threatening to staff working in the residences of the people we observe. In the past, staff members were concerned that their caregiving practices were the subject of our investigations or that there might be a record of their behavior that could be consulted. Assurances to the contrary could not dissuade them from this belief and could have resulted in atypical caregiving practices during our observations. Because the purpose of continuous observation is to understand behavior in nature, unnatural or artificial circumstances of caregiving should be avoided. The single major advantage of the videotape method is that tapes can be replayed to ensure that behavior has been appropriately counted or timed. This clearly contributed to, but is not the sole reason for, the increased time of the off-line approach. This important advantage was offset by a disadvantage of videotaping, which is that the observable field is limited by the angle of the camera and the ambient light of the environment. The focus of the camera on the individual often limits the ability to determine environmental features such as noise level and proximity of the individual to peers, staff, and reinforcers.

The system we chose for continuous observation is *The Observer for Windows* (Noldus Information Technology, 1991, 1997). Our application of this flexible software package is described in detail below. However, a software system similar to *The Observer* is the *Multiple Option Observation System for Experimental Studies* (*MOOSES*) (Tapp et al., 1995; see Chapter 6), which should be mentioned as a viable option for this kind of data collection. True to its name, *MOOSES* offers various options for the collection of continuous observational data. These options include event-based, interaction-based, duration, and interval recording of continuous observational data. These options can be mutually exclusive or they can be used in parallel to record a variety of individual and environmental factors. This system requires MS-DOS 3.0 (or later version) and a computer with 640 KB of RAM (hard drive optimal but not required). The user is able to tailor data collection and analysis by selecting from pull-down menus. To increase flexibility the authors (Tapp et al., 1995) included time-sampling options to accommodate a variety of research protocols.

In this chapter, we focus on our preferred computerized procedures for collecting observations of complex human behavior and describe them in some detail. A comprehensive comparison of systems is not attempted here. A recent summary description of 15 computerized methods of real-time observation (including our *ODAP* and our preferred choice, *The Observer*) is presented by Kahng and Iwata (1998; see Chapter 3).

HARDWARE

Among the first criteria we considered when we abandoned our proprietary system was the ability to use a real-time recording and scoring system in the field. Thus, the system had to be portable. We discovered quickly that a laptop computer was not viable for our purpose. Clumsy to carry and operate, laptop computers also are limited by short battery life. We needed a palmtop computer. We learned that accurately depressing the keys of a palmtop keyboard at high speed was not easy for all observers. Therefore, we adapted a larger 10-key keypad and needed a computer that could receive this input. The Hewlett-Packard 200LX (HP200LX) was chosen (Figure 4). Its dimensions are 6.3 inches by 3.4 inches by 1 inch, and it weighs 10 ounces. The HP200LX has an Intel 80C186 processor, an MS-DOS 5.0 operating system with 1–2 megabytes of internal RAM, a PCMCIA card slot (Type II), and a parallel RS-232 communications interface. The screen size is 125 by 53 millimeters, and it has a QWERTY keyboard. The HP200LX uses two AA batteries with an average life of 10 hours. The Event Recorder module on the HP200LX allows for a maximum of 16 classes of behavior and 999 behavioral elements. Our 10-key keypad, computer, and configuration codes are fitted onto a clipboard for field use (Figure 4). The system has functioned flawlessly for more than 4 years and logged more than 25,000 hours of data.

SOFTWARE

The first requirement of the software was that it run on a palmtop computer. There were only a few choices, and among them, *The Observer* from Noldus was superior. Several years ago when we began our study (1994), this software ran in a DOS environment. Noldus now has a Windows version that we have seamlessly adapted for our project.

The Observer is an established system for the collection, analysis, and management of data from direct observations. Sampling methods can be tailored to determine which individuals will be watched, when they will be watched, and how the behavior will be recorded. The sampling methods include the following:

Focal sampling (or continuous recording): Observation of one or more individuals for a specified time that produces an exact record of the process, including the time at which each instance of an event occurred and when a state began and ended. This is the method used in our study.

Instantaneous sampling (also called time sampling, scan sampling, point sampling, multimoment sampling, or simply interval sampling): The observation is divided into sample intervals for recording of an individual's behavior. This is used when few behaviors for many individuals (up to 120 can be observed simultaneously) are the focus of the study.

One-zero sampling: The observation is divided into intervals, but each behavior is scored regardless of whether it has occurred during the preceding interval.

Ad libitum sampling: This option is for recording as much as possible in a group of individuals.

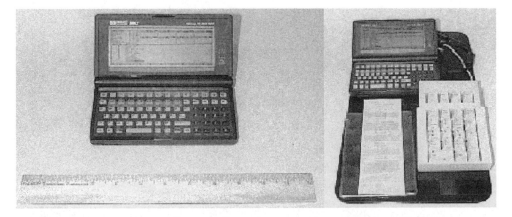

Figure 4.   Left, Palmtop computer used in field studies of behavior patterns. Right, System configured on a clipboard showing the palmtop computer, the larger keypad, and the container for scoring codes.

Data are entered directly into a palmtop computer (or from videotape off-line). Figure 5 illustrates how our focal-sampling configuration is displayed on the palmtop screen. Keystrokes on the palmtop keyboard, or the enlarged 10-key key-pad, signify the occurrence of an event (target behavior) and the clock time that each behavior of interest occurs. Each entry is checked against the user-defined configuration. Behavioral configurations can be simple or complex. The number of behaviors recorded is a function of the total number of keys or combinations of keys (up to three per combination) on the keyboard. For our purposes we have limited the number of events and states to 20. The configuration can be unique for each participant. Data entry errors can be corrected on-line or after a session has been completed. Notes and comments can be added through keyboard input and are stored with the data. This permits coding of unusual circumstances or qualifications during the observations. For instance, if the individual being observed disappears from sight or seeks privacy, a comment can be entered that explains the period of absence. A Pause function is used in our studies to provide programmed intervals of rest for the observers. The Pause function eliminates problems associated with artificial changes in behavioral states attributable to abrupt on/off discontinuities in observation time.

The Observer contains several useful analysis options (with *kappa* estimates due to be available in the fall of 1999 [Noldus Information Technology, personal communication, June 21, 1999]). A Time-Event Table provides a chronological listing of all recorded events. The output is two columns, one listing the clock time of occurrence and the other listing the behavioral category. The Time-Event Plot graphs behavioral data against time. This plot can be general, involving all behaviors, or focused on only one target behavior. A category of Elementary Statistics provides descriptive statistics about the frequency and duration of events or states. Lag Sequential Analysis is a useful option that describes how

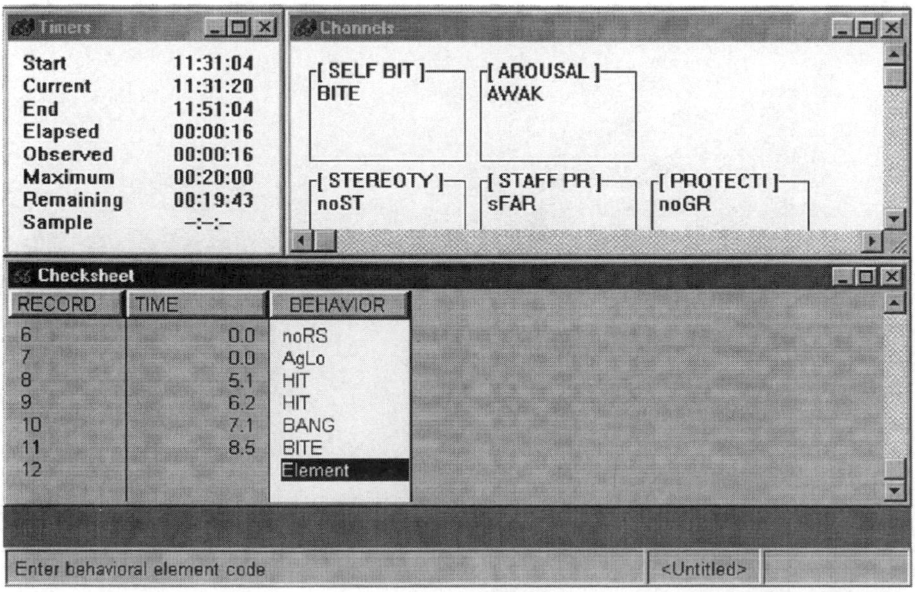

Figure 5.   Sample of a palmtop computer screen using The Observer.

often target events or states are preceded, or followed by, other selected events or states.

The Lag Analysis Statistics module of *The Observer* measures the relationship between classes of behavior as defined in the original data protocol. A lag analysis output table shows how many transitions occur between behaviors that have been defined as either antecedent or target events. What we call events (e.g., hit) and states (e.g., stereotypy) are here treated equally and simply called events. The duration of a state is ignored, and only the onset of a state behavior is counted. An antecedent behavior is any behavior or behaviors defined in the analysis as a preceding event. A target event is behavior or behaviors defined in the analysis as a following event. Therefore, the output table shows how many times a specified target behavior follows a specified antecedent event. This analysis can be further qualified with regard to the kind of transition that is counted based on either a time or a state lag. A *state lag sequential analysis* enumerates the number of times that a specified target event is the first event that follows a specified antecedent event. The analysis also reveals the number of times a given antecedent event immediately precedes a given criterion event. In a *time lag sequential analysis* the number of times are counted that a target event occurs within a specified period (e.g., 5 seconds) as the first event that follows an antecedent event. The key difference between the two is the addition of a time factor in the time lag sequential analysis. The amount of time specified as the transition period can vary from as little as .01 seconds to the duration of the entire observation period. In the latter case, the output should match that of the state lag analysis because no additional restraints have been put on the data. Examples of this are described below.

By analyzing many relationships between target behaviors and other events and states an index of preferred behavioral pathways can be characterized. For instance, we can determine the probability that stereotypy leads to SIB or that SIB results in changes in the environment. This is a powerful tool for examining the effects of treatments, such as pharmacological challenge, because complex interactions among behaviors may be more revealing about treatment than simple analyses of single target behaviors. These analyses are identical in purpose to those of Guess et al. (1993) and Emerson et al. (1995, 1996) described above.

Reliability estimates also are available when *The Observer* is used to collect continuous data. Reliability is an index based on the agreement between two observers. Instead of using discrete observation intervals to establish the basis of agreement, *The Observer* compares two records, one of which is designated the Master Record, for occurrences of events. For each event on the Master Record, the software searches for an identical event on the second record. Because events are recorded at a resolution of 100 milliseconds, it is virtually impossible to find an exact match. To solve this dilemma a temporal window variable is incorporated into the analysis options. The user can choose a tolerable temporal variation between records that is reasonable for synchronization. For our purposes, two observers equipped with separate recording systems observe the same individual for extended periods with a temporal window of 3 seconds. Any event or state change recorded by two observers within a 3-second period is considered to be identical.

We adapted *The Observer* output for analysis with the *Statistical Product and Service Solutions (SPSS*; 1998) program to enable a variety of statistical analyses, including computation of interobserver agreement based on intervals as in conventional partial interval recording. A rather elaborate macro was necessary to transform the unique *The Observer* configuration into a format that could be used by *SSPS*. For instance, *The Observer* lists output in two columns (described previously). One column lists the time any behavior occurred and the second column lists whether or not a behavior occurred, and if so, which behavior. Our macro (available from the authors) assigns each behavior a column and creates time bins along the rows. Our system will create any size time bin from absurdly small millisecond bins to bins of many hours. The interval (bin) size has little effect on Pearson estimates of reliability regardless of whether zero frequency intervals are included (see Table 2).

STUDY

In this 5-year study, behavior is observed for continuous 2.5-hour periods, two times a day (morning and afternoon), 4 days a week (Monday through Thursday) for 2 consecutive weeks, for a total of 40 hours per individual. All participants in the study were selected based on the criterion that they exhibited either SIB or agitated behavior on at least a daily basis so that the density of observations provided sufficient resolution for analysis of frequency, severity, topography, and periodicity. *The Observer* configuration was customized for each individual. Behaviors were assigned to specific keystrokes, and the legend describing each behavior–keystroke relationship was inserted in a plastic enclosure on the clipboard. Observers can refer to this legend, but we have learned that observers readily learn the sequence and rarely need to consult the legend. One reason for this is that events and states that are common among participants (e.g., stereotypy, activity level, noise level, peer and staff interactions) are assigned to the same key(s).

The observers are assigned to participants and are required to follow them for the duration of the recording session (2.5-hour periods). Observations last 20 continuous minutes and are followed by a 10-minute rest (for the observer). During the rest period, the system is "paused" to eliminate discontinuities and distortion in the data file.

Behaviors are grouped into classes of mutually exclusive categories (only one state is active at a time). Within a given class of behavior, when a state is turned on (e.g., individual asleep) the previous state in the same class (awake) is turned off. States that overlap (awake and individuals are outside) are placed in different classes that can occur simultaneously. States are scored as duration, i.e., the time in seconds that the individual is in the state. Events can occur within states, and their occurrence does not interrupt the timing of the state (i.e., events and states can coexist). Target behaviors (various forms of SIB, agitation), forms of activity,

Table 2.   Reliability coefficients based on interval data

Zero frequency	Time (seconds)			
	10	30	60	300
Included	.944	.964	.966	.993
Not included	.843	.925	.935	.991

location in space, social interactions, staff intervention, peer proximity, and noise level are examples of data recorded in this study.

ANALYSIS

For the purposes of illustration, data from one participant (ZX) with a high rate of occurrence of SIB are presented below.

Summary Statistics

The first analysis was a simple summary of SIB collapsed across days and weeks. The data in Figure 6 indicate that despite considerable variability from day to day, the first 30-minute interval in the morning was the period of highest risk for SIB. As the day continued the frequency of SIB decreased. These data were very useful for our purposes because we were interested in assessing biological changes (proopiomelanocortins, adrenocorticotropic hormone, endogenous opiates) associated with SIB. To assess the changes in proopiomelanocortins we drew blood immediately after a SIB episode. For this individual the optimal time for the phlebotomist to be stationed nearby for blood collection was during the first 2.5-hour period in the morning. During assessment of treatment effects we selected high-risk periods as preferred times for concentrated observations. Thus, for these purposes, collapsing the data across days and weeks provided important information about behavioral periodicity that informed aspects of the study.

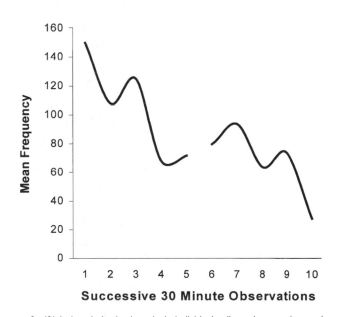

Figure 6.   Frequency of self-injurious behavior in a single individual collapsed across days and weeks. Despite substantial variation there is evidence that the highest risk for self-injurious behavior in this individual is during the first three observation periods (in the first 1.5 hours of the morning sessions). These data guide investigators to periods of highest risk for studies of biological factors.

Table 3.   Lag sequential analysis for *The Observer* data

Criterion event	10 Seconds			30 Seconds			60 Seconds		
	Number	Preceding target (%)	Following target (%)	Number	Preceding target (%)	Following target (%)	Number	Preceding target (%)	Following target (%)
Target event: Hit									
Hit	37	44.05	77.08	31	45.59	75.61	26	41.94	60.47
Bite	1	1.19	100.00	1	1.47	50.00	1	1.61	50.00
Ster	1	1.19	6.67	7	10.29	43.75	10	16.13	32.26
sPROX	0	0.00	0.00	0	0.00	0.00	2	3.23	7.41
sACT	0	0.00	0.00	0	0.00	0.00	1	1.61	5.56
Peer	0	0.00	0.00	1	1.47	16.67	2	3.23	25.00
None	45	53.57	50.00	28	41.18	48.28	20	32.26	50.00
Total	84			68			62		
Target event: Bite									
Hit	0	0.00	0.00	0	0.00	0.00	0	0.00	0.00
Bite	0	0.00	0.00	0	0.00	0.00	0	0.00	0.00
Ster	0	0.00	0.00	1	100.00	6.25	1	100.00	3.23
sPROX	0	0.00	0.00	0	0.00	0.00	0	0.00	0.00
sACT	0	0.00	0.00	0	0.00	0.00	0	0.00	0.00
Peer	0	0.00	0.00	0	0.00	0.00	0	0.00	0.00
None	1	1.47	1.11	0	0.00	0.00	0	0.00	0.00
Total	1			1			1		
Target event: Ster									
Hit	1	3.57	2.08	7	21.88	17.07	9	24.32	20.93
Bite	0	0.00	0.00	1	3.13	50.00	1	2.70	50.00
Ster	2	7.14	13.33	4	12.50	25.00	8	21.62	25.81
sPROX	2	7.14	13.33	4	12.50	22.22	7	18.92	25.93
sACT	0	0.00	0.00	1	3.13	6.25	2	5.41	11.11
Peer	0	0.00	0.00	0	0.00	0.00	2	5.41	25.00
None	23	82.14	25.56	15	46.88	25.86	8	21.62	20.00
Total	28			32			37		
Target event: sPROX									
Hit	0	0.00	0.00	1	4.55	2.44	3	9.68	6.98
Bite	0	0.00	0.00	0	0.00	0.00	0	0.00	0.00
Ster	0	0.00	0.00	0	0.00	0.00	6	19.35	19.35
sPROX	3	15.00	20.00	4	18.18	22.22	7	22.58	25.93
sACT	6	30.00	46.15	8	36.36	50.00	8	25.81	44.44
Peer	0	0.00	0.00	1	4.55	16.67	1	3.23	12.50
None	11	55.00	12.22	8	36.36	13.79	6	19.35	15.00
Total	20			22			31		
Target event: sACT									
Hit	0	0.00	0.00	0	0.00	0.00	3	13.64	6.98
Bite	0	0.00	0.00	0	0.00	0.00	0	0.00	0.00
Ster	1	7.69	6.67	1	10.00	6.25	5	22.73	16.13
sPROX	4	30.77	26.67	4	40.00	22.22	9	40.91	33.33
sACT	2	15.38	15.38	2	20.00	12.50	2	9.09	11.11

(continued)

Table 3. *(continued)*

Criterion event	10 Seconds			30 Seconds			60 Seconds		
	Number	Preceding target (%)	Following target (%)	Number	Preceding target (%)	Following target (%)	Number	Preceding target (%)	Following target (%)
Target event: sACT									
Peer	0	0.00	0.00	0	0.00	0.00	0	0.00	0.00
None	6	46.15	6.67	3	30.00	5.17	3	13.64	7.50
Total	13			10			22		
Target event: Peer									
Hit	1	20.00	2.08	1	20.00	2.44	2	33.33	4.65
Bite	0	0.00	0.00	0	0.00	0.00	0	0.00	0.00
Ster	0	0.00	0.00	0	0.00	0.00	1	16.67	3.23
sPROX	0	0.00	0.00	0	0.00	0.00	0	0.00	0.00
sACT	0	0.00	0.00	0	0.00	0.00	0	0.00	0.00
Peer	0	0.00	0.00	0	0.00	0.00	0	0.00	0.00
None	4	80.00	4.44	4	80.00	6.90	3	50.00	7.50
Total	5			5			6		
Target event: None									
Hit	9	24.32	18.75	1	5.26	2.44	0	0.00	0.00
Bite	0	0.00	0.00	0	0.00	0.00	0	0.00	0.00
Ster	11	29.73	73.33	3	15.79	18.75	0	0.00	0.00
sPROX	6	16.22	40.00	6	31.58	33.33	2	20.00	7.41
sACT	5	13.51	38.46	5	26.32	31.25	5	50.00	27.78
Peer	6	16.22	100.00	4	21.05	66.67	3	30.00	37.50
None	0	0.00	0.00	0	0.00	0.00	0	0.00	0.00
Total	37			19			10		
Total Target Events									
Hit	48			41			43		
Bite	1			2			2		
Ster	15			16			31		
sPROX	15			18			27		
sACT	13			16			18		
Peer	6			6			8		
None	90			58			40		

Relevant observational data for study participant ZX has been considered into behavior states Hit (number of hits), Bite (onset of biting), Ster (onset of stereotypic behavior), sPROX (staff proximity to individual), sACT (staff action/attention toward individual), Peer (peer interaction/touching), and None (no events occur). Each of these behaviors have been entered into a time series lag analysis in *The Observer* based on 10-second, 30-second, and 60-second time windows. Each behavior is defined in turn as both criterion and target events and then compared with each of the other behaviors. A target event is a behavior that follows a set of specified criterion or antecedent events. A criterion event is a behavior that precedes a specified target event. Preceding Target shows the percentage of the total number of transitions in which the specified criterion event immediately precedes the specified target event. Following Target shows the percentage of the total number of transitions in which the specified target event immediately follows the specified criterion event. For example, the top of the table shows Hit as the target event and all behaviors listed below that as criterion events. This is computed for 10-second, 30-second, and 60-second time windows. Therefore, 44% of the transition events that occur within 10 seconds before the target event Hit and 77% of the transition events that occur within 10 seconds after the criterion event Hit are hits.

Sequential Lag Analysis

Sequential lag analysis using various time lags has yielded interesting results. Table 2 shows behavioral data for our study participant condensed into behavior classes generally defined as Hit (number of hits), Bite (onset of biting), Ster (onset of stereotypic behavior), sPROX (staff proximity to participant), sACT (staff actions/attention toward participant), Peer (peer interaction or touching), and None (no events occur). Each of these behaviors was entered into a time series lag analysis in *The Observer* as both antecedent and target events, with 10-second, 30-second, and 60-second time windows. The Preceding Target column shows the percentage of the total number of behavioral transitions in which the specified criterion event precedes the specified target event within the given time window. For example, 44% of the transition events that precede hitting behavior within 10 seconds are other hitting behaviors. Two percent of these transitions are represented by biting and stereotypic behavior, whereas 54% of the 10-second transitions from criterion to target events have no behavior preceding a target event. The Following Target column shows the percentage of the total number of 10-second behavioral transitions in which the specified target event follows the specified criterion event within the given time window. For example, 77% of the events that follow hitting behavior within 10 seconds are other hitting behaviors. From the data in this column it is apparent that within 10 seconds hitting is followed by the onset of stereotypy and peer interaction 2% of the time and by nothing 19% of the time.

These same data are shown in Figure 7 with clear presentation of the effects of the lag window on transitional probabilities. It is clear that the different time lags (10, 30, and 60 seconds) produced different transitional lag percentages, but the general shape of the profiles is consistent. What is interesting is that the most common behavior to follow an episode of SIB was another episode of SIB for all

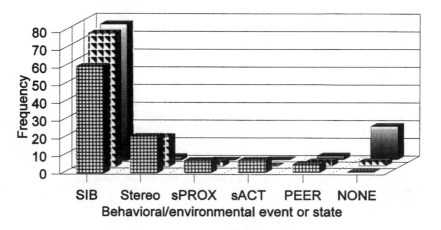

Figure 7.   Transitional percentages based on a time lag sequential analysis for 10-second, 30-second, and 60-second time intervals after self-injurious behavior (SIB; e.g., hitting). The most prominent event that occurs after a SIB episode is another SIB episode. This is accurate for all periods but especially for the shortest (10-second) time transition between events. Stereo, Onset of stereotypic behavior; sPROX, staff proximity to individual; sACT, staff action/attention toward individual; PEER, peer interaction or touching; NONE, no events occur. (■, 10 seconds; ▨, 30 seconds; ▦, 60 seconds.)

time lags. No events or states followed within 10 seconds of a SIB event for nine episodes, but the same was true for only one episode within 30 and 60 seconds. This means that only once during the observation period was there no event or state within 30–60 seconds after a SIB episode. One staff response was observable within the 60-second lag but not before. The lag sequential analysis for events preceding SIB indicated that no single event or state was most commonly related to SIB. The event preceding SIB with the highest frequency was another SIB event (as would be expected from the lag analysis of following events).

Reliability Estimates

Interobserver agreement reliability analysis is an important consideration when dealing with continuously sampled behavior data, particularly when behavior is observed in vivo without videotapes to consult. Figure 8 shows the pattern of agreement between two observers for a 17-minute epoch. Each diamond reflects detection of an event by an observer. The observers disagreed on events at 120 seconds and 660 seconds. Estimates of reliability were conducted initially using *The Observer*'s reliability module (described previously). The results are shown in Figure 9. As the window moves into times that are reasonable and may not reflect differences in human reaction time (i.e., 2 seconds or more) the agreement is consistently between 80% and 90%, which is perfectly acceptable.

Reliability coefficients also were calculated based on various time bins created by the *SPSS* macro (10, 30, 60, and 300 seconds). These data are presented with and without zero frequency intervals, or those intervals without any observable target behavior or target state change. During some periods of observation, zero intervals could be dominant. It was expected that the inclusion of zero intervals would greatly inflate reliability estimates because it was assumed that it was easier to agree that nothing happened. Moreover, fewer events happen at shorter intervals, which could lower reliability because the effects of disagreement would be magnified with low rates. Both of these expectations are reflected in Table 3, but they are inconsequential because the reliability estimates are uniformly high.

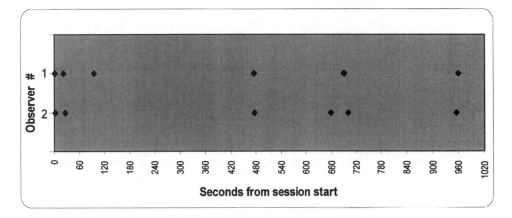

Figure 8. Stream of data from *The Observer* for two independent observers. Notice that there is disagreement at 120 seconds and 660 seconds.

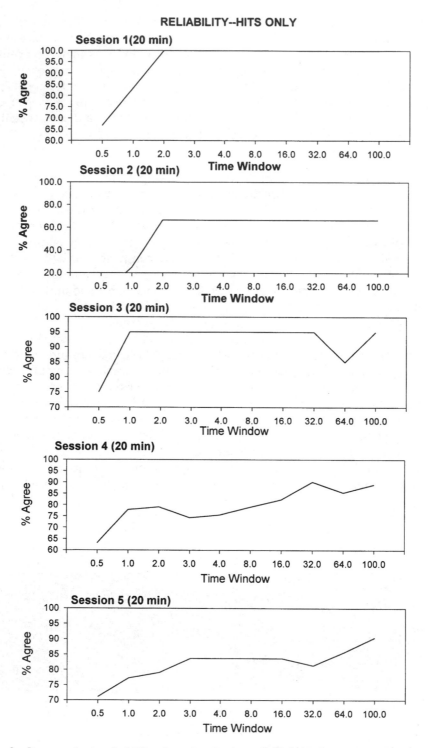

Figure 9.   Pearson estimates of reliability using various time intervals (bins). Very few events can transpire at .5 seconds, so the agreement is predictably low. However, as time intervals approach ranges in which human reaction times are less likely to account for errors, the estimates are between .80 and .90.

CONCLUSIONS

In previous studies we described the effects of pharmacological treatments on maladaptive behavior in individuals with developmental delays (Sandman et al., 1983, 1987, 1990, 1993, 1997). In each of these studies we observed behavior by scoring videotapes of epochs of behavior. In the early studies we used relatively crude scales and time sampling to describe and code behavior. In the more recent studies we developed our own computer-assisted system that improved the efficiency and reliability of our observations. The use of videotapes was time consuming, however, essentially tripling the time spent observing individuals. For our 5-year project, we adopted an on-line system and used palmtop computers in the field. In this chapter we have described this system and presented preliminary, but representative, data illustrating its promise. Very acceptable interobserver agreement and reliability can be obtained over a wide temporal range with the procedures we have used. In addition, we have presented examples of the assessment of complex behavior that may be more sensitive to pharmacological interventions than simple studies of single target behaviors. The time series studies permit analysis of both events leading to a target behavior (SIB) and events that follow the target behavior. As our examples indicated, changes in these behavioral pathways (transitional probabilities) suggest that repertoires of behavior and complex interactions with the environment could be influenced by pharmacological intervention. Thus, we have demonstrated that analysis of complex human behavior is technically feasible and a realistic goal for studies of treatment effects.

REFERENCES

Bakeman, R., & Gottman, J.M. (1986). *Observing interaction: An introduction to sequential analysis.* Cambridge, United Kingdom: Cambridge University Press.

Bakeman, R., & Quera, V. (1995). Log-linear approaches to lag-sequential analysis when consecutive codes may and cannot repeat. *Psychological Bulletin, 118(2),* 272–284.

Boccia, M.L., Scanlan, J.M., Laudenslager, M.L., Berger, C.L., Hijazi, A.S., & Reite, M.L. (1997). Juvenile friends, behavior, and immune responses to separation in bonnet macaque infants. *Physiology and Behavior, 61(2),* 191–198.

Campbell, M., Adams, P., Small, A.M., Tesch, L.M., & Curren, E.L. (1988). Naltrexone in infantile autism. *Psychopharmacology Bulletin, 24,* 135–139.

Campbell, M.C., Anderson, L., Small, A.M., Locascio, J.J., Lynch, N.D., & Choroco, M.C. (1990). NTX in autistic children: A double-blind and placebo controlled study. *Psychopharmacology Bulletin, 26,* 130–135.

Cohen, R. (1960). A coefficient of agreement for nominal scales. *Educational and Psychological Measurement, 20,* 37–46.

Conduct Problems Prevention Research Group. (1992). A developmental and clinical model for the prevention of conduct disorders: The FAST Track Program. *Development and Psychopathology, 4,* 509–527.

Conners, C.K. (1969). A teacher rating scale for use in drug studies with children. *American Journal of Psychiatry, 126,* 884–888.

Conners, C.K. (1985). Children's Psychiatric Rating Scale. *Psychopharmacology Bulletin, 21,* 765–770.

Duncan, S., & Sayre, R.E. (1991). C-QUAL: A system for computer-aided transcription of videotaped action sequences. *Behavior Research Methods, Instruments, and Computers, 23(4),* 505–512.

Eiler, J.M., Nelson, W.W., Jensen, C.C., & Johnson, S.P. (1989). Automated data collection using bar code. *Behavior Research Methods, Instruments, and Computers, 21(1),* 53–58.

Emerson, E., Reeves, D., Thompson, S., & Henderson, D. (1996). Time-based lag sequential analysis and the functional assessment of challenging behaviour. *Journal of Intellectual Disability Research, 40(3)*, 260–274.

Emerson, E., Thompson, S., Reeves, D., Henderson, D., & Robertson, J. (1995). Descriptive analysis of multiple response topographies of challenging behavior across two settings. *Research in Developmental Disabilities, 16(4)*, 301–329.

Forney, K.A., Leete, A.J., & Lindburg, D.G. (1991). A bar code scoring system for behavioral research. *American Journal of Primatology, 23*, 127–135.

Futrelle, R.P., & Potel, M.J. (1975). The system design for GALATEA: An interactive real-time graphics system for movie and video analysis. *Computer & Graphics, 1*, 115–121.

Gottman, J.M. (1981). *Time-series analysis: A comprehensive introduction for social scientists.* Cambridge, United Kingdom: Cambridge University Press.

Gottman, J.M., & Roy, A.K. (1990). *Sequential analysis: A guide for behavioral researchers.* Cambridge, United Kingdom: Cambridge University Press.

Guess, D., Roberts, S., Siegel-Causey, E., Ault, M., Guy, B., & Thompson, B. (1993). Analysis of behavior state conditions and associated environmental variables among students with profound handicaps. *American Journal on Mental Retardation, 97(6)*, 634–653.

Hall, S., & Oliver, S. (1997). A graphical method to aid the sequential analysis of observational data. *Behavior Research Methods, Instruments, and Computers, 29(4)*, 563–573.

Hetrick, W.P., Isenhart, R.C., Taylor, D.V., & Sandman, C.A. (1991). ODAP: A stand-alone program of observational data acquisition. *Behavior Research Methods, Instruments and Computers, 23*, 66–71.

Kahng, S., & Iwata, B.A. (1998). Computerized systems for collecting real-time observational data. *Journal of Applied Behavioral Analysis, 31(2)*, 253–261.

Knieps, L.J., Walden, T.A., & Baxter, A. (1994). Affective expressions of toddlers with and without Down syndrome in a social referencing context. *American Journal on Mental Retardation, 99(3)*, 301–312.

LeBoyer, M., Bouvard, M.P., & Dugas, M. (1988). Effects of naltrexone on infantile autism [Letter to the editor]. *Lancet, 1*, 158.

Linneman, J., & Walker, F.D. (1989). Reversal of self-abusive behavior with naltrexone. *Journal of Clinical Psychopharmacology, 9*, 444–449.

McGill, P., Hewson, S., & Emerson, E. (1994). *CTS: A Software Package for the Collection of Observation Data on Psion Organisers* [Software]. Canterbury, United Kingdom: Tizard Centre, University of Kent.

Noldus Information Technology. (1991). *The Observer:* A software system for collection and analysis of observational data. *Behavior Research Methods, Instruments, and Computers, 23(3)*, 415–429.

The Observer [Software]. (1997). Wageningen, The Netherlands: Noldus Information Technology.

Potel, M.J., Sayre, R.E., & MacKay, S.A. (1980). Graphics input tools for interactive motion analysis. *Computer Graphics & Image Processing, 14*, 1–23.

Sandman, C.A. (1990/1991). The opiate hypothesis in autism and self-injury. *Journal of Child and Adolescent Psychopharmacology, 1*, 235–246.

Sandman, C.A., Barron, J.L., & Coman, H. (1990). An orally administered opiate blocker, naltrexone, attenuates self-injurious behavior. *American Journal on Mental Retardation, 95*, 93–102.

Sandman, C.A., Barron, J.L., Crinella, F.M., & Donnelly, J. (1987). The influence of naloxone on the brain and behavior of self-injurious women. *Biological Psychiatry, 22*, 899–906.

Sandman, C.A., Datta, P., Baron, J.L., Hoehler, F., Williams, C., & Swanson, J. (1983). Naloxone attenuates self-abusive behavior in developmentally disabled clients. *Applied Research in Mental Retardation, 4*, 5–11.

Sandman, C.A., Hetrick, W.P., Taylor, D.V., Barron, J.L., Touchette, P., Lott, I., Crinella, F., & Martinazzi, V. (1993). Naltrexone reduces self-injury and improves learning. *Experimental and Clinical Psychopharmacology, 1*, 242–258.

Sandman, C.A., Hetrick, W.P., Taylor, D.V., & Chicz-DeMet, A. (1997). Dissociation of POMC peptides after self-injury predicts responses to centrally acting opiate blockers. *American Journal on Mental Retardation, 102(2)*, 182–199.

Saunders, R.R., Saunders, M.D., & Saunders, J.L. (1994). Data collection with bar code technology. In T.I. Thompson & D.B. Gray (Eds.), *Destructive behavior in developmental disabilities: Diagnosis and treatment* (pp. 102–116). Thousand Oaks, CA: Sage Publications.

Shores, R.E., Jack, S.L., Gunter, P.L., Ellis, D.N., De Breire, T.J., & Wehby, J.H. (1993). Classroom interactions of children with behavior disorders. *Journal of Emotional and Behavioral Disorders, 1,* 27–39.

SPSS, Inc. (1998). *Statistical Product and Service Solutions (SPSS), version 8.0* [Software]. Chicago: Author.

Tapp, J.T., & Walden, T.A. (1993). *PROCODER:* A professional tape control, coding, and analysis system for behavioral research using videotape. *Behavior Research Methods, Instruments, and Computers, 25(1),* 53–56.

Tapp, J.T., Wehby, J.H., & Ellis, D. (1995). A Multiple Option Observation System for Experimental Studies: MOOSES. *Behavior Research Methods, Instruments, and Computers, 27(1),* 25–31.

Walden, T.A. (1996). Social responsivity: Judging signals of young children with and without developmental delays. *Child Development, 67,* 2074–2085.

Willemsen-Swinkels, S.H.N., Buitelarr, J.K., Nijhof, G.J., & Van Engeland, H. (1995). Failure of naltrexone to reduce self-injurious and autistic behavior in mentally retarded adults. *Archives of General Psychiatry, 52,* 766–773.

V

Units of Analysis and
Quantitative Issues in
Analysis of Observational Data

18

Quantification Strategies in Behavioral Observation Research

Vicenç Quera and
Roger Bakeman

Interaction is a process during which the behavior of an individual (e.g., a mother) affects how another individual (e.g., her infant) behaves, which in turn affects how the former individual behaves. When interaction is observed systematically, behaviors are usually represented as sequences of codes. Codes always must be defined with a research problem in mind, for example, Do adult mothers tend to reduce their infants' fussing more effectively by cradling them than teenage mothers? This question requires that at least two different codes be defined, Mother Cradles Infant and Infant Cries. Codes must be defined objectively, and observers must be trained so that they use the codes reliably (Bakeman, in press; Bakeman & Gottman, 1997). Typically, more than just two codes are used because more than one research question relating the occurrences of different kinds of behaviors is posed.

Thus, data obtained by observers take the form of a sequence of code occurrences representing the interaction process that is being studied. Depending on how precise the research questions are, and which recording techniques are used, time can be represented just by the order in which codes occur (*event sequences* and *multievent sequences*), by the onset and offset times of the codes (*state sequences* and

The specifications discussed in this chapter are those of *SDIS-GSEQ* version 2.0. Bakeman and Quera (1992, 1995a) presented *SDIS-GSEQ* version 1.0. Note that all specifications in version 1.0 are included in version 2.0 as well, but version 2.0 contains many more features. *SDIS-GSEQ* runs under MS-DOS or as a MS-DOS program under Windows. A Windows version is under development. Both version 2.0 and the Windows version can be downloaded from http://www.gsu.edu/~psyrab/sg.htm.

timed-event sequences), or by the order of intervals containing code occurrences (*interval sequences*). Researchers can then ask whether certain codes tend to follow or precede some other codes (e.g., Do mothers tend to look at their infants after they start fussing?). Also, depending on the complexity of the codes, they can be represented as single-stream or multiple-stream sequences, the latter case permitting specific analyses of synchronicity between concurrent behaviors (e.g., Does the mother cradle her infant more often while it is fussing than while it is not?).

Sequential Analysis

Sequential analysis is a set of techniques devised to uncover the temporal patterns in sequences (e.g., Bakeman, 1978; Gottman & Roy, 1990; Sackett, 1979, 1987). Suppose that the codes Look at the Infant, Cradle the Infant, Touch the Infant, Talk to the Infant, Infant Cries, Infant Sleeps, and Infant Suckles have been defined, and the order in which the codes occurred (i.e., initiated) is recorded, thus providing event sequences. If mother and infant behaved randomly, i.e., if the mother's behavior did not affect the infant's behavior and vice versa, then every infant code would occur with its own unconditioned probability no matter which mother code preceded it, and every mother code would occur with its own unconditioned probability no matter which infant code preceded it.

To know if patterns exist in the sequence we must determine if the probabilities with which codes occur differ from their unconditioned probabilities (*global analysis*). If so, then we can determine which preceding or given codes are responsible for significant changes in the conditioned probability of a target code (*residual analysis*). For example, once we know that infant codes occur differently depending on which mother codes precede them, we can test whether the probability of code Infant Cries, conditioned to the previous occurrence of code Cradle the Infant, is significantly lower than its unconditioned probability. If so, we can say that Cradle the Infant "inhibits" Infant Cries. A global test such as Pearson's chi-square test can be used for the global analysis, and a sequential index such as an adjusted residual or a Yule's Q can be computed for each sequential pair of codes to gauge the strength of the association between them. A similar analysis can be done with mother codes as target and infant codes as given.

If mother and infant behaviors are coded as parallel streams, and code onset and offset times are recorded, a synchronicity analysis can be carried out. We can then test whether the probabilities with which target codes occur at each time unit, conditioned to the simultaneous occurrence of the given codes, differ from the unconditioned probabilities of the target codes at each time unit. If so, then we can say that synchronicity, or co-occurrence, patterns exist between mother and infant behaviors, and we can further analyze which codes tend to co-occur significantly by computing sequential indices.

Usually, researchers are interested not only in detecting patterns in some particular dyads or small groups but want to generalize those results to a population of dyads or groups, determine if dyads with different characteristics (e.g., teenage versus adult mothers) display different sequential or co-occurrence patterns, or discover whether a pattern that has been observed in a particular dyad is stable or stationary when the same dyad is observed at different times. Such applications imply that results from sequential analysis can be pooled only for those dyads or groups that are presumed or known to be homogeneous. Still, the homogeneity of sequential patterns should be tested before results are pooled by determining whether or not sequential indices are significantly different in those dyads that are assumed to be homogeneous.

Generally, long sequences of codes are necessary if conventional statistical tests are to be used on them. Also, researchers often need to explore the sequences in different ways before some research questions can be posed efficiently. Thus, a computer program that performs sequential analysis is often a necessity. *SDIS-GSEQ* is such a program (Bakeman & Quera, 1995a). *SDIS* verifies and compiles sequence data files, whereas *GSEQ* can perform a variety of sequential analyses and explorations according to specific commands entered by the user and export sequential indices to be analyzed further by other statistical software. This chapter presents the basic capabilities of *SDIS-GSEQ* and illustrates them with some examples. Examples of the use of *SDIS-GSEQ* for analyzing family interaction can be found in Bakeman and Casey (1995), and examples for analyzing engaged behavior of students with disabilities can be found in Logan, Bakeman, and Keefe (1997).

Software for Sequential Analysis

Several computer programs for sequential analysis have been developed since the mid-1980s (e.g., Arundale, 1984; Bakeman, 1983; Kienapple, 1987; Quera & Estany, 1984; Sackett, Holm, Crowley, & Henkins, 1979; Schlundt, 1982; Yoder & Tapp, 1990). However, these programs were usually designed with a specific purpose in mind, such as performing analyses tailored to a particular laboratory's research, or they could analyze a restricted kind of data. *SDIS-GSEQ* is a general-purpose program for sequential analysis that defines a standard, easy-to-use format or convention for sequential data that permits a variety of representations suited to various research needs.

SEQUENTIAL DATA TYPES AND *SDIS*

The *Sequential Data Interchange Standard* (*SDIS*) is a language designed to represent the different kinds of sequences of behavioral codes commonly obtained in interaction studies (Bakeman & Quera, 1992, 1995a). Several data formats are permitted by *SDIS*, each corresponding to a type of behavioral sequence and with different levels of complexity. *Event Sequential Data* (ESD) are the simplest; they consist of series of mutually exclusive and exhaustive (ME&E) codes with no onset or offset times. *State Sequential Data* (SSD) are series of single-stream or multiple-stream states. Onset and offset times are provided for each state, and states within a stream are ME&E, whereas states in different streams can co-occur. *Timed-Event Sequential Data* (TSD) consist of a mixture of momentary behaviors, for which occurrence times are known, and duration behaviors (or states), which have onset and offset times. In TSD, codes are not necessarily ME&E (i.e., there can be time units for which no code occurs at all as well as time units for which several codes occur simultaneously). *Interval Sequential Data* (ISD) represent behavior as series of intervals, such as those used when behavior is observed with a time-sampling technique. Each interval can contain one code, several codes (which can be interpreted as occurring simultaneously, provided that the time interval is small enough), or no code. *Multievent Sequential Data* (MSD) are series of complex events for which one or more codes are used (e.g., one code for speaker, another for content). Thus, codes are not mutually exclusive, because more than one code can characterize each event. As with ESD, no onset and offset times are provided for MSD.

Which data type is used depends not only on the particular questions that researchers want to answer but also on the available recording techniques. For example, if we are interested in patterns of synchronicity between verbal, vocal, and postural behaviors in mothers and infants, we could use video equipment to record them and subsequently code onsets and offsets of behaviors accurately. In that case, either SSD or TSD would suit our research needs. However, researchers interested in the sequential patterns of verbal interchange in dyads or small groups often record the order in which speaking turns occur and code each turn according to verbal content (i.e., who says what to whom). That is, a series of non-timed events are coded. In that case, ESD or MSD are useful. For example, if for each speaking turn several codes are used (e.g., speaker, content, emotional valence), then the sequence can be represented as a multievent sequence.

SDIS Data Files

SDIS requires that data be saved in ASCII data files using a specific syntax or set of conventions. For example, alphanumeric strings must be used for codes, and onset and offset times must be provided for those data types requiring them. Also, SDIS specifies how data for each observation session and each unit (i.e., individual, dyad, or group) must be entered and how design variables can be defined and used in the file. SDIS syntax is detailed fully in Bakeman and Quera (1992, 1995a).

Figures 1 and 2 show sections of two SDIS files containing ESD and TSD sequences, respectively. File COUPLES.SDS contains sequences of verbal interchange within couples. Each speaking turn is represented using just one code that identifies both the speaker and the verbal content. The data type is declared at the beginning of the file, and an optional declaration of code names, codes sets, and design variables can follow. In this example 12 codes are declared, 6 for wives (W) and 6 for husbands (H). The first character in each code indicates the speaker and the other characters indicate verbal content: complains (WCom, HCom), emotes (WEmo, HEmo), approves (WApp, HApp), empathizes (WEmp, HEmp), negates (WNeg, HNeg), and other (WOth, HOth). The first six codes are assigned to a set named Wife and the other six to a set named Husband. Also, two design variables are declared: Age, with two conditions, Young and Adult; and Type, with two conditions, Clinic and Control. Thus, data for each couple will be assigned to one of four possible combinations: Young and Clinic, Young and Control, Adult and Clinic, Adult and Control. Note that a semicolon indicates the end of a declaration.

Overview of SDIS Syntax

The general data structure in an SDIS file is as follows. Data for each unit (e.g., participant, couple) end with a slash (/). Within each unit, semicolons (;) can be used to separate consecutive observation sessions. Design information can be specified for each unit just before its slash. For example,

    ... data ... (Age = Young, Type = Clinic)/

assigns the data (up to the preceding slash) to the Young and Clinic design combination. Alternative syntax would be

```
Event                                          % Data type declaration
($Wife      = WCom WEmo WApp WEmp WNeg WOth)   % Code declaration
($Husband = HCom HEmo HApp HEmp HNeg HOth)
* Age = 1 (Young = 1 Adult = 2)                % Variable declaration
  Type = 2 (Clinic = 1 Control = 2);

<Young Clinic 1>
% Session #1 (1)
HApp WEmp WEmo HEmp WEmp WNeg WNeg HApp WEmo HEmo WEmp HEmp WCom HCom WCom HCom
WEmo HEmo WEmo HEmo WEmp HEmo WEmo HApp WEmp WEmo HApp HApp WApp HEmo WEmp HEmp
HEmo WEmo WEmo HApp HCom WNeg WNeg WCom HEmo WEmo WEmo WEmp HEmo WEmo HEmo WEmo
WEmo HEmp HNeg HOth HCom WOth WEmo WApp WApp HApp WEmp WEmo HEmp WCom HEmo
WEmo WCom HEmo WEmo HEmp WEmp WEmp HCom WCom HCom WNeg HCom WEmp HEmp WEmp
HEmp HEmo WEmo WEmp;

% Session #2 (2)
WEmo HEmo HEmp WEmo WApp HApp WEmp HEmo WEmo HEmo WEmp HNeg WEmp HCom WCom HNeg
HCom HNeg WEmp HEmp WEmp HEmp WEmp HEmp WEmo HEmo WEmo HEmo WEmo HApp WApp HApp
HApp WEmp HEmp WCom HEmp WEmp HEmo HNeg HApp HEmp WEmp HEmo HApp WApp WApp HEmp
WApp HCom WCom HCom HNeg WEmo HEmo WEmo HEmp WEmp;

% Session #3 (3)
HCom WEmo HEmo HEmp WEmp HApp WEmo HEmo WEmp WEmp HEmo WEmo HEmo WApp WApp HApp WEmp
HEmp WEmp WEmo HEmo HEmp WEmp WEmp HEmp WEmp HApp HApp WApp HApp WEmp HEmp HApp
WApp HApp WEmo HEmo WEmp HApp WApp HEmo HEmp WEmo HEmp WEmp HEmp WOth HApp WEmp
HApp WEmp HEmo HCom HEmp WEmp WEmo HEmo WEmo HEmp WEmp HEmp WEmp HEmp WEmo HEmo
WEmo (Young, Clinic)/

<Young Clinic 2>
% Session #1 (4)
WEmo HEmp WEmp HEmp HNeg WEmo HApp WEmo HEmo WEmp HEmo WEmo HEmo WApp HEmp WEmo
HNeg WEmp WEmo HEmo HEmp WEmp WEmo HEmo WEmo HApp WEmp WEmp HEmo HNeg HApp WNeg
HApp HCom WEmo HEmo WEmo HEmo HNeg WEmo WOth HEmo WEmo HApp WEmo HEmo WEmo HEmo
WEmo WApp HEmo WEmo HEmp WEmp HEmp WCom HApp HEmp WEmp HEmp;

. . .
```

Figure 1. An *SDIS* file containing event sequences of verbal interchange within couples. All codes are explained in the text. (File COUPLES.SDS.)

... data ... (Young, Clinic)/

or just

... data ... (1,1)/

provided that Young is the first Age condition and Clinic is the first Type condition, as in Figure 1. If design information is specified for a particular unit but not for its preceding units, then *SDIS* automatically assigns the preceding units to the conditions specified for that unit. Optionally, units can be labeled by enclosing a label within angle brackets (< and >) before their data. In Figure 1, data for the first couple are labeled <Young Clinic 1>. By assigning units to conditions, it is possible to request that *GSEQ* pool the results of sequential analyses over one or more of the declared variables. When units are labeled, *GSEQ* will use their labels to identify them when the results are not pooled over units.

As Figure 1 shows, event sequences are represented just by recording the codes in the order in which they occurred. In some cases a code can be repeated immediately after itself (as in ...HApp HApp...). However, that possibility depends on the coding decisions made by researchers. When verbal content is coded and two very similar or identical contents are issued consecutively by a speaker, the researcher can decide to code them either as two separate utterances

```
Timed                                                    % Data type declaration
($Mother = MPas MAct MRed) ($Infant = IQui IAct IFus)    % Code declaration
* Experience = 1 (No = 1 Yes = 2);                       % Variable declaration

<Dyad No 1>

MRed,00:00-01:07 MPas,01:25- MAct,01:37- MPas,01:48- MAct,02:12-02:27
MPas,03:19- MAct,03:33- MPas,04:24-04:27 MPas,05:28- MRed,05:30-
MAct,07:14-07:48 MPas,07:59- MRed,08:32-09:49 MRed,10:11-
MPas,22:00-22:22 MAct,22:34-
&
IAct,00:00- IQui,01:25- IAct,01:44- IQui,01:48-02:14 IAct,02:27-04:12
IAct,05:28- IFus,09:49- IAct,12:37- IFus,22:04- IQui,22:19- ,22:45;

MAct,00:00-00:19 MPas,00:25- MAct,00:50- MRed,03:46-03:55 MRed,04:39-
MAct,05:40- MRed,06:32- MAct,06:51- MPas,06:57-07:19 MPas,08:23-
MRed,08:35-08:41 MAct,09:56-09:57 MRed,11:04- MAct,13:08-13:53
MAct,16:27- MRed,18:23- MPas,23:06-23:31 MPas,23:32- MRed,23:35-23:41
MRed,25:13- MAct,25:17- MPas,25:27- MAct,25:56- MPas,26:03- MRed,26:30-
MAct,26:34-26:41 MAct,26:43- MRed,27:53- MAct,28:10-28:36 MPas,28:52-
&
IFus,00:00- IAct,00:19- IQui,00:25- IAct,00:49- IFus,01:27- IQui,03:31-
IFus,04:59- IQui,06:32-06:45 IAct,06:57-07:19 IAct,08:18- IQui,08:23-
IFus,08:37-08:41 IFus,10:56- IQui,13:48-14:02 IQui,16:41- IAct,16:45-
IQui,18:23- IAct,18:54- IQui,21:08- IFus,21:40- IQui,23:35-
IAct,23:47-23:56 IQui,25:17- IAct,26:43-27:49 IQui,28:40- ,28:54
(Experience=No)/

<Dyad No 2>

MPas,01:09-04:04 MRed,04:19-04:26 MRed,05:22-05:58 MRed,06:42-09:27
MAct,10:23- MPas,10:27- MAct,10:38- MPas,10:40- MAct,11:46- MRed,12:42-
MPas,13:24- MRed,14:20- MAct,15:13- MRed,15:49- MAct,18:04- MPas,19:52-
MAct,20:08- MRed,20:49- MPas,20:51- MRed,21:02-24:32 MPas,29:22-

. . .
```

Figure 2.   An *SDIS* file with timed-event sequences representing mother–infant interaction. All codes are explained in the text. (File MOMINF.SDS.)

or as a single utterance. In the latter case no codes would be repeatable in the data. Repeatability and nonrepeatability of codes in event sequences affect how data are analyzed subsequently by *GSEQ* and determine the statistical models to use. Some observation sessions can have start and end times, which are inserted at the beginning and the end of the sessions, respectively (a comma must precede the time). For those sessions with time information *GSEQ* can compute occurrence rates for the desired codes.

File MOMINF.SDS (Figure 2) contains timed-event sequences representing interaction between mothers and their infants. Six codes have been defined, three for the mothers (M): passive attending (MPas), active attending (MAct), redirecting (MRed); and three for the infants (I): quiet (IQui), active attending (IAct), and fussing (IFus). To indicate that the first three codes are ME&E their names are shown within parentheses in the declaration and given the name Mother. Likewise, the infants codes have been declared ME&E by enclosing them within parentheses and giving the set the name Infant. Also, variable Experience (meaning the mother's previous experience with children) is declared, with two conditions, No and Yes.

As Figure 2 shows, in TSD each item in a sequence is a pair of code and time, separated by a comma. States are indicated by specifying onset and offset times, separated by a hyphen, as in MRed,00:00-01:07. Offset times can be omitted when the onset time for the next code equals the offset time for the current code, as in

MPas,01:25- MRed,01:37-01:48. However, only onset times need to be specified for momentary codes. Additional conventions are permitted by *SDIS* for representing onsets and offsets of context, or background, codes. Code co-occurrence can be represented simply by stating overlapped times. For example, MPas,09:15-10:10 IAct,9:50-10:15 would indicate that codes MPas and IAct co-occur from time unit 9:50 to time unit 10:09 inclusive. Co-occurrences also can be represented in TSD by using multiple streams of codes within a session. In that case, consecutive streams must be separated by an ampersand (&), as shown in Figure 2. In that example, session end times are stated explicitly by preceding them with a comma, whereas session start times default to 0 unless they are stated explicitly.

Several time formats are permitted by *SDIS* (e.g., 8, 8:30, 8:30:14, 8:30.87). That is, one, two, or three fields can be used for representing time units. A colon (:) indicates that the next unit is a sixtieth of the preceding unit, whereas a period (.) indicates tenths, hundredths, or thousandths of the preceding unit. A common time format must be used throughout the data file, and interpretation regarding whether time units represent hours, minutes, seconds, or even video frames is left to the user.

Compiling and Plotting the Data

Once a data file has been composed with a text editor and saved as an ASCII file, it must be checked for errors using program *SDIS*. If the file contains no errors, *SDIS* will create a new file containing the data in compiled or MDS (i.e., modified SDS file) format, which can be processed subsequently by program *GSEQ* to perform sequential and descriptive analyses. During the compilation process program *SDIS* may note different kinds of errors. For example, in the file shown in Figure 2, codes MAct and MPas were declared to be mutually exclusive. If *SDIS* encounters data such as MAct,11:01-12:10 MPas,11:10-13:14, it will issue an error message indicating that codes overlap. Also, *SDIS* will report unrecognized codes (i.e., codes that are used in the data but were not declared at the outset), wrong times (i.e., onset times that are earlier than onset times for preceding codes), unexpected end of data (e.g., failure to close the last sequence with a slash), and so forth.

After the data are compiled it is often useful to inspect them graphically. Program *PLOT*, which is included with the *SDIS-GSEQ* software, represents MDS files in a grid of codes by time units (or by intervals or events, depending on the data type). Some co-occurrence and sequential patterns can reveal themselves in these plots. Also, inaccuracies and coding errors can be detected by visual inspection. Figure 3 shows a section of the plot corresponding to original file MOM-INF.SDS (Figure 2).

ANALYSIS OF EVENT SEQUENCES WITH *GSEQ*

GSEQ Command Files

Users communicate with program *GSEQ* by a specific command language. Command files can be composed manually, or the *GSEQ* Composer, a menu-driven utility, can be used. Either way, to request Lag 1 frequency tables and some associated sequential statistics for the example data in Figure 1, the following commands would be input to *GSEQ*:

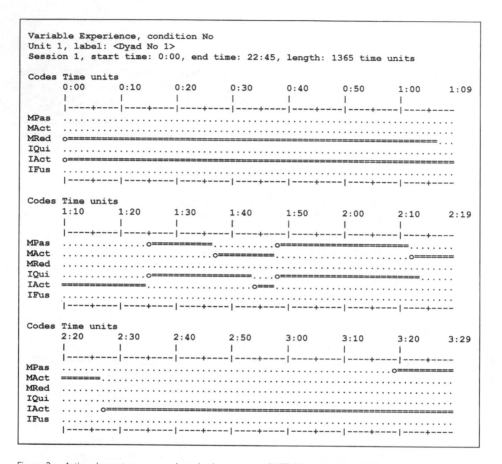

Figure 3.   A timed-event sequence plotted using program *PLOT*. All codes are explained in the text.

```
FILE "COUPLES";
POOL *;
STATS JNTF XSQ ADJR;
TARGET $Husband; LAG 1; GIVEN $Wife;
TARGET $Wife; LAG 1; GIVEN $Husband;
END;
```

The first command, FILE, indicates the data file to be analyzed. Command POOL specifies that results must be pooled over similar dyads (i.e., over couples that were previously assigned to a common design cell). In other words, in this case *GSEQ* will produce four tables of results, one for Young and Clinic couples, another for Young and Control couples, another for Adult and Clinic couples, and another for Adult and Control couples. If we were interested in obtaining just one table of results for young couples and another for adult couples (pooling over clinic and control dyads), we should specify POOL Type; instead, Type is a variable name declared in the data file.

Next, command STATS is used to specify which statistics must be computed for each table; in the example given, the statistics are joint or lag frequencies (JNTF), Pearson's chi-square (XSQ), and Haberman's adjusted residuals (ADJR) (which are similar but not quite identical to Allison & Liker's [1982] z-scores; see

Bakeman & Quera, 1995b). The TARGET/LAG/GIVEN commands define a table structure (the LAG command is used primarily with ESD, rarely with SSD or TSD, for which the WINDOW command is used instead). In this case, all husband codes act as target codes and all wife codes act as given codes. Lag 1 is specified, which indicates that *GSEQ* is being requested to tally how many times each husband code follows each wife code immediately. Alternatively, a list of all husband code names could have been specified explicitly as target codes and a list of all wife code names as given codes. For the second table requested in this example, wife codes act as target codes and husband codes act as given codes. Again, requesting Lag 1 for these ESD means that we are interested in determining how many times each wife code follows each husband code immediately. There is an alternative and shortest way of requesting those two tables:

TARGET $Husband; LAGS +1 -1; GIVEN $Wife;

Command LAG specifies two different tables. When lag is +1, GSEQ will tally how many times each husband code follows each wife code, as before; however, when lag is −1, it will tally how many times each husband code precedes each wife code, which is equivalent to tallying how many times each wife code follows each husband code.

Contingency tables defined using TARGET/GIVEN commands can be analyzed using standard statistical tools such as chi-square tests (which make sense only when the target and given codes are exhaustive). Arrangement of sequential data in contingency tables permits a more consistent statistical analysis (Bakeman & Quera, 1995b; Castellan, 1979) than the kind of tables originally advocated by Sackett (1979, 1987).

GSEQ Output

The commands specified in the preceding section would yield the Lag 1 frequencies for young and clinic couples shown in Table 1 (this is an example of *GSEQ* output). That is, of 410 transitions from a wife's verbal utterance to a husband's verbal utterance, 36 were transitions from wife complaints to husband complaints. Moreover, of 65 complaints emitted by wives, 36 were immediately followed by complaints emitted by husbands. Analogous interpretations can be made for other cells in the table.

Pearson's chi-square for this table is, according to GSEQ,

Lag 1. XSQ:

Pearson's Chi-square = 240.1927

Degrees of freedom = 25

Approximate p-value = 0.000000

Expected frequencies < 5 = 44.4%

Expected frequencies < 3 = 36.1%

Expected frequencies < 1 = 19.4%

It is a highly significant chi-square statistic, which indicates that, as a whole, husbands' verbal utterances were associated sequentially with previous wives' verbal utterances, or, in other words, that husbands' behavior tended to vary depending on previous wives' behavior. GSEQ also reports that 44.4% of table cells have expected frequencies that are less than 5, indicating that a greater sample size would be desirable in order to have confidence in the value of the chi-square. It should be noted that most of those small expected frequencies (not shown here) lie on the last row and column of that table, corresponding to codes WOth and HOth, whose total lag frequencies are very small (4 and 5, respectively). Deleting those two codes from the TARGET and GIVEN commands might be warranted.

When sequential association exists in a table overall it makes sense to probe for particular sequential patterns. To this end, *GSEQ* provides a table of Haberman's adjusted residuals, a kind of sequential index that, for every cell in the table, gauges the degree of departure of the observed from the expected frequency (i.e., the lag frequency in the cell if husband and wife behaviors are not associated at all). Provided that certain conditions hold (e.g., sample size is not too small) adjusted residuals can be roughly interpreted as normal z-scores. For the lag table shown in Table 1, *GSEQ* computed the residuals shown in Table 2. Adjusted residuals greater than or equal to +1.96 indicate that the given code tends to activate the target code, whereas adjusted residuals less than or equal to −1.96 indicate that the given code tends to inhibit the target code ($p < .05$; of course, other p values and their corresponding critical z values could be used). Absolute residuals less than 1.96 indicate that the effect is not statistically significant ($p > .05$). Thus, husbands tend to complain after wives complain (10.27) or negate (2.39) but not after they emote (−4.89), approve (−2.60), or empathize (−2.78).

When an adjusted residual does not meet the necessary conditions for a normal approximation *GSEQ* appends a colon to it. (In Table 2, all of the residuals in the last two rows and the last two columns might not approximate a normal distribution well.) This is caused by a small sample size but could also be caused by an unbalanced sample, e.g., when the relative frequency of a code is very large or very small (say, greater than 90% or less than 10%, respectively). When the sample size is too small or the sample is biased, p values for event-based lag frequencies can be computed using alternative exact methods (e.g., see program *PSEQ*; Bakeman, Robinson, & Quera, 1996).

Table 1.   Lag 1: Observed lag frequencies

| Given | Target | | | | | | Totals |
	HCom	HEmo	HApp	HEmp	HNeg	HOth	
WCom	36	7	4	16	2	0	65
WEmo	2	63	30	25	4	1	125
WApp	2	14	26	12	3	2	59
WEmp	10	29	13	76	6	0	134
WNeg	7	1	6	2	5	1	22
WOth	2	1	2	0	0	0	5
Totals	59	115	81	131	20	4	410

H, husband; W, wife; Com, complains; Emo, emotes; App, approves; Emp, empathizes; Neg, negates; Oth, other.

Table 2.   Lag 1: Adjusted residuals

Given	Target					
	HCom	HEmo	HApp	HEmp	HNeg	HOth
WCom	10.27	−3.38	−3.00	−1.38	−0.73:	−0.87:
WEmo	−4.89	6.67	1.43	−3.44	−1.04:	−0.24:
WApp	−2.60	−0.80	5.07	−2.07	0.08:	2.04:
WEmp	−2.78	−2.01	−3.56	7.49	−0.26:	−1.40:
WNeg	2.39:	−2.52:	0.91:	−2.36:	4.00:	1.75:
WOth	1.64:	−0.40:	1.14:	−1.54:	−0.51:	−0.22:

H, husband; W, wife; Com, complains; Emo, emotes; App, approves; Emp, empathizes; Neg, negates; Oth, other.

A colon appended to an adjusted residual value indicates that the adjusted residual does not meet the necessary conditions for a normal approximation.

ANALYSIS OF TIMED-EVENT SEQUENCES WITH *GSEQ*

Researchers representing their data as timed-event sequences are usually interested not only in the temporal order in which codes occur but also in the extent to which some codes overlap in time. If a Lag 1 analysis is performed in a timed-event sequence, tallies in the contingency table would represent time units (e.g., seconds). This could be an interesting approach when the average duration of codes is roughly one time unit, and when we are interested in detecting sequential patterns among codes. However, when codes tend to last much more than one time unit, and when several of them can co-occur, requesting a Lag 1 table for all codes as given and target codes would probably yield a trivial, and perhaps potentially confusing, result. If all codes have average durations much greater than one time unit, then tallies would concentrate in the main diagonal of the table, indicating a high degree of autocontingency; we would discover that codes have a high probability of repeating for many consecutive time units, which is not very informative. On the other hand, because columns and rows in a contingency table must correspond to mutually exclusive codes, if *GSEQ* detects that some of the target (or given) codes overlap it gives priority to the code that occurs first in the target (or given) list. Although this feature ensures that the table is a contingency table (and thus that statistics such as chi-square values can be adequately interpreted), it can obscure some sequential relationships.

Two-by-Two Tables

In timed-event sequences it is often much more interesting to analyze Lag 0 (or co-occurrence) patterns between codes. To do this, two-by-two tables can be specified for each pair of codes of interest, and statistics such as Yule's Q or Pearson's *phi* can be requested to assess the degree of association between codes (Bakeman, McArthur, & Quera, 1996). Also, new codes (or time windows) anchored with respect to existing codes can be defined using *GSEQ*, and Lag 0 associations between them can be evaluated (see next section).

The following commands request a co-occurrence analysis for the mother–infant data in Figure 2:

```
FILE "MOMINF";
POOL *;
```

```
STATS YULQ ADJR;
TARGET IQui &; LAG 0; GIVEN MPas &;
TARGET IQui &; LAG 0; GIVEN MAct &;
TARGET IQui &; LAG 0; GIVEN MRed &;
TARGET IAct &; LAG 0; GIVEN MPas &;
TARGET IAct &; LAG 0; GIVEN MAct &;
TARGET IAct &; LAG 0; GIVEN MRed &;
TARGET IFus &; LAG 0; GIVEN MPas &;
TARGET IFus &; LAG 0; GIVEN MAct &;
TARGET IFus &; LAG 0; GIVEN MRed &;
END;
```

Command POOL specifies that results must be pooled over dyads whose mothers have similar experience with children, i.e., two tables of results are requested, one for mothers with previous experience and another for mothers without previous experience. Nine Lag 0 two-by-two tables are defined. The first table has codes IQui and & (which *GSEQ* interprets as the residual code, i.e., any time unit in which code IQui does not occur) as targets and codes MPas and & (i.e., any time unit in which code MPas does not occur) as givens. Lag 0 here means that *GSEQ* must tally how many time units IQui and MPas, IQui and non-MPas, non-IQui and MPas, and non-IQui and non-MPas co-occur. Those tallies will then fill the cells of a two-by-two table. Note that when Lag 0 is requested, given codes can be specified as target codes and vice versa. Thus, in this example co-occurrence tables are requested for all combinations of infant and mother codes. For each table Yule's *Q* and adjusted residuals are computed.

GSEQ permits some repetitive commands to be specified in alternative ways. For example, those commands could have been written as follows:

```
FILE "MOMINF";
POOL *;
STATS YULQ ADJR;
TARGET IQui IAct IFus @; GIVEN MPas MAct MRed @;
END;
```

Command LAG has been omitted because by default *GSEQ* always tallies Lag 0 unless specified otherwise. The @ sign in the TARGET command tells *GSEQ* to create all possible tables with two target codes, the first being an infant code and the second the residual code; the same is true for the @ sign in the GIVEN command. Thus, nine two-by-two tables are requested.

The first table printed by *GSEQ* is shown in Table 3. There are five dyads (or units) assigned to the no-experience condition in these data. For those dyads a positive pattern of synchronicity exists between codes MPas and IQui, as Yule's *Q* is positive and close to 1 (as a measure of association, *Q* ranges from −1 to +1 and can be interpreted analogously to a correlation). The four cells in a two-by-two table always contain adjusted residuals that are identical in absolute value. Positive residuals in the main diagonal and negative residuals in the other cells indicate a positive association between codes. Thus, in this case mothers tend to attend passively while their infants are quiet. For mothers with previous experience the Yule's *Q* and adjusted residual values for those codes were .4097 and 18.33, respectively, as reported by *GSEQ*; these values also indicate a positive degree of co-occurrence.

Table 3. Adjusted residuals and Yule's Q for the no-experience condition

Pooling over 5 units (maximum 5 units per design cell).
Pooling over 10 sessions (maximum 2 sessions per unit).
Tallies are time units.
Lag 0. Adjusted residuals:

Given	Target IQui	&
MPas	37.16	−37.16
&	−37.16	37.16

Lag 0. YULQ:
    Yule's Q   = .7428
    Standard error = .0129

Nonsequential descriptive statistics often are useful when sequential data are being explored and as a help for clarifying objectives and research questions. Such statistics are provided by *GSEQ* as well. For example,

```
FILE "MOMINF";
POOL *;
SIMPLE ALL;
END;
```

would tell *GSEQ* to compute frequencies, durations, rates, average durations, and so forth for the codes in file MOMINF.MDS (the compiled version of file MOM-INF.SDS). Specification ALL is used to request a list of all possible descriptive statistics. For mothers without previous experience those commands would yield the results shown in Table 4.

In this table relative frequency equals frequency divided by total frequency, rate is expressed in number of occurrences per 60 time units, duration is expressed in the time units that were used in the data file, relative duration equals duration divided by the sum of code durations, probability is an estimate of the probability that a code occurs in any time unit and is computed by dividing duration by the total number of time units, and average duration equals duration divided by frequency. When codes are not mutually exclusive probability is more informative than relative duration, because probability indicates the proportion of observed time during which the codes occurred, whereas the total used to compute relative duration is the sum of code durations, which, when codes overlap, can exceed the actual observation time. Thus, when codes overlap the total probability can be greater than 1. In this example, mothers are redirecting their infants' attention 39% of the time, whereas infants are attending actively 36% of the time. Mothers attend passively during bouts that are shorter than their bouts of attending actively (average durations are 16.88 and 61.81 time units, respectively), whereas infants fuss during bouts that last 95.26 time units on average.

DATA MODIFICATIONS USING *GSEQ*

Once data have been described and sequential associations have been explored using *GSEQ*, it is often necessary to modify the original data to some extent to

Table 4.   Possible descriptive statistics for mothers without previous experience

Codes	Frequency	Relative frequency	Rate	Duration	Relative duration	Probability	Average duration
MPas	95	.1670	.2688	1,604	.0470	.0756	16.88
MAct	113	.1986	.3197	6,985	.2049	.3294	61.81
MRed	99	.1740	.2801	8,334	.2444	.3930	84.18
IQui	94	.1652	.2660	2,208	.0648	.1041	23.49
IAct	91	.1599	.2575	7,630	.2238	.3598	83.85
IFus	77	.1353	.2179	7,335	.2151	.3459	95.26
Totals	569	1.0000	1.6099	34,096	1.0000	1.6078	

Total number of time units = 21,206
M, mother; I, infant; Pas, passive attending; Act, active attending; Red, redirecting; Qui, quiet; Fus, fussing.

answer more complex questions. For example, after discovering that husbands tend to reciprocate wives by complaining after their wives complain (file COUPLES.SDS), we could ask, How do wives tend to respond to husbands after a cross-complaint? Also, once we know that mothers redirect infant attention while infant fussing occurs (file MOMINF.SDS), we could ask, Do mothers tend to redirect more after than before fussing starts, and does fussing tend to occur more before than after redirecting starts? In this case, we are trying to determine whether redirecting leads to fussing or vice versa.

GSEQ permits several kinds of data modifications, which are always performed by the program without altering the original file. Modified data can be saved for further analyses or analyzed subsequently using commands such as TARGET/GIVEN or SIMPLE. Some data modifications make more sense for certain data types than others. For example, commands RECODE, LUMP, and CHAIN are useful for event sequences. For the sequence

HEmp WCom HCom WOth HCom WCom,

the command

RECODE Complain1 = WCom HCom;

would tell GSEQ to analyze it as if it were composed of these codes:

HEmp Complain1 Complain1 WOth Complain1 Complain1.

Command

LUMP Complain2 = WCom HCom;

would have a similar effect, but codes that were recoded would be lumped together as

HEmp Complain2 WOth Complain2.

And command

CHAIN CrossComplain = WCom HCom;

would transform the original sequence into this one:

HEmp CrossComplain WOth HCom Wcom.

Note that the new code, CrossComplain, has been defined as a cross-complaint that is initiated by the wife, so the second instance of cross-complaining in those data would not be transformed. New codes defined with data modification commands can be used as target or given codes afterward. For example, these commands:

```
FILE "COUPLES";
POOL *;
RECODE Complain = WCom HCom;
SAVE "COUPLES1";
STATS JNTF;
TARGET HEmo HApp HEmp HNeg; LAG 1; GIVEN Complain &;
END;
```

would tell *GSEQ* to recode any complaint code into the new code Complain, save the modifications in a new data file, COUPLES1.MDS, and tally how many times codes HEmo, HApp, HEmp, and HNeg follow Complain and any non-Complain code (&).

Defining Time Windows

When concurrent codes are used, such as for SSD, TSD, ISD, and MSD, addition-al data modifications are permitted by *GSEQ*. They include AND, OR, NOT, NOR, and XOR, which perform logical operations between codes, and WINDOW, which creates new codes anchored to onsets and offsets of existing codes. Figure 4 shows examples of the logical modifications and compares them with RECODE and LUMP for a short timed-event sequence. Figure 5 shows different time periods

Figure 4.   Modification of concurrent sequential data. All codes are explained in the text.

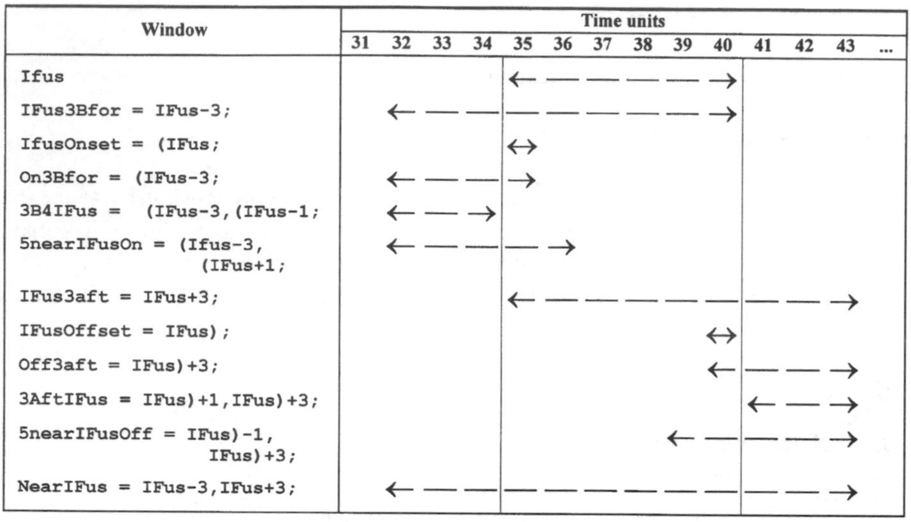

Window	Time units														
	31	32	33	34	35	36	37	38	39	40	41	42	43	...
IFus					←	—	—	—	—	→				
IFus3Bfor = IFus-3;		←	—		—	—	—	—	—	→				
IfusOnset = (IFus;					↔									
On3Bfor = (IFus-3;		←	—	—	→									
3B4IFus = (IFus-3,(IFus-1;		←	—	→										
5nearIFusOn = (Ifus-3, (IFus+1;		←	—	—	—	→								
IFus3aft = IFus+3;					←	—	—	—	—	—	—	—	→	
IFusOffset = IFus);										↔				
Off3aft = IFus)+3;										←	—	—	→	
3AftIFus = IFus)+1,IFus)+3;											←	—	→	
5nearIFusOff = IFus)-1, IFus)+3;									←	—	—	—	→	
NearIFus = IFus-3,IFus+3;		←	—	—	—	—	—	—	—	—	—	—	→	

Figure 5.   Definition of time periods with the WINDOW command. All codes are explained in the text.

that could be defined using the WINDOW command. For example, to determine whether mothers tend to redirect their infants' attention more after than before infant fussing starts, the following commands could be specified:

```
FILE "MOMINF";
POOL *;
WINDOW B4OnFuss = (IFus-5,(IFus-1;
WINDOW AftOnFuss = (IFus,(IFus+4;
STATS YULQ;
TARGET B4OnFuss AftOnFuss @; GIVEN MRed &;
END;
```

New codes B4OnFuss and AftOnFuss are two time periods comprising, respectively, the five time units before every onset of code IFus and the first five time units of every occurrence of code IFus. Note that (IFus denotes the onset of code IFus and that *SDIS* and *GSEQ* always consider time units to be discrete. Then, Yule's Q is requested for two Lag 0 two-by-two tables to assess how often MRed tends to co-occur with B4OnFuss and AftOnFuss (i.e., how often mothers redirect just before and just after infants start fussing). If the Yule's Q values differ greatly from one table to the other in their signs, their magnitudes, or both, then some evidence exists that the onset of infant fussing is associated with (i.e., affects or is affected by) the occurrence of mother redirecting.

EXPORTING *GSEQ* RESULTS

Pooling over individuals or dyads with similar characteristics assumes that the patterns that are being investigated are identical, or homogeneous, in all of them. However, in most cases it is necessary to analyze the data separately to determine that this assumption is true before proceeding to an analysis with pooled data. When no POOL command is specified, *GSEQ* prints one table of results per unit. For example, if Yule's Q for a two-by-two table is requested for the MOMINF.MDS file but no POOL command is included, then *GSEQ* will print 10 different Q values, one per unit or dyad in the data. If we are interested in comparing the five Q values for the experienced mothers with those for the nonexperienced mothers, we can perform a t-test. If requested, *GSEQ* can export any of the results into a format that is readable by a standard statistical package or a spreadsheet. Once exported, results can be further analyzed by any of these programs. For example, we could use *SPSS* to perform a t-test or an analysis of variance to determine whether some Yule's Q values differ significantly when experienced and nonexperienced mothers are compared. Sequential results, i.e., those specified by command STATS, can be exported using command EXPORT, whereas descriptive results specified by command SIMPLE can be exported using command SEND. The following commands tell *GSEQ* to export descriptive and sequential statistics for the MOMINF.MDS file:

```
FILE "MOMINF";
SIMPLE PROB;
SEND "MOMSIM" PROB SPSS;
STATS YULQ ADJR;
TARGET IFus &; GIVEN MRed &;
EXPORT "MOMYUL1" YULQ SPSS;
TARGET IFus &; GIVEN MAct &;
EXPORT "MOMYUL2" YULQ SPSS;
END;
```

For more information about *GSEQ* exportation capabilities, see Bakeman and Quera (1999).

CONCLUSIONS

The analysis of sequences of behavior is a necessary step for detecting patterns and describing the temporal structure of behavior. Sequential analysis can be applied in the study of the development of social skills and play in children, family relationships, interaction in clinical and educational settings, and communication processes. The essential requirement is that the process under study unfolds in time and can be observed objectively and systematically.

Interaction in dyads and small groups can be studied at various levels of resolution. To determine what participants think about their interaction, questionnaires and attitude scales can be used. However, when precise detail is needed about the process, and when objective measures are necessary, interaction is often observed and coded by external observers. This is usually a time-intensive task and typically requires the use of video equipment to record the behavior. Subsequently, trained coders observe the tapes carefully and code the sequence of behaviors, and probably their onset and offset times as well. Because generalization of results requires substantial amounts of data, usually more than one observation session is required for every dyad or group, and more than one group is observed, although a single unit (individual, family, etc.) can be observed multiple times. All this implies that researchers studying interaction often gather many data in the form of sequences for a single research.

The *SDIS* data language provides a common framework for representing sequential data. This is especially useful for interaction researchers, because standard statistical packages are not suited for analyzing the kinds of sequences they obtain. The *SDIS-GSEQ* programs are designed to analyze behavior sequences in a flexible and general way. Data can be obtained by direct observation of dyads, groups, or even individuals, either in experimental or nonexperimental settings, because *SDIS* permits representation of design variables. A variety of analyses are possible with *GSEQ*. Data can be described simply, to obtain measures such as frequency, duration, rate, relative frequency, or average duration for every behavioral code in the data. Lag sequential analyses can be carried out by defining sequential contingency tables for given and target codes; specifying lags; and requesting sequential statistics, such as chi-square, adjusted residuals, or Yule's Q. Users have complete control over which codes are included in the sequential tables and how they must be analyzed. Moreover, they can request that results be provided for pooled combinations of design variables. In addition, *GSEQ* permits several interesting data modifications, such as RECODE and WINDOW, which create new codes that can be analyzed subsequently using sequential techniques. New, more global codes can be created from existing codes using RECODE or LUMP, for example. In state, timed-event, and interval data the WINDOW command is especially useful for defining new codes linked to the onsets and offsets of existing codes. The new codes then can be included in subsequent Lag 0 (or synchronicity) analyses to detect, for example, possible sequential associations between a certain given code and some preceding and subsequent periods of some target code.

Results provided by *SDIS-GSEQ* belong to an *intermediate* level of analysis. Coding observed sequences can be viewed as a *low* level of analysis (in fact, a qualitative analysis). However, using analyses of variance or *t*-tests to determine differences in sequential association between dyads can be viewed as a *high*, and quantitative, level of analysis. *SDIS-GSEQ* performs quantitative analyses of the sequences and computes sequential indices that can be used for higher levels of analysis. Sequential indices such as Haberman's adjusted residuals and Yule's Q can be interpreted either as statistics testing deviations from the null hypothesis for some specific dyads or as descriptive indices of sequential association. If requested, *GSEQ* can export any of the statistics it computes to an external file that can be read subsequently by some program performing high-level analysis, such as *SPSS*.

In summary, *SDIS-GSEQ* contains tools for organizing sequential data in the form of sequential indices, and thus it can serve as a data reducer or bridge between raw data and conventional analyses such as analyses of variance and multiple regression. These are not automatic tools, and their use requires some skill and considerable thought, but the outcome can be useful insights into sequential processes no matter who is involved, whether mothers and infants, distressed couples, students with disabilities, or other humans or animals of research interest.

REFERENCES

Allison, P.D., & Liker, J.K. (1982). Analyzing sequential categorical data on dyadic interaction: A comment on Gottman. *Psychological Bulletin, 91*, 393–403.

Arundale, R.B. (1984). SAMPLE and TEST: Two FORTRAN IV programs for analysis of discrete-state, time-varying data using first-order Markov-chain techniques. *Behavior Research Methods, Instruments, and Computers, 16*, 335–336.

Bakeman, R. (1978). Untangling streams of behavior: Sequential analysis of observation data. In G.P. Sackett (Ed.), *Observing behavior: Vol. 2. Data collection and analysis methods* (pp. 63–78). Baltimore: University Park Press.

Bakeman, R. (1983). Computing lag sequential statistics: The ELAG program. *Behavior Research Methods and Instrumentation, 15,* 530–535.

Bakeman, R. (in press). Behavioral observations and coding. In H.T. Reis & C.K. Judd (Eds.), *Handbook of research methods in social psychology.* New York: Cambridge University Press.

Bakeman, R., & Casey, R.L. (1995). Analyzing family interaction: Taking time into account. *Journal of Family Psychology, 9,* 131–143.

Bakeman, R., & Gottman, J.M. (1997). *Observing interaction: An introduction to sequential analysis* (2nd ed.). New York: Cambridge University Press.

Bakeman, R., McArthur, D., & Quera, V. (1996). Detecting group differences in sequential association using sampled permutations: Log odds, kappa, and phi compared. *Behavior Research Methods, Instruments, and Computers, 28(3),* 446–457.

Bakeman, R., & Quera, V. (1992). SDIS: A Sequential Data Interchange Standard. *Behavior Research Methods, Instruments, and Computers, 24,* 554–559.

Bakeman, R., & Quera, V. (1995a). *Analyzing interaction: Sequential analysis with SDIS and GSEQ.* New York: Cambridge University Press.

Bakeman, R., & Quera, V. (1995b). Log-linear approaches to lag-sequential analysis when consecutive codes may and cannot repeat. *Psychological Bulletin, 118(2),* 272–284.

Bakeman, R., & Quera, V. (1999). Using GSEQ with standard statistical packages [On-line]. Available: www.gsu.edu/~psyrab/sg_exports_paper.htm

Bakeman, R., Robinson, B.F., & Quera, V. (1996). Testing sequential association: Estimating exact P values using sampled permutations. *Psychological Methods, 1(1),* 4–15.

Castellan, N.J., Jr. (1979). The analysis of behavior sequences. In R.B. Cairns (Ed.), *The analysis of social interactions: Methods, issues, and illustrations* (pp. 81–116). Mahwah, NJ: Lawrence Erlbaum Associates.

Gottman, J.M., & Roy, A.K. (1990). *Sequential analysis: A guide for behavioral scientists.* New York: Cambridge University Press.

Kienapple, K. (1987). Micro-analytic data analysis package. *Behavior Research Methods, Instruments, and Computers, 19,* 335–337.

Logan, K.R., Bakeman, R., & Keefe, E.B. (1997). Effects of instructional variables on the engaged behavior of students with moderate, severe, and profound disabilities in general education elementary classrooms. *Exceptional Children, 63,* 481–497.

Quera, V., & Estany, E. (1984). ANSEC: A BASIC package for lag sequential analysis of observational data. *Behavior Research Methods, Instruments, and Computers, 16,* 303–306.

Sackett, G.P. (1979). The lag sequential analysis of contingency and cyclicity in behavioral interaction research. In J.D. Osofsky (Ed.), *Handbook of infant development* (1st ed., pp. 623–649). New York: John Wiley & Sons.

Sackett, G.P. (1987). Analysis of sequential social interaction data: Some issues, recent developments, and a causal inference model. In J.D. Osofsky (Ed.), *Handbook of infant development* (2nd ed., pp. 855–878). New York: John Wiley & Sons.

Sackett, G.P., Holm, R., Crowley, C., & Henkins, A. (1979). A FORTRAN program for lag sequential analysis of contingency and cyclicity in behavioral interaction data. *Behavior Research Methods and Instrumentation, 11,* 366–378.

Schlundt, D.G. (1982). Two PASCAL programs for managing observational data bases and for performing multivariate information analysis and log-linear contingency table analysis of sequential and nonsequential data. *Behavior Research Methods and Instrumentation, 14,* 351–352.

Yoder, P.J., & Tapp, J.T. (1990). SATS: Sequential Analysis of Transcripts System. *Behavior Research Methods, Instruments, and Computers, 22,* 339–343.

19

Quantifying the Magnitude of Sequential Association Between Events or Behaviors

Paul J. Yoder and
Irene D. Feurer

Whether a behavior or event increases or decreases the probability of another behavior's or event's occurrence within the same observation session involves the sequential association of events. For example, if the investigator thinks that teacher instructions increase the probability of student self-injury (e.g., hitting his or her head on the wall) because self-injury helps the student avoid the teacher's unpleasant demands, then the motivating theory for research posits a close temporal (i.e., within a few seconds or within a few events) relationship between teacher instructions and student self-injury.

In such cases, the researcher needs an index or measure to quantify the extent to which the first behavior of interest (e.g., teacher instruction) is temporally related to the second behavior of interest (e.g., student self-injury). This index of sequential association is useful as the dependent variable in group statistical analyses (e.g., *t*-tests, regressions) or as the dependent variable that is analyzed in single-subject experiments (see Figure 1).

Given the number of indices of sequential association that various researchers have used (Bakeman & Adamson, 1984; Wampold, 1989; Yoder, Davies, & Bishop, 1994; Yoder, Klee, Hooshyar, & Schaffer, 1997), it is clear that it is more difficult than it first appears to identify an index that best reflects this sequential relationship and not other aspects of the observation session. When this index is influ-

---

This chapter was written while the authors were supported in part by National Institute of Child Health and Human Development Grant No. P30HD15052.

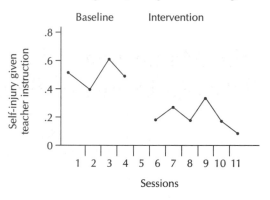

Randomized group experimental design

Group	Extent to which self-injury is sequentially related to teacher instruction within a session	
	Mean	Standard deviation
Experimental (*n* = 49 people)	.25	.17
Control (*n* = 52 people)	.50	.15

Single-subject experimental design

Figure 1.   Example of how indices of sequential association might be used for group and single-subject experimental designs.

enced by factors other than the degree of sequential association, Type I and Type II error rates can be elevated.

This chapter presents a detailed discussion of 1) the most common index of sequential association (i.e., the transitional probability of one type of behavior given the immediately preceding occurrence of another type of behavior), which is shown to be inappropriate for most applications of sequential analysis; 2) the consequences of using transitional probabilities as an index of sequential association; and 3) the conceptual underpinnings of a more appropriate index of sequential association, Yule's Q. We also describe a few of the other indices of association that have been used and indicate their limitations when used as indices of sequential association. Although much of this content has been touched on in other sources (Bakeman & Gottman, 1997; Bakeman, McArthur, & Quera, 1996), this discussion is unique in its level of detail and the extensiveness of the background material provided, which is needed to cover these issues thoroughly and in terms that are familiar to readers with limited experience with sequential analysis. These topics are important because transitional probabilities and other inappropriate indices of sequential association continue to be widely used. Our hope is that this more detailed discussion of the issues will aid proper interpretation of past studies using sequential analyses and increase the probability that future sequential analyses will use Yule's Q, not transitional probabilities, as the index of sequential association.

Our discussion of the issues and the examples we use to illustrate them will focus on situations and questions in which the second behavior of interest is predicted to occur immediately after the first behavior of interest (i.e., a forward lag 1 analysis). However, the general issues we discuss apply to research questions in which the first and second behaviors of interest are expected to occur simultaneously and to questions in which the second behavior is expected to occur one or more behaviors after the first behavior. Our discussion and examples will focus on analysis of momentary behaviors; however, one can also analyze seconds or intervals (Bakeman & Gottman, 1997).

Specifically, this chapter is arranged as follows:

1. We define the terms we use throughout the chapter.

2. We indicate the types of research questions that sequential analysis is best suited to address. In doing so we indicate why one might want to use sequential analysis.

3. We briefly indicate how one tallies sequences of behaviors into a two-by-two contingency table as part of a sequential analysis. This two-by-two table provides the basis for computations of all indices of sequential association discussed.

4. We illustrate why the transitional probability is not an appropriate index for most applications of sequential analysis.

5. We introduce Yule's Q and illustrate why it is superior to transitional probability as an index of sequential association.

6. Last, we indicate why other indices that have been used as indices of sequential association are not appropriate in most applications of sequential analysis.

DEFINITIONS OF TERMS USED IN THIS CHAPTER

The following terms will be used consistently throughout this chapter. In general, *sequential analysis* is concerned with sequences or simultaneous occurrence of coded events or of seconds or intervals in which a coded event has occurred. Conceptually, a *sequential association* occurs when two types of behaviors (e.g., teacher instruction and student self-injury) are temporally related within an observation session. An *index of sequential association* is a numeric expression of the extent to which the sequence of interest occurs during an observation session. To help us discuss the sequence of interest we call the hypothesized causal behavior or the hypothesized discriminative stimulus the *antecedent behavior*. The *target behavior* is the behavior that is hypothesized to be affected by the antecedent behavior. In our example about teacher instructions and student self-injury, teacher instruction is the antecedent behavior and student self-injury is the target behavior. A certain number of antecedent-target behavior sequences will occur by chance. Therefore, to correctly interpret an index of sequential association, we need some quantification of the chance occurrence of the sequence of interest. We call this value the *estimate of chance occurrences of the sequence.*

TYPES OF RESEARCH QUESTIONS THAT SEQUENTIAL ANALYSES CAN ADDRESS

Beginning students of sequential analysis may find it difficult to understand whether sequential analysis is well suited to a particular research question.

The first step to understanding the types of research questions that are appropriately addressed by sequential analysis is to understand the difference between *summary-level variables* and *sequential-level variables.*

It should be noted that the present use of the term "summary-level variables" distinguishes it from the term "summary statistic." To provide a contrast with sequential-level variables, in this chapter we use the term summary-level variable to mean the total frequency or probability of one behavior. In most applications, a summary statistic sums across people (e.g., the mean). In research designs with groups of participants (i.e., group designs) most research questions involving summary-level variables imply some type of association between two or more such variables or imply a mean difference between two or more groups or conditions.

For example, one might hypothesize that teacher instructions are aversive and increase the probability that children with mental retardation requiring extensive support will engage in self-injury (e.g., hitting their heads on the wall). If one is using summary-level variables, a first step to examining one aspect of this hypothesis would be to test whether the correlation between the number of teacher instructions to the children and the number of times the children engage in self-injury exceeds zero. Alternatively, in a single-subject experimental design the investigator typically examines graphs for possible differences between the trend or the level of a summary-level variable at baseline and in experimental phases. Under the same hypothesis, a researcher using a single-subject experimental design might examine graphs of the frequency of self-injury at baseline and during an experimental phase in which teachers were asked to reduce the number of their instructions. In such a study one would also verify that the teachers actually did reduce the frequency of their instructions in the experimental phase. In these examples, the two summary-level variables are 1) frequency of teacher instructions and 2) frequency of student self-injury. These measures fail to express anything about the sequence of teacher instructions and student self-injury. That is, we have not tested the part of our theory that predicts that teacher instructions have an almost immediate temporal relationship with self-injury.

Using a similar hypothesis with sequential-level variables in a group design, one might test whether the extent to which self-injury occurred immediately after teacher instructions was greater than one would expect by chance in the majority of teacher–student pairs. In this example this sequential measure quantifies the extent to which self-injury immediately follows teacher instructions. Thus, the part of our theory that predicts that teacher instructions have an immediate effect on self-injury is reflected in our choice of a sequential-level variable.

The main point is that sequential-level variables reflect a temporal association within an observation session. That is, the sequential-level variable quantifies the extent to which the target behavior (e.g., self-injury) occurs within a specified number of coded behaviors from the antecedent behavior (e.g., teacher instructions). The reader should note that it is important that the time period (e.g., within 5 seconds) or the number of coded behaviors (e.g., the next coded behavior) from the antecedent behavior be specified. Sequential analyses cannot be used to test the notion that the target behavior will occur within some unspecified time or number of behaviors after an antecedent behavior. Because sequential-level variables require the investigator to predict the number of events or the time window in which the target behavior will occur after the antecedent behavior, very specific temporal relationships can be tested. The degree of specificity implicit in sequential-level variables reduces the number of alternative explanations for the association of interest.

However, statistically significant or strong indices of sequential association are not proof that the antecedent behavior caused the target behavior to occur. Like other indices of association, indices of sequential association can be high because of some previously occurring or simultaneously occurring event (i.e., a spurious association). That is, sequences of teacher instructions and student self-injury may occur frequently because of preceding instances of student self-injury. For example, student self-injury may cause the teacher to provide instructions in an attempt to "redirect the student," and students who are self-abusing may tend to continue to engage in self-injurious behavior.

Many sequential analyses provide the basis for subsequent experiments by identifying potential causal variables. Alternatively, sequential analyses may reveal the mechanism by which an antecedent variable affects the target variable. For example, a sequential analysis might be used to demonstrate that teacher instructions have the strongest sequential association with student self-injury of all possible antecedents. To determine whether teacher instructions alter the probability of student self-injury, one needs to decrease teacher instructions in the context of a well-controlled group or single-subject experimental design and measure whether student self-injury decreases. Alternatively, a sequential analysis might be conducted after such an experiment to increase the precision of our notion of when self-injury is likely to occur relative to instances of teacher instruction. This step in the process would shed light on why teacher instructions increase the probability of student self-injury. As always, research design, not statistical techniques or whether the variable is sequential, determines the degree to which we can confidently infer that an antecedent behavior has a causal effect on a target behavior.

Sequential analyses are typically conducted in nonexperimental group designs. Three common nonexperimental group designs that may involve sequential-level variables are 1) correlational designs, 2) intact between-group comparisons, and 3) intraindividual comparisons between sequences. An example of a research question in a correlational design using a sequential-level variable is: Does the magnitude of the sequential association between teacher instructions and student self-injury vary as a function of the student's degree of mental retardation? A research question in an intact between-group comparison using a sequential-level variable is: Is the magnitude of the sequential association between teacher instructions and student self-injury greater in students with epilepsy than in similar students without epilepsy? An example of a research question in an intraindividual comparison between sequences would be: Is the magnitude of the sequential association between teacher instructions and student self-injury greater than that between teacher ignoring and student self-injury?

A promising but less common use of sequential-level variables is to use a randomized group experiment or a single-subject experimental design to determine whether a treatment affects the antecedent-target relationship. For example, in a randomized group experiment, an investigator might test whether the sequential association between teacher instructions and student self-injury is lower in students who receive a pharmacological treatment than in students in a control group. In a single-subject experimental design one might examine whether the level of the sequential association between teacher instructions and student self-injury is lower in the drug treatment phase than at baseline. See Figure 1 for illustrations of these two examples.

BASIS FOR INDICES OF SEQUENTIAL ASSOCIATION: THE TWO-BY-TWO CONTINGENCY TABLE

To compute any of the indices of sequential association it is useful to organize all possible pairs of behaviors into a mutually exclusive and exhaustive table with two rows and two columns (i.e., four cells). The method of how pairs of behaviors are tallied is sometimes difficult to understand initially. The reader is asked to consider the example in Figure 2 carefully while reading the general procedure by which pairs of behaviors are tallied into the cells of the two-by-two table. A convention used in the sequential analysis literature is to use the rows to categorize each pair of behaviors according to whether or not the antecedent behavior is the first behavior in the pair and to use the columns to categorize the same pair of behaviors according to whether the target behavior is the second behavior in the pair. The cell labels (A, B, C, and D) for the four cells in the two-by-two table in Figure 2 should be noted because these labels will be used below to aid presentation of the computational formula for the indices of sequential association. In Figure 2 each behavior pair is labeled using the label for the cell into which it is tallied. It should be noted that behavior pairs are tallied into the two-by-two table in such a way that one behavior pair "overlaps" the next behavior pair. That is,

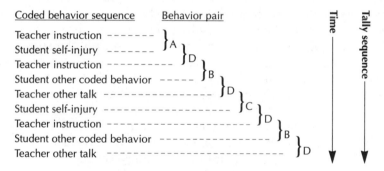

These pairs of behaviors are tallied into a two-by-two table as follows:

Behavior II

		Student self-injury	Any other student or teacher behavior	Total for rows
Behavior I	Teacher instruction	1 pair A	B 2 pairs	3 pairs
	Any other teacher or student behavior	1 pair C	D 4 pairs	5 pairs
	Total for columns	2 pairs	6 pairs	Total of 8 observed pairs*

Figure 2. The method used to tally pairs of behaviors into a two-by-two table. (*Analyzing just this portion of the session would not be sufficient to yield reliable indices of sequential association.)

except for the first and last behaviors, each behavior is considered both a first behavior and a second behavior (i.e., second in one pair and first in the next pair). Then, each of these overlapping pairs of behaviors is tallied into the appropriate cell in the two-by-two table. For more information on other measures of association for nominal data, see Reynolds (1984).

MOST COMMONLY USED INDEX OF
SEQUENTIAL ASSOCIATION: TRANSITIONAL PROBABILITY

Informal observation indicates that the most frequently used index of sequential association is the transitional probability of the target behavior following the antecedent behavior. This transitional probability is the proportion of instances of the antecedent behavior that are followed by an instance of the target behavior. In terms of the two-by-two table illustrated in Figure 2, the formula for this transitional probability is $A/(A + B)$. In the example in Figure 2 the transitional probability of self-injury given teacher instructions is $1/3$, or .33. Transitional probabilities are frequently used as an index of sequential association because they appear to be easy to interpret.

Unfortunately, if the investigator wishes to use sequential analysis to identify types of behavior that may increase the probability of target behaviors occurring, the correct interpretation of transitional probability is not as straightforward as it first appears. The problem is that observed transitional probabilities tell us nothing about the probability of the target behavior occurring after the antecedent behavior by chance processes. Although the exact computational method used varies, it is generally agreed that the estimate of the chance occurrence of the sequence is at least in part a function of the simple probability of the target behavior (Moran, Dumas, & Symons, 1992). The frequency of a behavior has meaning only if it is known how long the individual was observed or how many instances of other coded behaviors occurred in the session. For example, if self-injury occurs twice out of 1,000 instances of other child behaviors, it means something quite different than if it occurs twice out of 5 instances of other child behaviors. Therefore, we quantify the extent to which the target behavior occurs in terms of probabilities, not frequency. The *simple probability of the target behavior* is the number of times the target behavior occurs divided by the total number of pairs of coded behaviors. In the example presented in Figure 2 the simple probability of self-injury is $2/8$ or .25. Using the cell labels in Figure 2 it is computed as $(A + C)/(A + B + C + D)$.

Transitional probabilities are influenced by the simple probability of the target behavior, not just the sequential association of interest. Using classic measurement theory, one can decompose transitional probabilities as follows:

> Observed transitional probability is a function of the true sequential association plus the observed simple probability of the target plus measurement error.

All things being equal, the higher the simple probability of the target behavior, the higher the transitional probability by chance processes alone. For example, in an observational session in which the child is engaged in high rates of self-injury, self-injury will occur after teacher instructions very often by chance processes. This example makes it clear that an interpretable index of sequential association must be compared with an estimate of chance occurrences of the sequence. When applied to transitional probabilities used as an index of sequential association, interpretable transitional probabilities must be compared with the simple probability of the target behavior for that sequence.

Consider what happens when we remember that indices of sequential association are frequently used as the dependent scores in statistical analyses of a group of participants or in graphs used to examine a potential treatment effect in a single-subject experimental design (see Figure 1). Assuming that each participant has a different simple probability of the target behavior, even if the transitional probability for Participant A is the same as that for Participant B the meaning of the two transitional probabilities will vary. When transitional probabilities are used as indices of sequential association to test hypotheses, individual differences in the simple probability of the target behavior can cause elevated rates of Type I or Type II errors.

The probability of Type I error increases when the simple probability of the target event is systematically larger in conditions hypothesized to be associated with the strongest sequential dependencies (i.e., the "superior" level of the independent variable). Comparisons based on an index of sequential association that is not influenced by the simple probability of the target behavior are less likely to yield Type I errors. For example, if one compared the transitional probabilities in Table 1 across groups one would inaccurately conclude that the sequential association between teacher instructions and self-injury was stronger in children with mental retardation requiring extensive support than in children with mental retardation requiring intermittent support. When we take into consideration the simple probability of self-injury in the two groups we can see that the difference in transitional probabilities is largely a reflection of the difference in the simple probability of self-injury in the groups. Although it may be helpful to know that the simple probability of self-injury differs between groups, this is not our research question.

However, it is a different matter when the simple probability of the target behavior is systematically smaller in the condition or sequence or group or level of predictor in which the larger transitional probabilities occur. In such a case the difference between the true sequential associations compared will be sufficiently large to overcome the systematic influence of the difference in the simple probabilities of the target behaviors. For the sake of discussion, if there were actually a larger simple probability of self-injury in children with mild impairment than in children with severe impairment, the lower transitional probability of self-injury after teacher instructions in the children with mild impairment would have occurred despite the between-group difference in the simple probability of self-injury.

The probability of Type II error increases when we use transitional probabilities as an index of sequential association under conditions in which the simple probability of the target behavior varies randomly across the groups, conditions, or sequences to be compared or across values of the proposed predictor of the sequential association of interest. When the mean difference in the simple probabilities of two or more target behaviors is not significantly different from zero, we say that the simple probabilities are randomly distributed across the levels of the independent variable. When there is high variation in the simple probabilities of the target behaviors that are randomly distributed across the independent variable, transitional probabilities make it more difficult to detect the true difference in the sequential associations of interest compared with situations in which the index of sequential association is not influenced by differences in the simple probability of the target behavior (i.e., increased probability of a Type II error). For example, assume that we want to compare the sequential association of teacher instructions followed by self-injury with the sequential association of teacher instructions followed by student compliance in a group of students with mental retardation requiring extensive support. Assume further that about half of the students show a higher probability of self-injury and the other half show a higher probability of compliance. Even if there was a true stronger sequential association of self-injury after teacher instructions, we might not detect this difference because half of the students have "inflated" indices of sequential association attributable to their having higher simple probabilities of compliance.

TRANSITIONAL PROBABILITIES IN BACKWARD SEQUENTIAL ANALYSIS: A FREQUENT MISAPPLICATION

If a researcher wishes to determine the probable antecedent events of self-injury, a forward sequential analysis, like those discussed above, or a backward sequential analysis can be conducted. In this section, we discuss why the use of transitional probabilities as the index of sequential association in backward sequential analyses tends to result in more miscommunication than their use in forward sequential analyses designed to address the same research question.

By *backward sequential analysis* we mean that the investigator tallies the number of times that certain behaviors occur before the behavior of interest. For example, assume that we use theory to guide our decision to code several teacher behaviors that may increase the probability of self-injury (e.g., instructions, active ignoring, talking to other students, other talk to target student) because we ultimately want to reduce the instances of the associated teacher behaviors as part of an intervention to reduce self-injury. Just as one application of functional analysis requires that we ask teachers what tends to occur before student injury, we might observe which of these teacher behaviors tend to precede self-injury most often.

In a backward sequential analysis, we tabulate the sequence of behaviors into our two-by-two table moving backward in time. See Figure 3 for an illustration of this process using the same data that were presented in Figure 2. In accordance with backward sequential analysis principles, the tabulation of the first and second behaviors is reversed in Figure 3 compared with Figure 2.

Assume that we decide to use transitional probabilities as the index of sequential association (a common practice). It should be noted that the transitional probability of self-injury (i.e., the first behavior in a backward analysis) preceded by teacher instructions is $1/2$ or .50 (A/[A + B] in Figure 3). Note that the transitional probability of self-injury after teacher instructions (i.e., the first behavior in a forward analysis) is different: $1/3$ or .33 (A/[A + B] in Figure 2).

The primary source of the miscommunication is the mismatch between the motivation for conducting the study, the terms used in sequential analysis, and the backward sequential analysis process. The motivation for most studies using sequential analysis presumes a causal relationship between the antecedent and target behaviors. Causality progresses forward in time. The target or second behavior typically occurs after an antecedent or first behavior. For example,

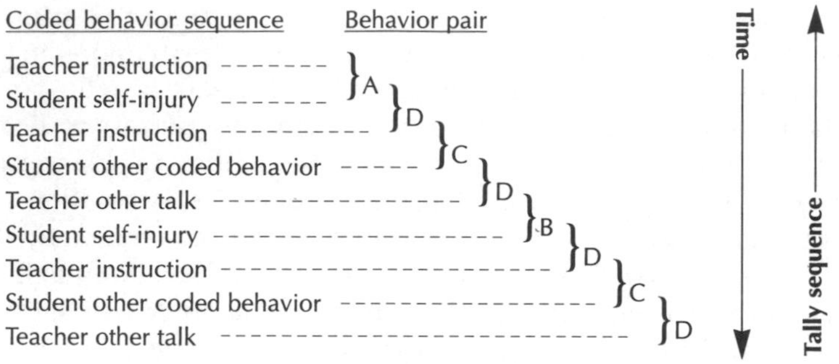

These pairs of behaviors are tallied into a two-by-two table as follows:

Behavior II

Behavior I	Teacher instruction	Any other teacher or student behavior	Total for rows
Student self-injury	1 pair A	B 1 pair	2 pairs
Any other student or teacher behavior	2 pairs C	D 4 pairs	6 pairs
Total for columns	3 pairs	5 pairs	Total of 8 observed pairs*

Figure 3. Backward sequential analysis of the data from Figure 2. (*Analyzing just this portion of the session would not be sufficient to yield reliable indices of sequential association.)

assume that we conduct a backward and forward analysis to identify the best candidates for antecedents of self-injury. The reason to conduct the study is to eventually reduce self-injury by reducing the occurrence of the antecedent behaviors of self-injury. The targets or second behaviors in a backward analysis to address this question are the possible antecedents. The target or second behavior in a forward analysis to address the same question is self-injury. Naïve readers might not realize that the target behaviors are typically different in the two or more sequences compared in this type of backward sequential analysis. In contrast, the target behavior is the same in the two or more sequences compared in a similar forward analysis. If the target behaviors are different, the simple probabilities of the two target behaviors are almost always different. As always, differences in the transitional probabilities are not interpretable by themselves when we compare transitional probabilities for sequences with different simple probabilities of the target behavior.

The issue is not whether backward sequential analysis has a place among our research tools. The issue is that many readers (and possibly many researchers) may be less aware of the greater potential for misinterpreting transitional probabilities as indices of sequential association in the context of backward sequential analysis than in the context of forward sequential analysis.

Unfortunately, use of transitional probabilities without reference to an estimate of chance occurrence is still frequent in the sequential analysis literature.

Some investigators consider such a use appropriate for "descriptive" purposes only (Bakeman & Gottman, 1997). However, we recommend against using transitional probabilities even for descriptive purposes because 1) readers frequently make implicit comparisons between transitional probabilities of sequences from different sessions or groups or with different target behaviors, and 2) Yule's Q provides a more interpretable descriptive index of sequential association in all of these situations.

In the final analysis, transitional probabilities are interpretable only when they are compared with an estimate of chance occurrences of the sequence of interest. One can do this by always including at least the simple probability of the target behavior (or some other estimate of the chance occurrence of the sequence; Moran et al., 1992) with the transitional probability. However, this practice is cumbersome at best. Alternatively, there is an index of sequential association that reflects a comparison with an estimate of the chance occurrence of the sequence: Yule's Q.

YULE'S Q: A BETTER INDEX OF SEQUENTIAL ASSOCIATION

Bakeman et al. (1996) documented many qualities of Yule's Q that make it a good alternative to transitional probabilities. In this section we present the conceptual meaning of Yule's Q and the statistic from which it is derived: the odds ratio. We present data that demonstrate that Yule's Q controls for the simple probability of the target and antecedent behaviors while quantifying the sequential association between antecedent and target behaviors. Thus, Yule's Q indicates whether the sequential association is larger or smaller than an estimate of the chance occurrence of the sequence of interest. By examining the odds ratio (the statistic on which Yule's Q is based) we illustrate the conceptual meaning of the estimate of the chance occurrence of the sequence of interest used by Yule's Q. Finally, we finish with a discussion of the minimum number of behaviors that one needs to reasonably interpret Yule's Q as an index of sequential association.

Odds Ratio and Yule's Q

Using the cell labels for the cells in the two-by-two tables in Figure 2, the computational formula for the odds ratio is A/B divided by C/D, which can be expressed as the cross-product ratio AD/BC (Reynolds, 1984). The odds ratio for the two-by-two table in Figure 2 is as follows:

$$\text{Odds ratio} = (1 \times 4)/(2 \times 1) = 4{:}2 = 2{:}1$$

This is interpreted to mean that self-injury occurs after teacher instructions twice as often as self-injury occurs after other behaviors. When there is no sequential association between the antecedent and target events the odds ratio is 1.0. In other words, there is an equal chance that the target event will occur after the antecedent behavior and after nonantecedent behaviors. Therefore, knowledge of the occurrence of the antecedent behavior does not help predict the occurrence of the target behavior. The possible range of the odds ratio is 0 to infinity. This asymmetry around 1 as an indication of statistical independence (i.e., no association) results in less clear communication of its meaning. Consequently, the odds ratio has been transformed into Yule's Q to make it more interpretable.

Using the cell labels for the two-by-two table in Figure 2, Yule's Q is computed as follows:

$$\text{Yule's } Q = (AD - BC)/(AD + BC)$$

In this formula, if the value of the A or D cell and the B or C cell is 0, an undefined number will result. Yule's Q cannot be computed in such cases. Using the two-by-two table in Figure 2 as an example (although this data set is too small to render Yule's Q interpretable), Yule's Q is computed as follows:

$$\text{Yule's } Q = (4 - 2)/(4 + 2) = 2/6 = .33$$

Yule's Q has a possible minimum of –1.0 and a possible maximum of 1.0, with 0 representing the null relationship between the antecedent and the target behaviors. Most readers find Yule's Q more interpretable than the odds ratio. However, the information that it conveys is identical to that of the odds ratio. Therefore, a Yule's Q of 0 means that the target is just as likely to occur after a nonantecedent behavior as after the antecedent behavior. A negative Yule's Q means that the target behavior occurs after the antecedent behavior less often than is estimated by chance processes alone. A positive Yule's Q means that the target behavior occurs after the antecedent behavior more often than is estimated by chance processes alone. Therefore, the Yule's Q for the data in Figure 2 indicates that the target behavior occurs after the antecedent behavior more often than one would expect by chance processes alone.

To demonstrate that Yule's Q is not affected by the simple probability of the target behavior, we computed Yule's Q values for self-injury after teacher instructions from the data in Table 1. The results are shown in Table 2.

In contrast to the results using transitional probabilities as the index of sequential association (Table 1), the data in Table 2 make it clear that the sequential association between self-injury and teacher instructions is greater in the children with mental retardation requiring intermittent support. Yule's Q reflects an implicit comparison with an estimate of the chance occurrence of self-injury after teacher instructions, whereas transitional probabilities do not. In addition, Yule's Q is not influenced by the simple probability of the target (or the antecedent) behavior. In fact, the computational formula of Yule's Q does not use the marginals of the two-

Table 1. Example of the improper use of transitional probabilities to compare sequential associations across groups

Group	Average transitional probability of self-injury after teacher instructions	Average simple probability of self-injury
Students with mental retardation requiring extensive support	.70	.72
Students with mental retardation requiring intermittent support	.04	.03

Table 2.   Comparison of Yule's Q and transitional probabilities for conditions that differ on the simple probability of the target behavior

Group	Average transitional probability of self-injury after teacher instructions	Average simple probability of self-injury	Average Yule's Q of self-injury after teacher instructions
Students with mental retardation requiring extensive support	.70	.72	−.11
Students with mental retardation requiring intermittent support	.04	.03	.34

by-two table at all. (The *marginals* are the far right cells for the rows and the bottom cells for the columns.) Yule's Q also is a more interpretable descriptive index of sequential association than transitional probabilities for backward sequential analyses. In fact, the value of Yule's Q is identical for both approaches. Yule's Q is computed on the basis of the products of the diagonal cells in the two-by-two table, and these products are equal in both forward and backward sequential analysis.

Because we are recommending that Yule's Q be used as a dependent variable in group designs with parametric inferential statistics, it is important to note whether distributions of Yule's Q usually meet the assumptions underlying the general linear model (GLM). For example, many GLM statistical procedures assume the residuals or errors to be normally distributed, and this assumption is much more likely to be met if the dependent variable is normally distributed. Noting the characteristics of the sampling distribution of Yule's Q is helpful in predicting whether samples of Yule's Q values will be normally distributed. Bakeman et al. (1996) described a sampling distribution of Yule's Q values and found the distribution to be approximately normally distributed and to possess a mean of approximately zero. This is exactly what one would wish for if Yule's Q is to be used as a dependent variable in parametric analyses.

Sufficient Behavior Samples to Interpret Yule's Q

Although Yule's Q is superior to transitional probability as an index of sequential association, one needs a sufficiently large behavior sample for Yule's Q to be interpretable. When we attempt to address our research questions with too few coded behaviors or too brief a behavior sample, we make it more difficult to detect a sequential association, particularly if the sequence does not occur frequently in our behavior sample.

Measurement theory tells us that short tests tend to be less reliable (i.e., they have greater measurement error) than longer tests. In observational research the data come from a behavioral observation session, not a test. When the behavior sample is small it is likely to contain more measurement error than larger samples, a point that has been demonstrated empirically (Bakeman, Quera, McArthur, & Robinson, 1997). The consequence of random measurement error is an increased probability of underestimating the true sequential association.

The notion of statistical power also provides a framework for understanding why small behavior samples increase the probability of underestimating the true level of sequential association. It is well known that larger sample sizes tend to increase statistical power (all things being equal). This is also true for sequential analysis. Unless the sequential association is very strong (i.e., the effect size is large) the probability of detecting a relationship that is actually present is relatively low when the behavior sample is short or the number of coded events is small. Unfortunately, there is no consensus on how power analyses may be applied to sequential analysis to help determine the minimum behavior sample size for a given study. All we have are rules of thumb to tell us how large the behavior sample needs to be. The bad news is that there are several rules of thumb. At this point researchers will have difficulty deciding which to use. The good news is that there is progress toward adequately defining which aspects of the session need to be considered when deciding how long the session must be to interpret Yule's Q accurately.

Earlier approaches used only the frequency of the antecedent and target behaviors. For example, one rule of thumb was to use Yule's Q only if there were at least five instances of both the antecedent and target behaviors (Bakeman & Gottman, 1997). The problem with considering only the frequency of the antecedent and target behaviors is that in sessions with infrequent occurrences of the antecedent and target behaviors longer sessions are necessary because many occurrences of the sequence are necessary to detect the association. The presence of many opportunities to observe the sequence of interest provides a better basis for quantifying the degree to which the sequence exceeds the estimate of chance occurrences of the sequence.

Therefore, such rules of thumb need to consider the total number of coded behaviors (or the length of the session) as well as the simple probability of the antecedent and target behaviors (Bakeman et al., 1997). The product of these three aspects of the session is used to compute the *expected value* in the A cell of the two-by-two table (i.e., the antecedent-to-target cell). For example, if the simple probabilities of antecedent and target behaviors are .20 and .40, respectively, and the total number of coded behaviors is 150, then the expected frequency for cell A is 12 (i.e., .20 × .40 × 150). Three values for the expected value for cell A have been proposed as rules of thumb: 5 (Bakeman & Gottman, 1997; Wickens, 1993), 10 (Bakeman et al., 1997), and 20 (Bakeman et al., 1997). Although we still do not have definitive guidance concerning when an estimated value of 5 is adequate, there is evidence that session lengths using the expected value of 10 as the rule of thumb are adequate when behavior coding is acceptably accurate (greater than 80% agreement with a perfectly coded session), the number of codes in the coding system is small (two or three), and the simple probabilities of the antecedent and target behaviors are approximately equal (Bakeman et al., 1997). Similarly, the most conservative approach to estimating the minimum length of the session (i.e., an expected value of 20) is needed when the number of codes is 10 or more, the simple probabilities of the antecedent and target behaviors are very different from each other, and coding judgments are likely to be less than 80% accurate (Bakeman et al., 1997).

OTHER INDICES OF SEQUENTIAL ASSOCIATION

We have demonstrated that the total frequency (i.e., the base rate) of the antecedent and target events must be controlled when quantifying the sequential association of interest. However, there are two other noteworthy considerations when selecting an index of sequential association: 1) the total number of coded behaviors must be controlled, and 2) the sampling distribution of the index must meet the assumptions of the GLM. All of the indices discussed below control for the base rates of the antecedent and target behaviors. However, they do not meet one of the two other criteria. As indicated above, the sampling distribution for Yule's Q has characteristics that are consistent with the assumptions of the GLM. In addition, Yule's Q is not affected by differences between individuals or sessions in the total number of coded behaviors because its computational formula does not use the sum of the row or column in a two-by-two table (i.e., marginals). We address the following alternative indices for sequential association: the probability value from a sampled permutation test, z-score, *phi* coefficient, and transformed *kappa*.

If one's data do not meet the rules of thumb for minimum length of session needed to interpret Yule's Q, Bakeman and Gottman (1997) recommend using the probability value associated with the sequence as an index of sequential association. This probability value is computed using a sampled permutation test (Bakeman, Robinson, & Quera, 1996). Briefly, a sampled permutation uses a computer program to count the number of times the target behavior occurs after the antecedent behavior in the observed session. Then, the computer program randomly shuffles the sequence of events and counts the frequency of occurrence of the sequence of interest again. This shuffle-and-count process is repeated 10,000 times to create an empirical probability distribution. The probability from such a process is the number of postshuffle counts of the sequence that exceed the observed count of the sequence divided by 10,000. For example, if 100 of the postshuffle counts are larger than the observed number of times the target follows the antecedent behavior in the real sequence of behaviors, the probability is .01.

The problem with using a probability value as an index of sequential association is that probability values are influenced by the total number of coded events in the sequence. This is true of all statistical significance tests; the sample size influences statistical significance. Therefore, one source of measurement error in using probability values as an index of sequential association is interindividual variance in the number of coded behaviors that occur during the sessions. As in our discussion of the consequences of measurement error in transitional probabilities, this type of measurement error can be random or systematic, with the corresponding consequences of Type II or Type I errors, respectively.

Another index of sequential association that increases when the total number of coded behaviors increases is the z-score (Bakeman & Gottman, 1997). Even when the sequential association is exactly the same, one can increase the z-score by simply increasing the length of the behavior sample. Yoder and Tapp (1990) illustrated this point by copying the same sequence of behaviors four times and concatenating the four samples into one sequence of coded behaviors. The z-score for the shorter behavior sample was half that for the longer behavior sample. In the past, a slight variation on the binomial z-score was used as an index of sequential association (Bakeman & Adamson, 1984). The same type of measurement error that was discussed for probability values occurs in this situation. It should be noted that the problems associated with using the z-score as an index of sequential association also apply to using log linear analysis or logit analysis to compare sequential associations (Bakeman, Adamson, & Strisik, 1989).

Another previously recommended index of sequential association, the *phi* coefficient (i.e., the correlation between two dichotomous variables), controls for the total number of coded behaviors (Yoder & Tapp, 1990), but this is also an unreliable index of sequential association. The *phi* coefficient can reach its theoretical maximum (i.e., 1.00) only when antecedent and target events occur at about the same frequency in a session (see Gorsuch, 1983). An analogous process restricts whether the *phi* coefficient can be –1.00. Readers familiar with the literature on *phi* coefficients (e.g., Reynolds, 1984) will recall that the frequency of the actual antecedent and target behaviors of interest (e.g., teacher instructions and student self-injury) influences whether the row and column totals are proportional to each other. For example, if the two-by-two table row totals are 20 and 80, and the column totals are about 40 and 160, then the marginals are proportional. The extent to which row and column totals are not proportional affects the possible maximum of *phi*, regardless of how strongly related the target and antecedent behaviors are (Gorsuch, 1983). When the difference between the frequency of the antecedent and target behaviors varies between individuals, the resultant *phi* coefficients will vary even when the underlying sequential relationship is identical. That is, different values of *phi* can represent the same strength of sequential association. Therefore, individual differences in the true sequential association are masked by the constraints that the differences in the relative frequencies of the antecedent and target events place on the *phi* coefficient.

One final index that has been suggested as an index of sequential association is transformed *kappa* (Wampold, 1989). Unfortunately, the sampling distribution of transformed *kappa* has been shown to be negatively skewed, and thus it is less desirable as a dependent variable in parametric analyses than Yule's Q (Bakeman et al., 1996).

CONCLUSIONS

We have presented a rationale for why Yule's Q is superior as an index of sequential association to transitional probability, probabilities from sampled permutation tests, z-scores, *phi* coefficients, and transformed *kappa*. Part of the rationale was to demonstrate that errors attributable to interindividual or between-session differences in the simple probability of the target behavior and the total number of coded behaviors can cause Type I or Type II errors. That is, when the confounding factor systematically varies with the other variables in the analysis or the phases of the single-subject experimental design, the reader is misled to believe that there is an effect when there is not one. In fact, we demonstrated that opposite conclusions can result from the use of inappropriate indices of sequential association. When the confounding factor does not vary with the levels of the other variables in the study and inappropriate indices of sequential association are used, one is less likely to find an effect that is actually present. The probability of either type of error is reduced by using Yule's Q.

REFERENCES

Bakeman, R., & Adamson, L. (1984). Coordinating attention to people and objects in mother–infant and peer–infant interaction. *Child Development, 55,* 1278–1289.

Bakeman, R., Adamson, L., & Strisik, P. (1989). Lags and logs: Statistical approaches to interaction. In M.H. Bornstein & J.S. Bruner (Eds.), *Interaction in human development* (pp. 241–260). Mahwah, NJ: Lawrence Erlbaum Associates.

Bakeman, R., & Gottman, J.M. (1997). *Observing interaction: An introduction to sequential analysis* (2nd ed.). New York: Cambridge University Press.

Bakeman, R., McArthur, D., & Quera, V. (1996). Detecting group differences in sequential association using sampled permutations: Log odds, kappa, and phi compared. *Behavior Research Methods, Instruments, and Computers, 28,* 446–457.

Bakeman, R., Quera, V., McArthur, D., & Robinson, B. (1997). Detecting sequential patterns and determining their reliability with fallible observers. *Psychological Methods, 2,* 357–370.

Bakeman, R., Robinson, B., & Quera, V. (1996). Testing sequential association: Estimating p values using sampled permutations. *Psychological Methods, 1,* 4–15.

Gorsuch, R.L. (1983). *Factor analysis* (2nd ed.). Mahwah, NJ: Lawrence Erlbaum Associates.

Moran, G., Dumas, J., & Symons, D. (1992). Approaches to sequential analysis and the description of contingency in behavioral interactions. *Behavioral Assessment, 14,* 65–92.

Reynolds, H.T. (1984). *Analysis of nominal data* (2nd ed.). Thousand Oaks, CA: Sage Publications.

Wampold, B.E. (1989). Kappa as a measure of pattern in sequential data. *Quality and Quantity, 23,* 171–187.

Wickens, T.D. (1993). Analysis of contingency tables with between-subjects variability. *Psychological Bulletin, 113,* 191–204.

Yoder, P.J., Davies, B., & Bishop, K. (1994). Reciprocal sequential relations in conversations between parents and children with developmental delays. *Journal of Early Intervention, 3,* 362–379.

Yoder, P.J., Klee, T., Hooshyar, N., & Schaffer, M. (1997). Correlates and antecedents of maternal expansions of utterances of children with language disabilities. *Clinical Linguistics and Phonetics, 12,* 23–41.

Yoder, P.J., & Tapp, J.T. (1990). SATS: Sequential Analysis of Transcripts System. *Behavior Research Methods, Instruments, & Computers, 22,* 339–343.

20

An Alternative Approach to the Sequential Analysis of Behavioral Interactions

Scott Hall and
Chris Oliver

As the previous chapters show, there are several tools available to the practicing behavior analyst to collect information about behavioral interactions. But how do we analyze these interactions? Skinner offered a useful starting point:

> We may analyze a social episode by considering one organism at a time. Among the variables to be considered are those generated by a second organism. We then consider the behavior of the second organism, assuming the first as a source of variables. By putting the analyses together we reconstruct the episode. The account is complete if it embraces all the variables needed to account for the behavior of the individuals. (1953, p. 304)

Suppose two people, A and B, were engaged in an interaction and that the behavior of A and B had been coded A and B, respectively. Considering the behavior of person A, we can calculate the conditional probability of B given A, $p(B \mid A)$ (i.e., the probability that B follows A) by tallying the total number of times that B followed A and dividing this number by the number of times that A occurred. As this conditional probability approaches 1.0 we can say with increasing confidence that A is *sufficient* for B (Fetterman, Killeen, & Hall, 1998). But the base rate of A may be low, and many Bs may be preceded by other events. We may infer how *necessary* A is for B by calculating the conditional probability of A preceding B. To

This chapter was supported in part by Grant No. IBN 9408022 from the National Science Foundation while the first author was at Arizona State University.

Thanks to Peter Killeen for his helpful insights.

do this, we need to tally the number of times that *A* preceded *B* and then divide this number by the number of times that *B* occurred.

Considering the behavior of person *B*, we can calculate the conditional probability of *A*, given *B* (i.e., the probability of *A* following *B*), by tallying the number of times that *A* followed *B* and then dividing this number by the number of times that *B* occurred. This would tell us how sufficient *B* is for *A*. Again, the base rate of *B* may be low, and many *A*s may be preceded by other events. We may infer how necessary *B* is for *A* by calculating the conditional probability of *B* preceding *A*. For this we need to tally the number of times that *B* preceded *A* and then divide this number by the number of times that *A* occurred.

WHY USE A NEW APPROACH?

A ubiquitous problem in the calculation of these conditional probabilities, however, and one that we have struggled with for many years, is this: Exactly what constitutes *preceding* and *following* when calculating the conditional probabilities of *A* preceding *B* or *B* following *A* in a behavioral stream in which *A* and *B* occur repeatedly? In other words, how far back or forward in time (or number of behavioral events) should we go to determine whether *A* is *antecedent* or *consequent* to *B*: 1 time interval (or 1 event), 10 time intervals (or 10 events), 100 time intervals (or 100 events)? We discovered that the most common approach to this problem is to define an arbitrary time or event *window* (i.e., a period of time or *event lag* keyed to the onset or offset of a particular behavior [Bakeman & Quera, 1995; Sackett, 1987]), usually 10 seconds or 10 events. For most research questions, however, it is unclear precisely what the size of the time or event window should be. For instance, some events may occur long after a particular behavior has occurred (see the literature on setting events [Wahler & Fox, 1981], establishing operations [Vollmer & Iwata, 1991], and delayed reinforcement [Hayes & Hayes, 1993] for examples), in which case the window may be too small to detect an effect. Moreover, any arbitrary window is insensitive to variations in the interval between occurrences of the behavior, so windows may sometimes overlap or repetitions of the same behavior may occur within the same window.

We believe we have developed a useful alternative approach that attempts to overcome this problem. The solution is to split the number of time units (or intervening events) between occurrences of a given behavior in half, assigning half of the time units (or event units) as antecedents and the other half as consequents. Figure 1 shows how this is done, given three occurrences of a hypothetical behavior *B*.

Once each period is defined in this way, we can determine where a second behavior occurs relative to each defined period by normalizing each period and converting the occurrence of a second behavior into percentiles. For instance, suppose a second behavior *A* occurred at the second time or event unit shown in Figure 1. With respect to the first consequent period of behavior *B*, *A* occurred during the first half of the period (i.e., at percentiles 0–50). By treating each occurrence of *A* in this way, a summary diagram showing the relative probability of *A* occurring in each period can be constructed. The purpose of this chapter is to consider this method of analysis applied to four data types—Event Sequential Data, State Sequential Data, Interval Sequential Data, and Timed Sequential Data formats (see Bakeman & Quera, 1995)—using some hypothetical data and a clinical

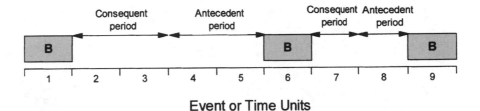

Event or Time Units

Figure I.   Definition of antecedent and consequent periods given three occurrences of a hypothetical behavior B.

example. We also consider the advantages and disadvantages of using our approach.

EVENT SEQUENTIAL DATA

Suppose we were interested in understanding the interactions commonly observed between a child who showed problem behavior and his teacher at school. First we would identify a number of relevant behaviors and record their occurrence. Let us say that X is the child's problem behavior, Y is the teacher's behavior, and other events or conditions are denoted by other codes. Hypothetical data, coded in Event Sequential Data format, are shown below:

    Event;
    Z D X Y Z D B X A X Y Z B Z X Y Z X Y Z D Z X Y Z
    C Z X A X Y D X Y Z B Z X Y Z D Z X A Z Y Z X Y Z
    /

A first question might be, Does the child's problem behavior produce a response from the teacher, or does the teacher's behavior produce problem behavior in the child? Put in causal terms, is X both necessary and sufficient for Y, or is Y both necessary and sufficient for X? Considering the teacher's behavior first, we can evaluate two of the four conditional probabilities (i.e., the conditional probability of X preceding Y and the conditional probability of X following Y). The first step is to split the number of event units between occurrences of Y in half, assigning half of the intervening event units as antecedent periods and the other half as consequent periods. In the event sequence shown in Figure 2 each antecedent period is marked by a left arrow, and each consequent period is marked by a right arrow.[1]

To equate epochs of different lengths (there are six event units between the first and second occurrences of Y and only four event units between the second and third occurrences of Y), each antecedent and consequent period is normalized and the location of a second behavior (in this case, X) within each period is converted into percentiles. For example, starting with the first antecedent period (i.e., event units preceding the second occurrence of Y) there are three antecedent event units. X occurs twice during this period, the first time occupying percentiles 0–33 and the second time occupying percentiles 67–100. For the next antecedent period (preceding the third occurrence of Y) there are two event units. X occurs once dur-

---

[1]Note that events leading up to the first occurrence of Y and leading from the last occurrence of Y are not defined, because the start and end of the session are artificially imposed by the observer.

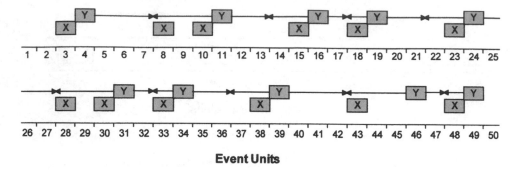

Event Units

Figure 2. Definition of antecedent and consequent periods given hypothetical behavior Y. The occurrence of X relative to these periods is also shown.

ing this period, occupying percentiles 50–100. X is the only antecedent event for the third antecedent period. In percentile terms, therefore, it occupies percentiles 0–100. For the fourth antecedent period, X is the second of two antecedent event units (occupying percentiles 50–100); for the fifth period, X is the first and third of three event units (occupying percentiles 0–33 and 67–100); for the sixth period, X is the only antecedent event (occupying percentiles 0–100). For the seventh period, there are two antecedent event units (with X occupying percentiles 50–100); for the eighth period, X is the first of three event units (occupying percentiles 0–33); and finally, for the ninth period, X is the only antecedent event (occupying percentiles 0–100).

The number of times that X preceded Y can now be tallied at each percentile. (For example, the number of times that X preceded Y at percentile 0 was six.) Once this is done the probability that X preceded Y at each percentile can be calculated by dividing these numbers by the number of antecedent periods. (At percentile 0, for example, the probability of X preceding Y was .67 [i.e., ⁶/₉].) A summary diagram showing the probability that X precedes Y at each percentile can then be constructed. The left panel of Figure 3 shows the resultant plot. (This panel also shows the probability of X following Y, calculated using the same procedure. In this case we determined the percentiles at which X occurred during the consequent periods.) In this case, X never occurred during the consequent periods of Y. The probability is therefore 0 throughout the period.

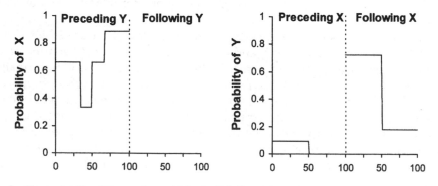

Figure 3. The probability of X preceding and following Y (left) and the probability of Y preceding and following X (right) at percentiles of event units for each period.

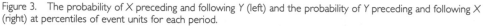

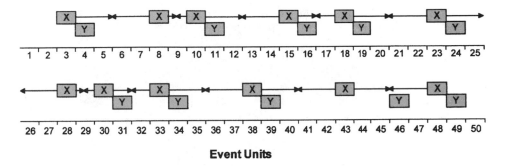

Figure 4. Definition of antecedent and consequent periods given hypothetical behavior X. The occurrence of Y relative to these periods is also shown.

We can see that the probability of X increases to about .9 immediately preceding Y. It appears, therefore, that X is necessary for Y. Because the conditional probability of X following Y is zero throughout the period, Y is not sufficient for X.

To calculate the remaining two conditional probabilities (i.e., to determine whether X is sufficient for Y and whether Y is necessary for X), we now consider the child's behavior. Using the same approach, antecedent and consequent periods are defined as shown in Figure 4.

First, we determine the percentiles at which Y occurred relative to X. (For example, for the first consequent period of X there are two consequent event units. Y occurs during the first of these units, occupying percentiles 0–50.) Once each consequent period has been examined in this way, the number of times that Y followed X is tallied at each percentile. As for Figure 3 the probability that Y follows X at each percentile can then be calculated by dividing these numbers by the number of consequent periods (11 in this example). A summary diagram showing the probability that Y follows X can then be constructed. The right panel of Figure 3 shows the corresponding plot. (It also shows the probability of Y preceding X, calculated by determining the percentiles at which Y occurred antecedent to X. Y occurs once during the eleventh antecedent period, occupying percentiles 0–50.) We can see that the probability of Y is 0 immediately preceding X. The probability of Y immediately following X is high, however. Y is not necessary for X, but X is sufficient for Y. Combining both analyses, we have identified that X is both necessary and sufficient for Y (i.e., problem behavior produces a response from the teacher).

STATE SEQUENTIAL DATA

Suppose that each event in the example data took two time units to occur. The sequence can be represented in State Sequential Data format as follows:

State;
Z,0 D,2 X,4 Y,6 Z,8 D,10 B,12 X,14 A,16 X,18 Y,20 Z,22 B,24 Z,26 X,28 Y,30 Z,32 X,34
Y,36 Z,38 D,40 Z,42 X,44 Y,46 Z,48 C,50 Z,52 X,54 A,56 X,58 Y,60 D,62 X,64 Y,66 Z,68
B,70 Z,72 X,74 Y,76 Z,78 D,80 Z,82 X,84 A,86 Z,88 Y,90 Z,92 X,94 Y,96 Z,98
/

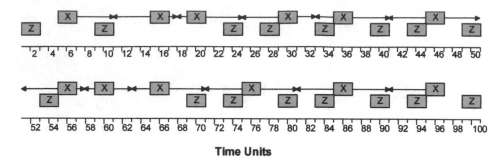

Time Units

Figure 5.   Definition of antecedent and consequent periods given hypothetical behavior X for the State Sequential Data. The occurrence Z relative to these periods is also shown.

If code Z represented times when the teacher was standing near the child, another research question might be, Does the presence of the teacher produce problem behavior (i.e., $Z \to X$), or does the problem behavior produce teacher presence (i.e., $X \to Z$)? As with the example under the previous "Event Sequential Data" heading, two of the four conditional probabilities can be calculated by first considering the behavior of one of the participants, for example, X. Time units antecedent and consequent to X are defined as shown in Figure 5.

Analysis proceeds as described above. Percentiles occupied by Z in each period relative to the occurrence of X are determined. By pooling across all antecedent periods, the probability that Z precedes X at each percentile can be calculated. Pooling across all consequent periods allows the calculation of the probability that Z follows X. The left panel of Figure 6 shows the corresponding plot. We can see that the probability of Z is approximately .6 immediately preceding X. The figure also shows that Z is 0 immediately following X. Z is necessary for X. X is not sufficient for Z.

To calculate the remaining two conditional probabilities (i.e., to determine whether Z is sufficient for X and whether X is necessary for Z), we next turn to analysis of behavior Z. Time units antecedent and consequent to Z are defined as shown in Figure 7. The right panel of Figure 6 shows the corresponding conditional probability plot. We can see that the probability of X is approximately .5 immediately following Z and is zero preceding Z. X is not necessary for Z. Z is sufficient for X. Combining both analyses, we have identified that Z is both necessary and sufficient for X (i.e., the presence of the teacher produces problem behavior).

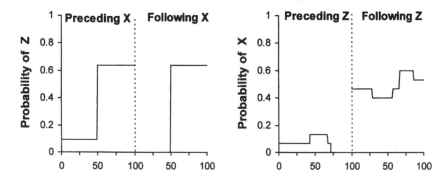

Figure 6.   The probability of Z preceding and following X (left) and the probability of X preceding and following Z (right) at percentiles of time units for each period.

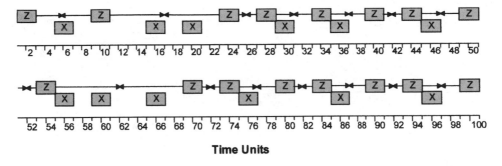

Figure 7.   Definition of antecedent and consequent periods given hypothetical behavior Z for the State Sequential Data. The occurrence of X relative to these periods is also shown.

INTERVAL SEQUENTIAL DATA

Suppose we had recorded the data in an interval format (e.g., in intervals of 10 time units). Interval Sequential Data can be represented as follows:

Interval = 10;
Z D, Z D X, Z X Y, Y Z, Z D, D B, B Z, Z, Z X A, A X, X Y, Y B, B Z, Z,
Z X Y, Y, Y Z, Z, Z X Y, Y, Y Z, Z, D Z, Z, Z X, Z X Y, Y Z, Z, Z C, C Z,
Z X A, X A Y, X Y, X Y D, X D Z, Z, Z X Y, X Y, Y B, B Z, Z X Y, X Y, Y Z, Z D, D Z, Z
   X A, X A Z, Z, Z Y, Z X, X Y, Y, Y Z, Z
/

Each interval is demarcated by a comma; codes within each interval are noted in the order in which they occur. For example, the hypothetical data listed above show that codes Z and D occurred in the first interval; codes Z, D, and X occurred in the second interval; and so forth. A research question might be, Does problem behavior (X) produce teacher vocalizing (Y), given that problem behavior (X) was preceded by teacher presence (Z) (i.e., $ZX \rightarrow Y$), or does a vocal response from the teacher (Y) produce problem behavior (X), given that problem behavior (X) was preceded by teacher presence (Z) (i.e., $Y \rightarrow ZX$)? Two of the four conditional probabilities can be calculated by nominating Y as the given behavior. Intervals antecedent and consequent to Y are defined as shown in Figure 8.

To represent the data in graphical form, percentiles of ZX relative to each period of Y are determined. Note that some behaviors occur during Y. Therefore, we can define three periods: antecedent, concurrent, and consequent. (For example, for the first concurrent period ZX occurs in the first of two intervals, occupying percentiles 0–50.) Once each antecedent, concurrent, and consequent period has been examined in this way a summary diagram showing the probability that ZX precedes, occurs during, and follows Y can be constructed. The left panel of Figure 9 shows this. ZX is necessary for Y. Y is not sufficient for ZX.

To calculate the remaining two conditional probabilities, occurrences of ZX are considered. Interval units antecedent and consequent to ZX are defined as shown in Figure 10. Following the procedure described above, the right panel of Figure 9 shows that the resulting conditional probability plot ZX is sufficient for Y. Y is not necessary for ZX. The sequence we have identified is $ZX \rightarrow Y$ (i.e., problem behavior produces a response from the teacher, given that problem behavior was preceded by teacher presence).

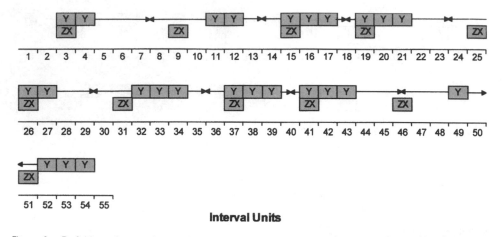

Interval Units

Figure 8.   Definition of antecedent and consequent periods given hypothetical behavior Y for the Interval Sequential Data. The occurrence of ZX relative to these periods is also shown.

TIMED SEQUENTIAL DATA

Suppose that we had collected the data in Timed Sequential Data format. The Timed Sequential Data can be represented as follows:

Timed X Y Z A B C D;
,1 Z,1-5) D,1-2) X,2-3) Y,3-4) D,5-6) B,6-7) Z,7-9) X,9-11) A,9-10) Y,11-12) B,12-13) Z,13-15) X,15 Y,15-17) Z,17-19) X,19 Y,19-21) Z,21-31) D,23 X,25-26) Y,26-27) C,29-30) X,31-35) A,31-32) Y,32-34) D,34-35) Z,35-37) X,37-38) Y,37-39) B,39-40) Z,40-41) X,41-42) Y,41-43) Z,43-51) D,44-45) X,46-47) A,46-47) Y,49 X,51-52) Y,52-54) Z,54-55) ,55)/

The first number after each code represents the onset interval of the code; the second number (following the hyphen) represents its offset interval. The right parenthesis indicates an inclusive offset interval. To evaluate whether ZX produces Y or whether Y produces ZX in timed sequential format, time units relative to Y would be defined.

As with the other examples, we can produce a plot for these data by determining when, relative to each period, ZX occurred. We leave it to the reader to determine whether the results would be equivalent to those obtained for the interval data in Figure 9.

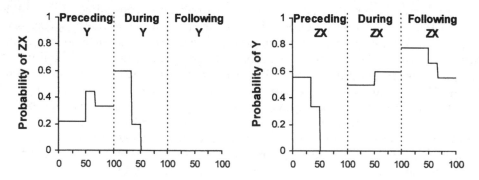

Figure 9.   The probability of ZX preceding, during, and following Y (left) and the probability of Y preceding, during, and following ZX (right) at percentiles of interval units for each period.

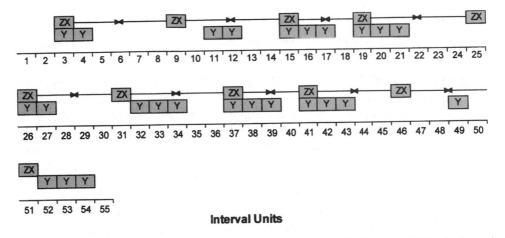

Interval Units

Figure 10. Definition of antecedent and consequent periods given hypothetical behavior ZX for the Interval Sequential Data. The occurrence of Y relative to these periods is also shown.

Case Example

Mike was a 7-year-old boy with Down syndrome who attended a local school for children with severe developmental disabilities. He had been referred to us for treatment of his aggressive behaviors, which were interfering significantly with his educational progress. As part of the assessment process, we collected 8 hours of observational data in his classroom over 3 days (see Oliver, Hall, & Nixon, 1999).

Observers collected data on an Olivetti Quaderno laptop computer using software that allowed several behaviors to be recorded simultaneously in continuous time (Repp, Harman, Felce, Van Acker, & Karsh, 1989). Data were subsequently saved in Timed Sequential Data format. The child behaviors we recorded were *aggression,* defined as forceful slapping or kicking of others, spitting, banging, and throwing of objects using the palm or the side of the hand to knock the object away; and *signing/vocalizing,* defined as hand gestures or signals usually accompanied by the words "go away," "no," or "bye-bye." In addition, a number of teacher behaviors were recorded: *instruction delivery,* defined as directions to complete a task, including physical prompts, verbal requests, and commands; *instruction removal,* defined as the discontinuation of instruction delivery for ten 1-second intervals (or whatever time was available between successive occurrences of instruction delivery, if instruction delivery recurred within ten 1-second intervals); *attention delivery,* defined as interactions with the participant, including touching, offering drinks or favorite items, talking, or blocking participant behavior; *attention removal,* defined as the discontinuation of attention delivery for ten 1-second intervals (or whatever time was available between successive occurrences of attention delivery, if attention delivery recurred within ten 1-second intervals). A second independent observer collected data during 20% of the observations. Agreements between observers were calculated on a 10-second interval-by-interval basis for the presence of each category, the onset of each category, and the offset of each category. All *kappa* indices were greater than .6.

Specifically, we set out to determine whether

1. Instructions were necessary and sufficient for aggression

2. Aggression was necessary and sufficient for instruction removal

3. Instructions were necessary and sufficient for signing/vocalizing
4. Signing/vocalizing was necessary and sufficient for instruction removal

Figures 11 and 12 show the resulting plots. Figure 11 shows the mean probability of instructions, attention, instruction removal, and attention removal preceding, during, and following Mike's aggression (left graphs) and the mean probability of aggression preceding, during, and following teacher instructions, attention, instruction removal, and attention removal (right graphs). From the left graphs, it appears that teacher instructions preceded Mike's aggression, and that instruction removal followed aggression. The right graphs show that Mike's aggression increased during teacher instructions and before instruction removal. Taken together, these data suggested that there may have been a probabilistic relationship between Mike's aggression and instruction removal. Figure 12 shows a similar relationship between Mike's signing, teacher instructions, and instruction removal, suggesting that instructions preceded signing and that instruction removal followed signing.

The results of this analysis were confirmed in a subsequent experimental assessment (see Oliver et al., 1999). Briefly, three conditions were devised in which the presence or absence of antecedent establishing operations were successively manipulated. In the first condition, EO-, Mike sat at the table next to the experimenter, was allowed to engage in a preferred activity (playing with plasticine), and received attention in the form of praise and comments. This was designed to simulate a nonprovoking environment, and little or no aggression was expected in this condition. In the second condition, EOdep, Mike sat at the table with the experimenter nearby, was allowed to engage in the preferred activity, but received very little attention. This was designed to simulate periods of low attention, and if Mike's aggression was provoked by low levels of attention, then high levels of aggression would be expected in this condition. In the third condition, EOav, Mike sat at the table with the experimenter and was prompted to engage in a nonpreferred activity (building towers with Lego bricks) using a three-step procedure consisting of sequential verbal, gestural (or modeled), and physical prompts. If Mike's aggression was provoked by instructions (as the sequential analysis suggested), then high levels of aggression would be expected in this condition. In all conditions there were no programmed social contingencies, i.e., in the EOav condition instructions were not terminated if Mike displayed problem behavior and/or signing, and in the EOdep condition attention did not follow problem behavior and/or signing. This was done because we did not want to inadvertently increase Mike's aggression to dangerous levels as a result of the programmed contingencies or to establish a new social function that did not exist previously. Figure 13 shows the results of the analysis.

Because Mike's aggression and signing/vocalizing increased only in the EOav condition, the data suggested that instructions reliably evoked aggression and signing/vocalizing and that, in the past, the behavior may have led to instructions being removed. This hypothesis was further supported by the fact that aggression and signing/vocalizing appeared to decrease across EOav conditions (i.e., the absence of the hypothesized maintaining contingency resulted in extinction). Treatment of Mike's aggression began immediately following this analysis.

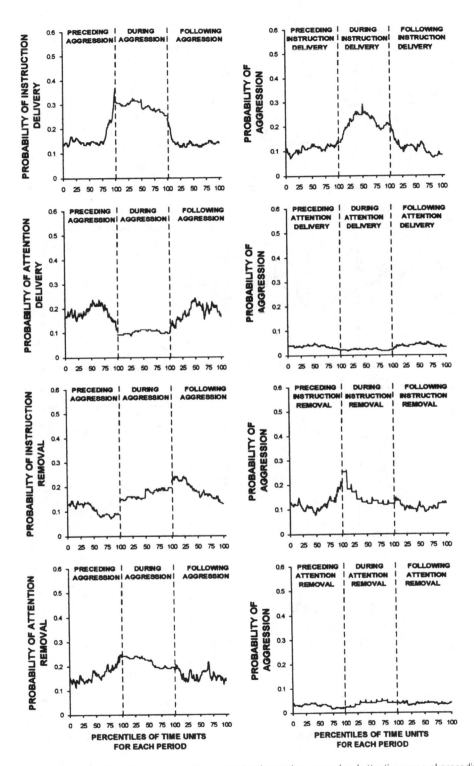

Figure 11.   The probability of teacher instructions, attention, instruction removal, and attention removal preceding, during, and following Mike's aggression (left) and the probability of Mike's aggression preceding, during, and following teacher instructions, attention, instruction removal, and attention removal (right) at percentiles of time units for each period.

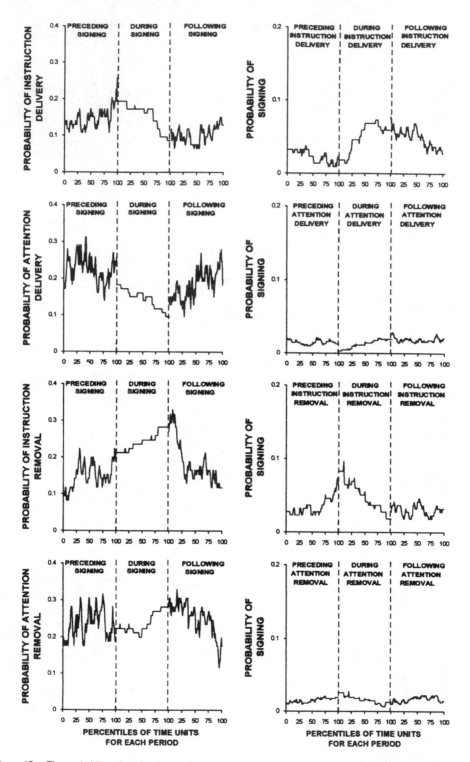

Figure 12.   The probability of teacher instructions, attention, instruction removal, and attention removal preceding, during, and following Mike's signing (left) and the probability of Mike's signing preceding, during, and following teacher instructions, attention, instruction removal, and attention removal (right) at percentiles of time units for each period.

Briefly, Mike's teacher was instructed not to remove demands when Mike showed aggression but to do so when he signed or vocalized. This met with some initial success, suggesting that our analysis was correct.

Although there are clearly some advantages to using our method to conduct sequential analysis, there may be some disadvantages. For instance, our method treats time (or event) periods between successive occurrences of a behavior as functionally equivalent to shorter periods, but we realize that this may not be the case. However, we are more likely to split time (or event units) along "natural line of fracture" if we let the data tell us where to divide time as opposed to guessing at where it should be divided. Of course, if the goal of the analysis is to determine whether a target behavior was more (or less) likely to occur within x seconds of a given behavior, then it is important to keep the time or event base. However, if an investigator wanted to determine whether a target behavior was either presented or removed relative to the occurrence of a given behavior (as in the case example above), then our alternative approach would be the more appropriate analysis.

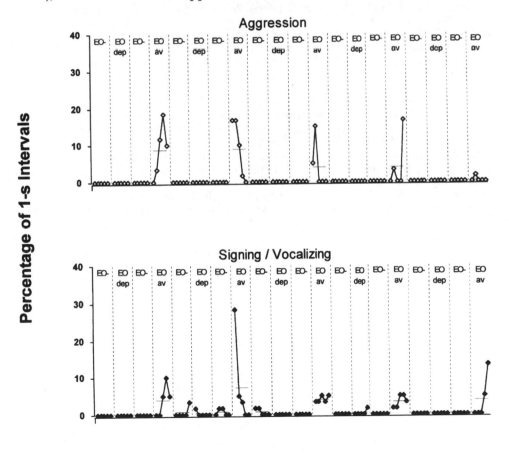

Figure 13.   Results of the brief experimental assessment. Upper panel: Percentage duration of aggression in each condition. Lower panel: Percentage duration of signing/vocalizing in each experimental condition. (From Oliver, C., Hall, S., & Nixon, L. [1999]. A molecular to molar analysis of communicative and problem behaviors. *Research in Developmental Disabilities, 20,* 208. Copyright © 1999. Reprinted with permission from Elsevier Science.)

Choosing the latter approach also would allow occurrences of a target behavior further removed in time or events from a given behavior to be included in the analysis.

We have attempted to make our approach relatively simple to follow and the data easy to interpret, in the hope that sequential analysis will no longer be an obstacle to practicing behavior analysts. Of course, we understand that naturalistic observational data are no substitute for carefully controlled experimental manipulations of independent variables. However, naturalistic observational data can provide a rich source of information about the determinants of behavior. We believe that our approach will help others to improve their understanding of behavioral interactions by uncovering the hidden structure of these systems.

REFERENCES

Bakeman, R., & Quera, V. (1995). *Analyzing interaction: Sequential analysis with SDIS and GSEQ*. New York: Cambridge University Press.

Fetterman, J.G., Killeen, P.R., & Hall, S. (1998). Watching the clock. *Behavioural Processes, 44,* 211–224.

Hayes, S.C., & Hayes, L.J. (1993). Applied implications of current JEAB research on derived relations and delayed reinforcement. *Journal of Applied Behavior Analysis, 26,* 507–511.

Oliver, C., Hall, S., & Nixon, J. (1999). A molecular to molar analysis of communicative and problem behaviors. *Research in Developmental Disabilities, 20,* 197–213.

Repp, A.C., Harman, M.L., Felce, D., Van Acker, R., & Karsh, K.G. (1989). Conducting behavioral assessments on computer-collected data. *Behavioral Assessment, 11,* 249–268.

Sackett, G.P. (1987). Analysis of sequential social interaction data: Some issues, recent developments, and a causal inference model. In J.D. Osofsky (Ed.), *Handbook of infant development* (2nd ed., pp. 855–878). New York: John Wiley & Sons.

Skinner, B.F. (1953). *Science and human behavior.* New York: Free Press.

Vollmer, T.R., & Iwata, B.A. (1991). Establishing operations and reinforcement effects. *Journal of Applied Behavior Analysis, 24,* 279–291.

Wahler, R.G., & Fox, J.J. (1981). Setting events in applied behavior analysis: Toward a conceptual and methodological expansion. *Journal of Applied Behavior Analysis, 14,* 327–338.

Index

Page numbers followed by "f" or "t" indicate figures or tables, respectively.